The CD-ROM Book

2nd Edition

Steve Bosak

Jeffrey Sloman

Revised by Dave Gibbons

QUE

The CD-ROM Book, 2nd Edition

Library of Congress Catalog No.: 94-67944

ISBN: 1-56529-957-4

97 96 95 94 5 4 3 2 1

Interpretation of the printing code: the rightmost double-digit number is the year of the book's printing; the rightmost single-digit number, the number of the book's printing. For example, a printing code of 94-1 shows that the first printing of the book occurred in 1994.

Publisher: David P. Ewing

Associate Publisher: Corinne Walls

Publishing Director: Brad R. Koch

Marketing Manager: Greg Wiegand

About the Authors

Jeffrey Sloman is a free-lance writer and consultant based in Franklin, Indiana. He is a contributing editor to *Windows* magazine, for which he writes the monthly Windows Networking column. His consulting practice includes all aspects of Microsoft Windows as well as marketing and strategic-direction support for high-tech companies. In a previous life, he worked at the Museum of Science in Boston, Massachusetts, where he designed and built electronic and electromechanical components for exhibits.

Steve Bosak has been writing about high technology and computers since the late '70s for a variety of publications, including *PC World*, *Byte*, and *Microsystems Journal*. He is director of the Professional Writing Program at Columbia College in Chicago. Interested readers can contact him on MCI Mail at `IDsbosak`.

Dave Gibbons is a former technical trainer and writer for DATASTORM Technologies in Columbia, Missouri, and LaserMaster Technologies in Eden Prairie, Minnesota. He began his professional writing career in chilly Cando, North Dakota, at age 16. Now a freelance writer and consultant, Dave spends much of his free time rock climbing on the Internet (`dgibbons@bigcat.missouri.edu`).

Credits

Title Manager
Thomas H. Bennett

Acquisitions Editor
Cheryl Willoughby

Acquisitions Assistant
Ruth Slates

Product Director
Jim Minatel

Technical Editor
Aaron Branham

Production Editor
Alice Martina Smith

Editors
Danielle Bird
Kelli Brooks
Christine Prakel
Linda Seifert

Editoral Assistant
Theresa Mathias

Book Designer
Paula Carroll

Production Team
Stephen Adams
Angela Bannan
Cameron Booker
Stephen Carlin
Chad Dressler
Elizabeth Lewis
Malinda Lowder
Steph Mineart
G. Alan Palmore
Kaylene Riemen
Caroline Roop
Kris Simmons
Marcella Thompson
Donna Winter

Indexer
Johnna VanHoose

Composed in *ITC Century Light* and *MCPdigital* by Que Corporation

Acknowledgments

Steve and Jeff would like to thank all the vendors, too numerous to name, who supplied products for evaluation in this book.

Dave would like to thank Ruth Slates, Jim Minatel, Chris Nelson, and Alice Martina Smith for all their help and support during this project. He also sends thanks to Xona and Alyse for Mufasa.

The editor would like to thank Dave (a Cando kind of guy) for his wit, conscientious effort to keep the book on schedule, and technical support on the mysteries of modems. Thanks, too, to Chris, a sedulous conduit.

Trademark Acknowledgments

Dedications

To Renée, Jonathon, Arnold, and Barbara.

—js

To Maureen and Ian for understanding where I disappear to for hours on end every night, and to Scott and Stephanie for their consummate game-playing skills and honest consumer opinions.

—sb

To my dad, who likes Liz's chili recipe.

—dg

Contents at a Glance

Table of Contents

3 How To Select CD-ROM Drives 29

Introduction

Thank you for buying *The CD-ROM Book, 2nd Edition*. This book is designed to help you learn about CD-ROM and the sort of technology available. It is written to answer three questions:

- ➤ What is CD-ROM?
- ➤ How do I use CD-ROM?
- ➤ What products are available in the CD-ROM arena?

We—the authors, editors, and designers of this book—have worked very hard to make this book especially helpful and easy to use. You will notice right away that this book looks different than other computer books. This difference in appearance is a product of the special features built into the book.

First is the easy-to-read double-column style, reminiscent of a magazine. We chose this layout because it is easier to read and nicer to look at. Second are the numerous sidebars (set off from the text) and margin notes (in a special place at the edge of the page). These devices help maintain a smooth flow of thought in the body of the book, while still providing related information, clarifications, and definitions where they can be useful. In the text, references to margin notes appear in a **special typeface** to alert you that a margin note can be found for that topic. This is a printed version of the hypertext found in electronic publications.

Another special feature of the book is the use of tables and icons that provide information at a glance. In places where products are discussed, specifications and classifications are right up front so that you can easily scan for items of interest. Where there are tables, features are marked with check marks ✔ and mean that the feature is part of that product; no check mark means that the feature is not available. This approach is familiar to users of graphical user interfaces like Windows and the

Macintosh; it lets you see what is not there as well as what is—so that you don't have to try to remember what *could be* there.

The book is designed to be used like a database, in a random-access fashion. Although you can read it from cover to cover, we don't expect you to. Instead, it is designed so that you can use it as a reference; each paragraph and chapter is substantially independent, with references to other information as needed. This means that if you are interested in some aspect of CD-ROM technology, you can look at just what you are curious about without jumping around or reading more than you want.

In a way, this book is an experiment. It represents a rethinking of books in the light of how we use information today. The book is designed to be as "interactive" as a printed book allows. We expect that the times you cannot find the information you need (to learn about what CD-ROM is, how it works, and what you can do with it) will be few.

What's New in the 2nd Edition

The first edition of *The CD-ROM Book* was a tough act to follow. For this second edition, we've made the following changes:

- Beefed up the networking coverage
- Added information on Macintosh CD-ROM and multimedia
- Covered the new higher-speed drives and other developments such as multimedia laptops
- Expanded the coverage of how CD-ROMs are created
- Included a chapter on choosing a multimedia computer or adding multimedia to your existing computer
- Covered how to troubleshoot CD-ROMs and multimedia
- Included CD-ROM reviews of the newest releases in all major categories

A Guide to Special Features

The margin notes in this book include icons that depict the nature of their contents. Most of them are related to the main body of text through words or phrases that appear in a **special typeface**. There are six types of margin notes:

What Is a Note?

A note is a piece of related information that would have been out of place in the text. Notes are designed to point out important ideas and concepts that might not otherwise be obvious.

What Is a Caution?

A caution is just what it says; it warns you about some aspect of the information provided in the text. Cautions help you avoid damage to equipment, data, or yourself.

EXPLANATION

What Is an Explanation?

An explanation is either a definition or a glossary-type entry. It is connected with some particular word or concept in the text.

RULE OF THUMB

What Is a Rule of Thumb?

The rule of thumb margin note includes a general rule about some piece of technology. It is used to help you make a decision when the rules are fuzzy and clear-cut recommendations are impossible.

TIP

What Is a Tip?

A tip is designed to make some processes easier. Tips are usually related to some particular action being described in the text.

CD-ROM BOOK AWARD OF EXCELLENCE

What Is an Award of Excellence?

In writing *The CD-ROM Book*, we came across products in all categories that stood out from the rest. We felt the need to recognize these special products beyond giving them our recommendation; these are the recipients of the Award of Excellence. There were no fixed criteria used to determine award winners; each was distinguished by some special characteristic that made the product an example to be followed. In each case, the logic for our decision is spelled out so that you can understand why the choice was made.

We feel the winners of *The CD-ROM Book* Award of Excellence are all examples of products that offer something exceptional. These products get our recommendation—as well as our admiration—for what they do well.

Icons without Text

A few icons used in the book are not accompanied by text. These icons indicate a fixed idea about a product, making the information easy to absorb without having to search the text.

Hardware products are rated graphically with a set of CD icons. These ratings reflect a relatively complex formula based on fact and opinion. The fact portion involves the tallying of points for various features and specifications. The opinion portion is an additional set of points we added, based on the drive's qualities relative to the rest of the field. The opinion portion of the score is worth about 1/3 of the total (although we could not overly influence the results, we could break ties).

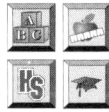

These icons are used with educational software and are intended to help you determine—at a glance—which applications may be of interest to you or your children. Notice that these four icons function like buttons on a toolbar: when they are dimmed, they do not apply to the product; when they are "active" (as all four of the icons shown here are), they do apply to the product. More than one icon may be "active" at the same time to indicate a range of ages.

What's in This Book

As innovative as this book may be, it *is* a book and books have chapters. Here's a run-down on what you will find in each chapter:

Chapter 1, "What Is CD-ROM?," introduces you to the fascinating world of compact disc read-only memory. What is it? Why do you need it? What do you need to know about the technology to keep up with the fast-changing world?

Chapter 2, "CD-ROM Specifications Explained," clarifies some of the most confusing aspects of CD-ROM technology. If you've ever wondered what "Yellow Book Specifications" have to do with CDs—or are looking for some comprehensible details about more complex issues—look no further.

Chapter 3, "How To Select CD-ROM Drives," describes more than 50 products. The specifications you need for each drive are presented consistently, making it easier for you to make an informed decision about the drive you need. We rate each drive to further assist your purchasing decision.

Chapter 4, "How To Install Your CD-ROM Drive," takes you through the doesn't-have-to-be-so-messy chore of introducing your computer to your new CD-ROM drive. You learn how to set jumpers on an adapter card, install the card, connect the drive, install the software drivers, and, finally, access data on a disc.

Chapter 5, "How To Network Your CD-ROM Drive," explains how to make your state-of-the-art CD-ROM drive available to everyone on the network. Perhaps more importantly, you learn why you'd want to. The chapter covers setting up your drive for use with Windows for Workgroups, Lantastic, LocalTalk, and NetWare, and explores some third-party solutions like CorelSCSI!, Microtest Discport, and MDI SCSI Express.

Chapter 6, "Troubleshooting," steps you through some efficient methods for finding—and fixing—problems in your CD-ROM installation.

Chapter 7, "What Is Multimedia?" introduces you to multimedia—a world made practical by the storage capacities of CD-ROM. Because a major element in multimedia presentations is audio sound, this chapter describes some of the best sound boards and speakers available.

Chapter 8, "How To Select a Multimedia Computer," lists several computers that come with multimedia capabilities, and multimedia upgrade kits that add CD-ROM, sound, and speakers to your existing computer. PCs, Macintoshes, and multimedia laptops are listed and rated.

Chapter 9, "CD-ROM in Business," groups application titles commonly found in business environments. General business, marketing, sales, law, accounting, finance, education, library-science, and medical application titles are described.

Chapter 10, "CD-ROM for Home Reference and Education," gives you an idea of the plethora of CD titles available in the reference and education realms. Imagine an entire shelf of encyclopedia volumes reduced to a single shiny disc, or a dictionary that pronounces *onomatopoeia* for you. Now imagine every document of importance to the history of the United States, all Shakespeare's works (in the Queen's English), and a French lesson that talks—and they all take up no more than a few inches of shelf space.

Chapter 11, "CD-ROM for After Hours," was the most fun for us to research. We're confident our information is good, thanks to the help of our expert consultants Scott and Stephanie. In this chapter, we talk about some of the best games on CD-ROM.

Chapter 12, "Copyright Law," presents specific information about copyright law—and copyright infringement—in clear language. Before you use parts of a CD-ROM in your next multimedia presentation, read this.

Chapter 13, "When One CD-ROM Isn't Enough," will be helpful when your thirst for data outgrows the capabilities of a single CD-ROM drive. This chapter describes options like CD-ROM changers, jukeboxes, arrays, and towers—and provides specifications for some of the available products.

Chapter 14, "Creating CD-ROMs," shows you several options for making your own discs for distribution or just for your own use. It covers multimedia authoring tools, CD-ROM recorders, and using professional pressing services.

Chapter 15, "CD-ROM on the Road: Going Portable," reassures those whose offices are the front seats of their cars that you really can take it with you. CD-ROM drives come in several packages that make transporting reams of data to remote locations as easy as taking the disc—and the drive—with you.

Chapter 16, "CD-ROM in the Family Room," draws the line between the CD-ROM drive used with your computer and the CD-ROM drive that may be hooked up to your television-based home-game system. Although these two systems—and the discs they use—are not fully compatible, you will want to know more about their differences.

Chapter 17, "Video on Disc: CD-ROM and Full-Motion Video," explains what full-motion video is and why CD-ROM makes the propagation of it possible. For real propeller heads, this chapter describes some of the video standards and code boards required for developing applications that make use of full-motion video.

Chapter 18, "The Future of CD-ROM," is more than an editorial. It provides some facts about the future of the CD-ROM industry, some tidbits about what's up-and-coming, as well as our opinions about the whole scenario.

The appendixes in this book contain lots of information tangential to the main flow of the text in the chapters. In these sections, you will find names and addresses of CD-ROM drive manufacturers, software developers and publishers, and hardware and software vendors. Some instructions for taking care of your precious data discs and some suggestions about where you can turn for additional information about CD-ROM round out the appendixes.

The Disc

As you've hopefully noticed by now, this book includes a real CD. Encoded in its plastic and metal layers are samples of over 40 Microsoft Home products you might like to experience (we would have said "look at," but the CD-ROM necessitates the use of a stronger word). The disc is compatible with Windows. You will find instructions for using the disc on the last page of this book, facing the disc itself.

Chapter 1

What is CD-ROM?

Before you begin a serious investigation into any new field, some familiarity with the terms used by people in that field is essential. Beginning your CD-ROM education is no exception. This chapter introduces you to CD-ROM terminology, briefly explains the evolution of the CD-ROM, and provides some reasons why you need to know more about this cutting-edge technology.

CD-ROM: A Brief History

In 1978, two companies—Philips and Sony—joined forces to produce the audio compact disc (CD). Philips had already developed commercial laser-disc players, and Sony had a decade of digital recording research under its belt. The two companies were poised for a battle—the introduction of potentially incompatible audio laser disc formats—but they came to terms on an agreement to formulate a single audio technology.

Sony pushed for a 12-inch disc. Philips wanted to investigate smaller sizes, especially when it became clear that they could pack an astonishing 12 hours of music on 12-inch discs.

By 1982, the companies announced their standard, which included the specifications for recording, sampling, and above all, the 5-inch format we live with today. To be specific, the discs are 12 centimeters in diameter. As legend has it, this size was chosen because it could contain Beethoven's Ninth Symphony (about 72 minutes).

With the continued cooperation of Sony and Philips through the 1980s, additional specifications were announced concerning the use of CD technology for computer data. These recommendations have evolved into the computer CD-ROM drives we use today. Where engineers once struggled to find the perfect fit between disc form-factor and the greatest symphony ever recorded, software developers and publishers are cramming these little discs with the world's information.

Understanding and using this CD-based cornucopia of knowledge can enrich your business, your career, and your leisure. The technology is affordable and easy to add to an existing PC.

A Library on Your Desk

Within minutes of inserting a compact disc into your computer, you have access to information that may have taken you days, or even weeks, to find a few years ago. A wealth of science, medicine, law, business profiles, and educational materials—every conceivable form of human endeavor or pursuit of knowledge—is making its way to aluminum-coated, 5-inch plastic discs called **CD-ROMs**, or compact disc-read only memory.

EXPLANATION

CD-ROM

The CD-ROM (compact disc-read only memory) is a read-only optical storage medium capable of holding 660 megabytes of data (approximately 500,000 pages of text), about 70 minutes of high-fidelity audio, or some combination of the two. The CD-ROM is very similar to the familiar audio compact disc and can, in fact, play in a normal audio player. The result, however, is noise, unless audio accompanies the data on the CD-ROM. When accessing data, a CD-ROM is somewhat faster than a floppy disk, but considerably slower than a modern hard drive. The term *CD-ROM* refers to both the discs themselves and the drive that reads them.

Although only dozens of CD-ROM discs, or titles, were published for personal computer users in all of 1988, the Software Publishers Association estimates that in 1993, publishers offered over 3,000 individual titles, containing data and programs ranging from worldwide agricultural statistics to preschool learning games. Individual businesses, local and federal government offices, and small businesses also publish thousands of their own, limited-use titles every year.

The Infinite Index

Aside from the sheer avalanche of data available on CD-ROM, this medium of delivering information has unique properties. Imagine, for example, a 300-volume library of classic literature with an *infinite index* that offers the ability to search and perform a cross-reference on every work in a text. By entering the word **Dickens**, for example, you can see a list of all the Dickens titles on the CD—no more remarkable than the traditional card catalog found in your neighborhood library. But if you then narrow your search by typing **work house**, you see an index listing of every passage in every Dickens work that mentions the words *work house*. Finding the Shakespeare play that contains the quotation, "Alas, poor Yorick!" is as simple as typing it in. Within seconds, the software whisks you to that famous graveside passage in Hamlet.

Because every word, number, or symbol on a disc can be located in seconds, information that might take hours to retrieve in printed form is merely a few keystrokes away on a PC equipped with a CD-ROM. Suppose, for example, that you need to find the address and phone number of your friend, with nothing more to go on than his or her name. To complicate matters, you have no idea what city or state he or she is in, which means that the phone company and a phone directory is of no use—even if your local library stocks every phone book in the country! By using a single directory CD, you can type **Smith** and instantly see how many people match that name (see fig. 1.1).

As you can see, the nearly limitless way in which you can use CD-ROMs to search for data makes them even more approachable and useful, in many cases, than their printed counterparts.

The Talking Papyrus

When the Egyptians began using papyrus—man's first paper—to record information, it was a technological innovation. It sounds funny now, but it's true. Where previous cultures had used rocks, wood, tree bark, and cave walls to inscribe information, the papyrus allowed the Egyptian culture to leapfrog its predecessors in information technology. The papyrus was easier to store, easier to read, and certainly more portable than the stone tablets being lugged around.

But the most useful feature of papyrus was its ability to store a virtually unlimited amount of information; a collection of scrolls could contain a lengthy piece of work, not possible with other "technologies" from the past. Scrolls eventually evolved into handwritten books, then the printed books of today.

But CD-ROMs have upped the ante. Although the book you're holding right now contains over 100,000 words, the enclosed CD can hold millions of words, with room to spare for audio and video.

Even if CD-ROMs were strictly limited to publishing text, you have already seen how powerful the medium is in locating the tiniest bits of information. Although this electronic papyrus has nearly unlimited potential for text indexing and retrieval, its capabilities do not end with the printed word.

The same CD-ROM technology that offers the full text of Shakespeare, business databases, and an entire dictionary all on one CD is capable of *speaking* to you as well. Publishers of CD-ROMs have begun to take advantage of the audio capabilities of the data CD technologies in inventive ways. The same CD that holds text can also simultaneously incorporate audio—speech, music, or sound effects—to enhance its text presentations.

Perhaps you've always been a bit reluctant to use the word *forte* because you are not sure how it's properly pronounced. If you look up *forte* in Microsoft's Bookshelf for Windows CD-ROM, you are presented with the screen shown in figure 1.2.

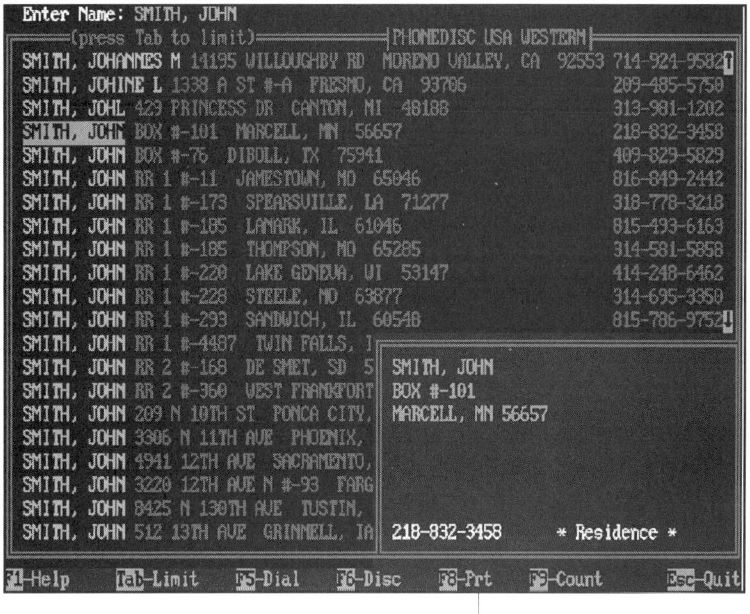

FIGURE 1.1

Using this telephone directory CD-ROM, all you need is a name to find the addresses and phone numbers of all those who have that name.

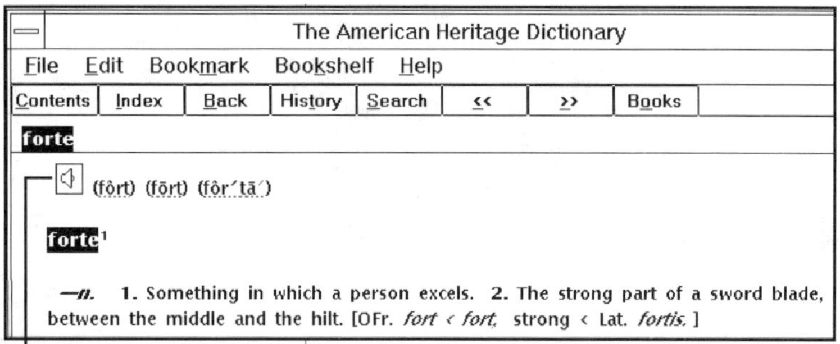
The American Heritage Dictionary
File Edit Bookmark Bookshelf Help
Contents Index Back History Search << >> Books
forte
(fôrt) (fōrt) (fôr′tā′)
forte¹
—n. 1. Something in which a person excels. 2. The strong part of a sword blade, between the middle and the hilt. [OFr. fort < fort, strong < Lat. fortis.]

Forte is pronounced when you click this icon.

FIGURE 1.2

Clicking the speaker icon next to the definition provides you with a spoken pronunciation of that bothersome word, recorded by a professional elocutionist. Public speaking can now be your forte.

EXPLANATION

Multimedia

Although *multimedia* is a general term with no clear definition, in the context of CD-ROM the word refers to a combination of at least two of the medium's capabilities to present information (for example, the use of text and sound or pictures and sound). The term *MPC* (Multimedia PC), on the other hand, has a clear definition. MPC is a specification for hardware and software for multimedia presentation of information.

Art, Photos, and Video

CD-ROM can also provide visual information: a full-color image of *Guernica* as you read a short biography of Picasso; photos of Saturn taken by the Voyager spacecraft when you reference an article on unmanned space exploration; or a film clip—complete with sound—of President Nixon's resignation speech when you read about Watergate.

Complex theories and mechanisms can be explained and demonstrated through animation and narration. Databases of visual information can be searched as effortlessly and endlessly as their written counterparts by using index information provided on the disc.

This combination of text, sound, graphics, and animation on CD-ROM is called **multimedia**. Multimedia is explained in greater detail in Chapter 7, "What Is Multimedia?"

The use of multimedia CD-ROMs for PCs is just beginning to be explored by innovative publishers. The years ahead will see a tremendous growth in both the number and variety of titles.

What's Playing on CD-ROM?

Each CD-ROM has a capacity of over 600 megabytes of storage. In terms of data, that capacity is roughly the equivalent of 500,000 pages of text. With all this available storage, single CD-ROMs can pack an enormous amount of data. The variety is staggering, as the following list shows:

- Every listing from all the Yellow Pages throughout the United States
- Full-color maps containing every street in the country
- Facsimile numbers for all publicly held businesses and all government institutions
- A visual tour of the Smithsonian Institution
- A 21-volume encyclopedia, complete with full-color pictures, illustrations, sound annotations (see fig. 1.3), and full-motion video clips

With all this cheap, efficient storage power, virtually every facet of life is already being transformed by this technology:

- Businesses are using CD-ROM technology for marketing and marketing research, business reference, and lead generation.

- Schools have adopted CD-ROM for referencing and as an exciting new tool for interactive education.
- Scholars use CD-ROM technology to cut research time and to publish data for a fraction of the cost of paper-bound materials and publications.
- The government is in the process of converting massive amounts of paper documents to CD-ROM in an effort to conserve space and preserve its archives.
- At home, CD-ROMs can replace shelves of reference materials, add a new dimension to a child's learning, and transform your PC into a multimedia playground with the most visually stunning games and entertainment software yet developed.

Now that you have an idea of what CD-ROM technology can do on your PC, you should understand how it works.

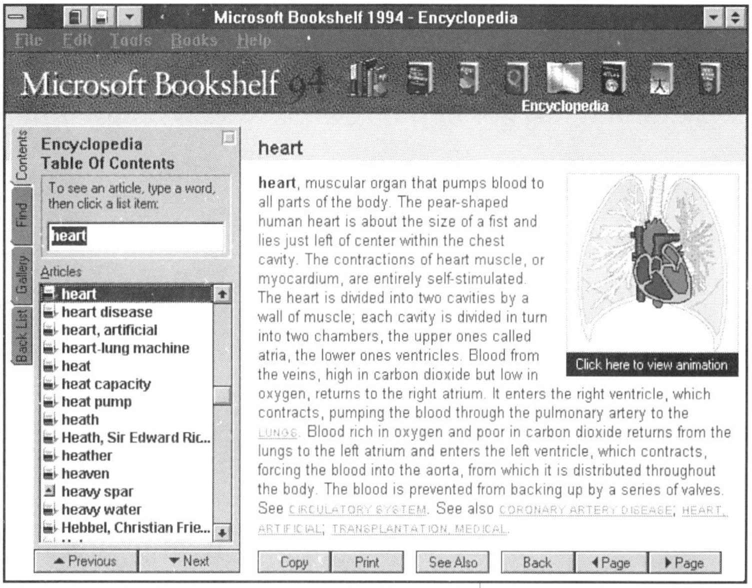

FIGURE 1.3

The text article on the human heart is accompanied by an animation of a heart in action. A voice-over explains the action as it proceeds.

Compact-Disc Technology

Although identical in appearance to audio CDs, computer CDs store both data *and* audio. The CD drives that read the discs when attached to PCs also bear a strong resemblance to an audio CD. The methods of handling discs, inserting them into the CD drive, and ejecting them when finished are all familiar to anyone who has used an audio CD. Both forms of CD operate on the same general mechanical principles.

The disc itself, nearly 5 inches in diameter, is made of a polycarbonate wafer. The wafer's base is coated with a metallic film, usually an aluminum alloy. The aluminum film is the portion of the disc that the CD-ROM drive reads for information. The aluminum film, or strata, is then covered by a **plastic coating** that protects the underlying data.

Mass-Producing CD-ROMs

Although a laser is used to etch data onto a master disc, this technique is impractical for the reproduction of hundreds or thousands of copies of the disc. Each production of a master disc can take more than 30 minutes to encode. In addition, master discs are made of materials that aren't durable enough for continued or prolonged use. In fact, unless you are using a CD-R (CD-Recordable) or CD-WO (CD-Write Once) for mastering discs or storing data, the material used for master CDs is made of glass. Only the CD-R and CD-WO drives use metal-coated discs for making masters or writing data.

continues

NOTE

Handling CD-ROMs

You should handle CD-ROM media with the same care you afford a photographic negative. The CD-ROM is an optical device and degrades as its optical surface becomes dirty or scratched. If your drive uses a *caddie*—a container for the disc that rules out the need to handle the disc itself—you should purchase a sufficient supply of caddies to reduce disc handling.

For more information on maintenance, see Appendix F, "Care and Feeding of CD-ROMs."

FIGURE 1.4

A CD-ROM is composed of layers of plastic, polycarbonate, and aluminum.

continued

For limited-run productions of CDs, an original master is coated with metal in a process similar to electroplating; once the metal is formed and separated from the master, the metal imprint of the original is used to stamp copies, not unlike the reproduction of vinyl records. This process works effectively for small quantities, but eventually the stamp wears out.

To produce a large volume of discs, a three-step process is employed:

1. The master is, once again, plated and a stamp is produced.
2. This stamp is used to create a duplicate master, made of a more resilient metal.
3. The duplicate master is used to produce numerous stamps.

This technique allows a great many production stamps to be made from the duplicate master, preserving the integrity of the original encoding. It also allows the mass-production discs to be made from inexpensive materials. The CDs you buy are coated with aluminum after they are stamped into polycarbonate; then they are protected with a thin layer of plastic. The thin, aluminum layer that coats both the etched pits and smooth surfaces enables the reading laser to determine the presence or absence of strongly reflected light.

This mass-manufacturing process is identical for both data and audio CDs.

CDs, in some respects, are similar to an older technology, the phonograph record (which the CD has made nearly obsolete). On a CD, microscopic pits stamped into a polycarbonate layer and coated with aluminum replace the vinyl record's grooves. These pits are called **data bits**.

Reading back the information is a matter of reflecting a low-powered laser off the aluminum strata. A receiver or light receptor notes where light is strongly reflected and where it is absent or diffused. Diffused or absent light is caused by the recorded pits in the CD. Strong reflection of light indicates no pit—an area called a *land*. The light receptors within the player collect the reflected and diffused light as it is refracted from the surface. As the light sources are collected from the refraction, they are passed along to microprocessors that translate the light patterns back into data or sound.

Compact discs resemble their old vinyl predecessors in yet another way: CD tracks are not concentric circles across the surface, but one long spiral of pits and lands leading from the disc's center, just as a phonograph record's long groove leads toward the label of the record. This spiral of CD data is nearly three miles long.

When a CD—audio or data—seeks a bit of data from the disc, it looks up the address of the data from a table of contents and positions itself near the beginning of this data across the spiral, waiting for the right string of bits to flow past the laser beam.

Inside Data CD-ROM Drives

The microprocessor that decodes the electrical impulses—or pits and lands of the disc's reflected light—is the key difference between music and data compact players. This decoder must pass along digital information to a digital target—a PC. The audio CD player, on the other hand, must pass along digital information to an analog processor—a stereo amplifier.

EXPLANATION

Data Elements: Bits, Nybbles, and Bytes

The term *bit* is a contraction of BInary digiT. A bit is the atomic—smallest, indivisible—element used to represent data in a computer's memory. A bit is binary, that is, it can have only one of two values: 1 or 0. BIts are grouped together to represent symbols and for easier manipulation. The most common grouping is eight bits, called a *byte*. One byte can represent 256 different values. In the case of text, these values are the 256 characters in the American Standard Code for Information Interchange (ASCII). A *nybble* is four bits or one-half byte. The nybble is useful only in some obscure cases but certainly shows that at least some computer scientists have a sense of humor.

A CD-ROM drive has internal components that operate in the following manner:

1. The *laser diode* emits a low-energy beam toward a reflecting mirror.
2. The *servo motor*, on command from the microprocessor, positions the beam onto the correct track on the CD-ROM by moving the reflecting mirror.
3. After the beam hits the disc, its refracted light is gathered and focused through the first lens beneath the disc, bounced off the mirror, and sent toward the beam splitter.
4. The *beam splitter* directs the returning laser light toward another focusing lens.
5. The last lens directs the light beam to a *photo detector*, which converts the light into electrical impulses.
6. The incoming impulses are decoded by the microprocessor and sent along to the host computer as data.

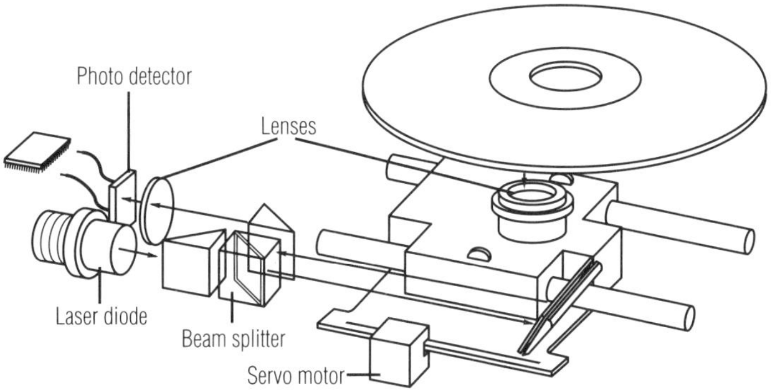

FIGURE 1.5

The internal components of a CD-ROM drive.

Although the simplicity of data or binary language seems to imply that a data CD optical reader would need to be less sensitive to incoming signals than an audio CD reader, that is not the case. Because the encoding pits on a data CD are uniform in size, the presence or absence of the pitting must be measured precisely, thereby signaling the 1 or 0 of binary code. Even one **misreading** of the space or pit can cause the entire data file to lose integrity, or become useless. Therefore, the tracking mechanism—the motor that moves the laser beam across the surface—and the receptors of the refracted light must be more tightly integrated with each other and more accurate in reading the recording surface than those in an audio CD reader.

In the case of an audio CD, missing data can be "interpolated." That is, the information follows a predictable pattern that allows you to guess the missing value. For example, suppose that a series of three values—10, 13, and 20—are stored on an audio disc. If the middle value is missing because of damage or dirt on the CD's surface, you can interpolate a middle value of 15, which is midway between the values 10 and 20. Although this guess is not exactly correct, in the case of an audio recording, it is not noticeable to the listener. If those same three values appear on a CD-ROM in an executable program, there is no way to guess the correct value for the middle sample. Interpolation cannot work because executable program data follows no natural law for the data in a series of values. To guess that the missing value is 15 is not just slightly off, it is completely wrong.

Because of the need for such precision, CD-ROM drives for PCs were later to market than their audio counterparts. When first introduced, CD-ROM drives were too expensive

EXPLANATION

Error Correction

To prevent a single scratch or flaw in a CD-ROM from destroying the disc's value, an error-correction scheme is used. The CD-ROM uses a scheme called *Reed-Solomon ECC* (Error Correcting Code). This code works by storing the data on the disc more than once, allowing the recovery of a missing bit (or bits) by using the surrounding data. A key element to error correction is error detection. An error-detection algorithm (a mathematical "mechanism") allows the drive to identify damaged data and employ the error-correcting code.

for widespread incorporation. In addition, drive manufacturers were slow to adopt standards, causing lag time in the production of CD-ROM titles. Without a wide base of software to drive the industry, acceptance was slow.

As this book will show, the game has changed considerably. Software titles are pouring out from major commercial, academic, and government publishers, and small and large businesses are adding this powerful technology to their competitive arsenals. Drive manufacturers have improved their products, moved to more standard interfaces, and dropped their prices. When data CD-ROM drives were first introduced, only three or four manufacturers made all the available drives, but now there are dozens of suppliers.

With greater competition, better mass-manufacturing techniques, and increased demand, some drives can be purchased today for less than $200. Many drive systems include a bundle of CD-ROM software discs, making the purchase even more attractive.

Chapter 2

CD-ROM Specifications Explained

If you are considering the purchase of a CD-ROM drive, you have undoubtedly been bombarded with advertising lingo and the conflicting advice of competing advertisements. What do you look for in a CD-ROM drive? How do you know exactly what a CD-ROM drive can do? How do you know whether drive X is better than drive Y? Unlike searching the Personal section of the local paper for the perfect mate, there are some standards used in advertisements for CD-ROM drives. This chapter helps you determine what all the hype means.

Drive Attributes

When purchasing a CD-ROM drive for your PC, you should consider three distinct sets of attributes of CD-ROM drives:

- The drive's specifications
- The format or formats it is capable of reading
- The interface it requires for connection to your **computer**

The variance in any of these categories is enormous; in fact, single vendors offer entire lines of drives that vary in performance specifications, format-reading capabilities, and the type of adapters they can use to connect to your computer. For these reasons, drive prices vary widely. First-generation CD-DA drives, for example, are available for as little as $100. You'll probably be disappointed in the drive's performance and capabilities, however, and may be better off looking elsewhere. Before you buy, know the drive's characteristics.

This chapter discusses all three drive characteristics, giving you a better understanding of what type of drive you need to buy.

NOTE

Which Computer Are We Talking About?

Throughout this book, the term *PC* refers to any personal computer—Apple Macintosh, IBM PC-compatible, or any other. The entire term *PC-compatible* is used when information is specific to the PC-compatible platform.

EXPLANATION

Data Transfer Rate

Data transfer rate is the rate at which data moves from its resting place on storage media (such as the CD-ROM) to a place where it can used by your application. It is a *rate* because it is measured as a quantity over time. The higher the data transfer rate, the better.

RULE OF THUMB

Recommended Transfer Rate Minimum: 300 KB/s.

EXPLANATION

Access Time

Access time is the measure of time it takes the CD-ROM drive to find a particular point on the disc. Because the current position of the laser pickup influences how long it takes for the drive to locate a particular point, access time is expressed as an average. CD-ROM drives have access times far greater than typical hard drives because of the large size of the laser unit. The smaller the access time, the better.

CD-ROM Drive Specifications

Drive specifications tell you the drive's performance capabilities. If you're shopping for a sports car, for example, and the dealer tells you the car can accelerate from a standing stop to 60 miles per hour in 6 seconds, you know you've got a hot car. The car's horsepower, displacement in liters, and number of cylinders and valves are also specifications you use to determine how fast the car can run.

CD-ROM drive specifications tell the shopper much the same thing. Typical performance figures published by manufacturers are the data transfer rate, access time, internal buffers (if any), and the interface used.

Data Transfer Rate

The **data transfer rate** tells you how much data the drive can read from a data CD and transfer to the host computer when reading one large, sequential chunk of data. The standard measurement in the industry is kilobytes per second, usually abbreviated as KB/s. If a manufacturer claims a drive can transfer data at 120 KB/s, it means that the drive can read a sequential stream of data at the rate of 120 kilobytes per second—once the drive has come up to speed.

Note that this is a sustained and sequential read—not access across the data disc from different portions of the platter. In other words, the read is taking place as one long gulp of data from a single continuous track, rather than random accesses from various parts of the disc. Obviously, the data transfer specification is meant to convey the drive's peak data-reading capabilities. A higher rate of transfer might be better, but a number of other factors come into play.

A higher transfer rate might not be useful if the software accessing the data or the PC using the data does not need the information in such high volume.

If you expect to run a variety of CD-based software on your system, you need a drive with a high data transfer rate. Applications that employ full-motion video, animation, and sound require high transfer rates; you'll be disappointed in the results of a slower drive.

Access Time

A CD-ROM drive's access time is measured the same as it is for PC hard drives. In other words, the **access time** is the delay between the drive receiving the command to read and its actual first reading of a bit of data. The time is recorded in milliseconds (ms); a typical manufacturer's rating may be listed as 350 ms.

The amount of time it takes to perform a series of random reads from a number of different positions on the disc is called the *average access time;* the true access time depends entirely on where the data is located on the disc. Positioning the read mechanism at a portion of the disc near the narrower center of the disc gives you a faster access time than positioning it at the wider outer perimeter. Access times quoted by many manufacturers are an average taken by calculating a series of random reads from a disc.

Obviously, a faster average access time is desirable, especially when you are relying on the drive to locate and pull up data quickly. Access times for CD-ROM drives are steadily improving; these advancements are discussed later in this chapter.

Note that these average times are significantly slower than those for PC hard drives, ranging from 500 to 200 ms (compared to 20 to 10 ms on a typical hard disk). Most of the speed difference lies in the construction of the drive itself; hard drives have multiple read heads and platters and range over a smaller surface area of media. CD-ROM drives have only one laser read beam that must be positioned over the entire range of the disc. In addition, the data on a CD is organized in a long spiral from the inner edge outward. When the drive positions its head to read a "track," it must estimate the distance into the disc and skip forward or backward to the appropriate point in the spiral. Reading off the outer edge requires a longer access time than reading off the inner segments because the head has to travel further before it can find the data.

One way to visualize a CD-ROM data disc is to think of a phonograph record; the record, like the CD, holds data in a spiral down the platter. New tracks, or songs, are merely different segments along the spiral. CDs and records differ in one significant way, however; the CD's spiral of data moves from the inside toward the outer edge as it fills with data (the analog spiral of the phonograph record moves from the outer edge inward).

Buffer

Some drives are shipped with internal buffers, or caches of memory, installed on-board. These buffers are actual memory chips installed on the drive's board that allow data to be staged or stored in larger segments *before* being sent to the PC. A typical buffer for a CD-ROM drive is 256 kilobytes (KB). There are several advantages to having buffer memory on the CD-ROM drive. Buffers can ensure that the PC receives data at a constant rate; when an application requests data from the CD-ROM disc, the data is probably scattered across different segments of the disc. Because we know that the drive has a relatively slow access time, the pauses between data reads may cause a drive to send data to the PC sporadically. You may not notice this problem in typical text applications, but a slower access-rate drive coupled with no data buffering is very noticeable—even irritating—in the display of video or some audio segments. In addition, a drive's buffer, when under the control of sophisticated software, can read and have ready the disc's table of contents, making the first request for data faster to find on the disc platter.

Interface

A CD-ROM's **interface** is the physical connection of the drive to the PC's expansion bus. The interface is an important element—the pipeline of data between the drive and the computer.

SCSI Standard Interfaces

SCSI, or the *Small Computer System Interface*, refers to a group of adapter cards that conforms to a set of common commands. These adapter cards also allow computer users to string a group of devices along a chain from a single adapter, avoiding the complication of inserting new adapter cards into the PC bus slots every time a new hardware device, such

RULE OF THUMB

Recommended Access Time: 350 ms or better.

RULE OF THUMB

Recommended Buffer: 256 KB or better.

EXPLANATION

Interfaces

In the world of computers, interfaces are everywhere. An *interface* is simply a place where information moves from one system to another—for example from a CD-ROM drive to the computer's memory for use by an application, or from the computer to a printer for hard copy. The user interface—where you type and use your mouse—is where the data is moved between the computer and you.

EXPLANATION

SCSI Commands

SCSI commands are low-level requests, acknowledgments, and signals passed from the PC to the peripheral device with which it is communicating. SCSI commands may be as simple as finding all connected devices or asking whether a device is busy or idle. If devices, host adapters, and software drivers all use the same commands that are implemented the same way across all hardware, you've avoided another standards war and entered nirvana.

TIP

CorelSCSI!

Corel Corporation, the same company that who brings you CorelDRAW!, has done more than any single company to help standardize SCSI on the PC. By taking Adaptec's ASPI interface and creating a standard set of requirements for it, Corel *certifies* hardware for compatibility. Corel's own product, CorelSCSI!, provides drivers for a wide array of SCSI devices at a single low cost. If you want or need to use SCSI, check out CorelSCSI!.

For manufacturer information on CorelSCSI!, see Appendix D, "Where To Buy: Hardware and Software Vendors."

RULE OF THUMB

Recommended Interface: SCSI-2 or ASPI compatible.

as a tape unit or additional CD-ROM drive, is added to the system. These traits make SCSI interfaces preferable for connecting peripherals such as a CD-ROM drive to your PC.

All SCSI adapters are not created equal. Although they may share a common command set, they can implement these commands differently—or not at all—depending on how the adapter's manufacturer designed the hardware. Furthermore, although the adapter may use **SCSI commands** to operate the CD-ROM drive, it may not allow the chaining of devices, defeating one of the chief purposes of implementing a SCSI interface.

SCSI-2 and ASPI

As is usual with standards, the original SCSI specification did not take into account the rapid enhancements to the technology involved. Changes to the amount of data that SCSI devices are expected to move, and the sophistication of the devices themselves, required enhancements to the original specification.

The SCSI-2 standard incorporates several enhancements, including the following:

- SCSI Fast, a special high-speed mode that greatly increases *throughput* (the amount of data moved on the SCSI bus).
- SCSI Wide, an enhancement that adds a second cable. This cable is used to widen the data bus to 32 bits, which also enhances throughput.
- Scatter/Gather, intelligent data reads and writes that minimize seek times by scheduling activity based on the data's physical location under the control of the SCSI host adapter.

The Advanced SCSI Programming Interface (ASPI) standard was designed by Adaptec—a manufacturer of SCSI host adapters—to ease the development of SCSI hardware device drivers. ASPI provides a standard software interface to the host adapter hardware. A SCSI device manufacturer can write a single, ASPI-compatible device driver that works with any ASPI-compatible host adapter or interface card made by Adaptec or another manufacturer.

The ASPI standard interface is made possible by the **ASPI driver** for a particular host adapter. The ASPI driver is a small device driver that translates the peculiarities of a particular manufacturer's hardware into the standard ASPI interface.

Nonstandard SCSI

Some drive manufacturers ship their own controller cards with their drives. These controllers may be called SCSI, but may not be compatible with the ASPI or SCSI-2 specifications. When a manufacturer claims a drive has or comes with a SCSI interface, you may be getting far less than you need.

If you don't intend to install multiple SCSI devices, however, a proprietary controller or adapter is acceptable. Just beware of the limitations on expansion and compatibility.

CD-ROM Disc and Drive Formats

As was explained in Chapter 1, compact discs are pitted to encode the binary bits 0 and 1. Without a logical organization to this disc full of digits, however, the CD-ROM drive and PC would be at a loss to find any discernible data in all those numbers. To this end, the data is encoded to conform to particular standards. When a drive encounters particular patterns, it—and the PC—"recognize" the organization of the disc and find their way around the platter. Without standard data formats, the CD-ROM industry would be dead in the water; vendors of particular discs and disc drives would be producing incompatible discs and drives, thereby limiting the number of units that could be sold.

Formats are also needed to advance the technology. For example, hard rubber wheels and no suspension were fine for the first automobiles that cruised along at the breakneck speed of 30 miles per hour. But hitting a pothole at 60 miles per hour in such a vehicle could cause serious damage to the vehicle—and the riders. Consequently, inflatable tires and shock absorbers became a necessary component of the modern car.

Similarly, the standards for disc formats have evolved. The first compact data discs stored only text information that was relatively easy to encode. Graphics produced a greater challenge, and the standards evolved to incorporate them. The use of animation with synchronized sound, and then live-motion video, called for other expansions to the standards in which CDs store data.

Advanced CD-ROM standards are still evolving. Multiple vendors are deploying a number of different techniques for expanding the capabilities of CD-ROM technology. These techniques can be incompatible with each other or immature in their development. Consequently, acceptance of some of these newer standards by software vendors is essential to the widespread use of these newer standards. You need to be familiar with these issues before you purchase a drive; consider the formats that the drive is capable of reading—both now and in the future.

The majority of drives available today, however, do comply with earlier CD-ROM formats, ensuring that the vast library of CD-ROM applications currently available can be used on these newer drives.

First Data Standard: ISO 9660

Manufacturers of the first CD-ROM data discs produced their discs for one particular drive. In other words, a data disc produced for company A's drive could not be read by anyone who had purchased company B's drive; the disc was formatted for each manufacturer's drive. Obviously, this incompatibility stalled the industry's development. Philips and Sony—the original collaborators for the standards incorporated in audio CDs—developed the "Yellow Book" specifications for data CD-ROMs.

As an extension of the way in which audio data was stored on disc, the Yellow Book specification details how data can be organized on a disc for later retrieval. The International Standards Organization (**ISO**) refined this specification in such a way that every vendor's drive and disc would expect to find a table of contents for a data disc. This is known as a *Volume Table of Contents*, and in theory is similar to a standard book's table of contents. ISO 9660

EXPLANATION

ISO

The International Standards Organization is a committee responsible for developing standards that favor international trade by ensuring compatibility among manufacturers.

did not completely solve compatibility problems, however. The incorporation of additional data to aid and refine the search for data on a disc, as well as to format the data blocks, was still left to each separate vendor's design.

Books, Books, Everywhere...

Colors of books are used to define CD-ROM specifications because of the binders in which the specifications were originally held. The Yellow Book specification, for example, gets its name because the specifications were originally contained in a yellow binder. Following is a list of the book colors and a brief description of the CD-ROM format specifications they contain.

Color	Description
Red	Audio
Yellow	Data (CD-DA)
Green	CD-I (Philips), CD-ROM-XA
Orange	Recordable (CD-WO, CD-R)

High Sierra Format

EXPLANATION

CD Tracks

CD data is all on one long spiral track. *Track* refers to the sectors or segments of data along the spiral.

It was in the interest of all manufacturers to resolve the compatibility issue. In a meeting in 1985 at the High Sierra Hotel and Casino in Lake Tahoe, California, leading manufacturers of CD-ROM drives and CD-ROM discs came together to resolve the differences in their implementations of the ISO 9660 format.

The agreement became known as the *High Sierra format*, and is now a part of the ISO 9660 specification document. This expansion enabled all drives to read all ISO 9660-compliant discs, opening the way for the mass production of CD-ROM software. Adoption of this standard also enabled disc publishers to provide cross-platform support for their software, easily manufacturing discs for DOS, UNIX, and other operating system formats. Without this agreement, the maturation of the CD-ROM marketplace would have taken years longer and stifled the production of available ROM-based information.

The exact and entire specifications for how to format the CD media is complex, strewn with jargon you may never need, and superfluous to your understanding of drive capabilities. You should know the basics, however, because they give you a glimpse at the inner workings of retrieving data quickly from such an enormous well of data.

To put basic High Sierra format in perspective, the disc layout is roughly analogous to a floppy disk. A floppy has a system track that not only identifies itself as a floppy and its density and operating system, but also tells the computer how it's organized—into directories, and within the directories, into files.

Basic CD-ROM formats are much the same. The initial **track** of a data CD identifies itself as a CD and begins synchronization between the drive and the disc. Beyond the synchronization area lies a system area that details how the entire disc is structured; as a part of the system area, the disc identifies the location of the volume area—where the actual data is held. The system area also contains the directories of this volume, with pointers or addresses to various named areas. A significant difference between CD directory structures and DOS directory structures is that the CD's system area also contains direct addresses of files within their subdirectories, allowing the CD to seek a specific location on the spiral data track.

CD-DA (Digital Audio)

Data drives that can read data *and* audio are called CD-DA. Virtually any data drive now being sold can read both types of discs. When you insert a disc, the drive reads the first track of the disc to determine what type is loaded. Most drives ship with **audio CD** software that allows you to play audio CDs from your PC (shareware and freeware utilities to control audio CDs are also readily available on on-line services). You can use headphones, or if you have installed a sound card, you can connect speakers to the system. Some external drives ship with standard left/right audio plugs; just plug them into any external amplifier.

PhotoCD

Kodak first announced the PhotoCD in 1990 but did not make it available until 1992. Kodak is now shipping in quantity the home CD drives that display your own photographs on your television. You merely drop off a roll of film at a participating Kodak developer and later take home a PhotoCD and drop it into your Kodak PhotoCD-compatible disc player. But what's a PhotoCD-compatible player?

Because virtually all data-ready CD drives can also interpret audio, it's no surprise that the Kodak PhotoCD players can play audio discs. The player merely reads the first track and determines what type of disc you've fed it. The real breakthrough is in the drive's capability to determine whether the data disc contains one, two, or dozens of individual photo "sessions."

CD Sessions

Remember from the discussion of the High Sierra format (earlier in this chapter) that each data disc holds a Volume Table of Contents (VTOC) that tells the CD reader where—and how—the data is laid out on the disc. CD data had, until this point in its evolution, been single-session in its encoding. In other words, when a CD master disc was created, all the data that would ever reside on the disc was recorded in a single session. Neither the format nor the media contained any provision for returning later to append more information. The PhotoCD format—along with the XA and CD-I formats covered in "CD-ROM-XA Extended Architecture," later in this chapter—not only allows for multiple sessions, but allows multiple sessions to be read back on a fully PhotoCD-capable CD-ROM drive. The drive must be capable of finding the multiple VTOCs associated with the appended sessions, however.

Volume Table of Contents

Disc ID	Data Block 1 Address	Data Block 2 Address	Data Block 3 Address	etc...

FIGURE 2.1

The basic organizational format of a CD-ROM.

This is where some confusion arises. When Kodak first released the PhotoCD, the company maintained that a drive must be CD-ROM-XA-compliant to use PhotoCD. As of January 1992, however, Kodak tested non-XA drives with new software drivers and okayed them as single-session PhotoCD-compatible. In other words, many of the drives shipping right now—in fact, a majority of the drives—may be perfectly suited to reading PhotoCD discs that contain a single session of photos. The drive can recognize only the first session, however, and ignores any data or subsequent volume entries made after the initial session.

Almost all PC-based CD-ROM drives, if supplied with the proper device driver and Kodak-based software, can read single-session

TIP

Hearing Your CD-ROM

Even the least expensive CD-ROM drives are likely to be able to play audio from a CD, but some have only a headphone jack on the front of the drive unit. You can use a simple cable to connect an amplifier to this jack. The cable is readily available at electronic supply or discount stores. Just ask for a 1/8-inch stereo phone-plug-to-RCA-plug cable.

TIP

Using PhotoCD

Although PhotoCD can be used as the modern equivalent of the slide show when the discs contain photos of your vacation, this technology is also a wonderful opportunity for DTP (desktop publishing) enthusiasts and other desktop document creators. Even if you have a scanner and can create your own images, you probably can't duplicate the quality and convenience of the PhotoCD. For the pros and semipros, Kodak's offering may be a liberating technology.

For a lot more information about PhotoCD, see Chapter 16, "CD-ROM in the Family Room."

PhotoCD images, and many can also read multisession PhotoCDs. Kodak is licensing the "viewer" portion of its software so that it can be incorporated into existing software packages. Special filters—or decoders—will be added to desktop publishing, word processing, and PC-paint software to enable you to import PhotoCD images into documents created using these packages.

Kodak has plans to incorporate synchronized audio and text into its existing photo format. To take advantage of these capabilities, the drive that reads these advanced discs must be XA-compatible. In addition, drives must be XA-compatible to read any disc that contains multiple recordings.

As of this writing, almost all CD-ROM drives can read Kodak PhotoCD discs in at least single-session mode, but many can read multisession discs as well. Philips CD-I home entertainment systems and the Kodak systems can also use multisession discs. To take advantage of multisession capabilities and to use audio and text on a PhotoCD for the PC, you must have an XA-compatible CD-ROM drive.

How Do They Do It? PhotoCD Production

When you drop off your roll of film, the Kodak developers process the film, just as they do normally. After the negatives are made, however, the process goes high-tech. Using high-speed UNIX operating-system-based SUN SparcStations, the negatives are scanned into the SparcStation using ultra-high resolution scanners. To give you an idea of the amount of information each scan carries, one color photograph can require 15 to 20 megabytes of storage space. After the image is stored on disc, it is compressed using Kodak's own custom software. The compressed, stored images are then encoded onto special writeable CDs. The finished product is packaged in a familiar CD case and shipped back to your local developer for pickup.

Even though these scanned images occupy an enormous amount of media space, the capacity of CD technology can easily carry 100 photos—at the highest possible resolution. (See table 2.1 for more details.) Because most of us rarely have this many photos developed at the same time, Kodak developed the system in conjunction with Philips so that multiple sessions can be recorded on one disc. You can have your Thanksgiving photos developed and recorded to disc in November, for example, and bring the same disc back in late December to have other holiday photos added. You can continue to bring in the same disc until it is full.

Table 2.1 PhotoCD Resolutions

Resolution (in Lines)	Uses
256 by 384	Fine for most conventional TVs and low-resolution VGA adapters.
512 by 768	Good for color Macintosh video or S-VHS TVs and VGA adapters with 1 MB or more of memory.
1024 by 1536	Beyond current TV technology but ready for high-definition TV; even high-end graphics cards can't use all the data.
2048 by 3072	Beyond TV or current personal computer capacities but useful for print media.

EXPLANATION

Backwards Compatibility

Backwards compatibility means that a new or improved system or technology can work with its predecessors. Backwards compatibility is very important to vendors as they design new products. Consumers do not want their supply of data, media, equipment, or the like to become suddenly obsolete. Backwards compatibility, however, is a double-edged sword. In order to ensure this compatibility, trade-offs are always made, and these trade-offs generally mean that the new technology does not achieve its full potential.

CD-ROM-XA Extended Architecture

CD-ROM-XA, or eXtended Architecture, is **backwards-compatible** with the earlier High Sierra or ISO 9660 CD-ROMs. It adds another dimension and added capabilities to the world of CD-ROM technology.

Interleaving

CD-ROM-XA drives employ a technique known as *interleaving*. The XA specification calls for the ability to encode on disc whether the data directly following an identification mark is graphics, sound, or text. Graphics may include standard graphic pictures, animation, or full-motion video. In addition, these blocks can be *interleaved*, or *interspersed*, with each other. For example, a frame of video may start a track and be followed by a segment of audio that accompanies the video, which in turn is followed by yet another frame of video. The drive picks up the audio and video sequentially, buffers the information in memory, and then sends it to the PC for synchronization.

In short, the data is read off the disc in alternating pieces and then synchronized at playback so that the result is a simultaneous presentation of the various kinds of data.

Mode 1 and Mode 2, Form 1 and Form 2

To achieve the level of sophistication dictated by the XA specification, the CD format is broken up so that the data types are layered. Mode 1 is CD data *with* error correction (ECC). Mode 2 is CD data *without* error correction. The Mode 2 track, however, also allows what are called **Form 1 and Form 2** tracks to exist—one after the other—to allow for interleaving. These interleaved tracks may include their own error correction and may be any type of data.

For a drive to be truly XA-compatible, the Form 2 data encoded on the disc as audio must be ADPCM audio. Therefore, the drive or the SCSI controller must have a signal processor chip that can decompress the audio during the synchronization process.

FIGURE 2.2

CD-ROM-XA architecture adds the ability to "interleave" different types of data.

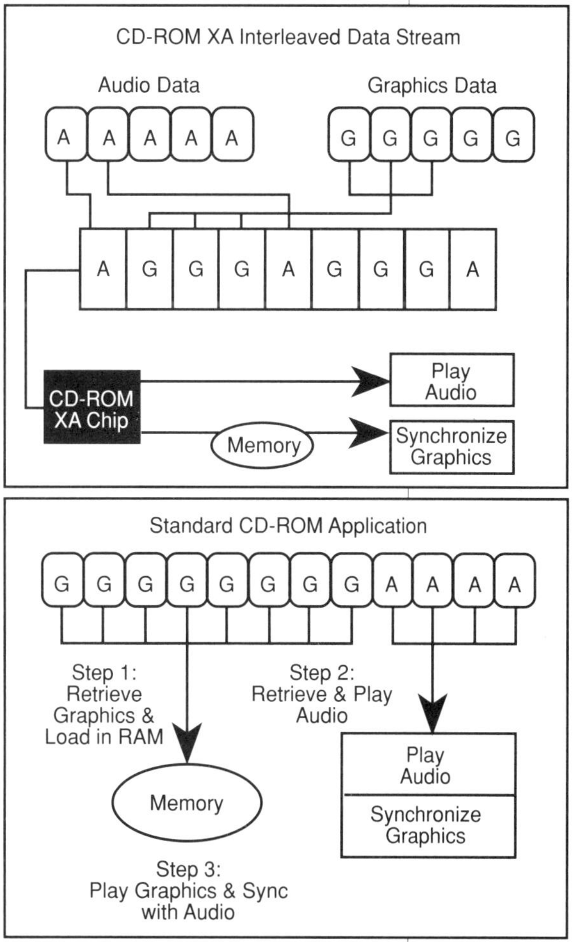

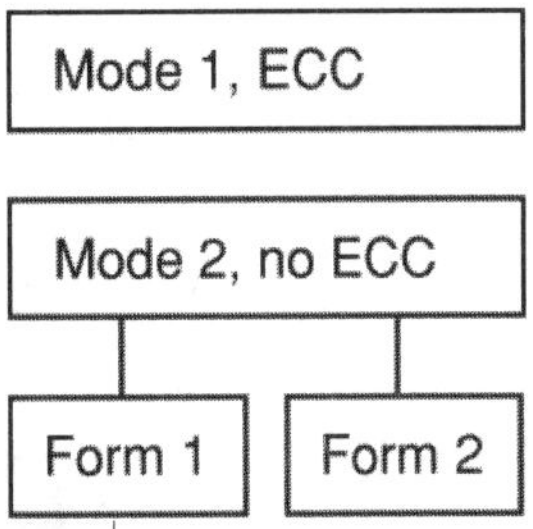

FIGURE 2.3

A simple schematic of the use of modes and forms in a CD-ROM-XA format. Both modes can be used on one disc.

EXPLANATION

Forms and Modes

The terms *Form 1* and *Form 2* refer to two separate audio and video tracks that can be interleaved in Mode 2. Because Mode 1 doesn't expect interleaved data, Form 1 and Form 2 have no effect on it.

TIP

Using CD-R

Although writeable CD-ROM may not be ready for consumer prime time, it is a great business tool. CD-R has two important applications. First is desktop database publishing, in which the high capacity and low cost of CD-ROM media make small production runs of large databases possible. The second application is internal or external distribution of large amounts of data. This application is useful to organizations that must distribute a great deal of data to only a few locations—not enough to justify the production of a normal CD-ROM. This data could be a catalog, an inventory, or even executable programs.

What all this translates into is that drives currently available may be *partially* XA-compliant. They may be capable of interleaving data and reading multisession discs but may not have the ADPCM audio component on the disc or its controller.

Manufacturers may claim that their drives are "XA-ready," which means that they are capable of multisessions and Modes 1 and 2 and Forms 1 and 2 reading, but they do *not* incorporate the ADPCM chip. Software developers, including Kodak, have yet to produce many XA software titles. IBM has a few under its Ultimedia program, but others have not yet hit the market.

If you purchase a drive that is fully mode-compatible, form-compatible, and capable of reading multiple sessions, you may have the best available at this time. The XA specification is currently waiting for acceptance. Audio and video interleaving *is* possible without full XA compliance, as MPC applications under Microsoft Windows demonstrate.

CD-R

Sometimes known as CD-WORM and CD-WO, the **CD-R** format allows you to write your own CDs.

As with mastering any CD, data must be laid out or formatted before it is recorded to the CD-R unit. Often, this layout is performed on a PC with large hard disks or other magnetic and removable media.

The CD-R is not quite the CD you might expect, however. Instead of the recording beam burning pits into a metallic or glass strata, the CD-R media is coated with a dye that has the same reflective properties as a "virgin" CD disc—in other words, a CD reader sees an unrecorded CD-R disc as one long land without any pits (lands and pits are described in Chapter 1, "What Is CD-ROM?"). When the recording laser begins to burn data into the CD-R media, it heats the gold layer and the dye layer beneath. The result of heating these areas causes the dye and gold areas to diffuse light in exactly the same way that a pit does on a glass master disc or a mass-produced CD. The reader is fooled into thinking a pit exists; there is no actual pit, however—just a spot of less-reflective disc caused by the chemical reaction of heating the dye and gold.

Golden Memories: Gold Metal in CD-ROMs

The Kodak PhotoCD discs you receive from a developer look like bright gold. This regal color is not a marketing gimmick; the discs actually contain a film of gold. The Kodak PhotoCD system is a variant of the CD-R recorder. Your memorable photos are, in fact, etched in gold.

Many of the newer-model CD-R units support all the formats covered in this chapter: from ISO 9660 through CD-ROM-XA. In addition, these drives also read the formats, serving as a ROM reader. Prices have fallen, but they're still around $3,000. A number of models are discussed in Chapter 14, "Creating CD-ROMs," which covers capabilities, price, and the cost of recordable CD-R media.

Other Standards and Designations

When discussing CD-ROM drives, applications, and software, a number of additional standards and terms may be used. The following sections are a round-up discussion of these standards and designations.

Multimedia CD-ROM

Multimedia is not a specific standard but a descriptive term. Any CD that incorporates text with graphics or sound or video is, by definition, multimedia. **Multimedia CDs** exist for DOS, Macintosh System 7, MegaDOS, Windows, and UNIX operating systems and may be available in many different formats.

MPC CD-ROMs

A consortium of hardware and software manufacturers led by Microsoft Corporation announced the formation of the Multimedia PC Marketing Council at Fall COMDEX in 1991. This council described the recommended platform for implementing multimedia on PC-compatible systems; as more manufacturers joined the council, applications and hardware conformed to the proscribed specifications. The council has produced two separate standards: MPC Level 1 and MPC Level 2.

The MPC Council recommends the following minimum performance requirements for MPC Level 1-compatible CD-ROM drives:

- CD-DA drive with external audio output. ("External audio output" can be as simple as a headphone jack. Most drives have headphone jacks and a 4-pin audio edge connector or standard RCA audio plugs.)
- 150 KB/s transfer rate, required for animation or video.
- 500 ms access speed. This rate is unrealistically low, however. Most drives have much better access rates; if you use a lot of graphics and video, you'll want a drive with better performance than 500 ms.

The standards for MPC Level 2 drives are more in-line with today's CD-ROM drive market. MPC Level 2 specifications include all the MPC Level 1 requirements with some modifications:

- 300 KB/s transfer rate. The council recommends that drives achieve this rate using less than 60 percent of the CPU's time.
- Under 400 ms access speed.
- XA-ready.
- Multisession PhotoCD compatible.

Far from being an exact specification or format for data, MPC CD-ROM is a convention for storing audio, animation, video, and text for synchronization under Microsoft Windows using data received from an MPC-compliant

NOTE

Using Terms Correctly

As a rule of thumb, *multimedia CD-ROM* is a term used to describe any disc that uses multiple media. Other specifications and terms are more specific to operating systems or CD-ROM disc formats.

For a lot more information on multimedia, see Chapter 7, "What Is Multimedia?"

To find out about multimedia at home, see Chapter 16, "CD-ROM in the Family Room."

CD-ROM. Microsoft has developed Windows Application Programmer's Interface software, which allows CD-ROM software manufacturers to organize data on their CDs so that information can be passed to Windows for processing.

Note that discs labeled *MPC* or *MPC2* run only under Microsoft Windows 3.0 (with the Microsoft Multimedia Extensions) or higher. If a drive meets either level of the MPC Council recommendation for performance, it can run MPC CD-ROMs under Windows.

MultiSpin and High-Speed Drives

Audio drives deliver sound at a preset transfer rate (150 KB/s) to the Digital to Analog Converters (DACs).

MultiSpin drives, a term coined and trademarked by NEC, Inc., allow the drive to **spin faster** and deliver data at rates far higher than the audio equivalent. There is no reason why the computer must restrict itself to receiving data at the slower audio rate if the CPU, memory, and application software are capable of handling faster data rates.

NEC's line of double-speed drives were the first on the market in 1992, but now double-speed drives are commonplace. It should be no surprise that these drives deliver data to the PC at roughly twice the speed of earlier CD-ROMs. Particular applications, such as live-motion video, especially benefit from this technology—data is delivered in a constant stream, allowing the PC to process the video frames at a smoother rate. Some drives without double-speed (or faster) technology, especially those that have no buffering capabilities, deliver video in a jerky and uneven manner.

The newest drives on the market are faster yet, delivering data at three or four times the original rate. NEC makes a triple-speed drive, and several manufacturers now make quad-speed drives (a technology introduced by Pioneer). Although most currently available discs aren't designed to take advantage of this higher speed (Microsoft's newest titles are), more quad-speed compatible discs are being produced all the time.

EXPLANATION

Spinning Speeds

The CD format was originally designed to store audio, not data. For audio reproduction, the speed at which the disc spins must send the data to the DACs—Digital to Analog Converters, which turn the digital information stored on the disc into the sound you hear—at a rate that provides the data when it is needed for the sound. This data rate is fixed, even though the disc spins more slowly at its center—where the data starts—than at its outside edge. The laser speed varies to compensate for the higher angular velocity that the larger diameter at the edge causes. This speed is perfect for audio; for data, however, the faster, the better. New drives can adjust themselves to higher spinning speed for data or the standard speed for audio.

Other Drive Features

Given all the technical specifications such as transfer rates, buffers, and interfaces, you must also evaluate other aspects of a drive's construction, design, and manufacture when choosing a CD-ROM.

Drive Seals

Dirt is your CD-ROM's biggest enemy. Dust or dirt, when it collects on the lens portion of the mechanism, can cause read errors or severe performance loss. Many manufacturers seal the lens and internal components in airtight enclosures away from the drive bay. Other drives, while not sealed, have double dust doors—one external and one internal—to keep dust from inside the drive. These features help prolong the life of your drive.

Caddies

Some CD-ROM drives require that you first insert the CD into a caddie and then insert the caddie into the drive. Some drive manufacturers, however, have built-in caddies—drawers that slide out when you push the Eject button. The disc is merely inserted into the drawer. Both methods have pros and cons.

Caddieless Drives

CD-ROMs without caddies require you to spend less time fumbling around with your CDs—and save you the money you'd otherwise spend on caddies. This method has two slight hitches, however. First, you must make certain that the CD drawer is kept very clean; the easiest way to foul the reading of disc—and potentially damage a drive—is to introduce dirt into the mechanism. Second, if the drawer hinge fails, you must send the entire drive in for repair.

Drives with Caddies

You need a phone number for a business in Los Angeles, so you open the CD case for your American Business Phone Book CD. You eject the CD already in the drive, remove it, and replace it in its case. You take out the Phone Book CD and insert it into the caddie. Then....

You get the picture. Using caddies is a time-consuming bother if you deal with a number of different CDs. This inconvenience is the big drawback to caddies. The individual caddies are easy to clean; when they show signs of wear, you simply throw them away. You can pick up caddies for about five or six dollars each; it's worth the small investment to buy each of your most-used CDs its own caddie.

Self-Cleaning Lenses

If the laser lens gets dirty, so does your data. The drive spends a lot of time seeking and reseeking—or finally giving up. **Lens-cleaning discs** are available, but built-in cleaning mechanisms are now included on some model drives. You may want to consider this feature, particularly if you work in a less-than-pristine work environment or, like us, you have trouble keeping your desk clean—let alone your CD-ROM drive lens.

Internal versus External: Some Considerations

You need to consider whether you want an internal or external drive. Think about where and how you intend to use your CD-ROM drive. What about the future expansion of your system? There are pluses and minuses to both drive types. Take a look at some of the issues covered in the next sections.

External Enclosures

Drives with external enclosures tend to be rugged, portable, and large—in comparison to their internal versions. They're also typically more expensive. Buy an external drive if you have the space and are considering or already own other external SCSI peripherals you can chain to the same adapter. You may also consider an external drive if you want to move the drive easily from one PC to another. If each PC has its own SCSI adapter, you simply unplug the drive from one adapter and plug it in to the other.

TIP

Cleaning Your Drive's Lens

The collimating lens on the laser pickup assembly tends to get covered with dust, which can cause errors. If your drive is not self-cleaning, special CDs are available that, when inserted into a CD drive, use a soft brush to dust the drive's lens. These CDs are available at audio and discount stores.

For more information about caring for your discs and drives, see Appendix F, "Care and Feeding of CD-ROMs."

Internal Enclosures

Internal drives clear off a portion of your desk. Buy an internal drive if you already have internal SCSI devices you can chain to your adapter, have ample drive bay space, or intend to keep the CD-ROM drive exclusively on one machine.

Chapter 3

How To Select CD-ROM Drives

You now have a good idea what a CD-ROM drive can do for your personal and business computing. There's one problem: where once there were only a handful of CD-ROM drives to choose from, now there are dozens, with new models and manufacturers releasing new products virtually every month. These drives can vary widely in performance, design, and construction. This chapter compares many of the currently available CD-ROM drives.

How To Use This Chapter

In this chapter, you find descriptions of many kinds of CD-ROM drives. Because there are so many different brands available, this chapter narrows the search down to some of the best. Every drive in the chapter is worth looking at, but some stand out above the others. Drives are rated with a number of compact-disc icons. The maximum rating is five icons (rounded to the nearest half icon); drives that appear with no icon ratings are average drives. The rating system considers the performance and specifications of the drive; a subjective "value" score was added to the overall total. This value score factors in our opinion of the drive based on price, quality, features, and how it compares with the available field. This rating is designed to help you narrow the choices available; it is not foolproof or scientific.

Because advertisements aren't always consistent in what they tell you about the product, this chapter incorporates specification charts into the descriptions of the various products. The charts provide the same information about each product so that you can compare all the important aspects of the drives before you make a purchasing decision.

A special icon, called the Award of Excellence, is used to mark superlative products (we explain why these products are cream of the crop in the margin-note text accompanying the award icon).

Apple

Cupertino, California, giant Apple Computer has recently replaced its single-speed PowerCD and CD 150 with the double-speed AppleCD 300 Plus, available in internal and external versions. The specifications for both drives are impressive, as is their mid-range retail price.

RULE OF THUMB

Drive Speeds

Even if the drive's speed rating isn't in the name, it's easy to tell whether a drive is single-speed, double-speed, triple-speed, or quad-speed just by looking at its transfer rate:

Single-speed:	150 KB/s to 155 KB/s
Double-speed:	300 KB/s to about 350 KB/s
Triple-speed:	450 KB/s
Quad-speed:	600 KB/s

TIP

Suggested Retail Prices—Don't Believe 'Em

As you might guess from the name, the *Manufacturer's Suggested Retail Price* (MSRP) is just that: a suggestion. The manufacturers take the price they charge dealers and add an estimated (and usually *very generous*) markup, and make that their MSRP. Most dealers, especially in the computer industry, charge less than the MSRP—usually *much* less. The price the dealer charges is the *street price*. The Mitsumi double-speed CD-ROM drive, for example, has an MSRP of $199, but we've seen street prices as low as $100. The charts in this chapter include the MSRP for each drive, but check magazines and dealers for street pricing. Don't be scared away by a higher-than-average MSRP until you've checked with the real world.

AppleCD 300e Plus

External

✔ PC compatible	
✔ Macintosh compatible	
✔ MPC Level 2 compliant	
✔ PhotoCD, single session	
✔ PhotoCD, multisession	
Interface:	
✔ SCSI	
✔ SCSI-2	
Proprietary	
Average access time	<290 ms
Transfer rate	342 KB/s
Buffer	256 KB
Audio:	
✔ Standard RCA jacks	
✔ Headphones	
4-pin CD audio out	
Suggested list price:	$314

Comments: Although both the 300e Plus and 300i Plus are "MPC-compatible," the 300e Plus is the only real choice for Windows users. Unlike the 300i Plus, it includes the full complement of audio controls that are absent from most PC-compatible systems.

AppleCD 300i Plus

Internal

✔ PC compatible	
✔ Macintosh compatible	
✔ MPC Level 2 compliant	
✔ PhotoCD, single session	
✔ PhotoCD, multisession	
Interface:	
✔ SCSI	
✔ SCSI-2	
Proprietary	
Average access time	<290 ms
Transfer rate	342 KB/s
Buffer	256 KB
Audio:	
Standard RCA jacks	
Headphones	
✔ 4-pin CD audio out	
Suggested list price:	$314

Comments: Good price, but you may run into additional installation charges if you have a dealer add it to your existing Mac. Skip this one if you're a PC-compatible user—it doesn't have the audio controls you need because it's designed for Macs (most of which have those controls built in).

CD Technology

Based in Sunnyvale, California, CD Technology's primary product is its CD Porta-Drive, a lightweight, portable Mac- and PC-compatible CD drive (see fig. 3.1). CD Technology claims that, unlike other portable or lightweight CD-ROM drives, its drive is free from possible contamination because of a "quadruple seal" approach: the outside power supply is sealed, the drive mechanism is sealed, an additional barrier is provided with the popular "garage door-style" disc opening, and a self-cleaning lens mechanism adds another level of contamination protection. The drive is based on the Toshiba XM-3401 mechanism, one of the fastest on the market. The unit is light—a mere three pounds—and has a standard SCSI connection.

The suggested price includes drive, caddie, power supply, enclosure, and instructions. SCSI cards are sold separately by CD Technology, but Adaptec, Future Domain, and Procom SCSI adapters should be fine, with appropriate drivers for the Toshiba.

The internal Porta-Drive model comes with a caddie and a standard SCSI flat ribbon cable with connectors for three SCSI devices (with three connectors, you can "daisy chain" devices on the cable). Although the company offers standard 8-bit and 16-bit SCSI adapters, virtually any SCSI card supported by CorelSCSI! should work. Because this drive is essentially a Toshiba drive, the SCSI kit supports it.

FIGURE 3.1

The CD Porta-Drive T3401 from CD Technology.

SCSI Adapters without SCSI Cards

CD Technology sells a parallel-to-SCSI adapter—a SCSI-on-the-printer-port solution for the external drive—making it possible to easily attach the drive to a notebook computer that has no slot available for a SCSI card, or for users and system administrators who are squeamish about opening up PCs and messing with SCSI interface cards.

CD Technology Porta-Drive Model T3401

External (Portable)

- ✔ PC compatible
- ✔ Macintosh compatible
- ✔ MPC Level 2 compliant

- ✔ PhotoCD, single session
- ✔ PhotoCD, multisession

Interface:

- ✔ SCSI
- ✔ SCSI-2
- Proprietary

Average access time	200 ms
Transfer rate	330 KB/s
Buffer	256 KB

Audio:

- ✔ Standard RCA jacks
- ✔ Headphones
- 4-pin CD audio out

Suggested list price: $700

Comments: Yes, that's the real suggested list price, but this drive has a few things that make it worth a look. It has won a slew of major awards from Macintosh and PC magazines and endorsements from big names like Microsoft and IBM. And it's a portable, which always jacks up the price a little.

CD Technology Model T3402-INT

Internal

- ✔ PC compatible
- ✔ Macintosh compatible
- ✔ MPC Level 2 compliant

- ✔ PhotoCD, single session
- ✔ PhotoCD, multisession

Interface:

- ✔ SCSI
- ✔ SCSI-2
- ✔ Proprietary

Average access time	200 ms
Transfer rate	330 KB/s
Buffer	256 KB

Audio:

- Standard RCA jacks
- Headphones
- ✔ 4-pin CD audio out

Suggested list price: $500

Comments: The T3402 has an impressive transfer rate and access time but its price is a little high. Most of CD Technology's sales are direct (not through stores), so you may have a tough time finding a better price.

Chinon

Chinon America, Inc., carries a full line of CD-ROM drives, multimedia upgrade kits, and 3.5-inch Magneto Optical drives. Although primarily known in this country as a manufacturer and supplier of printers, the Chinon CD-ROM drive line covers PC and Macintosh platforms, with both internal and external versions (see fig. 3.2).

The CDX-535 comes with a power supply, one CD caddie, and documentation. An optional PC Interface Package bundles an 8-bit SCSI card, SCSI cable, Microsoft MSCDEX extensions, and documentation.

The Macintosh Interface Package, an added option, includes Mac drivers, a connector cable to the Mac SCSI bus, and CD Play Software.

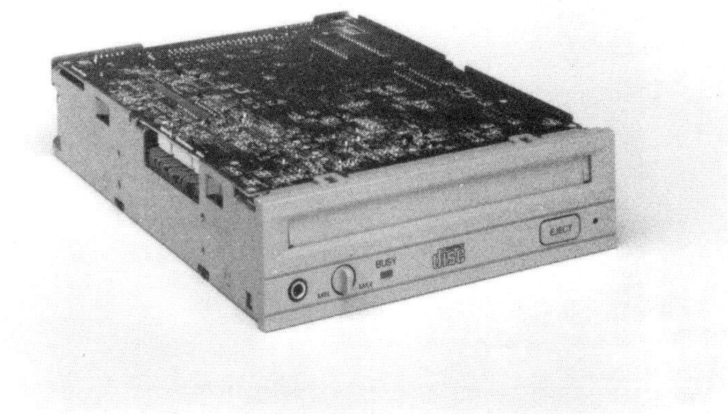

FIGURE 3.2

The Chinon CDS-535 double-speed cached drive.

Chinon CDS-535

Internal

✔ PC compatible
✔ Macintosh compatible
✔ MPC Level 2 compliant

✔ PhotoCD, single session
✔ PhotoCD, multisession

Interface:
✔ SCSI
✔ SCSI-2
Proprietary

Average access time	280 ms
Transfer rate	300 KB/s
Buffer	256 KB

Audio:
Standard RCA jacks
✔ Headphones
✔ 4-pin CD audio out

Suggested list price: $379

Comments: There's nothing really extraordinary about this drive, but there aren't many strikes against it, either (except possibly the price).

Chinon CDX-535, PC

External

✔ PC compatible
Macintosh compatible
✔ MPC Level 2 compliant

✔ PhotoCD, single session
✔ PhotoCD, multisession

Interface:
✔ SCSI
✔ SCSI-2
Proprietary

Average access time	280 ms
Transfer rate	300 KB/s
Buffer	256 KB

Audio:
✔ Standard RCA jacks
✔ Headphones
4-pin CD audio out

Suggested list price: $429

Comments: This drive is about average in its specs, with a slightly higher price than comparable drives.

Chinon
CDA-535, Mac

External

PC compatible	
✔ Macintosh compatible	
MPC Level 2 compliant	
✔ PhotoCD, single session	
✔ PhotoCD, multisession	
Interface:	
✔ SCSI	
✔ SCSI-2	
Proprietary	
Average access time	280 ms
Transfer rate	300 KB/s
Buffer	256 KB
Audio:	
✔ Standard RCA jacks	
✔ Headphones	
4-pin CD audio out	
Suggested list price:	$795

Comments: Street price on this drive is much lower (hundreds lower, in fact).

Creative Labs

The big name in sound cards, Creative Labs recently expanded their multimedia offerings with two CD-ROM drives—a double-speed from Panasonic and a triple-speed from NEC. Both are offered in kit form, with all the interface cables, manuals, and the Creative Labs Power Graphics CD. The included CD (with Aldus Photostyler SE, Altimira Composer, Aldus Gallery Effects, Kai's Power Tools, and HSC Digital Morph) is possibly the most impressive feature of the double-speed drive because its specs are average at best. The triple-speed kit is an external NEC drive with a SCSI interface, so you know it's powerful and reliable.

Creative Labs OmniCD Double Speed Kit

Internal

✔	PC compatible	
✔	Macintosh compatible	
✔	MPC Level 2 compliant	
✔	PhotoCD, single session	
✔	PhotoCD, multisession	
	Interface:	
	SCSI	
	SCSI-2	
✔	Proprietary	
	Average access time	280 ms
	Transfer rate	300 KB/s
	Buffer	64 KB
	Audio:	
	Standard RCA jacks	
✔	Headphones	
✔	4-pin CD audio out	
	Suggested list price:	$399.95

Comments: Although the drive has run-of-the-mill specs for a double-speed drive, it is the only drive that works with some of the Sound Blaster cards. Newer cards from Creative Labs offer other drive interfaces as well (some even include SCSI), but if you have a Sound Blaster that has only a Creative Labs CD-ROM interface, consider this kit.

Creative Labs Omni3X Kit

External

✔ PC compatible
✔ Macintosh compatible
✔ MPC Level 2 compliant

✔ PhotoCD, single session
✔ PhotoCD, multisession

Interface:
✔ SCSI
✔ SCSI-2
Proprietary

Average access time	195 ms
Transfer rate	450 KB/s
Buffer	256 KB

Audio:
✔ Standard RCA jacks
✔ Headphones
4-pin CD audio out

Suggested list price:	$599.95

Comments: NEC offers the same drive for less, but Creative Labs does include an impressive CD with its kit.

Hitachi

The Hitachi company has been in the CD-ROM drive business since the beginning, producing some of the first and fastest drives in the early market. They have a wide range of drives; in fact, no other vendor offers such a wide product line. The Hitachi drives are high quality, easy to install and configure, and have very competitive prices (see fig. 3.3).

In their extensive line of internal and external drives, Hitachi has a model and price range for virtually any user or organization.

With a larger buffer than the 1900S and a SCSI interface, the Hitachi 1950S CD-ROM drive can be a good choice for multimedia systems with standard SCSI. The drive meets MPC Level 2 specifications, includes automatic lens cleaning, and the buffer should ensure smooth video playback.

FIGURE 3.3

An Hitachi CD-ROM drive.

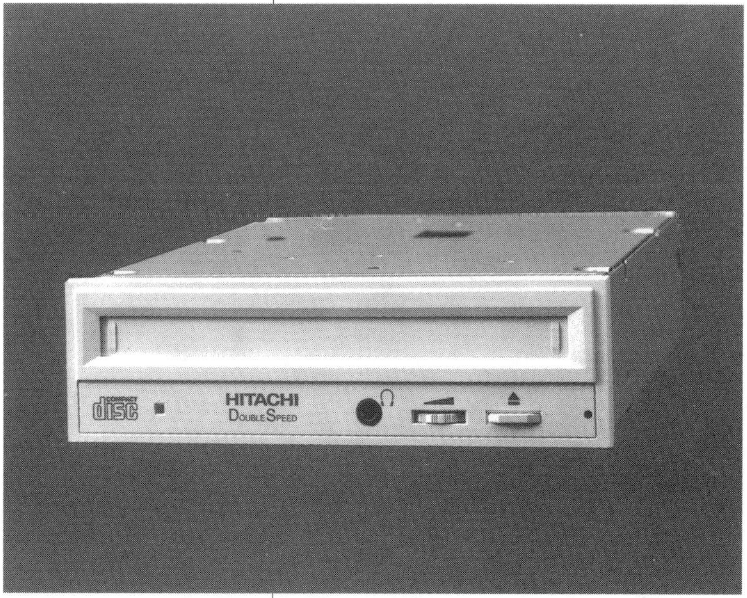

The CDR-1950S is a solid, basic, MPC or Macintosh CD-ROM drive.

Installation kits are available for Mac, PC, and PS/2 MCA bus machines.

Hitachi CDR-1750S

External

✔	PC compatible
✔	Macintosh compatible
	MPC Level 2 compliant
✔	PhotoCD, single session
	PhotoCD, multisession
Interface:	
✔	SCSI
	SCSI-2
	Proprietary

Average access time	320 ms
Transfer rate	153.6 KB/s
Buffer	64 KB

Audio:	
✔	Standard RCA jacks
✔	Headphones
	4-pin CD audio out

Suggested list price: $600

Comments: This is one of the very few single-speed drives we listed, mostly because of its SCSI interface and relatively quick access time. Many of today's CD-ROM titles are still made for single-speed drives, and the $600 MSRP is nowhere *near* what you'll find on the street. Look for single-speed drives like this one at $100 or less.

Hitachi CDR-1900S

Internal

✔	PC compatible
✔	Macintosh compatible
✔	MPC Level 2 compliant
✔	PhotoCD, single session
✔	PhotoCD, multisession
Interface:	
✔	SCSI
✔	SCSI-2
	Proprietary

Average access time	260 ms
Transfer rate	300 KB/s
Buffer	128 KB

Audio:	
	Standard RCA jacks
✔	Headphones
✔	4-pin CD audio out

Suggested list price: $670

Comments: Like the Hitachi CDR-1750S, the Hitachi CDR-1900S has an oversized MSRP but a more reasonable street price.

Hitachi CDR-1950S

Internal

- ✔ PC compatible
- ✔ Macintosh compatible
- ✔ MPC Level 2 compliant

- ✔ PhotoCD, single session
- ✔ PhotoCD, multisession

Interface:

- ✔ SCSI
- ✔ SCSI-2
- Proprietary

Average access time	235 ms
Transfer rate	307 KB/s
Buffer	256 KB

Audio:

- Standard RCA jacks
- ✔ Headphones
- ✔ 4-pin CD audio out

Suggested list price: $670

Comments: Low access time, higher-than-average transfer rate, and adequate cache combine to make this a competitive drive, but even at under $500 on the street, it's a little overpriced.

Hitachi DR-6700

Internal

- ✔ PC compatible
- ✔ Macintosh compatible
- ✔ MPC Level 2 compliant

- ✔ PhotoCD, single session
- ✔ PhotoCD, multisession

Interface:

- SCSI
- SCSI-2
- ✔ Proprietary Hitachi Bus

Average access time	260 ms
Transfer rate	300 KB/s
Buffer	128 KB

Audio:

- Standard RCA jacks
- ✔ Headphones
- ✔ 4-pin CD audio out

Suggested list price: $515

Comments: This drive is hard to find and doesn't compare favorably to others in its price range. Look at the Hitachi CDR-6750 for better performance at a better price.

Hitachi CDR-6750

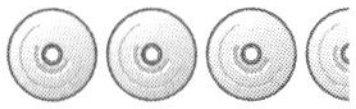

Internal

- ✔ PC compatible
- ✔ Macintosh compatible
- ✔ MPC Level 2 compliant

- ✔ PhotoCD, single session
- ✔ PhotoCD, multisession

Interface:
- ✔ SCSI
- ✔ SCSI-2
- Proprietary

Average access time	245 ms
Transfer rate	307 KB/s
Buffer	256 KB

Audio:
- Standard RCA jacks
- ✔ Headphones
- ✔ 4-pin CD audio out

Suggested list price: $515

Comments: The CDR-6750 sells for around $350 on the street. The specs are a little better than average, and you get a SCSI-2 interface instead of a proprietary Hitachi Bus interface.

Liberty Systems

Liberty is best known for bundling a variety of mass-storage devices with SCSI and parallel-to-SCSI interfaces. Liberty specializes in removable media drives such as Syquest systems and high-end optical products. Liberty's portable CD-ROM reader is a Toshiba drive in a Liberty enclosure with parallel-to-SCSI, Mac, and standard PC SCSI connection options. This portable prices out much lower than CD Technology's portable, based on the same Toshiba XM-301 drive mechanism, so if you want a solid portable at an attractive price, take a look at the Liberty drive.

The 115CD-P has a parallel-port SCSI and a price of $799. All systems—Mac, PC, or parallel—ship with cable, power cord, and software for drive installation. An optional padded carrying case is $29.

Liberty Systems 115 Series

External (Portable)

✔ PC compatible	
✔ Macintosh compatible	
✔ MPC Level 2 compliant	
✔ PhotoCD, single session	
✔ PhotoCD, multisession	
Interface:	
✔ SCSI	
✔ SCSI-2	
Proprietary	
Average access time	200 ms
Transfer rate	300 KB/s
Buffer	256 KB
Audio:	
✔ Standard RCA jacks	
✔ Headphones	
4-pin CD audio out	
Suggested list price:	$649

Comments: Liberty sells direct; that $649 price is for real.

Media Vision

One of the leaders in the multimedia arena, producing sound cards, multimedia upgrade kits, and CD-ROM titles, Media Vision has recently branched into the CD-ROM drive market with its Reno drive. Touted as the "first personal CD-ROM player," Reno detaches from its SCSI adapter module to become a portable audio CD player. Both the SCSI adapter and the drive draw power from NiCad AA batteries (8 for the SCSI adapter, 4 for the drive) or the included 12-volt AC adapter.

On the technical end, the Reno is no slouch, offering one of the fastest access times among double-speed drives—180 ms.

Media Vision Reno

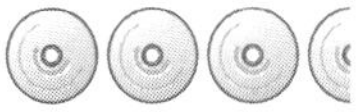

External (Portable)

✔ PC compatible	
✔ Macintosh compatible	
✔ MPC Level 2 compliant	
✔ PhotoCD, single session	
✔ PhotoCD, multisession	
Interface:	
✔ SCSI	
✔ SCSI-2	
Proprietary	
Average access time	180 ms
Transfer rate	306 KB/s
Buffer	64 KB
Audio:	
✔ Standard RCA jacks	
✔ Headphones	
4-pin CD audio out	
Suggested list price:	$349

Comments: As of this writing, the Reno was barely available and severely backordered. Look for price changes and availability problems for a while, especially with Media Vision's well-publicized financial troubles.

Mitsumi

Although Mitsumi drives are fairly new to store shelves, they're already in a lot of households—with other brand names on their faces. Their drives are quick and very inexpensive, and they come standard with a caching driver. All Mitsumi's commercial drives are internal and include an interface card.

Mitsumi has always had a proprietary interface instead of a SCSI interface. The drives are so popular, many third-party sound cards include the Mitsumi CD-ROM interface. Future products from Mitsumi will also be non-SCSI, but they'll be even more standardized. As of this writing, Mitsumi is planning to move most of their drives to an IDE interface. A Mitsumi rep we spoke with said a lot of the CD-ROM manufacturers are migrating over to IDE because SCSI devices are so expensive for the consumer to add to their systems. Prices for the new kits are not yet set, but the rep said he expects them to be very close in price to the current kits.

The Mitsumi drive is caddieless and double-sealed against dust. It includes all cables, manuals, caching-driver software, and an interface card. By the time you read this, a low-cost quad-speed version may also be available, but speculations are so sketchy as of this writing, we can't say anything about specs or pricing.

Mitsumi Double Speed

Internal

✔ PC compatible	
Macintosh compatible	
✔ MPC Level 2 compliant	
✔ PhotoCD, single session	
✔ PhotoCD, multisession	
Interface:	
SCSI	
SCSI-2	
✔ Proprietary	
Average access time	250 ms
Transfer rate	300 KB/s
Buffer	32 KB (up to 128 with caching driver)
Audio:	
✔ Standard RCA jacks	
✔ Headphones	
4-pin CD audio out	
Suggested list price:	$199

Comments: Mitsumi's drives are solid and very inexpensive. Look for IDE drives in the near future.

NEC

NEC was a pioneer in bringing CD-ROM to the desktop. NEC's CD art-gallery disc was one of the first commercially available and useful applications, which clearly demonstrated to most users the capabilities of CD technology for computing. NEC was also first in providing double-speed drives, a technology that NEC refers to as *MultiSpin*. As you know, double-speed drives give PCs more muscle when processing multimedia video and animations, making PC video a smooth, more life-like representation than the jerky, out-of-sync playback you experience on drives with 150 KB/s transfer rates. Today's NEC drives are leaders in triple-speed and quad-speed operation.

Macintosh Drivers with NEC

If you're a Mac user, make certain that you have the latest drivers for the NEC when using System 7 or above. Some users have experienced problems with their PostScript interpreters when using older NEC drivers, and the problem is particularly difficult to track down unless you know what to suspect.

NEC's two-year warranty and reputation for quality make NEC a good choice in high-speed drives. Its prices on triple-speed drives compare favorably with some prices on double-speed drives.

FIGURE 3.4

The NEC MultiSpin 4XPro (top) and the NEC MultiSpin 3XP (bottom left) and the NEC MultiSpin 3XE (bottom right).

NEC MultiSpin-3XE

External

✔ PC compatible
✔ Macintosh compatible
✔ MPC Level 2 compliant

✔ PhotoCD, single session
✔ PhotoCD, multisession

Interface:
✔ SCSI
✔ SCSI-2
Proprietary

Average access time	195 ms
Transfer rate	450 KB/s
Buffer	256 KB

Audio:
✔ Standard RCA jacks
✔ Headphones
4-pin CD audio out

Suggested list price: $495

Comments: The MSRP on this triple-speed drive is below several double-speeds. If you're looking for something in the $400 street price range, you can't beat the NEC triple-speeds.

NEC MultiSpin-3XI

Internal

✔ PC compatible
✔ Macintosh compatible
✔ MPC Level 2 compliant

✔ PhotoCD, single session
✔ PhotoCD, multisession

Interface:
✔ SCSI
✔ SCSI-2
Proprietary

Average access time	195 ms
Transfer rate	450 KB/s
Buffer	256 KB

Audio:
Standard RCA jacks
✔ Headphones
✔ 4-pin CD audio out

Suggested list price: $465

Comments: See the earlier comment on the NEC MultiSpin-3XE and the Award of Excellence we gave to NEC triple-speed drives. 'Nuff said.

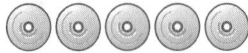

NEC MultiSpin-3XP

External (Portable)

- ✔ PC compatible
- ✔ Macintosh compatible
- ✔ MPC Level 2 compliant

- ✔ PhotoCD, single session
- ✔ PhotoCD, multisession

Interface:
- ✔ SCSI
- ✔ SCSI-2
- Proprietary

Average access time	195 ms
Transfer rate	450 KB/s
Buffer	256 KB

Audio:
- ✔ Standard RCA jacks
- ✔ Headphones
- 4-pin CD audio out

Suggested list price: $415

Comments: The lowest-priced triple-speed, this portable model has everything going for it—speed, quality, and affordability.

NEC MultiSpin-4XPro

External (Portable)

- ✔ PC compatible
- ✔ Macintosh compatible
- ✔ MPC Level 2 compliant

- ✔ PhotoCD, single session
- ✔ PhotoCD, multisession

Interface:
- ✔ SCSI
- ✔ SCSI-2
- Proprietary

Average access time	180 ms
Transfer rate	600 KB/s
Buffer	256 KB

Audio:
- ✔ Standard RCA jacks
- ✔ Headphones
- 4-pin CD audio out

Suggested list price: $995

Comments: Nice specs, but other manufacturers have hit the quad-speed market at a much lower price point.

CD-ROM BOOK
AWARD OF EXCELLENCE

NEC Triple-Speed Drives

All the NEC 3X drives are impressive, but the MultiSpin-3XP portable model is stunning (especially the price). Even though these drives are brand new as of this writing, street prices are already reasonable ($350 to $400 in most cases) and the power is unbeatable in this price range.

Philips LMS

Philips invented CD-ROM. The company does well in recordable, **CD-I**, and portable optical technologies. It's no surprise that Philips' CD-ROM drives are some of the best in the business, nor that many manufacturers are repackaging the Philips mechanism in multimedia PCs and in their own enclosures. The Colorado-based Laser Magnetic Storage (LMS) company was a subsidiary of Philips and is now Philips LMS—the consumer arm of the company.

Not surprisingly, given its inventive nature, Philips LMS makes drives with a little more innovation than most others. On some models, for example, a motorized caddie smoothly ejects the disc. To play audio CDs, you don't need to load a special software utility—just press the volume knob to play the first track, press it again to skip to the second track, and so on. Other features include a good-sized volume control and easy-to-read LEDs. Another salient feature of the LMS line is of great importance—price. The Philips LMS CD-ROM line is very reasonably priced.

All LMS retail drive packages come with an adapter card, cables, and all necessary installation software.

According to a company spokesperson, Philips LMS is the only U.S.-based manufacturer of CD-ROM drives. The company sells drives through distributors and OEM relationships with other vendors.

EXPLANATION

CD-I

Philips' CD-Interactive technology lets you play games, do research, and play audio and PhotoCDs—all through your television set. CD-I compatible CD-ROM drives can play those CD-I titles on your computer. See Chapter 16, "CD-ROM in the Family Room," for more information on CD-I.

FIGURE 3.5

The Philips LMS CM206 and CM207 double-speed drives have motorized disc trays for loading CDs and a very attractive $199 suggested list price.

Philips LMS CM206

Internal

✔ PC compatible
  Macintosh compatible
✔ MPC Level 2 compliant

✔ PhotoCD, single session
✔ PhotoCD, multisession

Interface:
  SCSI
  SCSI-2
✔ Proprietary

Average access time	<325 ms
Transfer rate	307-352 KB/s
Buffer	64 KB

Audio:
  Standard RCA jacks
✔ Headphones
✔ 4-pin CD audio out

Suggested list price: $199

Comments: This drive (like several similar ones from Philips LMS) shows up in multimedia upgrade kits a lot. Its specs are better than average and its price is better than some lower-quality drives.

Philips LMS CM207

Internal

✔ PC compatible
  Macintosh compatible
✔ MPC Level 2 compliant

✔ PhotoCD, single session
✔ PhotoCD, multisession

Interface:
  SCSI
  SCSI-2
✔ Proprietary

Average access time	325 ms
Transfer rate	307-352 KB/s
Buffer	128 KB

Audio:
  Standard RCA jacks
✔ Headphones
✔ 4-pin CD audio out

Suggested list price: $199

Comments: Another quick, low-priced drive.

Philips LMS CM215

Internal

✔ PC compatible	
Macintosh compatible	
MPC Level 2 compliant	
✔ PhotoCD, single session	
✔ PhotoCD, multisession	
Interface:	
✔ SCSI	
✔ SCSI-2	
Proprietary	
Average access time	360 ms
Transfer rate	153.6-176.4 KB/s
Buffer	64 KB
Audio:	
Standard RCA jacks	
✔ Headphones	
✔ 4-pin CD audio out	
Suggested list price:	$299

Comments: An older product from Philips LMS, this is one of the fastest single-speeds around. Don't be fooled by the MSRP, either—if you can find this drive, it'll be much cheaper.

Plextor

The Plextor (formerly Texel) line has much to offer. The drives are rugged, fast, easy to install, and give excellent performance for the money. All models—including the multimedia kits—are an exceptional value for such quality products. The Plextor drives support all the CD-ROM formats you can use on a PC or Mac at the time of this writing, and further improvements and enhancements are scheduled in the near future for this drive line. Although the name *Plextor* may not be a PC-household word yet, that may change soon. For the money, the quad-speed drives are the best. Period. If you're in the market for PhotoCD, MPC, and a standard SCSI interface drive, you cannot go wrong purchasing Plextor's quad-speeds or even the double-speed drives.

For the price, the Plextor 4Plex drive cannot be beat. If you're considering an internal quad-speed drive, you cannot find a better value.

FIGURE 3.6

Two 4Plex drives from Plextor.

AWARD OF EXCELLENCE

Plextor

Plextor's quad-speed drives are priced right and come with thoughtful additions like a full 1 MB internal cache. They're built right. If you're looking for top-of-the-line performance (regardless of your budget), look no further.

Plextor 4Plex

Internal

- ✔ PC compatible
- Macintosh compatible
- ✔ MPC Level 2 compliant

- ✔ PhotoCD, single session
- ✔ PhotoCD, multisession

Interface:

- ✔ SCSI
- ✔ SCSI-2
- Proprietary

Average access time	235 ms
Transfer rate	600 KB/s
Buffer	1 MB

Audio:

- Standard RCA jacks
- ✔ Headphones
- ✔ 4-pin CD audio out

Suggested list price: $599

Comments: When we tabulated the scores of all the drives in this chapter, the 4Plex line blew all our numbers away. We promised we'd use a maximum of five disc icons, but the numbers warranted almost twice that. Incredible specs, incredible price.

Plextor 4Plex

External

- ✔ PC compatible
- ✔ Macintosh compatible
- ✔ MPC Level 2 compliant

- ✔ PhotoCD, single session
- ✔ PhotoCD, multisession

Interface:

- ✔ SCSI
- ✔ SCSI-2
- Proprietary

Average access time	235 ms
Transfer rate	600 KB/s
Buffer	1 MB

Audio:

- ✔ Standard RCA jacks
- ✔ Headphones
- ✔ 4-pin CD audio out

Suggested list price: $649

Comments: See the comment on the Plextor 4Plex internal drive. We tried to get the publisher to give this drive an 8-1/2 disc-icon rating.

Plextor DoubleSpeed PLUS

External

- ✔ PC compatible
- ✔ Macintosh compatible
- ✔ MPC Level 2 compliant

- ✔ PhotoCD, single session
- ✔ PhotoCD, multisession

Interface:
- ✔ SCSI
- ✔ SCSI-2
- Proprietary

Average access time	240 ms
Transfer rate	335 KB/s
Buffer	64 KB

Audio:
- ✔ Standard RCA jacks
- ✔ Headphones
- ✔ 4-pin CD audio out

Suggested list price:	$409

Comments: Although not nearly as exciting as Plextor's other offerings, this double-speed drive still offers a low access time and high transfer rate.

Plextor DoubleSpeed PLUS

Internal

- ✔ PC compatible
- Macintosh compatible
- ✔ MPC Level 2 compliant

- ✔ PhotoCD, single session
- ✔ PhotoCD, multisession

Interface:
- ✔ SCSI
- ✔ SCSI-2
- Proprietary

Average access time	240 ms
Transfer rate	335 KB/s
Buffer	64 KB

Audio:
- ✔ Standard RCA jacks
- ✔ Headphones
- ✔ 4-pin CD audio out

Suggested list price:	$299

Comments: If you purchase caching software to make up for the smaller buffer, this quick double-speed drive is a good choice.

Procom Technology

Procom is perhaps best known for its SCSI Xelerator adapters, which are put to good use in these CD-ROM packages. The drives are based on mechanisms from Toshiba, NEC, and Sony. The drives and drive/adapter bundles sold by Procom are a great value (see fig. 3.7).

All Procom systems have electronic caddie ejection—vastly preferable over the mechanical ejection mechanisms, which jam and often malfunction. The caddie can be ejected by software command as well.

The Procom SiCD-DS is a fast double-speed internal drive, especially when used with a Procom adapter and CorelSCSI!. A fabulous access rate, a high transfer rate, and a hefty 256 KB buffer make this drive a real multimedia racehorse.

Procom's triple-speed offerings, the SiCDN-3x and MAC-CD-3x, are reasonably priced, with respectable specifications (not surprisingly identical to NEC's triple-speed drives on which they are based).

FIGURE 3.7

The double-speed drives from Procom are a good value for such high-end performance.

Procom SiCD-DS

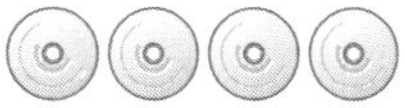

Internal

✔	PC compatible	
	Macintosh compatible	
✔	MPC Level 2 compliant	
✔	PhotoCD, single session	
✔	PhotoCD, multisession	
	Interface:	
✔	SCSI	
✔	SCSI-2	
	Proprietary	
	Average access time	200 ms
	Transfer rate	330 KB/s
	Buffer	256 KB
	Audio:	
	Standard RCA jacks	
✔	Headphones	
✔	4-pin CD audio out	
	Suggested list price:	$545

Comments: Fast but expensive.

Procom MCD-DS

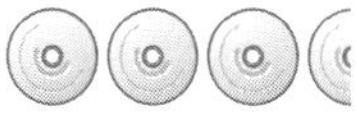

External

✔	PC compatible	
	Macintosh compatible	
✔	MPC Level 2 compliant	
✔	PhotoCD, single session	
✔	PhotoCD, multisession	
	Interface:	
✔	SCSI	
✔	SCSI-2	
	Proprietary	
	Average access time	200 ms
	Transfer rate	330 KB/s
	Buffer	256 KB
	Audio:	
✔	Standard RCA jacks	
✔	Headphones	
	4-pin CD audio out	
	Suggested list price:	$665

Comments: This drive has everything a double-speed needs—but at a quad-speed price.

Procom PXCDP-DS

External	
✔ PC compatible	
Macintosh compatible	
✔ MPC Level 2 compliant	
✔ PhotoCD, single session	
✔ PhotoCD, multisession	
Interface:	
✔ SCSI	
✔ SCSI-2	
Proprietary	
Average access time	320 ms
Transfer rate	300 KB/s
Buffer	64 KB
Audio:	
✔ Standard RCA jacks	
✔ Headphones	
4-pin CD audio out	
Suggested list price:	$315
Comments: Although this is one of Procom's lowest-priced drives, its run-of-the-mill speed and price aren't up to the competition.	

Procom PICDP-DS

Internal	
✔ PC compatible	
Macintosh compatible	
✔ MPC Level 2 compliant	
✔ PhotoCD, single session	
✔ PhotoCD, multisession	
Interface:	
✔ SCSI	
✔ SCSI-2	
Proprietary	
Average access time	320 ms
Transfer rate	300 KB/s
Buffer	64 KB
Audio:	
Standard RCA jacks	
✔ Headphones	
✔ 4-pin CD audio out	
Suggested list price:	$265
Comments: Low price for a SCSI double-speed, but nothing too impressive.	

Procom SiCDN-3x

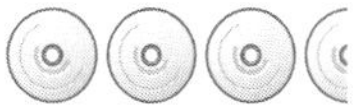

Internal

✔	PC compatible	
	Macintosh compatible	
✔	MPC Level 2 compliant	
✔	PhotoCD, single session	
✔	PhotoCD, multisession	
Interface:		
✔	SCSI	
✔	SCSI-2	
	Proprietary	
Average access time		195 ms
Transfer rate		450 KB/s
Buffer		256 KB
Audio:		
	Standard RCA jacks	
✔	Headphones	
✔	4-pin CD audio out	
Suggested list price:		$565

Comments: A NEC triple-speed in a Procom box at a higher MSRP than NEC? It's a high-quality drive, but find out what the extra cost buys you.

Procom SiCD-TDS

Internal

✔	PC compatible	
	Macintosh compatible	
✔	MPC Level 2 compliant	
✔	PhotoCD, single session	
✔	PhotoCD, multisession	
Interface:		
✔	SCSI	
✔	SCSI-2	
	Proprietary	
Average access time		250 ms
Transfer rate		300 KB/s
Buffer		64 KB
Audio:		
	Standard RCA jacks	
✔	Headphones	
✔	4-pin CD audio out	
Suggested list price:		$355

Comments: Nothing outstanding.

Procom MCDN-3x

External

✔ PC compatible
Macintosh compatible
✔ MPC Level 2 compliant

✔ PhotoCD, single session
✔ PhotoCD, multisession

Interface:
✔ SCSI
✔ SCSI-2
Proprietary

Average access time	195 ms
Transfer rate	450 KB/s
Buffer	256 KB

Audio:
✔ Standard RCA jacks
✔ Headphones
4-pin CD audio out

Suggested list price: $685

Comments: Another repackaged NEC triple-speed. Great drive, but you might want to save a couple hundred dollars and buy it from NEC.

Procom MCD-TDS

External

✔ PC compatible
Macintosh compatible
✔ MPC Level 2 compliant

✔ PhotoCD, single session
✔ PhotoCD, multisession

Interface:
✔ SCSI
✔ SCSI-2
Proprietary

Average access time	250 ms
Transfer rate	300 KB/s
Buffer	64 KB

Audio:
✔ Standard RCA jacks
✔ Headphones
4-pin CD audio out

Suggested list price: $465

Comments: The access time is good, but everything else is average.

Procom MAC-CD-DX

External

	PC compatible	
✔	Macintosh compatible	
✔	MPC Level 2 compliant	
✔	PhotoCD, single session	
✔	PhotoCD, multisession	
Interface:		
✔	SCSI	
✔	SCSI-2	
	Proprietary	
Average access time		320 ms
Transfer rate		300 KB/s
Buffer		64K
Audio:		
✔	Standard RCA jacks	
✔	Headphones	
	4-pin CD audio out	
Suggested list price:		$399

Comments: Average specs, above-average price.

Procom MAC-CD-3x

External

	PC compatible	
✔	Macintosh compatible	
✔	MPC Level 2 compliant	
✔	PhotoCD, single session	
✔	PhotoCD, multisession	
Interface:		
✔	SCSI	
✔	SCSI-2	
	Proprietary	
Average access time		195 ms
Transfer rate		450 KB/s
Buffer		256 KB
Audio:		
✔	Standard RCA jacks	
✔	Headphones	
	4-pin CD audio out	
Suggested list price:		$649

Comments: Another version of the NEC triple-speed at a higher MSRP than NEC.

Sony Corporation

Sony sells double-speed drives and higher-end units for multimedia applications. The drives—internal and external—first shipped in the summer of 1993. Many sound cards support the Sony Bus interface (used in the CDU-33A), so you may find a better deal on a bare drive than on one that includes the Sony Bus interface card. The newer drives use standard interfaces—the CDU-55S uses SCSI and the soon-to-be-released CDU-55E uses IDE.

Sony CDU-33A

Internal

✔	PC compatible	
	Macintosh compatible	
✔	MPC Level 2 compliant	
✔	PhotoCD, single session	
✔	PhotoCD, multisession	
Interface:		
	SCSI	
	SCSI-2	
✔	Proprietary	Sony Bus
Average access time		320 ms
Transfer rate		300 KB/s
Buffer		64 KB
Audio:		
	Standard RCA jacks	
✔	Headphones	
✔	4-pin CD audio out	
Suggested list price:		$219.95

Comments: This is Sony's award-winning drive, which won the hearts of several top magazine editors some time ago. Scheduled to be phased out in favor of the CDU-55E, the CDU-33A is currently being discounted through all major channels. You can find this drive for less than half its retail price if you look around.

Sony CDU-55S

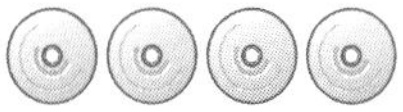

Internal

- ✔ PC compatible
- Macintosh compatible
- ✔ MPC Level 2 compliant

- ✔ PhotoCD, single session
- ✔ PhotoCD, multisession

Interface:

- ✔ SCSI
- ✔ SCSI-2
- Proprietary

Average access time	220 ms
Transfer rate	360 KB/s
Buffer	256 KB

Audio:

- Standard RCA jacks
- ✔ Headphones
- ✔ 4-pin CD audio out

Suggested list price:	$259.95

Comments: Sony calls this drive a "2.4 speed" because of its unusually high transfer rate. Low price, low access time, and standard SCSI interface make this drive a good choice.

Sony CDU-55E

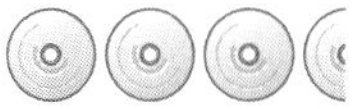

Internal

- ✔ PC compatible
- Macintosh compatible
- ✔ MPC Level 2 compliant

- ✔ PhotoCD, single session
- ✔ PhotoCD, multisession

Interface:

- SCSI
- SCSI-2
- ✔ Proprietary (ATAPI)

Average access time	250 ms
Transfer rate	342.2 KB/s
Buffer	256 KB

Audio:

- Standard RCA jacks
- ✔ Headphones
- ✔ 4-pin CD audio out

Suggested list price:	Not Available

Comments: Sony's new ATAPI (IDE interface) drive is currently available only to other manufacturers, but Sony plans to release it to the public soon. Retail prices are not available as of this writing.

Toshiba

The Toshiba XM-3401B is an internal speed demon that is perfect for multimedia applications, PhotoCD, and full-motion video. The price is reasonable when you consider its features and performance.

The Toshiba TXM-3401E is a great drive for any application dealing with full-motion video (look at its transfer rate and 256 KB buffer); but this external version of the Toshiba is a high-end drive, with a higher-than-average price.

The TXM-4101A is Toshiba's portable version of the double-speed drive, with specifications identical to the internal and external models.

Toshiba XM-3401B

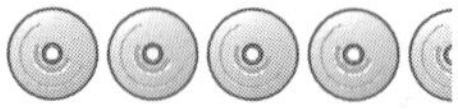

Internal

- ✔ PC compatible
- ✔ Macintosh compatible
- ✔ MPC Level 2 compliant

- ✔ PhotoCD, single session
- ✔ PhotoCD, multisession

Interface:

- ✔ SCSI
- ✔ SCSI-2
- Proprietary

Average access time	200 ms
Transfer rate	330 KB/s
Buffer	256 KB

Audio:

- Standard RCA jacks
- ✔ Headphones
- ✔ 4-pin CD audio out

Suggested list price:	$425

Comments: Fast and reasonable street price (under $300).

Toshiba TXM-3401E

External

- ✔ PC compatible
- ✔ Macintosh compatible
- ✔ MPC Level 2 compliant

- ✔ PhotoCD, single session
- ✔ PhotoCD, multisession

Interface:
- ✔ SCSI
- ✔ SCSI-2
- Proprietary

Average access time	200 ms
Transfer rate	330 KB/s
Buffer	256 KB

Audio:
- ✔ Standard RCA jacks
- ✔ Headphones
- 4-pin CD audio out

Suggested list price: $545

Comments: This is a fast drive and it has a street price that's much more realistic than MSRP.

Toshiba XM-4101B

Internal

- ✔ PC compatible
- ✔ Macintosh compatible
- ✔ MPC Level 2 compliant

- ✔ PhotoCD, single session
- ✔ PhotoCD, multisession

Interface:
- ✔ SCSI
- ✔ SCSI-2
- Proprietary

Average access time	320 ms
Transfer rate	300 KB/s
Buffer	64 KB

Audio:
- Standard RCA jacks
- ✔ Headphones
- 4-pin CD audio out

Suggested list price: $265

Comments: An average, entry-level, double-speed drive.

Toshiba TXM-4101L

External

✔ PC compatible	
✔ Macintosh compatible	
✔ MPC Level 2 compliant	
✔ PhotoCD, single session	
✔ PhotoCD, multisession	
Interface:	
✔ SCSI	
✔ SCSI-2	
Proprietary	
Average access time	320 ms
Transfer rate	300 KB/s
Buffer	64 KB
Audio:	
✔ Standard RCA jacks	
✔ Headphones	
4-pin CD audio out	
Suggested list price:	$360

Comments: Another average double-speed drive, but one that's priced a little out of its class.

Toshiba TXM-4101A

External (Portable)

✔ PC compatible	
✔ Macintosh compatible	
✔ MPC Level 2 compliant	
✔ PhotoCD, single session	
✔ PhotoCD, multisession	
Interface:	
✔ SCSI	
✔ SCSI-2	
Proprietary	
Average access time	320 ms
Transfer rate	300 KB/s
Buffer	64 KB
Audio:	
✔ Standard RCA jacks	
✔ Headphones	
4-pin CD audio out	
Suggested list price:	$415

Comments: Nothing too impressive here. Look at the Toshiba XM-3401B for better performance at a similar (or even better) price.

Chapter 4

How To Install Your CD-ROM Drive

You've read Chapter 3 and decided on the drive you want. You ordered it. It has arrived at your doorstep. What next?

Installation of a CD-ROM drive is as difficult—or as easy—as you make it. If you know a little about SCSI interface devices such as your CD-ROM drive, and plan ahead, the installation should go smoothly.

This chapter walks you through the installation of typical internal and external CD-ROM drives. It also includes tips and pointers that often aren't included in the manufacturer's installation manuals. Even after you've installed the hardware, however, you need to do more than turn on the drive and toss in a CD. You first must load special software, called a *driver*, onto your computer. Relax—this chapter also walks you through the software installation. The first few sections deal with PC-compatibles, and the last section is just for Macintoshes.

Preparing the Adapter Card

Regardless of the type of installation—internal or external drive—you need to check your CD-ROM drive's interface card (typically a SCSI card, a sound card, or an IDE interface) before installation. If you use an external drive that plugs into the parallel port, you can skip this section.

Static Protection

Static electricity is the enemy of your electronic equipment. Sensitive CMOS (Complimentary Metallic Oxide Semiconductor) components are easily damaged by static discharge—a static "shock" can have as many as 250,000 volts! This problem is particularly severe when humidity is low—like in the winter. You can avoid damage by taking some simple precautions:

continues

continued

- Leave your PC plugged into (but turned off!) a *grounded* outlet and touch the exposed metal case of the power supply to discharge any static charge built up in your body.
- Better yet, buy a static discharge wrist strap (inexpensive versions are available from Radio Shack and other electronics suppliers). *Do not attempt to make your own; wrist straps require special safety features to prevent potentially fatal shocks.* By wearing the wrist strap, you will continuously drain your static charge.
- Try to work in an uncarpeted room, if possible.
- Remember that static discharge damage is not always *immediately* fatal to your equipment. Without some precaution, you can do damage that may show up only after some use of the device.

Carefully remove the adapter card from its protective, antistatic bag (if the card came in one).

Lay out the card on the antistatic bag; the IC chips, transistors, and processors should be face up; the external connector should be to your right. Virtually all documentation for adapter cards assumes that the cards are oriented this way when you configure them.

NOTE

Getting All or Most of the Settings

Some proprietary SCSI host adapters may have some, all, or just a few of these settings available. In any case, jot down whatever defaults are listed in the manual.

The single most important step in installing any device, including a new CD-ROM drive, is properly *configuring*, or making the correct settings for, the adapter card in front of you. If you pay special attention to this part of the installation, you'll avoid 90 percent of the problems with installing new devices.

Check the adapter's documentation for the default settings of the card. These specifications are generally indicated in a list near the beginning of the documentation or by notation throughout the manual. *Don't* worry about pin settings, jumpers, or anything else—just copy the default settings to a piece of paper. Look for the following default settings:

- IRQ
- DMA channel
- I/O address or memory address
- Adapter SCSI ID (SCSI cards only)

Don't panic! You don't need to know exactly what each of these settings means. In any event, we'll provide explanations along the way....

The following is a typical list of default settings for a CD-ROM adapter:

IRQ: 11
DMA channel: 5
I/O address: 330
SCSI ID: 7 (Only on SCSI cards)

Don't worry if your **settings** are different; we discuss each of the settings in this chapter.

If you want to avoid hair pulling, teeth gnashing, and general frustration, you must now check the CD-ROM adapter card default settings for possible conflicts with other cards already installed in your PC. You *cannot* have two cards with the same settings for IRQ or DMA. If you do, I/O address or the drive—and possibly your PC—will lock up or operate erratically.

A War Story

After performing a hasty installation of a drive two years ago, my machine booted just fine. My printer, on the other hand, began to spew page after page of blank paper. A quick check of the card showed I had set the CD-ROM SCSI adapter for IRQ 7, the same interrupt channel my printer card was set for.

Here are some cards you should check to make sure that your CD-ROM settings do not duplicate the IRQ, DMA, and I/O port address settings for these cards:

- Network interface cards (Ethernet, ARCNet, and so on)
- Sound cards
- Scanner interfaces
- Internal modems and fax modems
- Other cards for hard drives, external storage devices, or any other added peripherals such as tape-backup units

If you value your time and your sanity, keep a record handy of these important settings for all your adapter cards. Write down the current settings on a piece of paper, for example, and tape that paper into the PC's owner manual or inside your PC's case. This way, any time you add a new adapter card or must reconfigure one already installed, you'll have a reference. Otherwise, you may find yourself pulling out every peripheral adapter in your machine to check its settings. Obviously, any time you add a new card or change the settings of one installed, change your note card. (For more information about upgrading your computer, and how to maintain a list of settings for your computer, see *Upgrading and Repairing PCs*, 3rd Edition, published by Que Corporation.)

If you did not keep records for previously installed devices and need to check for existing settings, refer to each card's documentation. You may also purchase a PC diagnostic software program—many are currently available. These programs scan installed adapter cards for occupied interrupts and DMA channels. QA/Plus, WIN Sleuth, and Quarterdeck's Manifest are some popular choices. Recent Microsoft operating systems (Windows 3.1, DOS 5.x, and DOS 6.x) include Microsoft System Diagnostics, a capable system sleuth for showing IRQ, DMA, and I/O assignments. Some drives come with software that searches for a free IRQ, DMA, and I/O address (Sony is a good example).

Make a note of any conflicts. It will probably be easier to change the defaults on the CD-ROM adapter, which is already out of the PC and sitting in front of you. But don't make changes yet. Just take notes.

The next step is to make sure that the defaults listed in the manual are, in fact, the defaults actually set on the board. Everyone makes mistakes, including your adapter-card's manufacturer. Although this type of error is relatively uncommon, it's best to double-check the manual's default listings against the physical defaults set on the card before you've gone too far into the installation process.

Jumpers and Switches

Adapter-card configurations are set with *jumpers*—tiny plastic-covered shunts that fit over pin-pairs on the adapter card. The rows of

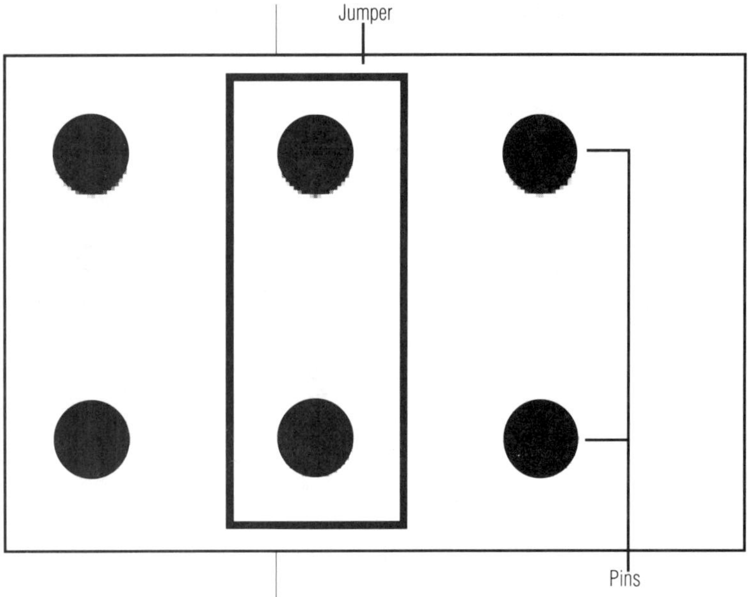

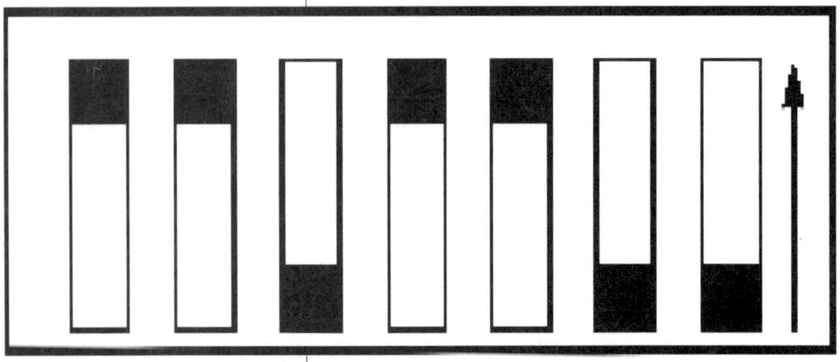

FIGURE 4.1, top

Jumper banks.

FIGURE 4.2, bottom

Some adapters use DIP switches rather than jumpers to set configuration options.

jumper pins may run left to right or up and down across the card. Configuring the board is a matter of having the jumpers on or off a pair of pins.

These rows of jumper pins are labeled with a letter and a number, such as J5 or W1. Your adapter-card manual or pamphlet has a diagram of these jumper rows, or *banks*, as they're called (see fig. 4.1). Carefully check the pin settings against your manual. Make sure that pins are jumpered where they should be. Just as important, make sure that there are no extra jumpers on any of the pins.

DIP Switches

Some adapter manufacturers, such as Adaptec, configure the cards using rocker switches—called *DIP switches*—instead of jumpers (see fig. 4.2). DIP is an acronym for *Dual Inline Package*, which refers to the configurations of the pins on the switch's "package." This configuration places the electrical connections in an industry-standard layout. The pins are lined up on the top and bottom of the switches in two rows (dual, inline).

As you're checking the **jumper blocks**, make sure that you are checking the correct bank of jumpers; there may be a number of banks of blocks on the card. After you verify that the pins are set to the correct defaults, you're ready to resolve any possible interrupt conflicts.

Irksome IRQs

The most common cause of a system lock-up after an installation is an IRQ conflict. Avoid problems up front by making sure that you have no conflicts now. Table 4.1 lists common IRQ numbers and which ones are typically open. Remember that you may already have an installed card occupying one of these interrupt request lines. In addition, if you have an 8-bit card, you are further restricted in the number of available IRQs: from 0 to 7 only.

If you find a conflict, consult your adapter-card manual for help selecting a different IRQ. To set up the adapter card to use a particular IRQ, remove or move a jumper from one pin-pair to another. Although you can remove jumpers with your fingers, you risk handling chips that may be near the jumpers. It's better to use a pair of tweezers (especially handy are those included in a computer tool kit) to carefully remove the jumper. Reset the jumpers according to the manual's diagrams for the new IRQ.

IRQs

The letters IRQ are shorthand for *Interrupt ReQuest*. An IRQ is part of the hardware architecture of the IBM PC, which is an "interrupt-driven" design. IRQs are used by hardware to notify the microprocessor—your PC's CPU (Central Processing Unit)—that some service is needed. If IRQs were not used, the CPU would have to wait for the completion of the current hardware activity before it could move on to another task. To make this clearer, let's look at how this works in the case of a CD-ROM drive connected with a SCSI adapter.

When an application needs some data from the CD-ROM drive, it requests the information from the operating system (OS). The OS, in turn, makes the request to the CD-ROM drive through the adapter. The CD-ROM drive receives the request through the host adapter and goes off to find the requested data. This operation is not instantaneous; it takes some time for the drive to do its job. To us, it is almost no time, but to the CPU it is a long time indeed. The CPU could keep asking the adapter if the data was available, a technique called *polling*, but this would be a waste of time that the CPU could use to service other requests from programs and hardware. Instead of polling the drive, the CPU does some real

NOTE

Adapter Cards without Jumpers

Newer adapter cards from Proc Technology, Adaptec, and Future Domain are virtually jumperless. Your particular adapter card may not have jumpers; it may have rocker-switch (DIP-switch) settings or software-selectable interrupts. With the latter cards, you use software to set open DMA and interrupt channels; you make settings on the card entirely from the keyboard. If we're all very lucky, most hardware manufacturers will soon be shipping software-configurable adapter cards.

Table 4.1 Common IRQ Assignments

IRQ	Use
IRQ 0	Timer Interrupt
IRQ 1	Keyboard Interrupt
IRQ 2	Cascade to IRQ 9
IRQ 3	COM 2 or COM 4
IRQ 4	COM 1 or COM 3
IRQ 5	LPT 2 (parallel printer port—available for new cards if you only have one parallel port)
IRQ 6	Floppy Disk
IRQ 7	LPT 1 (parallel printer port)
IRQ 8	Real Time Clock
IRQ 9	Cascade to IRQ 2
IRQ 10	Available to user
IRQ 11	Available to user
IRQ 12	Mouse Port on PS/2 (may be available)
IRQ 13	80x87 Math Coprocessor (may be available on 386s)
IRQ 14	Hard Disk
IRQ 15	Available to user

work, like handling the movement of the mouse pointer, accepting keystrokes, and the like.

When the data is finally ready for the CPU, the adapter gets the attention of the CPU by "pulling on" an IRQ—the one to which it is connected. The CPU knows, by referring to the **device driver**, that the particular IRQ it just detected is associated with the host adapter. The CPU then completes the request the application made for data by receiving the data that is now waiting at the host adapter. Although this explanation is simplified, it should give you some idea what is going on in your machine.

EXPLANATION

Device Drivers

Device drivers are specialized pieces of software that let programs interface with (talk to) hardware devices. They're always available in memory to intercept signals from the software and translate those signals into commands for the hardware. Some devices, like a standard hard drive or floppy drive, don't need a device driver; nonstandard devices like CD-ROM drives and sound cards do require them. The device drivers are typically included with the hardware or the operating system.

You may also hear IRQs referred to as "interrupt *levels*." This is because, in IBM-PC compatible machines, IRQs have priority levels: 0 is the highest priority and 15 is the lowest. The IRQs are serviced in the order of their priority. When PCs were equipped with relatively low-powered microprocessors, this priority system was critical, and you had to choose an IRQ that provided a high-enough priority for your purpose. Today, machines are much more powerful, so prioritization is no longer a concern.

DMA Conflicts

DMA, or Direct Memory Access, settings have less serious consequences than IRQ settings when they are in conflict. A typical symptom of a DMA conflict is no response from one of the cards in conflict. For example, if you have a sound card and a CD-ROM SCSI card set for the same DMA channel, one—or both—of the cards may not function. Check DMA settings on the cards, but be aware that getting the proper DMA channel may require more than one jumper setting (you may have to change two or three jumpers to change the DMA channel). The Adaptec 1540 SCSI card, for example, has a default DMA of 5, but jumpers pertaining to the DMA selection are on jumper block 5 *and* on jumper block 9. To set all DMA jumpers to the same DMA channel on the Adaptec card, you must set DMA Channel Select, DMA Request, DMA ACKnowledge, and DMA INTerrupt Request on these two separate blocks.

EXPLANATION

DMA

Direct Memory Access (DMA) is a technique that speeds up access to memory for expansion cards. Because it avoids the intervention of the CPU, this technique is "direct." There are seven DMA channels in an IBM-AT compatible machine.

Most cards come set with a default of DMA channel 5. This should be fine for most PCs because few other adapter cards occupy these channels. Some of the newer, 16-bit sound cards have DMA channel 5 set as the default, however, making them likely culprits in any conflict with your CD-ROM adapter cards.

I/O Port Addresses

No two cards can live at the same **I/O port** address. More importantly, I/O port addresses are really base addresses—they describe the *starting address* the card occupies. The full range of the memory address must be taken into consideration when resolving conflict with other cards. For example, if a sound card occupies memory address 220, you may assume that a SCSI card can exist at address 230. But this is not necessarily so. If the sound card's memory range is 220 to 235, you've just introduced a conflict.

We've noticed some typical conflicts of late in the way types of adapter cards are shipped in their default state. Most CD-ROM adapter cards ship with base I/O port addresses of 220, 300, or 330. Many sound boards and internal fax modem cards may also occupy these addresses in their default configurations. Network interface cards are often set in the 300 to 360 range by default, too. If you need to change your I/O port address to resolve a conflict, make certain that you know the *range* of the possible conflict.

Typical symptoms of I/O conflict are similar to those that occur with DMA conflicts: one or both of the cards in conflict does not respond. Another symptom of memory conflict is disconcerting, but harmless: your machine may go through the boot process of checking memory, loading drivers, and so on, get to the end of the boot, and then reboot all over again. If this happens, you can be certain you have an I/O port conflict.

Installing the Card and Attaching the Drive

After you configure the card correctly, resolve all potential conflicts, and are thoroughly tired of looking at the manual's hazy diagrams for jumper blocks, you're ready to insert the card into the PC.

Selecting a Slot

To begin, turn off the power to the computer. Unscrew the case cover and remove it. Look at the available or unoccupied slots in your PC bus. These card slots may come in 8-bit, 16-bit, or 32-bit lengths (8-bit slots are the shortest and 32-bit slots are the longest and usually the last slots in the case). If your CD adapter is an 8-bit adapter, it has one set of gold edge-connectors; the 16-bit cards have two sets—one short and one long. Make the most of the real estate inside your PC case. Don't put an 8-bit card in a 16-bit slot unless you have no other choice—you may want that 16-bit slot later on for a true 16-bit card. Unscrew from the back of the PC the slot cover for the bus slot you've selected. Hang onto this screw.

Hold the card by its top edges and slide it firmly into the expansion bus; the connector edge should be facing through the open slot in the back of the PC chassis. Press down firmly. You'll feel the card *seat* itself—pop into the connector. Be careful not to press down too hard—you might damage the motherboard under the connector. Make sure that the card is evenly seated, front to back. Some SCSI cards have cable hooks on either side of the outside connector that can get in the way when you put the card into the slot. If one of these hooks gets caught between the chassis and the card, you'll have a difficult time seating the card properly. Move the hooks straight up, parallel with the connector, so that they slide easily through the slot in the back of the PC.

Gently move the adapter flange with its slotted top away from the screw hole in the PC chassis. Put the screw from the slot plate (the one you saved when you removed the slot cover) into the hole and give it a few turns—enough to start it solidly. Slide the card flange under the screw and secure it firmly. By starting the screw into the chassis first and then sliding the card into place beneath it, you avoid the problem of trying—often without luck—to align the adapter bracket flange and PC chassis hole for the screw. A common hassle here is dropping the **screw** into the PC case while trying to secure the card. Keep a flashlight handy to peer between the cards and locate dropped screws; those tweezers you used for changing jumpers can come in handy to carefully remove misplaced screws. If you've grounded yourself, you won't do any damage if you're careful in removing a dropped screw.

For the hardware-squeamish, the worst part is over. If you're lucky enough to have chosen

EXPLANATION

I/O Ports

An I/O (Input/Output) port is just what its name says: a port for the movement of data. I/O ports allow the operating system to communicate with adapter cards in the computer's bus. The addresses used by these ports are arbitrary memory locations to which the adapter's hardware is mapped. In other words, the adapter gives the appearance that its hardware resides at the selected address. The "memory space" used by the PC for I/O ports is completely separate from that used by RAM (Random Access Memory), where programs are stored, and ROM (Read Only Memory), where system software is stored.

CAUTION

Loose Screws

Never, under any circumstances, leave loose or dropped screws in the computer case. They inevitably short something out, doing severe damage to your main PC board and any cards in the expansion bus.

correct IRQ, DMA, and I/O address settings, you won't have to touch the hardware any more.

Do not replace the cover of the PC yet. If some lingering conflicts exist or the card is not fully seated in the slot, you may need to do more inside work. You can replace the PC case after you've installed the drive, rebooted the system, installed the driver software, and (whew!) tested the drive...not before.

Attaching the CD-ROM Drive

Once the card is in and properly seated, you can hook the card to the drive. Depending on your configuration—external or internal—read the appropriate section that follows.

External CD-ROM Drives

Unpack the CD-ROM drive carefully. When you purchase an external drive, you should receive the following items:

- External drive
- Power cord
- Cable (if the card came bundled with the drive)
- Floppy disks with device driver software
- Operator's manual

This is the bare minimum to get the drive up and running. You may also find a CD caddie, a manual or pamphlet for the adapter card, and, possibly, a sampling of CDs to get you started.

Configure and check the adapter card as described in "Preparing the Adapter Card," earlier in this chapter.

Take a look at your work area and the cable that came with the drive. Where will the drive find a new home? You're limited by the length of the cable. Find a spot for the drive and insert the power cable into the back of the drive unit. Make sure that you have an outlet, or preferably a free socket in a surge-suppressing power strip into which you can plug the new drive.

Plug one end of the supplied cable into the connector socket on the drive, and one onto the connector on the adapter card in the PC. External SCSI drives have two connectors on the back—either connector can be hooked to the PC (see fig. 4.3); we'll discuss the extra connector later in this chapter. Use the guide hooks, if they're provided, to secure a SCSI cable to both the drive and adapter connector. Some SCSI cables supplied with Future Domain 16-bit controllers have a microconnector for the adapter end that simply clips into place. Non-SCSI cables usually attach with thumbscrews.

If you have a SCSI drive, you need to read the sections on SCSI IDs, chains, and termination, later in this chapter. Otherwise, turn on the power for the drive and the PC and install the driver software according to your adapter manual.

Internal CD-ROM Drives

Unpack the internal drive kit. You should have the following pieces:

- Internal drive
- Power cord (some kits don't contain power cords because extra ones are usually leading out of the PC's power supply)

- Interface board (not all manufacturers include an interface board, so you may have to purchase one —or a compatible sound card—separately)
- Internal ribbon cable
- Floppy disks with device driver software
- Operator's manual
- Drive rails or mounting screws

Your manufacturer also may have provided a power-cable splitter—a bundle of wires with plastic connectors on each of three ends. A disc caddie and owner's manual may also be included.

Configure and check your card according to the instructions in "Preparing the Adapter Card," earlier in this chapter. Make sure that the PC is turned off and that the cover is off. There's not a lot of spare room inside a PC, so you may want to attach the ribbon cable to the drive and feed it through the open drive bay before you continue. If you'll be inserting the adapter card between other cards, however, you should connect the ribbon cable to the adapter card before installing it.

The ribbon cable should be identical on both ends. You'll find a red stripe or dotted line down one side of the outer edge of the ribbon cable. This stripe is the pin-1 designation; it gives you a visual cue that the cable is connected properly into the card and into the drive. Occasionally, the connectors have a number 1 printed on them, or an arrow on pin 1, as well. If you're lucky, the manufacturer supplied a cable with notches or keys along one edge of the connector. With such a key, there is only one way to insert the cable into the card and drive. You must hook up an unkeyed cable according to the pin-1 designation.

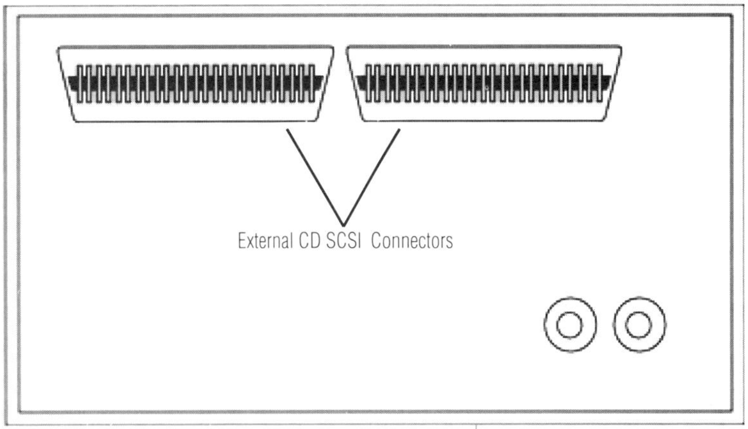

FIGURE 4.3

External CD-ROM drive SCSI connectors.

Finding the connector for a proprietary interface (like some from Sony, Mitsumi, Panasonic, and Hitachi) is easy—it's either on the included interface card or on your sound card. Pin 1 should be marked with the number 1 on the card. Look for a double row of pins on the card and match up the ribbon cable's pin 1 with the card's pin 1.

If you're installing an IDE-based drive, look for a double row of pins on the card that is connected (with a different ribbon cable) to your hard drive. Pin 1 should be marked with a 1 on the card itself. Attach the free end of the CD-ROM drive's ribbon cable to that connector.

The connector on SCSI adapter cards is a double row of 50 brass-colored pins. In small print along the base of these pins are at least two numbers: 1 and 50. Aligning the ribbon cable's marked edge over pin 1, carefully—and evenly—insert the ribbon cable connector (see fig. 4.4).

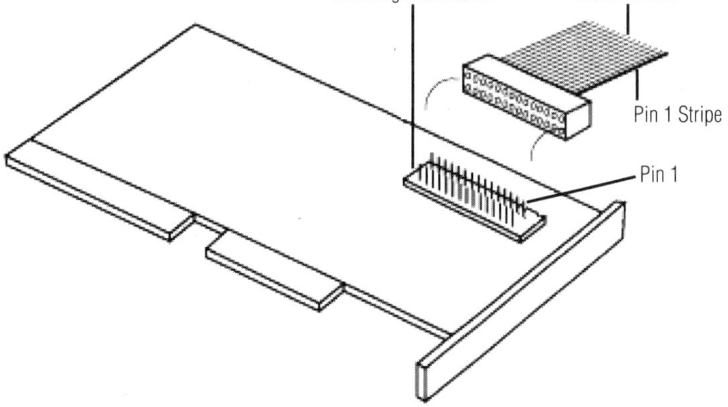

FIGURE 4.4

Ribbon cable connection to a SCSI adapter.

Now insert the adapter card into an open expansion slot in the PC, leaving the drive end of the cable loose. Choose one of the drive bays at the front of the machine for the internal drive. Make sure that the bay is easily accessible and not blocked by other items on your desk—you'll be inserting the CDs here, and you'll need the elbow room.

Remove the drive bay cover. Inside the drive bay is a metal enclosure with screw holes for mounting the drive. If the drive has mounting holes along its side and fits snugly into the enclosure, you won't need mounting rails. If it's a loose fit, however, mount the rails along the sides of the drive with the rail screws and then slide the drive into the bay. Secure the drive into the bay with four screws—two on each side. If the rails or drive don't line up evenly with the four mounting holes, make sure that you use at least two screws—one mounting screw on each side. Because you will insert and eject a lot of CDs over the years, making sure that the drive is mounted securely is a must.

Find the striped side of the ribbon cable and align it with pin 1 on the drive's edge connector. To determine which is pin 1, refer to either the diagram in your owner's manual or to the designation on the connector itself.

The back of the CD drive has a power connector outlet. Inside the case of your PC, at the back of the floppy or hard disk, are power cords in a bundle—two black, one red, and one yellow—attached with plastic connectors to the floppy and hard drives. You may already have a free power connector laying open in the case. Plug the open connector into the back of the power socket on the CD-ROM drive (these connectors go in only one way). If you do not have an open connector, use a power-cable splitter (see fig. 4.5), provided by the manufacturer or available at an electronics store. To install the splitter, disconnect a floppy drive power cord, attach the splitter to the detached power cord, and plug one of the free ends of the splitter into the floppy drive and the other end of the splitter into the CD-ROM drive.

If you'll be using your CD-ROM drive for audio CDs, you'll probably want to connect the drive's 4-pin audio connector to your sound card. It's not a requirement—you can listen to the audio CDs through the drive's headphone jack, if it has one—but it's handy to be able to play audio CDs through your sound card and whatever speakers and audio equipment you have connected to it. This connection also lets you sample directly from audio CDs, if you have the appropriate recording software. Find the 4-pin audio connector on your sound card and attach one end of the audio cable to it. Attach the other end of the audio cable to the 4-pin audio outputs on the CD-ROM drive. In most cases, these cables fit only one way on the connectors.

If you have a SCSI drive, you need to read "SCSI Chains: Internal, External, and a Little of Both," the next section in this chapter, for final installation information.

Do not replace the PC cover yet—you need to make certain that everything is running perfectly before you seal the case. You're now ready to turn on the computer. For the drive to work, however, you need to install the software drivers.

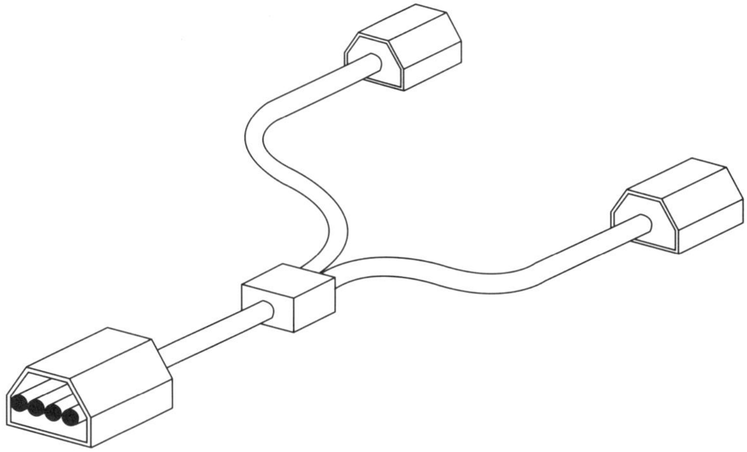

FIGURE 4.5

Power cord splitter and connector.

SCSI Chains: Internal, External, and a Little of Both

Remember that one of the primary reasons for using a SCSI controller for your CD-ROM drive is that you can chain several peripherals to one adapter card—preserving card slots inside the PC and limiting the nightmare of tracking IRQs, DMAs, and memory addresses.

You can add scanners, tape-backup units, and other SCSI peripherals to this chain (see fig. 4.6). There are only a few things to keep in mind: chief among them is SCSI termination.

ID Numbers for SCSI Devices

The SCSI specification states that up to seven devices (in addition to the SCSI interface card) can be connected together. To distinguish between the devices, each device in the chain has a unique ID number. The SCSI card is typically set to ID 7 or 0; to be on the safe side, set the CD-ROM drive and other devices to unique IDs from 1 to 6. As long as each device has its own unique ID, the devices can go in any order—you can have a chain with ID 7 for the first device, ID 3 for the next, ID 5 for the next, ID 2 for the next, and so on. For the examples in this chapter, we use SCSI ID 6 for the drive and ID 7 for the interface card.

The first rule of SCSI device chaining is simple: each end of the SCSI chain must be terminated: the first device must contain a termination resistor and the last must also have a terminator attached. All devices between the first and last should be free of any terminator.

The second SCSI rule is that all SCSI devices must be set to a unique ID number. For the external drive installed in an example earlier in this chapter, the SCSI adapter was set for ID 7 and the CD-ROM drive was set for ID 6. Any additional SCSI devices added must take the IDs 0, 1, 2, 3, 4, or 5. (If you have a SCSI hard drive, as a rule, most SCSI hard drives occupy SCSI ID 1; if you have SCSI hard drives, be certain that you do not set the CD-ROM drive or other devices to occupy a hard drive SCSI ID number.) Remember that the SCSI adapter card takes an ID, and its default is usually ID 7 or 0.

EXPLANATION

SCSI Termination

Signals on the SCSI bus have a high enough frequency to act as radio waves. When a radio signal travels down a wire, it reflects back from the end unless it finds an "impedance match." The terminators on the SCSI bus are used to absorb these reflections, which would otherwise interfere with legitimate SCSI signals and cause errors.

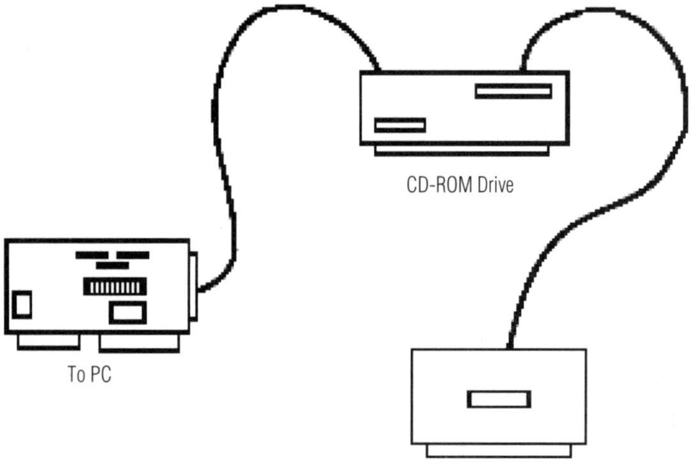

FIGURE 4.6

A SCSI chain of devices on an adapter card.

TIP

Internal Termination for External Drives

Some external drives have *internal termination*. In other words, the manufacturer installed terminating resistors—much like the ones installed on the adapter card—onto the drive's IC board inside the drive case. If your drive has internal termination, you *must not* put a terminator cap on the external connector. Check the manual that came with your drive to ensure that the drive has no internal termination. Thankfully, few external drives are internally terminated. Naturally, if your drive is internally terminated, it must be the last device in the chain—any devices past it aren't able to send or receive any signals.

Example One: All External SCSI Devices

Suppose that you've installed a CD-ROM drive and added a tape device to the chain with the extra connector on the back of the CD-ROM drive. The first device in this SCSI chain is the adapter card itself. All SCSI cards have a series of long, ceramic-tipped components plugged into the board in a group of two or three components. These are the **terminating resistors** for the card (see fig. 4.7). From the card, you've run an external cable to the CD-ROM drive, and from the CD-ROM drive, you've added another cable to connect the CD-ROM drive to the back of the tape unit. The tape unit must be terminated as well, because it's the last device in the chain. Only the first and last devices—the SCSI card and the tape drive, in this example—must be **terminated**. Most external units are terminated with a *SCSI cap*—a small connector that plugs into the unused external SCSI connector.

These **external drive** connectors come in two varieties: a SCSI cap and a pass-through terminator. The cap plugs over the open connector and covers it. The pass-through terminator, however, plugs onto the connector and has an open end into which you can plug a SCSI cable. Unless your drive uses DIP switches for termination (as NEC drives do), this type of connector is essential if your external drive has only one SCSI connector—you can plug in the drive *and* make sure that it's terminated by using only one connector.

Example Two: Internal Chain and Termination

The same SCSI termination and ID rules apply to internal chains as they do to external chains: all the internal devices must have unique SCSI ID numbers and the first and last devices must be terminated. In the case of internal devices, however, you must check for termination. Internal devices have terminating resistors or packs similar to the ones installed on the adapter card. If you install a tape unit as the last device on the chain, for example, it must have resistors on its circuit board. If you place a CD-ROM drive in the middle of this chain, its resistors must be removed. The adapter card, at the front end of the chain, should keep its resistors: ***do not*** remove them.

Example Three: Internal and External SCSI Devices

If you mix and match external and internal devices, follow the rules for assigning SCSI ID and termination outlined in "SCSI Chains:

Internal, External, and a Little of Both," earlier in this chapter. In the third example, shown in figure 4.8, an internal CD-ROM drive is terminated and set for SCSI ID 6; the external tape unit is also terminated and assigned SCSI ID 5. The SCSI adapter itself is set for ID 7, and—the most important point—its terminating resistors have been removed.

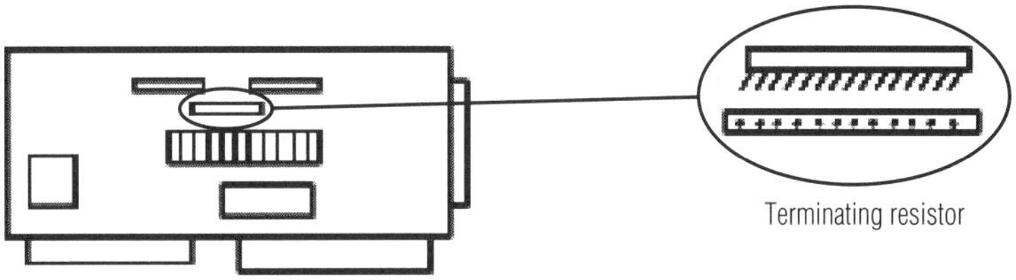

FIGURE 4.7

SCSI adapter-card terminating resistors.

Removing Resistors

Be careful when handling the adapter card—static discharge can damage the IC chips contained on the card. Make sure that you ground yourself before you start. Additionally, never hold the card by its edge connectors. Chip pullers—specially made tweezers found in most computer tool kits—are especially useful in removing resistor packs from adapter cards and from internal peripherals such as CD-ROM drives. The resistor packs have very thin teeth that bend easily; once bent, they're really tough to straighten out and reinsert.

Installing Driver Software

After you configure the adapter card correctly, insert it into the PC, and ensure that the drives are connected and terminated properly, you're ready for the last step: installing the CD-ROM software.

Putting CD-ROM Software on the PC

If you purchased your drive as a drive/adapter-card bundle, the manufacturer has included the appropriate software disk and documentation for installing the software. If you purchased your drive and card separately, the software components you need may have come with the adapter card. In any case, the CD-ROM drive needs three software components to operate on a PC:

- An adapter driver (SCSI only)
- A driver for the specific CD-ROM drive you've installed
- MSCDEX—Microsoft CD Extensions for DOS

The first two drivers—the SCSI adapter driver and the CD-ROM driver—are loaded into your system at start-up by placing command lines in the CONFIG.SYS file. The MSCDEX, or DOS extension, is an executable file added to the system through the AUTOEXEC.BAT file.

Installing the SCSI Adapter Driver

Each SCSI adapter model has a specific driver that allows communications between the PC and the SCSI interface. This driver should have been provided with your SCSI drive and adapter kit. Documentation should also have been included, which walks you through the installation of the software. You can manually add the SCSI device driver to your CONFIG.SYS file.

NOTE

Terminating Resistors

Most internal SCSI devices ship with terminating resistors on board. Check the user manuals for the locations of these resistors. There may be one, two, or even three resistors on any given device.

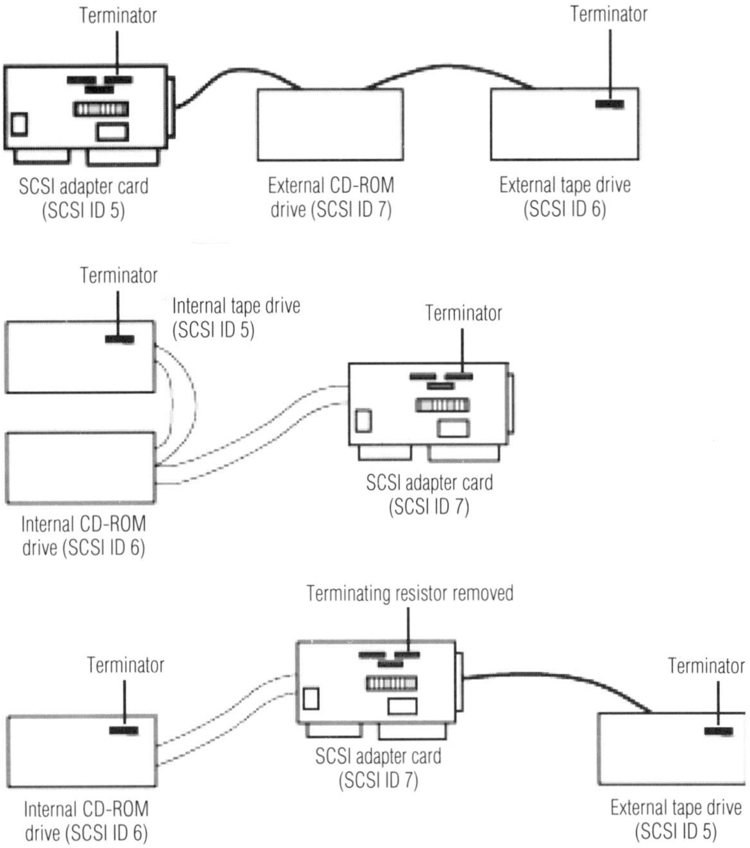

FIGURE 4.8

Examples of SCSI termination.

To add the SCSI device driver to your CONFIG.SYS file, go to the top of the CONFIG.SYS file. Use the DEVICE= statement to add the name and path of the driver:

```
DEVICE=C:\DRIVERS\MYSCSI.SYS
```

In this sample statement, C:\DRIVERS is the drive and directory to which the SCSI device driver, MYSCSI.SYS, has been copied. Some drivers have option switches or added commands that, for example, allow you to view the progress of the driver being loaded. Option switches are usually added to the end of the DEVICE= statement.

Installing the CD-ROM Device Driver

The CD-ROM device driver, as well the SCSI adapter driver, should be a part of your basic installation kit. If not, contact the drive's manufacturer for the proper CD-ROM device driver for your SCSI card or CD-ROM drive.

For SCSI drives, the device driver should come with an installation program that prompts you for the memory I/O address for the SCSI adapter on which you installed the CD-ROM drive. The *device driver* allows communication with the drive through the SCSI bus to your PC. For non-SCSI drives, the driver installation procedure usually prompts you for the card's address, DMA, and IRQ. You may also be prompted for other options such as what size **memory buffer** to use. Installation programs add a line similar to the following to the CONFIG.SYS file:

```
DEVICE=C:\DRIVERS\MYCDROM.SYS
    /D:mscd001
```

In this sample statement, C:\DRIVERS is the drive and directory that contains the driver MYCDROM.SYS, the CD-ROM driver for your specific CD-ROM drive. The /D:mscd001 option after the statement designates this CD-ROM driver as controlling the first (001)—and only—CD-ROM drive on the system. This portion of the device-driver statement identifies the drive as a Microsoft DOS Extensions CD-ROM (MSCDEX designates CD-ROM drives in this fashion: mcs001, mcs002, and so on).

Installing the Microsoft CD Extensions File

The Microsoft CD Extensions file allows DOS to identify and use data from CD-ROMs attached to the system. Because the original DOS had no provisions for this technology, "hooks" for handling this unique media are not a part of the basic operating environment. Using Microsoft CD Extensions is convenient for all the software components involved. As CD-ROM technology changes, the MSCDEX file also can be changed, independent of the DOS system. For example, most PhotoCD, multiple-session CD-ROM drives require MSCDEX.EXE Version 2.21 (or later), which has been modified from earlier versions to accommodate the newer CD format. MS-DOS Version 6 includes MSCDEX Version 2.22.

MSCDEX.EXE should be in the software kit that came with your drive. If not, obtain the latest copy directly from Microsoft. The latest version of CD Extensions is also available on CompuServe in the Microsoft forum. If you are a registered user of the DOS operating system, MSCDEX is free. Read the licensing agreement that appears on the disk or in your manual for the proper licensing of MSCDEX files.

Your installation software should add to your AUTOEXEC.BAT file a line similar to the following:

```
C:\WINDOWS\MSCDEX.EXE /d:mscd001
```

In this sample statement, C:\WINDOWS is the drive and directory to which the MSCDEX.EXE file has been copied. MSCDEX assigns a DOS name or drive letter to the CD-ROM drive when it is installed. The /d:mscd001 portion of the statement tells MSCDEX the DOS name or drive of the device defined by the **CD-ROM device driver** in the CONFIG.SYS file. In this example, the DOS name is d: (the D drive).

Sound complicated? Don't worry. As long as these three drivers are loaded properly in the system, the CD-ROM drive will operate as transparently as any other drive in the system.

MSCDEX.EXE has a variety of options or switches you can add to its command line in the AUTOEXEC.BAT file. Table 4.2 lists these switches.

Getting Ready for Lift-Off

Your drive should come with installation software that copies the device-driver files to the hard drive and adds the necessary command lines to the CONFIG.SYS and AUTOEXEC.BAT files. After the drivers are loaded and the files are modified, you can reboot the machine and look for signs that all went smoothly in the software installation.

If you have a SCSI drive, the SCSI driver is the first to load. You see an on-screen message from the driver that includes the software version number and the model of the SCSI adapter card it found.

Then the CD-ROM adapter driver loads, showing its software version and the drive it supports.

Finally, MSCDEX loads, telling you the buffer size, the memory allocated to the drive, and what DOS drive letter has been assigned to the CD-ROM drive.

EXPLANATION

Memory Buffers

If your drive includes a buffering driver (also called a *caching driver*), you can tell it what amount of the computer's RAM to use as a memory buffer—a place to store commonly accessed data like the disc's table of contents. See Appendix C, "Useful CD-ROM Utilities," for more information about memory buffers.

NOTE

Driver Names

The MSCDEX and CD-ROM device driver names must match (for example, they both must be msc000 or msc001—the defaults provided by most installations are used in this example). As long as the two names are the same, the drivers can "find" one another.

Table 4.2 Switches for the MSCDEX.EXE File

Switch	Function
/V	This option is called Verbose; causes the screen to display at startup information about memory allocation, buffers, drive-letter assignments, and device-driver names.
/L: <*letter*>	Designates which DOS drive letter is assigned to the drive. For example, /L:G assigns the drive letter G to the CD-ROM drive. Two conditions apply: You must not have another drive assigned to that letter and the LASTDRIVE= statement in the CONFIG.SYS file must be equal to or greater than the drive letter assigned here. For example, LASTDRIVE=G is fine, but LASTDRIVE=F causes an error if you attempt to assign the letter G to the CD-ROM drive with the /L: switch.
/M: <*buffers*>	Specifies the number of sector buffers. Allows you to buffer data from the CD-ROM drive. This switch is useful if you want faster initial access to the drive's directory. Buffer values of 10 to 15 are more than enough for most uses—any more is overkill. Because each buffer is equal to 2 KB of memory, a /M:10 buffer argument, for example, takes 20 KB of memory. Note that the buffer allocation does not significantly increase the overall performance of the drive—just DOS's initial access to the drive and the access of large data blocks when the drive is gulping down live-motion video, for example. You can't turn a 400 millisecond drive into a speed demon by adding a 200 KB buffer. With no /M: argument added, MSCDEX uses a default of 6 buffers, which is fine for most PCs and CD-ROM drives.
/E	Loads the buffers into DOS's expanded memory, freeing space in the conventional 640 KB. Early versions of MSCDEX—anything below Version 2.1—do not load into expanded memory. You must have DOS 5.0 or higher for this option to load into high memory.
/S	Enables you to share your CD-ROM drive on a peer-to-peer network, like Windows for Workgroups.
/K	Kanji support for Japanese software.

Once you're sure that the software is loaded correctly, test the drive by inserting a CD into the disc caddie and loading it into the CD-ROM drive. Type **DIR/W G:** at the DOS prompt to see a directory of the CD you just inserted (see fig. 4.9). (If your CD has been assigned a drive letter other than G, use that drive letter instead.)

You can log on to the CD-ROM drive just as you can on to any DOS drive. CD-ROM drives look like network drives to the operating system; they support any DOS commands that work on a network drive and that do not write to the drive. CDs, remember, cannot be overwritten, erased, or formatted.

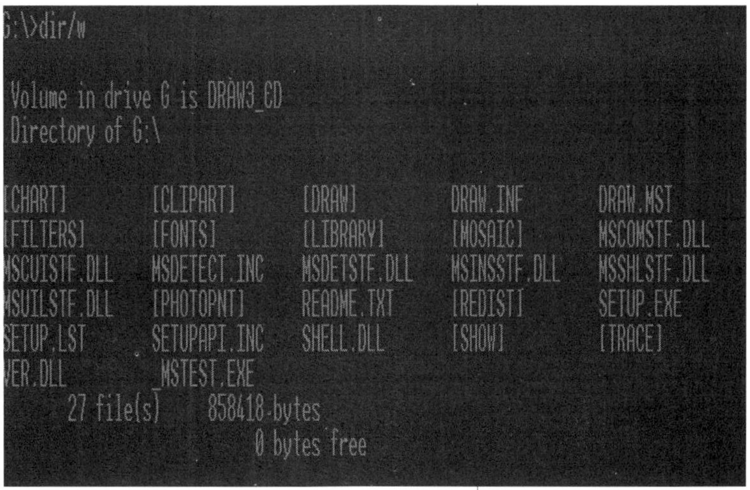

FIGURE 4.9

The directory of a CD after installing the drive.

If you have logged on to the CD-ROM drive and can receive a directory of a sample CD, you're all set. The drive is correctly installed.

Now you can power down the PC and replace the cover.

Using a CD-ROM in Microsoft Windows

Once you add a CD-ROM drive to your system, Windows knows about it through DOS. You'll suddenly find a few changes in your Windows environment. Open the File Manager by double-clicking its file-cabinet icon. You see the new CD-ROM drive icon among the old, familiar drive icons across the top of the window (see fig. 4.10). Notice that the CD-ROM drive icon is highlighted with a miniature CD drive and disc and that the drive carries the title *CD-ROM*. The DOS Extensions mentioned earlier tell Windows the media type (removable, read-only) of your new drive.

Using Media Player

You can set your CD-ROM player to play audio CDs as you work in Windows. You first must hook your drive to a sound card and speakers or connect the CD's audio ports to a stereo. Go to the Windows Control Panel by selecting the Control Panel icon from the Main group; select the Drivers icon from the Windows Control Panel. If you do not see [MCI]/CDAUDIO among the files in the drivers list, insert the Windows Installation disk that contains the CDAUDIO driver, choose Add, and double-click Unlisted or Updated Driver from the menu at the top of the screen. At the prompt, type the drive letter of the Windows Installation disk. After the driver appears in the Control Panel list, double-click it to add it to the Windows configuration, and then exit the Drivers and Control Panel windows.

Double-click the Media Player icon; from the Devices area of the screen, select CD. A list of the track numbers on the audio CD installed in the CD-ROM drive appears along the bottom edge of the Media Player window. The controls in Media Player are similar to those on an audio CD player, including track select, continuous play, and pause (see fig. 4.11). You can configure Media Player to display the CD audio line in either tracks or time duration by choosing the Scale option from the menu at the top of the screen.

Many drive manufacturers supply DOS-based CD audio players with their systems. Check your installation manual and software disks for these utilities.

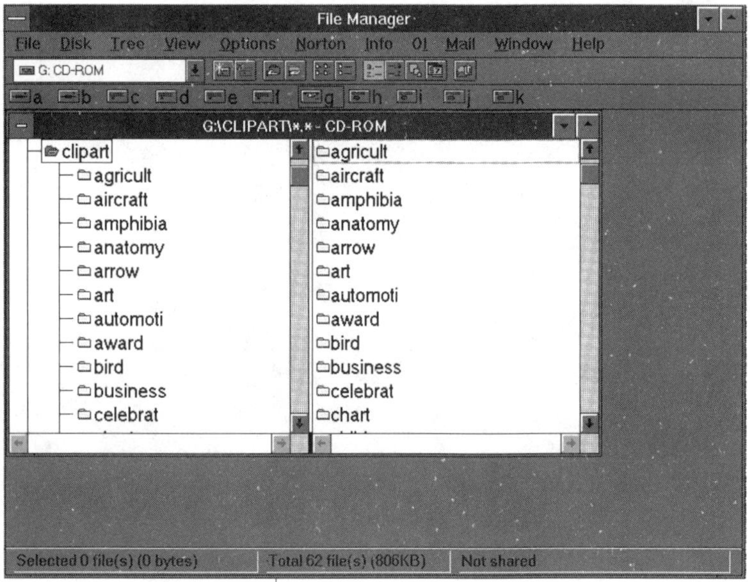

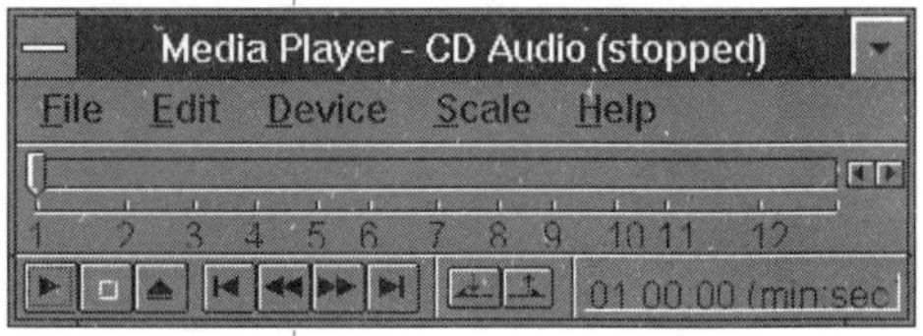

FIGURE 4.10, top

The CD-ROM icon is automatically added to the Windows File Manager window.

FIGURE 4.11, bottom

The Media Player with an audio CD loaded.

Installing CD-ROM Drives on a Mac

For a detailed, step-by-step view of this procedure—along with photographs detailing the steps—see *Upgrading Your Mac Illustrated* (published by Que). This book also covers installing an internal CD-ROM drive in a Mac.

Installing a CD-ROM Drive for a Macintosh

Apple was one of the first personal computer manufacturers to realize the potential of SCSI—the fast interface that lets you chain up to seven devices together off a single port. Almost all **Macs** now come with standard SCSI ports, so most Macintosh peripherals (including CD-ROM drives) are SCSI-based. This section assumes that you're installing an external SCSI CD-ROM drive on your Mac.

The two most important things to keep in mind with SCSI peripherals are these:

- Each device in the chain has its own address
- Both ends of the chain must be terminated

Your SCSI CD-ROM drive has two identical ports, or SCSI connectors, on the back of it (as shown in fig. 4.3, earlier in this chapter). When you run a SCSI cable from your Mac directly to one of these ports, you form the first link in what could be a seven-link chain of SCSI devices (like scanners, hard drives, or tape-backup units). The other port on your SCSI device plugs into either another SCSI cable (only if you have another device to add to the chain) or a terminator (if it's the last device in the chain—even if it's the only device). Although we said "both ends" of the SCSI chain had to be terminated, you have to worry only about the far end—the other end is automatically terminated inside your Mac.

The SCSI address (or SCSI ID) is usually set with DIP switches or a dial. Check your drive's documentation to see how you can set the address. The SCSI ID must be different than any other link in the chain; 0 is usually a bad choice for a SCSI ID number—ID 0 is typically used by internal hard drives. If your CD-ROM drive is the only device in the chain, set it for SCSI ID 1; check any other SCSI devices you have and set the CD-ROM drive's ID number to the lowest number that's not already taken.

Follow these steps to get your CD-ROM working with your Mac:

1. Attach the drive to your SCSI chain. Set its address according to the guidelines in the preceding paragraph.

2. Make sure that the chain is properly terminated. See "SCSI Chains: Internal, External, and a Little of Both," earlier in this chapter, for a complete explanation of SCSI termination.

3. Connect your CD-ROM drive to its power supply.

4. Connect the audio out connectors from the CD-ROM drive to the Mac's audio input port (the one with the microphone) using the audio connector supplied with your drive. If your drive did not come with this audio connector, you can get one at most electronics or computer stores (see fig. 4.12).

5. Start your Mac. When you see the desktop, place the floppy disk with the CD driver in the floppy drive.

6. Run the installer program. Most CD-ROM software has a simple installation program that copies the appropriate drivers into the System Folder (see fig. 4.13). If you see only data files on the floppy disk (and there is no installer program), check for a README file with instructions. If you can't find a README file, just drag the files from the floppy disk into the Extensions folder.

7. Restart your Mac.

If there is a disc in the CD-ROM drive, the CD-ROM drive icon should show up on your desktop along with your hard drive icons. The CD-ROM drive icon works just like the hard drive icons, except that (obviously) you can't change the files. See Chapter 5, "How To Network Your CD-ROM Drive," for instructions on

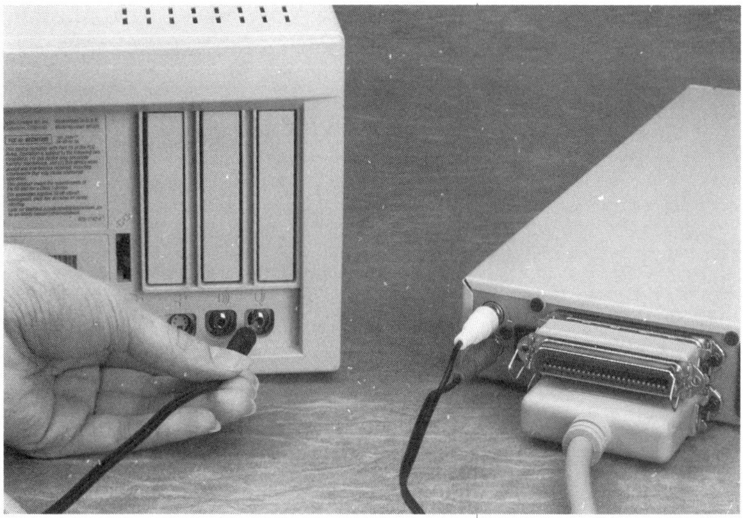

FIGURE 4.12, top

Connecting the audio cable to the Mac.

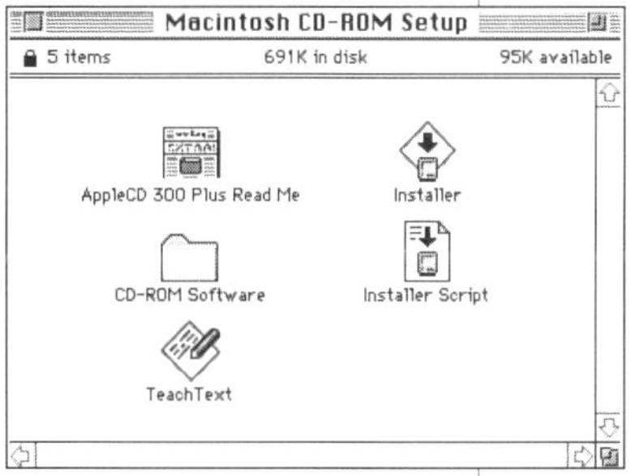

FIGURE 4.13, bottom

The driver disk for the AppleCD 300 Plus. In this example, the CD-ROM Software folder contains the actual drivers, but you can use the Installer to copy them automatically to your system.

accessing the CD-ROM drive through AppleTalk.

Moving Onward

Your hardware is all set. You're ready to explore the thousands of CD-ROM titles available. Look through the coming chapters for our selections of a few of the best titles released to date.

Other chapters in this book show you how to share your CD-ROM drive across various networks and how to add multimedia capabilities to your system. The addition of a CD-ROM drive is the cornerstone for many new additions to your system.

Congratulations! You've entered the information age of CD-ROM!

Chapter 5

How To Network Your CD-ROM Drive

Computer networks are no longer just for large companies and educational institutions. Peer-to-peer networks like Lantastic and Windows for Workgroups make networking a real possibility for the ever-more-common multi-computer household.

In this chapter, you learn how to make CD-ROM drives available across a network so that all users can access CD-ROM data. Take careful note of CD-ROM software licensing agreements before networking any CD-ROM-based application: the very act of providing shared access to the CD over a network may violate the terms of the software license.

Networking and CD-ROM Drives

There are two basic reasons to provide networked access to a CD-ROM drive:

1. The cost of a CD-ROM drive prevents the purchase of enough drives for all users.

2. Many or all the users on the network must share a database stored on CD-ROM.

EXPLANATION

Types of Networks

A *peer-to-peer* (or just *peer*) *network* is a network of computers that all have equal status. Theoretically, all computers can be both clients and servers on a peer network. Practical management considerations, however, usually dictate the dedication of a particular machine to do the bulk of the server work. Peer networks contrast with *client/server networks*, in which a dedicated file server provides file and print services to clients called workstations.

A *file server* is a computer whose disk drives are used by workstations on the network for common and private storage of files. A *client* is a computer that uses the services of a file server. Print services include giving clients access to print *queues* that allow clients to send print jobs to a printer.

Three of the **networks** reviewed in this chapter (Windows for Workgroups, Lantastic, and LocalTalk) are appropriate for home and small-business networks. If you are a Windows user, Windows for Workgroups probably makes the most sense for you. If you stay in DOS most of the time, look at Lantastic. Naturally, Mac users will utilize LocalTalk in small networks. This chapter also covers Novell's CD-ROM support for larger DOS, Windows, and Mac (or any combination) networks.

As you've already seen, when you add a CD-ROM drive to your computer, the software drivers make it look like just another disk drive. Networking a CD-ROM drive uses the same idea—the physical drive becomes another logical drive on the network. The users won't see any difference between using files from the CD-ROM drive across the network and using files from a remote hard drive.

Physical and Logical Drives

A *physical drive* is the actual piece of hardware—the part you can kick. A network file server, for example, can have one or more CD-ROM drives, several hard disk drives, and other physical devices attached to it. That computer knows how to access each physical device through its internal addressing scheme.

Network software uses its own addressing and naming scheme to refer to physical devices on one or more machines. The name of a CD-ROM drive on one file server, for example, might be CUSTOMER_DATABASE_1 or Clipart or anything else (within the network software's naming limitations, that is). These names are *logical drives* (or logical devices), meaning that they don't literally exist outside of the network software. You can give a logical name to practically anything, including sets of files on a physical drive (a subdirectory, for example) or even a combination of drives—it is not unusual to see two or three large drives on a file server combined into a single logical drive.

This chapter walks through CD-ROM installation with some popular networking software packages. If you keep a few simple steps in mind, you can successfully network a CD-ROM drive on just about any type of network:

1. Test the drive locally first. Make sure that the CD-ROM drive works correctly *without the network* before you try to get it to work *with* the network. The network should be completely out of the picture—not only without the software drivers, but even to the point that the network card is out of the machine, if possible.

2. Test the CD-ROM drive locally with the network loaded. Make sure that with the network card and local network drivers loaded, you can still successfully use the CD-ROM drive.

3. Publish the CD-ROM drive. When you're sure that the drive works on the local machine even when the network is active, you can *publish* the drive (make it available across the network).

Taking these steps in this order can save you a lot of headaches. It's tempting to install the network and CD-ROM drive at the same time, but if you flip the switch and something doesn't work, you'll have too many possible suspects—you won't know if the drive works at all, if you've got a software or hardware conflict between the drive and the network, or if you've got a conflict with some other piece of hardware or software on the local machine.

Using a CD-ROM Drive with Windows for Workgroups

For Windows users, Windows for Workgroups (WFW) is a great way to get connected. WFW is actually a version of Windows with built-in peer networking capabilities. This program lets a Windows workstation share its disk drives, including CD-ROM, and printers. It's a snap to install, and it can run alongside Novell NetWare.

Novell NetWare and CorelSCSI! Pro

Although Windows for Workgroups is a fine way to provide some level of CD-ROM sharing over a NetWare network, there is more than one native solution you can use to connect the CD-ROM drive to a NetWare file server or to provide CD-ROM services through specialized hardware. One very good solution (which brings other benefits as well) comes from Corel Corporation in the form of CorelSCSI! Pro. CorelSCSI! is an amazing product that provides ASPI-compatible device drivers for just about any optical-drive device, including CD-ROM, R/W optical disk drives, and WORMs.

The Pro version of the product also comes with many NetWare drivers and utilities, including software to share CD-ROM drives from the file server.

For more information about how to contact Corel, see Appendix D, "Where To Buy: Hardware and Software Vendors."

One of the best things about WFW is its ease of installation (most of the time—as with any other piece of technology, you'll hear a few horror stories if you poke around enough). Its installation program is very good at determining your hardware setup and configuring itself appropriately. If you are installing Windows for Workgroups for the first time, as a pilot, or just between two workstations, the best choice is to buy the WFW Starter Pack (available from your Microsoft dealer). The Starter Pack includes software for two stations, two NICs (Network Interface Cards), two BNC T connectors and terminators (required for the connection), and a 25-foot cable.

The included NICs use Ethernet, a networking standard that allows the stations to communicate at a very high data rate: 10 MB/s (**megabits** per second). This rate is faster than the disk drive of an ISA (Industry Standard Architecture, or AT-style) machine can move data.

Ethernet can run over a variety of cable types. The simplest to implement is 10Base2, which uses a coaxial cable. 10Base2 gets its name because its two conductors share an axis, one running through the center of the other. This cable is very similar to the cable used for your cable-TV connection, with slightly different electrical properties.

The 10Base2 standard is the most economical way to network for smaller groups because the addition of a station requires only a T connector and a segment of cable. The cable terminates in BNC connectors. These connectors are industry-standard bayonet locking connectors. Setting up the physical cabling requires only a little understanding and no special technical skills.

You are also very likely to hear about the 10BaseT standard. This cabling scheme uses UTP (Unshielded Twisted Pair), which is very similar to the wiring used in telephone systems. This system has advantages for larger systems but requires extra hardware in the form of *hubs* or *concentrators*.

As far as WFW is concerned, once the CD-ROM drive is correctly installed, it is just like any

NOTE

Bytes or Bits?

LAN speeds are generally measured in mega*bits* per second; data transfer rates from disk drives and the like are generally measured in mega*bytes* per second.

EXPLANATION

Ethernet

Ethernet is one of many standards used in computer networking. It is essentially a description of how the signal should look on the wire. Nearly every NOS (Network Operating System, the software that provides network services) out there, from the simplest to the most complex, can use Ethernet.

Ethernet was developed by Xerox Corporation at their Palo Alto Research Center (known as PARC). It has been adopted as the most prevalent standard for networking and is used by the largest computer network in the world, the Internet, which connects literally millions of computers worldwide.

other disk drive on the network. Sharing a CD-ROM drive with WFW is almost completely transparent to the user. Even installation is essentially transparent.

Installing a CD-ROM Drive with WFW

The first step in the installation of the CD-ROM drive on a Windows for Workgroups network is to install the drive so that it works with DOS. You must be sure that you have the appropriate driver software installed. You'll need all of these drivers:

- The driver for the CD-ROM adapter (if you are using SCSI/ASPI, this is the ASPI driver for the SCSI adapter)
- The ASPI driver for the CD-ROM drive (SCSI only)
- MSCDEX (Microsoft CD-ROM Extensions) or its equivalent—like CorelSCSI!'s CORELCDX

The next step is to install Windows for Workgroups; if you are already using Windows, you can perform an upgrade. During this process, WFW notices that you have a CD-ROM installed and does a couple of things for you automatically: it updates the MSCDEX file to version 2.22 (required if you want to share the CD-ROM drive) and it adds the /S (share) switch to the MSCDEX command line.

WFW, NetWare, and CD-ROM Drives

WFW is a great way to share a CD-ROM drive on a NetWare network, but one very common problem can drive you crazy if you don't catch it: Microsoft provides a special, WFW-compatible driver called MSIPX so that you can access your NetWare file server. If other stations are to share your drive, you must place MSCDEX *after* Net Start, but *before* MSIPX in the AUTOEXEC.BAT file. If you don't, workstations attempting to share the CD-ROM drive get an error message instead of a file list when they try to look at the drive in File Manager.

Amazingly enough, that's all it takes. If you already have Windows for Workgroups installed, just install the CD-ROM drive for DOS and make these changes yourself:

1. If your MSCDEX version is not 2.21 or higher (or the replacement for MSCDEX provided by Corel), update it. You can find the 2.21 version on the WFW distribution disks.

2. Add the /S switch to the MSCDEX command line in AUTOEXEC.BAT.

Sharing the CD-ROM Drive with WFW

Making your CD-ROM drive available to other users on the network is simple once you install the drive. Open File Manager and follow these steps:

1. In the toolbar at the top of the screen, click the icon for your CD-ROM **drive** (or the one you want to share, if you have more than one). The icon has a picture of a CD on it. A file list from the CD-ROM in that drive appears (see fig. 5.1).

2. Click the Share button in the toolbar (or choose Share As from the Disk menu) if you want to generally share the drive so

CAUTION

Running Out of Drive Letters

If you're working with a large WFW network, you may have already used up all available drive letters (C through Z) on shared drives or directories before you try to access the CD-ROM drive. You may have to drop one of the drives you're already sharing in order to free a drive letter for the CD-ROM drive.

that, for example, others can place disks in the drive and use them. (The Share button shows a little hand and a file folder.) After you click the Share button, the Share Directory dialog box appears (see fig. 5.2).

If you intend to share only a specific directory on a specific disc, make that directory the current directory by clicking it in the right pane of the display, and then click the Share button.

3. In the Share Directory dialog box, tell WFW just what to do by filling in the form provided:

The Share Name is the name that others on the network see when they browse for the drive. You can call the drive anything you like, but make the name something clear like *Joe's CD-ROM Drive.*

The Path line is filled in for you, so leave it alone.

Use the Comment line to specify a comment for others to see.

The Re-share at Startup checkbox determines whether this share is a persistent share. A *persistent share* is automatically remade the next time you start WFW. You probably want this to happen (which is why this is the default). If you don't want this share to be made the next time you start WFW, click the box to deselect the option. Some drives generate an error message if there is no disc in them at startup when this option is selected. The error message is nothing more than an annoyance and doesn't hurt anything.

The Access Type group of radio buttons determines what sort of access users have to the drive. For normal drives, this feature is important, but because users cannot write to the CD-ROM drive, you can ignore this option (it can only be Read-Only for a CD-ROM drive).

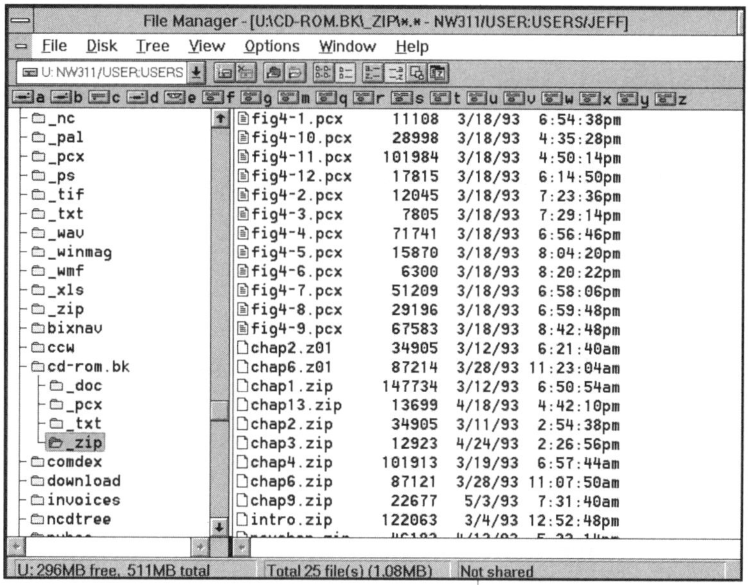

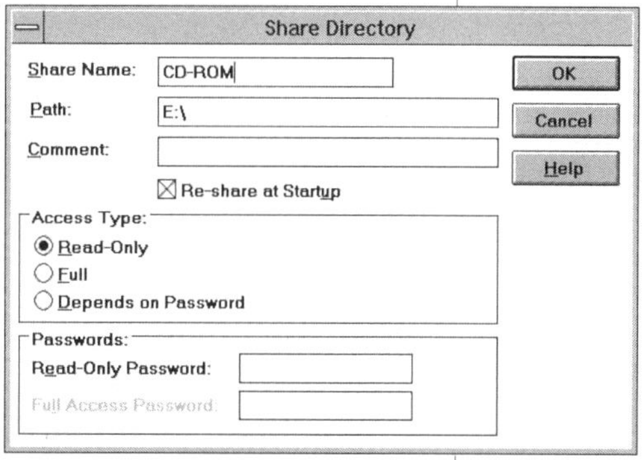

FIGURE 5.1, top

WFW's File Manager is the control center for sharing and connecting drives.

FIGURE 5.2, bottom

The Share Directory dialog box.

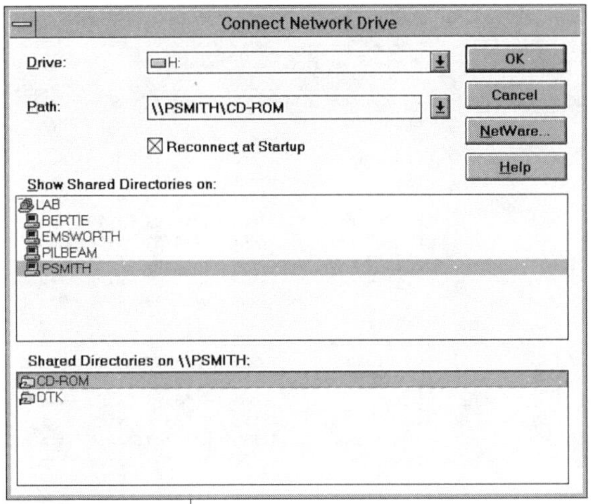

FIGURE 5.3

The Connect Network Drive dialog box lets you browse for and connect to drives owned by other users.

The Passwords options let you set a password that users who want to share your drive have to type. The password is the same for everyone who uses the drive and should not be considered particularly secure.

4. After you fill in the Share Directory dialog box, click the OK button to complete the operation. Your drive is now available to others in the workgroup.

> **Licensing**
>
> Just because you *can* share a CD-ROM disc does not mean you are allowed to. Please carefully read the license agreement that came with the disc to make sure that you comply with its terms before allowing multiple users to access the CD-ROM at the same time. Some applications can detect when they are running across the network and refuse to work.

Connecting to Another CD-ROM Drive with WFW

It is just as easy to access someone else's drive with WFW as it is to make your drive available to others in the workgroup. The process involves File Manager and a few simple operations:

1. Click the Connect button (the first button) on the toolbar in the WFW File Manager window or choose Connect Network Drive from the Disk menu. The Connect Network Drive dialog box appears (see fig. 5.3).

2. Fill in the appropriate options in the Connect Network Drive dialog box:

   Use the Drive combo box to choose the drive letter assigned to the shared CD-ROM drive. The combo box defaults to the next available drive, but you can choose another. Your choice must be no higher in the alphabet than the LASTDRIVE= statement in your CONFIG.SYS file.

   The Path combo box is filled in automatically as you browse for the CD-ROM drive. You can ignore it for now.

   The Reconnect at Startup checkbox serves the same purpose as its partner in the Share Directory dialog box: it decides whether the connection is persistent (automatically remade the next time you start Windows). A noncritical error may occur if there is no disc in the drive when you start Windows; a dialog box appears to allow you to continue.

3. In the Show Shared Directories On list box, locate the machine on which the drive you want to access is located and click its icon. This list box allows you to browse for **shares** on other machines in your workgroup and is where you find the CD-ROM drive you want to share. Each machine on the network is listed in this box with both an icon and a name.

4. After you select a machine, the pane in the bottom half of the dialog box displays any directories available on that machine. Click on the CD-ROM drive's share. With any luck, the share has been given an obvious name. This action fills in the Path combo box you ignored earlier. If you know exactly what you want and where it is (if you're a propeller head), you can skip the browsing and type the path in the Path box directly.

5. Click the OK button and supply the password, if one is requested. Now you can access information on the CD-ROM drive you chose.

Understanding Performance Issues

Windows for Workgroups makes sharing CD-ROM drives easy and relatively inexpensive. It also brings the added benefits of sharing other drives and printers. The downside, however, is that you may suffer performance degradations on both the CD-ROM-based application and on the machine sharing it.

Become familiar with the problem signs so that you can decide whether you need to purchase another CD-ROM drive and use it directly. The first sign is **poor performance** of CD-ROM applications that move lots of data from the CD. Applications that use complex graphical images, sound, or other multimedia-style elements may show problems. You may also see some slowing of applications on the host machine during access.

NOTE

What's a Share?

A *share* is a path that the machine's user has given other users access to through WFW. It can be the entire drive or just a directory.

Of more concern is the fact that some applications with timing-critical sections geared around audio or animation sequences may lock up if you attempt to run them across the network. This problem is less common now than it was when multimedia applications were first created, but watch for it so that you don't mistake it for another problem.

TIP

How To Correct Some Performance Problems

You may be able to correct the slow-down problem somewhat by using the Performance Tuning adjustment available in the Windows Control Panel. This slider control lets the machine's owner select the priority of foreground over background operations.

Using a CD-ROM Drive with Lantastic

Lantastic is another peer-to-peer networking product that comes in two flavors: DOS and Windows. Actually, the Windows version of Lantastic is simply a Windows interface to the network. If you want to enable networking under Windows, you must load the basic Lantastic network drivers before starting Windows (after Windows loads, the Lantastic for Windows drivers are initiated).

Sharing a CD-ROM Drive with Lantastic

Sharing a CD-ROM drive with other members of your workgroup under Lantastic is a fairly straightforward procedure. Carry out the following steps on the machine to which the CD-ROM drive is physically connected.

Regardless of the installation—DOS or Windows Lantastic—you must take the following preliminary steps:

1. Make sure that all SCSI, CD-ROM, and DOS drivers for the CD-ROM drive are installed and functioning properly. To make sure that the CD-ROM drive is properly installed, use the DOS prompt to switch to that drive and get a directory of files on a disc in that drive.

2. Install Lantastic. Make sure that all members of the workgroup can access and share selected drives.

3. Remove the MSCDEX command from your AUTOEXEC.BAT file.

4. In the STARTNET.BAT file (which contains commands to start Lantastic), make sure that the MSCDEX command originally found in the AUTOEXEC.BAT file falls between the Lantastic REDIR and SERVER command lines. For example, position the MSCDEX statement as follows:

```
REDIR SERVER1
MSCDEX.EXE /D:MSCD0001 /L:D
SERVER
```

5. Save the STARTNET.BAT file.

6. Type **NET_MGR** at the DOS command line and press Enter to access Lantastic's Network Resource Manager.

7. Select Shared Resources Management from the menu. A list of resources pops up on the screen.

8. Press the Insert key, type an identifying name for the CD-ROM drive—up to eight characters long (for example, **MY_CDROM**)—and press Enter.

9. When NET_MGR asks you for the true link, or true name, for the CD-ROM drive, type the DOS drive name (for example, type **D:** or **E:**).

10. That's it! Press the Escape key to exit the menus and NET_MGR. Each workstation on the peer network can now access the shared CD-ROM drive.

Connecting to Another CD-ROM Drive with Lantastic

Once you set up the CD-ROM drive to be shared across the Lantastic network (as described in the preceding section), you must connect each workstation that is to share the CD-ROM drive to the drive over the network. To connect a workstation to the shared drive, follow these steps on the machine that is to access the drive:

1. Type **NET** at the DOS prompt and press Enter to access Lantastic's Peer NET program.

2. Select Network Disk Drives and Printers from the Main Functions menu.

3. Select the drive designation you want the CD-ROM to use under that machine's Lantastic sessions. Suppose that the workstation has two floppies and one hard drive (that is, it has drives A through C); you may want to make the CD-ROM drive D. Specify the DOS drive name you want the CD-ROM drive to become for this workstation and press Enter.

4. The next list displays available servers. Select the server physically connected to the CD-ROM drive you want to access. For example, if the machine to which the CD-ROM drive is physically connected is called EMSWORTH, select EMSWORTH as the server to which you want to connect.

5. Select the CD-ROM drive from the list of available drives on the selected server and press Enter. The name you select here is the same name you gave to the drive when you accessed Lantastic's Network Resource Manager, selected Shared Resources Management, and pressed Insert (refer to the preceding section for more information about setting up a drive to be shared on Lantastic).

6. Press the Escape key to back out of all menus and return to the DOS prompt.

Once you install Lantastic for Windows, you'll find that all Lantastic's Network Manager tools now show the shared CD-ROM drive. You need do no additional work under the Windows version of the interface.

Using a CD-ROM Drive with Novell NetWare

NetWare LAN administrators and users have a number of ways to attach CD-ROM drives and applications to their networks so that they can share network-licensed CD-ROM applications. The majority of these solutions involve attaching the CD-ROM drives directly to a NetWare server, running special NetWare Loadable Modules (NLMs) to access the drives through the SCSI interface, and then allowing network access to the drives for groups of users. This sounds like a relatively painless process, but in real life, it isn't. SCSI conflicts, NLM incompatibilities, and myriad other complications often arise.

This section shows you how to load the Novell CD-ROM NLM and how to use a third-party solution (Microtest's discport) to make the process a little smoother.

Installing CD-ROM Support in NetWare

NetWare includes an NLM (Network Loadable Module) for CD-ROM support. The NLM makes the CD-ROM drive look like any other NetWare volume and gives you many of the same access functions (mount, dismount, and so on).

Although we describe a simpler third-party solution in the next section (Microtest's discport), CD-ROM setup over NetWare is pretty easy—if you're lucky. As we mentioned earlier, adding a CD-ROM drive to a server introduces a whole new world of potential hardware and software conflicts. If you'd rather not worry about these potential troubles, try discport. If, however, your server is stable and you don't anticipate any problems (or if you're lucky enough to get the server with the CD-ROM preinstalled), try Novell's CD-ROM support. To set up a CD-ROM driver with Novell's native CD-ROM support, follow these steps:

Table 5.1 CD NLM Command-Line Switches

Switch	Function
DEVICE LIST	Shows the CD-ROM drives that are available from the server. Also shows the number of each device, its status (active/inactive and mounted/dismounted), its name, and its volume name.
VOLUME LIST	Similar to the DEVICE LIST switch but shows the volume name before the device name; does not show the active/inactive status.
MOUNT [*device number* or *volume name*] [/mac] [/nfs] [/G=*x*] [/R] [/Z]	Mounts the specified drive. Only the first option (the *device number* or *volume name*) is required. The other switches perform these functions: /mac — Adds Macintosh Name Space Support /nfs — Adds NFS Name Space Support /G=*x* — Sets the volume group access rights (*x* is the number listed from the GROUP command—see below) /R — Prevents NetWare from rebuilding a directory and file structure for the volume each time the drive is mounted (saves a significant amount of time in the mounting process); to use this option, make sure that the drive has been mounted once, and an image stored on the SYS volume /Z — Ignores all zero-length files when building the file structure
DISMOUNT [*device number* or *volume name*]	Dismounts the specified device.
CHANGE [*device number* or *volume name*]	Allows you to change the disc in the drive.
DIR [*device number* or *volume name*]	Shows the directory of the CD-ROM drive.
GROUP [*group name* and *group number*]	Lets you configure group access to the drive.

1. Make sure that the drive works. In the case of NetWare, this may involve testing the drive on a DOS-based machine other than the server. If possible, however, test the CD-ROM drive locally on the server.

2. Load the NetWare driver for your CD-ROM drive. This driver is provided by the interface card's manufacturer.

3. Load the CD-ROM NLM; the NLM is called **CD** and takes the arguments listed in table 5.1. You must know the device number or volume label of the drive you want to use. You can find that information with either the CD DEVICE LIST or CD VOLUME LIST command. If you find that your drive is device number 3, for example, the command to load the NLM looks like this:

   ```
   CD MOUNT 3
   ```

   After a long pause (during which NetWare builds its file and directory map of the drive), NetWare tells you it has mounted the drive with read-only access.

discport

Thankfully, someone has done something to ease the pain of networking CD-ROMs under NetWare.

Microtest has come up with an ingenious hardware and software package that makes the installation and networking of CD-ROM drives under NetWare 3.11 as easy as installing a drive in a single PC. The product is called discport and retails for about $795 ($995 for the Token Ring version)—and is worth every penny.

The package consists of a discport "black box" that houses an Ethernet port, a SCSI port, a CD-ROM SCSI cable, a power supply, and software. Installation is this simple:

1. Plug the Ethernet port on the discport box into the network on any available Ethernet socket.

2. Plug your standard (SCSI-2) CD-ROM drive into the SCSI port on the discport box.

3. Plug the power cord into the discport box and into a power outlet.

4. Install the discport software.

That's it!

Drives can be chained—up to seven CD-ROMs on each discport box. And to make management easy, you don't have to attach the discport box to the server; you can put it anywhere out on the LAN where authorized users can change discs.

It's the software that makes this package really hum, however. One of the most confusing issues for NetWare LAN users is how to find the CD-ROM applications out on the network. The masterful discport Windows and DOS end-user software displays a list of all CD-ROMs available to users—with familiar application names rather than cryptic volume labels.

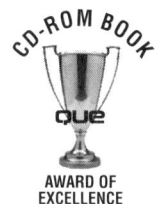

CD-ROM BOOK
AWARD OF EXCELLENCE

discport

Don't even think about networking CD-ROMs under NetWare without Microtest's discport. It's *the* easiest way to add CD-ROM capabilities to NetWare, period. Now, if every SCSI device were this easy to configure....

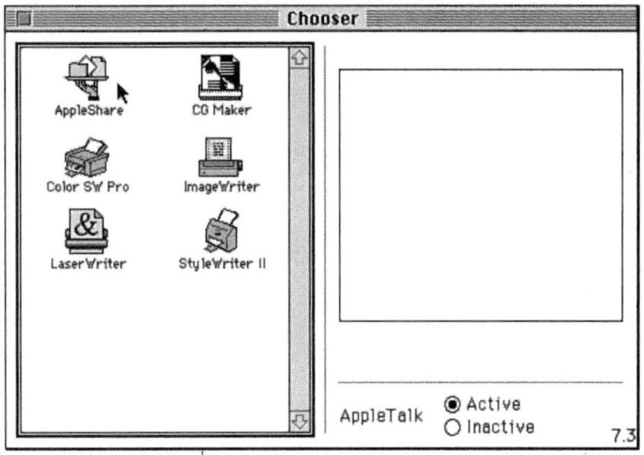

FIGURE 5.4

Select the AppleShare icon in the Chooser. The available servers will appear in the box on the right.

Network administrators can control who has access to CD-ROMs and can assign members of a workgroup as CD-ROM managers, allowing them to change CDs and publish the applications to others within their group.

This is a fabulous product at a great price. Don't network without it.

Using a CD-ROM Drive on a Mac Network

Macintosh has always been silently envied by PC network administrators. Say what you will about AppleTalk, it's simple enough for just about anybody to operate.

Like your hard drives, the CD-ROM drive is a named volume on your Mac. You can give it any name you want (be creative—you're using a Mac, after all). When another user picks your machine in their Chooser, they see the CD-ROM's name in the list of volumes.

Follow these easy steps to network your Mac's CD-ROM drive:

1. Follow the instructions in Chapter 4 for installing your CD-ROM drive; make sure that the drive works on the local machine before you try to share it across the network. As a quick test, try copying some files from the CD-ROM to your hard drive.

2. From another machine on the same AppleTalk network, open the Chooser. Pick the AppleShare icon (see fig. 5.4).

3. Pick your machine from the list of servers in the right side of the Chooser. You may have to type a password for that server to get to the next dialog box. (If the target machine doesn't show up in the Chooser, enable File Sharing on the machine and wait a minute or so before you reopen the Chooser.)

4. In the Volumes dialog box (which has the name of the server at the top), click the CD-ROM's volume name and click OK. The drive's icon should appear on your desktop.

That's all. You can work with files and programs from the remote machine just like you can with the local machine. In fact, sharing a CD-ROM drive is even a little less stressful than sharing a hard drive—you don't have to worry about someone else deleting or changing any of the files on the CD-ROM.

Chapter 6

Troubleshooting

You've installed your new CD-ROM drive, flipped all the switches, and...something's wrong. Maybe everything works until you try a certain disc, or you can hear your game's music but can't hear the characters talk.

This chapter tells you how to track down problems. It also lets you know when you should throw in the towel and call for help. The last section lists some common problems and gives you some ideas for fixing them.

Troubleshooting Basics

When you have a problem with your computer, it's not unusual to get scared (you're probably looking at a couple thousand dollars you've invested—what if it's all fried?) or frustrated (you know, when you start pressing keys really hard and saying nasty things to the screen). Troubleshooting is very easy and logical, but it's not easy to think logically when you're upset. Before you start fixing it, take some time to relax. This chapter has many helpful tips, and you can always call your drive's manufacturer if you can't find the problem yourself. When you're confident you can proceed logically, you can start your troubleshooting process.

Here's a quick rundown of the troubleshooting process:

1. Define the problem clearly.

2. Focus on the elements that could cause that problem and check each in turn.

3. Try *one solution at a time*, documenting your work as you go.

The following sections show you how each of those steps works and how you can troubleshoot efficiently.

Defining the Problem

The first step to solving a problem is to have a problem—a *clearly defined problem*, that is. Even if you don't want to do any fixing on your own and call the hardware manufacturer, the service person will ask you to describe the problem right at the start. Get as specific as you can. "My CD-ROM doesn't work," is a poorly defined problem. "Every time I try to run a movie from Compton's Interactive Encyclopedia, my computer locks up," is much better. Defining the problem might take some time, but it more than makes up for the time you'd spend otherwise trying to solve a poorly defined problem.

When you're defining the problem, first try to re-create it. As you know if you've worked with computers for a while, some problems happen one time and disappear forever after you **reboot** your computer. Don't waste time chasing down a one-time glitch—until you can reproduce the problem, it's not a problem. Try to remember everything you did before the problem occurred—and do the same things again after you reboot your computer. If the problem pops up again, you should be able to clearly define it.

TIP

Reboot First

Some problems are one-time things. Reboot your computer and try to retrace the steps you made just before the problem showed up. With any luck, the problem will have disappeared and you can chalk it up to computer gremlins.

Professional troubleshooters always ask two questions: "What happens?" and "When does it happen?" So even if you're solving your problem on your own, make sure that your explanation includes a *what* and at least one *when* (preferably more). The *what* is the symptom, like "my computer locks up," or "the screen colors go all weird." *Whens* for that fact are modifiers that make the *what* more clear, like "when I try to play a music CD," or "when I get to this part of the program." A clear description of a problem might look like this:

> "My sound card buzzes when I print from Windows."

In severe problems, the *when* might be "whenever the computer is turned on," or even "all the time."

Listing the Suspects

The goal of troubleshooting is to locate the source of the problem—and the most common way of narrowing down the suspects is to eliminate the impossible. As Sherlock Holmes might have said, "When you eliminate the impossible, whatever is left—no matter how improbable—is the reason your computer locks up when you play Wing Commander."

As you eliminate potential problems, start big. For example, don't check the physical surface of the CD-ROM for scratches first (that's a very tiny component of the whole process). A better approach is to identify the major components and see which could cause your symptoms.

These are some of the major components of running multimedia software from your CD-ROM drive:

- The software on the CD-ROM disc
- The physical CD-ROM disc
- The CD-ROM drive
- The cables from your drive to your computer
- The interface card
- The interface card's software drivers

- The CD-ROM drive's software drivers
- The operating system
- The operating system's software for the CD-ROM's application (like a QuickTime driver for movies)
- Any other hardware components used by the CD-ROM's application (like a sound card) and its software drivers, cables, and external components (like speakers)

It's a long list, but there aren't too many problems that will find causes in *each* of these elements. The idea is to find the elements that *could* cause your problem. If your problem is "My screen goes blank when I try to play an animation file in my encyclopedia," for example, the problem is probably not with any of your computer's cables, the CD-ROM drive, the interface card (or its drivers)—if there was a problem with one of those areas, you wouldn't be able to use the encyclopedia software at all.

Once you've narrowed down the field (eliminated the impossible), you can focus on finding the specific cause.

Figure out ways to eliminate each remaining component—or several at once if possible. For example, you can eliminate the physical CD-ROM disc as a culprit by trying a different animation file from that disc or trying an animation file of the same type from another disc. These tests also help eliminate other variables. If another animation file from the same disc works, you know that the animation drivers in the operating system work. However, if animation files from a different disc also fail, you know the problem isn't with the software on the first disc.

Write down everything you try. A record of what you've tried and what happened when you tried it is especially valuable if you end up asking someone else for help, but it will also help you keep your logic straight.

When you think you've found the problem, verify it by approaching it from the other side. Ask yourself what other things would be affected by that particular failure. Continuing with the animation example, if you determine that the problem is in the animation drivers, you can verify it by trying to play other animation files.

Fixing the Problem

By now, you know which component is causing your problem, so you're about halfway home. The most important thing to keep in mind when *fixing* a problem is to try one—and *only one*—solution at a time. This serves two purposes:

1. When the problem goes away, you know exactly what fixed it
2. You reduce the risk of fixing the problem and breaking something else at the same time

If you have a problem with your interface card conflicting with another card, for example, don't change its IRQ *and* address at the same time. Murphy's Law dictates that your base address is fine when you've got an IRQ conflict and vice versa—if you change them both, you're sure to fix the one that was broken and break the one that worked.

Trying one solution at a time also implies that if your attempt doesn't work, you should undo it. For example, if you try a different IRQ for the interface card and the problem doesn't go away, switch back to the original IRQ before you try other solutions.

As you did when you were eliminating suspects, keep a record of every solution you've tried. This keeps you from trying the same thing twice and definitely helps if you call someone else in to help fix the problem.

Working with Technical Support

The manufacturer of your CD-ROM drive (or an authorized third-party service company) should be able to help you track down problems, try solutions, and repair or replace any defective hardware. Check the manuals that came with your equipment for a Technical Support or Authorized Service Center number, and call it when you're ready for outside help. You may also be able to reach those sources through a BBS, an on-line service like CompuServe, or with a fax.

The following sections show you what to do before you call and what to expect from the company.

Before the Call

If you've followed the guidelines from earlier in this chapter and *written everything down*, you'll make life easier for yourself and the technician you work with. If you didn't write everything down, you should have at least this information on hand:

- The last thing you did before the problem happened
- The serial number or registration number for your product
- The make and model of your drive and its interface card
- For DOS users: a printed copy of your CONFIG.SYS and AUTOEXEC.BAT files

Make sure that you can get the problem to happen again even after you turn the computer off and back on. You may also want to check out some of the very common (and slightly embarrassing) simple causes of problems:

- The drive is not plugged in
- The drive is not connected to the interface card
- The drive is not turned on
- There is no disc in the drive

- The disc in the drive is not for your computer type (for example, you have a PC and the disc is for a Mac—check the package)

Know What To Expect

When you talk with a technical support person, you should have an idea what you're getting into. Realistic expectations on your part will make the session easier for both of you.

It is perfectly reasonable for you to expect these things:

- Help with the specific product you purchased from that company, but not with products from other companies—your CD-ROM drive manufacturer probably won't be able to help you install Microsoft Office from a CD-ROM.
- Repair or replacement service as outlined in your product's manual. Read that section before you call so that if there's a charge for shipping or a standard repair period, it won't be a surprise.
- Courteous service, even if you're not able to answer all the technical questions they ask. Don't worry—the technicians can walk you through actions over the phone that give them the answers they need.

Common Symptoms, Causes, and Solutions

This section lists some of the common problems you find when working with CD-ROM drives and multimedia software. It also gives you a few possible causes (and corresponding solutions) for each problem.

Symptom	Possible Causes and Solutions
You can't see the directory of the disc, or you can't run any programs from the disc, or the disc doesn't appear on your Macintosh desktop or in Windows' File Manager, or the drive doesn't appear to work at all.	There is no disc in the drive, or the disc is upside down. The drive is not plugged in or turned on. The disc caddie isn't seated properly or (for caddieless drives) the tray isn't pushed in all the way. Eject and reinsert the disc. The disc in the drive is for another type of computer. Check the packaging. The CD-ROM driver didn't load at startup. On a Macintosh, you see an × through the driver's icon or no icon at all. On a PC, you see an error

continues

Symptom	Possible Causes and Solutions
	message when the driver tries to load (usually something like `Bad or missing C:\CDROM\CD.DRV`). Make sure that the file exists at the specified location. Try reinstalling the driver software. Does the drive work with a different disc? If so, it could be a bad disc. Try the disc-resuscitation techniques listed in Appendix F, "Care and Feeding of CD-ROMs." If you've just installed the drive and it doesn't work with *any* discs, it could be a hardware or software conflict. See Chapter 4, "How To Install Your CD-ROM Drive," for instructions on setting up your CD-ROM's hardware and software. If the drive has been working but stopped all of a sudden, something has probably changed. Did you add a new program or utility? Did you add a piece of hardware? Try restoring the computer to the way it was before you made the change. If that works, investigate possible hardware or software conflicts and try different settings.
You see the directory for the disc you just ejected instead of the disc you just put in.	If you're using Windows File Manager, you have to click on the drive's icon (under the menu bar) before you see the new directory. Otherwise, it's a caching problem. Unload and reload the caching software or restart your computer.
You can't read certain types of discs on your Macintosh.	Make sure that the disc is made for the Macintosh and not for MPC, Windows, or DOS. System 7.x uses several drivers in the Extensions folder for CD-ROM support. If one of those drivers is missing, you can read some discs but not others. Common examples of driver files are High Sierra File Access, ISO 9660 File Access, and Audio CD Access. Reinstall the software.

Symptom	Possible Causes and Solutions
Your animations don't work but the programs on the same CD work fine.	The animations could be trying to set up your video for a mode it doesn't support—for example, too many colors or an unsupported resolution. Check the disc's system requirements to see whether it needs a different video mode. You may be able to set your existing hardware up for a different video mode by using different system drivers. The animation driver in your operating system is the wrong version for the animations, or it is missing or corrupt. Check the disc's documentation to see what animation driver it needs (a certain version of QuickTime or Video for Windows, for example). Reinstall the driver.
Your video files hesitate, jump around, or cause the sound to break up.	Your system isn't fast enough to play all the frames in the video at the same speed as the accompanying audio. It either has to drop frames from the video (which usually lets the audio play at full speed but makes the video hesitate or jump around) or it plays all the frames and breaks up the audio. You may be able to solve this problem with a disc cache or a different video driver. If that doesn't help, you may want to invest in a video accelerator card.
You just installed a CD-ROM program and now Windows doesn't work.	Many CD-ROM programs change your Windows setup by adding new drivers or switching to a different video mode. They usually ask permission during their installation process—but sometimes they don't. Try running Windows Setup (type **SETUP.EXE** from DOS) and setting Windows back to its original settings—which usually means **resetting** its video driver to VGA from whatever it was changed to.

continues

CAUTION

Fixing One Problem May Cause Another

Be aware that resetting the video mode may cause the CD-ROM application not to work. If this happens, rerun the installation program for the CD-ROM application and see whether it gives you the option of using your default video. If this option is not available, call the technical support number for the application or the manufacturer of your video card to see how you can get the combination to work.

Symptom	Possible Causes and Solutions
You upgraded to a quad-speed drive, but your game didn't get any faster.	Discs must be specifically made to take advantage of the quad-speed drive. Most discs (at the time of this writing) aren't, so most of the applications won't get much faster. If the disc *is* quad-speed compatible, you may have to change the software drivers to recognize the new drive.
When you plug in your speakers, you can't hear the sound effects from your Mac multimedia CDs—even though you can hear the music.	The two sounds come from different sources: the music comes from your CD-ROM player's audio ports, and the sound effects come from the Mac's audio ports. Your speakers probably have plugs for the regular RCA jacks on the back of the drive as well as a 1/8-inch stereo plug (like the plug on a pair of Walkman-type headphones). That second plug is usually the culprit—it's supposed to go into the back of your Mac, but it fits just right in the CD-ROM drive's headphone jack. If you put that plug in the front of your CD-ROM drive instead of the back of your Mac, you won't hear the sound effects. Insert the 1/8-inch stereo plug into the audio out jack on the Mac and the problem will be solved.
Your new external CD-ROM drive works but now your (pick one) scanner, tape backup, or other peripheral doesn't work.	Most likely a SCSI ID or termination problem. See Chapter 4, "How To Install Your CD-ROM Drive," for information about setting up SCSI devices. If the external drive also included a new interface card, you could be having a hardware conflict with an existing card or a software driver conflict. See Chapter 4 for hardware and software setup information.

Chapter 7

What Is Multimedia?

Although the focus of this book is CD-ROM technology, this chapter examines another closely related concept, and one of the most exciting developments in personal computing in the last five years: multimedia. CD-ROM is not a requirement for multimedia on a PC, but its impressive capacity makes data-intensive multimedia applications practical. Little short of a CD-ROM can deliver the raw storage capacity required for these ambitious, exciting software packages.

Most multimedia applications, however, require more than just a CD-ROM drive to be effective. The addition of a sound card, for example, is essential for most multimedia applications.

In this chapter, we explain the basic components of multimedia. The following chapter shows you some specific hardware options, like multimedia-ready computers, upgrade kits, and individual multimedia components (sound cards, speakers, and so on.).

Understanding Multimedia

Multimedia on a computer is any application that employs more than one medium to convey information. The following list runs through the possible combinations for multimedia presentations from the least to the most complex:

Text with graphics
Text with photos
Text with sound
Text with animation
Text with video
Graphics with sound
Photos with sound
Animation with sound
Video with sound

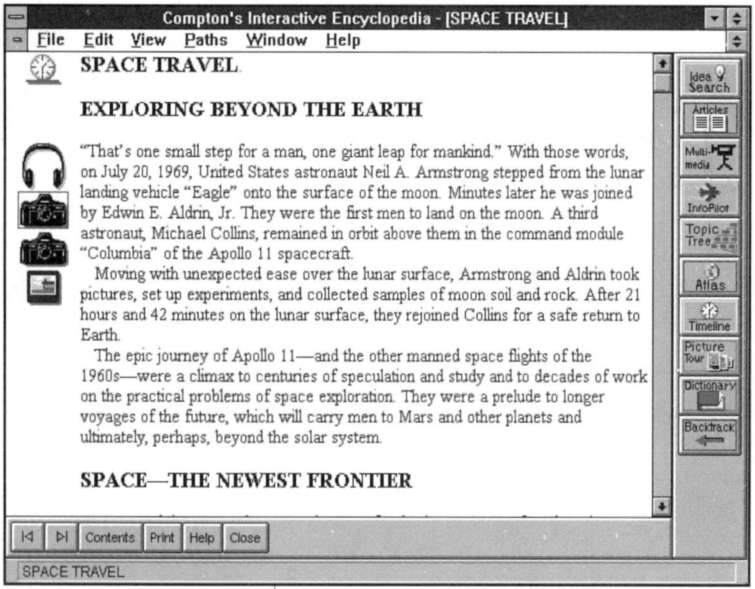
Compton's Interactive Encyclopedia - [SPACE TRAVEL]
File Edit View Paths Window Help
SPACE TRAVEL
EXPLORING BEYOND THE EARTH
"That's one small step for a man, one giant leap for mankind." With those words, on July 20, 1969, United States astronaut Neil A. Armstrong stepped from the lunar landing vehicle "Eagle" onto the surface of the moon. Minutes later he was joined by Edwin E. Aldrin, Jr. They were the first men to land on the moon. A third astronaut, Michael Collins, remained in orbit above them in the command module "Columbia" of the Apollo 11 spacecraft.
Moving with unexpected ease over the lunar surface, Armstrong and Aldrin took pictures, set up experiments, and collected samples of moon soil and rock. After 21 hours and 42 minutes on the lunar surface, they rejoined Collins for a safe return to Earth.
The epic journey of Apollo 11—and the other manned space flights of the 1960s—were a climax to centuries of speculation and study and to decades of work on the practical problems of space exploration. They were a prelude to longer voyages of the future, which will carry men to Mars and other planets and ultimately, perhaps, beyond the solar system.
SPACE—THE NEWEST FRONTIER
Idea Search
Articles
Multi-media
InfoPilot
Topic Tree
Atlas
Timeline
Picture Tour
Dictionary
Backtrack
Contents
Print
Help
Close
SPACE TRAVEL

FIGURE 7.1

Compton's Multimedia Encyclopedia, showing an article with graphics enhancement.

CAUTION

The *Multimedia* Buzz Word

The term *multimedia* is a buzz word, like *new* or *improved*, that can be construed to mean something as simple as a word processing document. Because of this ambiguity, the term itself is subject to abuse. Don't count on the word *multimedia* to mean anything in particular when it appears on a software package or elsewhere. Look for terms that are specific and unambiguous, such as MPC (discussed later), when shopping for software.

Enhancing Multimedia

Most multimedia applications on PCs are still primarily text-based with multimedia aspects added to them. For example, figure 7.1 is from Compton's Multimedia Encyclopedia. Next to the great article on space exploration that occupies most of the screen, notice the icon that represents a multimedia enhancement to the article. Clicking this camera icon displays a picture of an Apollo moon landing.

Sound enhancements to articles are handled similarly. Figure 7.2 is an example from Quanta's Consumer Information CD. By clicking the headphone icon next to the backache article, you can hear a brief spoken introduction to the text. Other text-based multimedia applications incorporate animation, video, and video with sound.

Many multimedia applications are not text-based, however. They use graphics, sound, animation, and/or video. CD-ROM-based games and education applications may consist entirely of animation and sound.

Understanding Storage Requirements

In terms of complexity and required storage, the **media** used in multimedia applications have a broad range.

Text files with graphics images are the base level of multimedia. Text and graphics in one file or presentation on a PC require relatively little storage space. For example, a five-page report about the increased sales of baseball bats to the Pacific Islands that includes three-color bar charts consumes no more than 100 KB of disk space.

If you present the same information in a five-minute graphic slide-show format with a dubbed stereo soundtrack of music to accompany the graphics, however, the presentation blossoms into a sound-with-graphics multimedia presentation that requires nearly 40 MB of storage space.

Table 7.1 gives some rough estimates of how storage hungry various multimedia elements are.

It's easy to see from these kinds of numbers that the use of multimedia in mass-produced applications requires the storage capacity of CD-ROM.

Enabling Technology

In the world of technology, an innovation in one area sometimes leads to radical changes in other technologies. These new technologies are called *enabling technologies.* CD-ROM is an enabling technology. The compact-disc media can record any form of digital information—and any sort of information can be encoded digitally. As long as standards are in place for the orderly recording and playback of the information, CD-ROM technology can deliver all forms of information. For these reasons, CD-ROM enables multimedia to be widely distributed and exploited in a variety of applications. In the case of multimedia, the CD-ROM allows the digital storage of sound and images. This technique is replacing the traditional method of analog recordings and 35mm transparencies or overhead foils.

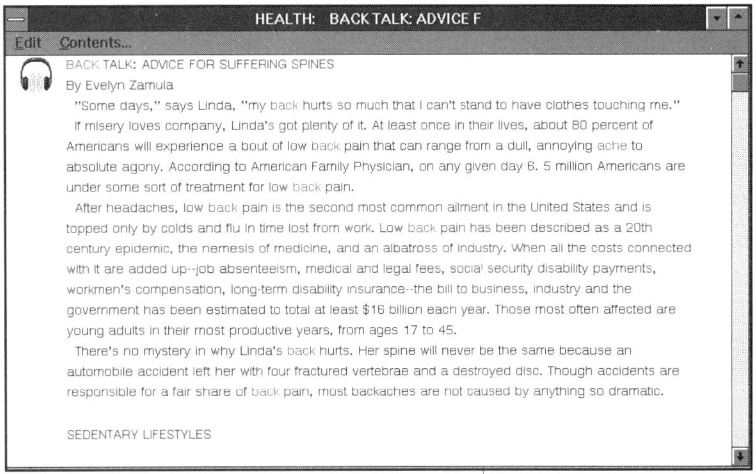

HEALTH: BACK TALK: ADVICE F
Edit Contents...
BACK TALK: ADVICE FOR SUFFERING SPINES
By Evelyn Zamula
"Some days," says Linda, "my back hurts so much that I can't stand to have clothes touching me."
If misery loves company, Linda's got plenty of it. At least once in their lives, about 80 percent of Americans will experience a bout of low back pain that can range from a dull, annoying ache to absolute agony. According to American Family Physician, on any given day 6. 5 million Americans are under some sort of treatment for low back pain.
After headaches, low back pain is the second most common ailment in the United States and is topped only by colds and flu in time lost from work. Low back pain has been described as a 20th century epidemic, the nemesis of medicine, and an albatross of industry. When all the costs connected with it are added up--job absenteeism, medical and legal fees, social security disability payments, workmen's compensation, long-term disability insurance--the bill to business, industry and the government has been estimated to total at least $16 billion each year. Those most often affected are young adults in their most productive years, from ages 17 to 45.
There's no mystery in why Linda's back hurts. Her spine will never be the same because an automobile accident left her with four fractured vertebrae and a destroyed disc. Though accidents are responsible for a fair share of back pain, most backaches are not caused by anything so dramatic.
SEDENTARY LIFESTYLES

FIGURE 7.2

Quanta's Consumer Information CD, showing an article with audio enhancement.

Looking at the MPC Standards

MPC (Multimedia PC) standards were created by a consortium of companies including Microsoft Corporation. This group met and developed a list of requirements for hardware designed to be used in multimedia presentations. This list is a great advantage to you as a multimedia consumer. It guarantees that if you own an MPC, you can successfully run any application labeled with the MPC logo. The basic requirements for a Level 1 MPC are as follows:

- CPU: 386SX (or better)
- RAM: 2 MB (more is *definitely* better)
- Disk drives: Floppy disk—3.5" high-density; Hard disk—30 MB (or larger)
- CD-ROM with CD-DA output
- MPC-compliant sound card
- VGA display adapter (or better)
- 101-key keyboard

EXPLANATION

Media

The term *media* (plural) or *medium* (singular) is used in two ways that can be easily confused. One sense is the *storage medium,* such as the CD-ROM disc itself. The other sense is the *presentation medium,* such as the graphics, text, and sound. You may see both senses in the same paragraph, so pay careful attention to context to avoid confusion.

Table 7.1 Storage Requirements

Multimedia Element	Amount of Storage Space Required
One minute of audio, mono	700 KB
One minute of audio, stereo	1.5 MB (more at audio CD-quality)
One minute of animation	2.5 to 5.5 MB
One minute of video	20 to 30 MB, compressed

- Mouse (with a minimum of two buttons)
- Joystick (not all applications use this)
- Serial, parallel, and MIDI (Musical Instrument Device Interface) ports

MPC Level 2 incorporates all the specifications of Level 1, with some modifications:

- CPU: 486SX (or better)
- RAM: 4 MB (8 MB recommended)
- Hard disk: 160 MB or larger
- CD-ROM drive with 300 KB/s minimum data rate (using no more than 60% of the CPU's time) and average seek time under 400 ms. The drive must also be XA-ready.
- 16-bit wave audio support at 44.1 KHz, mono and stereo.
- VGA display (640x480 pixels) or better with at least 65,536 colors (16-bit video).

The Role of Sound Cards in Multimedia

All CD-ROM drives for PCs are capable of playing standard CD audio, so why the need for yet another piece of hardware? The trouble with sound is that there are many techniques for providing digital audio for applications; CD audio (CD Digital Audio, or CD-DA) is just one of them. For one thing, CD-DA eats up enormous disc space. In a multimedia application that requires sound, video, text, and graphics, even the CD-ROM's enormous storage capacity can be stretched to the max. Also, the synchronization of audio with video or animation is technically more difficult with CD audio. To get around some of these drawbacks, software developers use a variety of audio recording techniques to provide voice, sound effects, and music. Sound cards offer an effective means of taking CD-ROM-based audio and synchronizing it for multimedia applications.

The following sections provide some basic information about sound-card technology. For specifics on some of the sound cards on the market today, see the next chapter, "Choosing a Multimedia PC."

Digital Audio and What Is Covered Here

The field of digital audio and the creation of multimedia presentations is vast—too big to cover thoroughly in this book. This book assumes that you want information to help you purchase an appropriate audio card to play back multimedia applications. Therefore, it covers only audio that pertains directly to your purchase of a sound board as a compliment to your CD-ROM drive.

If you're going to delve heavily into the creation of your own multimedia presentations, this section of the book provides basic background on audio, but doesn't give you all the information you need to create applications.

Sound Sources

Unfortunately, not all sound is created—or reproduced—equally on a PC. The recording, creation, and reproduction of sound can be handled in a variety of ways with a number of different technologies. The following sections explain the differences between these technologies and their relative merits.

Sampled Sound

Analog sounds—sounds that exist in the physical, real world—are vibrations of air. In effect, these sounds are waves of differing heights and widths. Additionally, analog sound is continuous, so the wave's modulations blend from beginning to end, without interruption, throughout the sound event. When you drop a pot lid on the floor, the analog sound of the crash goes through many peaks, valleys, and gradually diminishing spikes until the sound disappears altogether.

Digital recording onto CDs is *sampled audio*. Instantaneous snapshots of the original sound are taken at regular intervals, encoded to digits, and captured to the recording media. The greater the rate at which the sound is sampled, the more closely the digital recording resembles the original.

Figure 7.3 represents, in a graphic wave format, a single analog cough. If the cough is sampled at a low rate, the resulting wave might look like the wave shown in figure 7.4. Notice that many of the peaks and valleys have not been captured. The second sample may not even be discernible as a cough when played back because so much information is missing.

Taking many more samples of the sound gets us closer and closer to the original analog sound. There is a diminishing point of returns, however, because each sample needs storage space. Theoretically, you can sample an analog sound into infinity—but you also need infinite storage space. Luckily, the human ear is not infinitely capable of discerning sound quality.

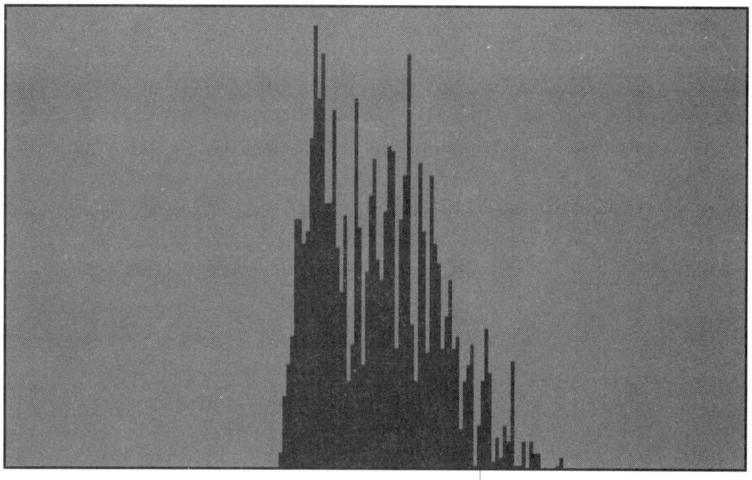

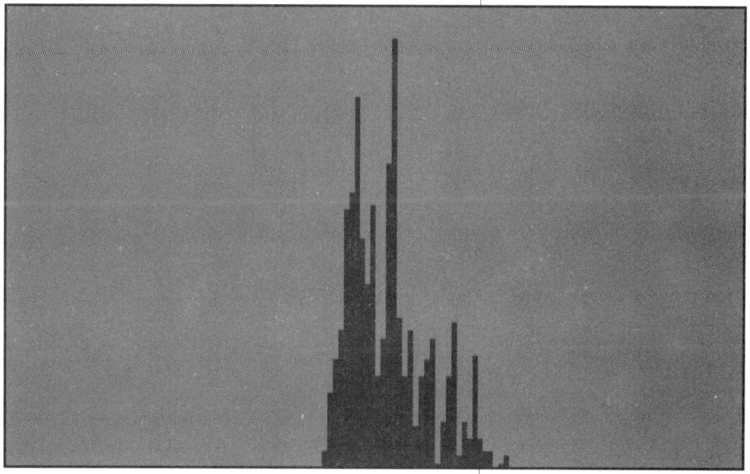

The more complex a sound is, the greater the sample rate that must be used to reproduce it accurately. Human speech, for example, is capable of a fairly limited range of sounds and can be reproduced with a relatively low sample rate. Music, on the other hand, is complex and requires a higher sample rate if it is to be reproduced without noticeable loss of sound quality.

FIGURE 7.3, top

An analog representation of a cough.

FIGURE 7.4, bottom

A sample of a cough, with fewer samples recorded.

By understanding these inherent characteristics of different types of sounds, software developers can utilize the most appropriate sample rates to capture multimedia audio, reducing significantly the CD-ROM space needed to record voice-overs, music, and sound effects.

Sample rates are expressed in **kilohertz** (KHz), which is the number, in thousands, of samples per second. Some typical sample rates are 11, 22, and 44 KHz. The highest, 44 KHz, is the rate of CD audio recordings. This rate was established as a result of an idea called the *Nyquist limit*, which says that the highest frequency that can be reproduced is one half the sample rate. Therefore, the theoretical high-frequency limit of a CD recording is 22 KHz (22,000 Hz). This frequency is just about the upper limit of human hearing and is considered high fidelity.

NOTE

Hertz and CPS

The technical term for *CPS* (cycles per second) is *Hertz*. It is named after Heinrich Hertz, a German physicist. The prefix *kilo* multiplies the value by one thousand; the prefix *mega* multiplies it by one million.

8-Bit and 16-Bit Sound

In addition to sample rate, the data bits available for capturing sound also come into play. Eight-bit samples are capable of representing a wave in one of 256 possible states. Sixteen-bit samples, on the other hand, can express over 65,000 possible states, dramatically expanding the recording's **dynamic range**.

EXPLANATION

Dynamic Range

Although sample rate (time-domain resolution) determines the frequency response of a digital recording, the number of bits in each sample (amplitude-domain resolution) determines the *dynamic range*. The dynamic range is simply the difference between the quietest and loudest reproducible sounds. A 16-bit recording, when compared to an 8-bit recording, has a superior dynamic range.

Obviously, 16-bit cards are superior in dealing with sound samples. Only 16-bit cards can deliver 44 KHz, CD-audio-quality sound through the PC. In addition, some hardware manufacturers are currently shipping cards that support 12-bit sound. All cards do not record and play back at the same resolution; for example, some cards can record only at 8-bit resolution but can play back 16-bit sound files.

Sound Encoding

In addition to employing sampled sounds to create audio in digital format, software and hardware can compress or encode that digital data even more, enabling better use of the CD storage space. One standard for encoding these sound bits is called PCM (Pulse Code Modulation). The sound board uses a DAC (Digital to Analog Converter) to take the digital information representing the sound and convert it to analog signals for speakers and, ultimately, your ears.

ADPCM (Applied Differential Pulse Code Modulation) is a refinement of PCM that provides more efficient encoding than PCM and is a part of the CD-ROM-XA (Extended Architecture) specification. To date, however, few applications use ADPCM digital encoding, and not many sound boards have ADPCM chipsets on them. ADPCM may become the standard for multimedia sound encoding in the future, however, for a number of reasons. First, ADPCM requires much less storage space compared to conventional PCM encoding. ADPCM-enabled multimedia applications can store up to 16 times more audio information than is possible with the PCM method, leaving more space for text, graphics, and video. Perhaps the most important reason behind the use of ADPCM, however, is that the sound can be effectively interleaved with other data types under the XA format. Present multimedia applications must use PCM or CD audio; these formats must be clearly defined on the disc as a separate audio track or stored in a sound file.

Different Sound Formats

All sounds are not created equal. The actual sounds themselves are represented in different formats in multimedia applications. Just as sample rates affect the quality of a recording, so does the manner in which the sound is generated. The following sections describe the available formats and point out the drawbacks and merits of each in representing sound in multimedia applications.

FM Synthesis

FM, or *frequency modulation*, synthesis is used in the development of sound effects and synthesized music. Synthesized music is the music most people commonly refer to as *computer music* because it generally lacks the richness expected from natural sounds (although it does use a technique very similar to the way real sounds are produced). All the tones and effects are produced by mixing and modulating simple tones in different patterns with specialized hardware. One pattern may provide a cymbal-like crash, for example, and another pattern may produce a musical tone.

Because the variety and complexity of tones is limited by the synthesizer's capabilities, nuances or shadings of sound are generally beyond the capabilities of the relatively simple synthesizers supplied on sound boards. As a consequence, these sounds have limited appeal but are perfectly suited to certain background and sound-effect functions in multimedia presentations. Earlier FM synthesis cards provided only 10 or 11 simultaneous sounds or voices, but most cards now use 20-voice stereo chipsets (the minimum you settle for in a synthesis-based sound card).

MIDI

MIDI is short for Musical Instrument Digital Interface and really is not a method for recording music as much as it is a way for recording commands to be sent to a musical instrument (like a keyboard). A MIDI file—often designated with the extension MID—contains references to notes, not an actual recording of the music itself. When MIDI-compatible sound cards read the MIDI files, the cards take the references and look them up in a MIDI table. The table indicates which sound should be played for each reference. For example, the MIDI table may define a cymbal crash as number 55. When the sound card reads a MIDI file and sees the reference to 55, it provides the cymbal sound. You can play MIDI files through the FM synthesis (described in the preceding section) or you can tie MIDI files to a ROM-based sample of real sounds with the ROM chips residing on the sound board.

Wavetable Synthesis

Some higher-end sound cards produce sounds with a technique called *wavetable synthesis*, where on-board ROM-based memory chips carry actual recordings of instruments. These recordings are stored according to the MIDI standard table and can be referenced in that way. ROM-based samples sound more real than their mechanically synthesized counterparts and include all the nuances of live musical instruments.

Providing ROM-based memory chips capable of holding the range of musical instruments and sounds in the MIDI standard, however, requires expensive chips and technology. Sample-based sound cards are more expensive than their synthesized cousins, but you may find the difference worth the added expense. Also, as mass manufacturing and competition heats up even more in the sound-card market, prices will fall to reasonable levels.

WAVE

PCM and ADPCM (described in "Sound Encoding," earlier in this chapter) are techniques for digitally ***encoding*** sounds; WAVE is a ***file format***, that is, a standard way to store encoded data. WAVE files are digital recordings, just like CD audio, but they are saved in file form rather than recorded on a CD track. WAVE files usually have the extension WAV, but this extension is not required. WAVE files can be stored in 8-bit or 16-bit format and can be recorded at 11, 22, or 44 KHz. Many current multimedia titles rely on applications reading a WAVE file and playing it at the same time that a graphics or photo file is displayed.

Storing a sound in WAVE format on CD is not the most productive use of the CD space, but it provides independence for the audio element. The WAVE file can be assigned or used by any application at any time and need not be a synchronized, interleaved part of the multimedia application. The key asset of WAVE files is their versatility; they can reside on the hard drive, floppy drive, or CD-ROM.

WAVE files created by different applications may be in different file formats, much as graphics formats may differ. Files created with Sound Blaster software, for example, have a VOC extension and must be converted to WAVE format for use with Microsoft Windows WAVE applications.

A Sound Summary

Now that you know where all the sound is coming from on PCs these days, keep a few things in mind when purchasing a sound board with a CD-ROM interface:

- Music scores stored in MIDI files sound only as good as the on-board capabilities of the card you buy. Some cards use FM synthesis and others use real samples of instruments. Sampled sound is superior in quality to synthesized sound, but you pay for the improvement. Even those cards that use instrument samples have differing qualities; some use samples at the 44-KHz range and others use 22-KHz samples.

- Only 16-bit sound boards are capable of playing or recording full CD-audio quality 44-KHz WAVE files and CD audio tracks.

- Cards that offer compression techniques (such as ADPCM) may be positioned for use in multimedia applications that use the CD-ROM-XA specification. On-board compression of audio is also a plus if you plan to record your own sound; you can conserve hard disk storage space with such features.

Chapter 8

How To Select a Multimedia Computer

CD-ROM has become synonymous with multimedia. Because video, audio, and high-resolution graphics take up so much storage space, CD-ROM is just about the only way to distribute multimedia games and programs inexpensively. This chapter is about the *other* pieces of the puzzle—a CD-ROM drive alone isn't enough for multimedia: you need sound capabilities, speakers, and a powerful computer.

Whether you want to add multimedia capabilities to an existing computer or buy a computer with those functions built in, this chapter shows you how to do it. This chapter covers how to choose a new multimedia-capable Macintosh or **MPC**, a multimedia kit, or the individual components to make up your own multimedia kit. Along the way, we'll tell you some things to look out for, and some important things to consider when you're deciding what to buy.

This chapter is devoted to desktop computers. For multimedia you can take with you, see Chapter 15, "CD-ROM on the Road: Going Portable."

Important Features in a Multimedia Computer

As with any other major buying decision, purchasing a multimedia computer takes a little forethought and research. You obviously have to know what you're looking for before you start looking. This section lists some of the elements to look for in a multimedia computer; these are the same elements you should consider upgrading if you are modifying an existing computer.

EXPLANATION

MPC

Generally, *MPC* stands for Multimedia Personal Computer, but MPC also refers to two performance standards for PC-compatible computers with multimedia hardware. The two MPC specifications are explained in Chapter 7, "What Is Multimedia?"

NOTE

What's in a Logo?

The MPC or MPC2 logo means that the product it adorns complies with one of two different specifications. Generally speaking, a program disc with the MPC2 logo on its packaging will not run (or run with difficulty) on a computer that features the older MPC logo. Chapter 2, "CD-ROM Specification Explained," lists the specifications for both the original MPC and the newer MPC Level 2 products.

TIP

When a Faster Processor Is Better

If your main interest in CD-ROM is databases rather than high-performance multimedia, invest in a faster processor instead of additional RAM or high-end video.

First off, all multimedia computers are not the same. Even if they carry the **MPC or MPC2 logo** (specific to PC-compatibles), that only guarantees that they meet the *minimum* MPC or MPC Level 2 specifications. A suitably equipped 486SX with 4 MB of RAM can carry the MPC2 logo—as can a decked-out Pentium with 16 MB of RAM—but the 486SX won't offer anything close to the Pentium's performance level.

Multimedia presentations generally tax three of the major elements in your computer—video, memory, and processor, in that order. When you're buying a multimedia computer or upgrading an existing computer, keep those functions in mind and you're likely to get significantly more performance for your investment. For example, if upgrading to a slightly **faster processor** and upgrading to 8 MB more memory each costs $500, you're much better off getting more RAM. More RAM makes your operating system use the hard disk much less—even the fastest processor can't make up for the slowdown caused by frequent hard disk access. The best price/performance deal is usually an accelerated video card, which can speed up your system's video performance between 8 and 32 *times* (accelerated video cards can be found for between $150 and $500).

Generally speaking, if you buy an MPC, you get a PC-compatible computer (usually a 486SX or better) with these additional components:

- Super-VGA graphics capabilities (a Super-VGA monitor may or may not be included in the purchase price, but you'll need one to take advantage of an SVGA card—hooking up a standard VGA monitor to the SVGA card won't cut it)
- Sound card
- CD-ROM drive
- Speakers

Don't assume that a mail-order advertisement for a "multimedia computer" or "multimedia-ready computer" (without the MPC or MPC2 logo) is going to have all these components. Verify with the dealer which **components are included** and ask for the specifications for each component. If the computer carries an MPC or MPC2 logo, you already know it meets the minimum specifications set forth by the MPC council.

Even entry-level Macintoshes have several multimedia sound functions built in, and you don't have to worry about substandard clones (yet), so if you're looking for a multimedia Mac, you'll only need these additional pieces:

- Color graphics
- CD-ROM drive
- Speakers (which you may not need to add—some Macs have them built into the case)

Apple also makes multimedia kits that allow you to upgrade Macs that weren't born with these capabilities.

On the higher end, Apple makes AV (audio visual) Macs that come with audio and video input/output ports, onboard digital signal processors, and telecommunications functions.

Multimedia Computers

The following sections describe some multimedia-capable computers from major manufacturers; the sections include lists of included equipment and suggested retail prices. Contact the manufacturers directly for current pricing and offerings.

Apple

Apple offers several multimedia Macs. You might say all Macs are multimedia capable—even the lower-end models offer some sound functions right out of the box, and the operating system includes animation support—but to take advantage of the multimedia titles currently available on CD-ROM, you'll need a few things beyond these basics.

All current Macs (except some PowerBooks) support color displays. If your Mac doesn't come with 24-bit color support, you'll have to add a high-end video card to use the ultra-high resolution and 24-bit graphics found in many multimedia titles.

You'll also need a CD-ROM drive; Apple makes a good double-speed drive that's competitively priced (see Chapter 3, "How To Select CD-ROM Drives"). The internal model is available as a factory option on any Mac with an empty 5.25-inch drive bay, and you can add the SCSI model to any model with a SCSI port (which is everything but the Duo, and you can get a Duo docking station with a SCSI port for $250 to $500).

For stereo speakers, you can use just about any model on the market because stereo-capable Macs (610, 650 and 950 Quadras and all AVs and PowerMacs) include standard RCA-type jacks. Apple's AudioVision 14 monitor is an interesting combination of color video and audio. It has stereo speakers built into the bottom of the casing, a condenser microphone at the top, and a 14-inch high-resolution color Trinitron screen.

The AV models (Quadra 660AV and 840AV, Power Macintosh 6100AV, 7100AV, and 8100AV) include higher-end video and sound processing functions and double-speed CD-ROM drives. They all include stereo input and output (some nonAV models have stereo output with mono input), a digital signal processor, and video input ports for a VCR or camcorder in addition to the standard video output ports.

Compaq

Compaq's 3-year warranty and reputation for quality makes this computer a popular choice for businesses; the company's new pricing strategy is starting to help them move into the home market.

The multimedia element in Compaq's systems is their Multimedia Solution Paq. The current Paq includes a double-speed CD-ROM drive, a Creative Labs Sound Blaster 16 audio card, stereo speakers, a microphone, and eight CD-ROM titles—Microsoft Works, Microsoft Encarta, Quicken, Time Almanac, Professor Multimedia, Home Remedies, Space Adventure, and Dinosaur Adventure, but the title list could change at any time. Add $499 to any of the systems listed below for the Multimedia Solution Paq.

TIP

No Magic MPC Design

Only the most specialized manufacturers design multimedia computers from the ground up—most MPCs are just regular computers with preinstalled multimedia kits. You can usually check the prices of the same computer without multimedia capabilities and compare it to the MPC version. You may find you come out ahead by purchasing the nonMPC version and adding your own multimedia kit (see the list of multimedia kits later in this chapter).

The Compaq ProLinea line of computers are high-performance systems with integrated local bus Super-VGA and 14-inch Super-VGA monitors. Most systems include TabWorks, an intuitive replacement for the Windows Program Manager. The entry-level multimedia-ready ProLinea is the 4/33s, a 486SX-33 with 4 MB of RAM and a 200-MB hard drive; it retails for $1,475. The ProLinea MT has 4 MB of RAM and a 340-MB hard drive; it is available in a 486SX-33 model ($1,725) or a 486DX2-66 model ($2,299).

Dell

Dell has consistently been a technology leader, and their current crop of computers is no exception. One of the first companies to take advantage of the new 486SX2 processor, Dell now offers several capable machines under the $2,000 mark.

The multimedia option on Dell's computers is better than average, too. For $399, you can add a Panasonic double-speed CD-ROM drive, Peavey stereo speakers, and a Creative Labs Sound Blaster 16 sound card to any of Dell's desktop PCs.

The entry-level machine on Dell's Dimension line is the 433SV, a 486SX-33 with 4 MB of RAM, a 340-MB hard drive, accelerated local bus video, and a VGA monitor—pretty basic, but only $1,149. The next step up is the 450SV, a 486SX2-50 with 4 MB of RAM, a 340-MB hard drive, accelerated local bus video, and a Super-VGA monitor, at $1,299. The 466V is a 486DX2 with 8 MB of RAM, a 340-MB hard drive, accelerated local bus video, and a 15-inch Super-VGA monitor, at $1,599—even with the $399 multimedia kit, it's a very impressive sub-$2,000 system.

Gateway 2000

Known throughout the industry as "the Cow Company," Gateway 2000 has made news recently for something other than their Holstein-spotted packaging—they're now including a double-speed CD-ROM drive *standard* on every system.

Budget-minded buyers can add a 16-bit Sound Blaster-compatible sound card and two Labtec speakers for around $100, but serious multimedia enthusiasts should look at the higher-end Wavetable Audio Multimedia kit. The Wavetable kit is a 16-bit wavetable card (which supports practically every standard, including Sound Blaster, AdLib, and MIDI), two Altec Lansing shielded speakers, an Altec Lansing subwoofer, MidiSoft Sound Explorer and Time Warner's Aegis software, and a PhotoCD sampler from Corel, all for about $275 when you buy a system from Gateway.

Basic systems (with the CD-ROM drive, but without the sound kits) start at $1,299 for a 486SX-33 with 4 MB of RAM, a 340-MB hard drive, local bus Super-VGA graphics, a 14-inch Super-VGA monitor, and Microsoft Works Multimedia Edition. A mid-range system that's great for multimedia is their P4D-66—a 486DX2-66 with 8 MB of RAM, a 540-MB hard drive, PCI local bus video, a 15-inch Super-VGA monitor, and Microsoft Office Pro software, all for $2,299.

Gateway's Family PC series is designed specifically around multimedia. These machines include the basic 16-bit sound card with stereo speakers, Super-VGA local bus graphics, a 14-inch Super-VGA monitor, a 340-MB hard drive, Microsoft Works, Microsoft Encarta, Microsoft Baseball, Microsoft Money, Microsoft

Golf, and a Corel PhotoCD sampler. The 486SX-33 version (which includes 4 MB of RAM) is $1,499; the 486DX2-66 version (with 8 MB of RAM) is $1,999.

IBM

Since the release of its PS/1 line, IBM has been consistently delivering powerful, reasonably priced multimedia systems for the home market. As part of its many recent efforts to become more nimble and competitive in the marketplace, IBM has started integrating the best third-party equipment into its equipment instead of insisting everything be made by IBM. The new ValuePoint Performance line is a good example; it uses Media Vision's 16-bit Jazz sound cards and third-party double-speed CD-ROM drives.

A basic ValuePoint Performance 486SX-33 with 4 MB of RAM and a 270-MB hard drive is $1,620. Add the Media Vision 16-bit sound card, a double-speed CD-ROM drive, stereo speakers, and a microphone, and the total goes up to $1,960. A 486DX2-66 version with 8 MB of RAM and a 364-MB hard drive is $2,775.

The PS/1 remains popular with home users and schools, partly because of its competitive pricing. For example, you can get a 486SX-25 with 4 MB of RAM, a 170-MB hard drive, a Sound Blaster 16 sound card, stereo speakers, and several CD-ROM titles for $1,549. This setup includes Compton's Interactive Encyclopedia, the Mayo Clinic's Family Health disc, Monologue for Windows, and King's Quest VI.

Multimedia Kits

Multimedia kits do for computers what TV dinners do for meals: save you time and money by putting all the pieces in one handy package—if you're willing to accept their combinations. Quality is not a problem in most kits—all the multimedia kits listed here include top-quality components and titles—and the savings are respectable, so you're likely to come out ahead even if you decide you don't want two of the fifteen discs in a particular kit.

Most kits include at least a CD-ROM drive (all the kits shown here include a double-speed or faster drive), a sound card, stereo speakers, and some CD-ROM titles. Some include a microphone and a joystick as well.

The two leaders in multimedia kits are Creative Labs and Media Vision, both better known for their sound cards than anything else. Most of the other companies that sell multimedia kits are mail-order retailers whose "kits" are really just the individual components sold as a **package deal**.

If you're looking for a quick, inexpensive way to get started with multimedia, these kits are it.

Apple

This is the sole Mac-compatible kit in our list. Partially because Macs come with so many multimedia functions right out of the box, Mac users are more apt to buy the few missing pieces (a CD-ROM drive and speakers)

CAUTION

Where Are the Instructions?

Some of the mail-order kits available are just individual components bundled together. Don't look for instructions on getting all the pieces to work together or one-stop technical support. Still, you can find some good deals on industry-standard components if you're willing to tackle the installation on your own.

individually. Apple's Multimedia Kit includes the AppleCD 300 Plus double-speed CD-ROM drive (internal or external model), a pair of AppleDesign Powered Speakers II (the budget model), and Apple headphones. The kit also comes with a selection of CD-ROM titles that changes depending on where you live and when you buy.

This kit is impressive for its flexibility as well as its Apple quality. Because you can get an external CD-ROM drive and all the other components to plug into existing ports, you can use the kit to bring multimedia functions to just about any Mac, even if it doesn't have NuBus slots or drive bays.

Creative Labs

Sound-card pioneer Creative Labs has now branched into CD-ROM drives, speakers, and other multimedia equipment. All the hardware in their kits bears the Creative Labs brand name except for the NEC triple-speed drive in the Digital Edge 3X kit.

At $999, the Sound Blaster Digital Edge 3X multimedia kit is one of the most expensive kits listed in this chapter, but for high-speed multimedia, it's well worth a look. It is based on a SCSI-2-compatible NEC triple-speed drive and a Sound Blaster 16 SCSI-2 card (with a DSP chip), and includes amplified stereo speakers and a condenser microphone. The impressive list of titles in the current kit includes Quicken Deluxe, the New Grolier Multimedia Encyclopedia, Rebel Assault, Aldus PhotoStyler SE, Altamira Composer, Kai's Power Tools, Gallery Effects, and Speed, but titles could change at any time. Creative TextAssist and several sound utilities are also included.

The Edutainment CD 16, at $599, is a similar kit with a Creative Labs double-speed drive. It includes amplified stereo speakers, a microphone, and a Sound Blaster 16 card. Also included are Quicken Deluxe, the New Grolier Multimedia Encyclopedia, Rebel Assault, Aldus PhotoStyler, 3-D Dinosaur Adventure, Travel Adventures, Digital Morph, Kai's Power Tools, and Gallery Effects.

Gamers should check out the Game Blaster CD 16 kit, listed at $549. It includes a Creative Labs double-speed CD-ROM drive, a 16-bit Sound Blaster card, a high-performance joystick, and amplified stereo speakers. Some of the game titles include Rebel Assault, Return to Zork, Iron Helix, and Sim City 2000. The kit also includes the New Grolier Multimedia Encyclopedia, presumably to help you analyze the climate of your simulated cities.

The Sound Blaster Discovery 16 CD is a capable entry-level kit, retailing at $449. The Creative Labs double-speed drive and 16-bit Sound Blaster card are the same ones you find in other kits, but the stereo speakers are not amplified. This kit includes the New Grolier Multimedia Encyclopedia, Aldus PhotoStyler SE, Altimara Composer, Kai's Power Tools, Digital Morph, and Gallery Effects.

Media Vision

Despite its well-publicized financial troubles, Media Vision continues to expand into new areas of multimedia. The company recently released two full-motion video-based games with live actors (see our review of Critical Path in Chapter 11, "CD-ROM for After Hours"), and has now introduced a portable double-speed CD-ROM drive that transforms into a battery-powered audio CD player—the Reno drive, highlighted in Chapter 3, "How To Select a CD-ROM Drive."

One nice touch from Media Vision is the installation video included with each kit. The company also offers toll-free technical support seven days a week.

Media Vision changes CD-ROM titles periodically, but some of the titles found in its kits as of this writing are Return to Zork, Iron Helix, Mad Dog McCree, Mega Rock Rap'n'Roll, Undersea Adventure, Richard Scarry's Busy Town, and Media Vision's own hits: Critical Path, Forever Growing Garden, and Quantum Gate. Most kits include Compton's Interactive Encyclopedia as well.

Like Creative Labs' triple-speed kit, Media Vision's top offering centers on a NEC triple-speed drive. This kit also includes amplified stereo speakers, a microphone, Media Vision's 16-bit sound card, and 15 titles.

The Reno drive is the heart of Media Vision's Premium Deluxe kit, available for PC or Mac at $599. Both kits come with amplified stereo speakers, headphones, a carrying case for the portable drive, and 15 CD-ROM titles. The PC kit also includes Media Vision's 16-bit sound card and a microphone.

At $499, the Super Deluxe Multimedia kit is an affordable but full-featured kit. It has a double-speed, caddieless CD-ROM drive, a 16-bit sound card, microphone, amplified stereo speakers, and 15 titles.

Rounding out Media Vision's kits is the Family Deluxe Multimedia kit, which sells for $399. Its specs are the same as the Super Deluxe kit, except that it doesn't have a microphone and includes only 9 CD-ROM titles.

Assembling the Pieces Yourself

Multimedia kits are convenient and usually inexpensive, but much of the time you have to compromise something in the bargain: you may not want the bundled CD-ROM titles, or the kit may offer one mediocre component (typically the speakers) that you end up replacing anyway. Even though you'll probably pay more for the individual pieces, you may be happier with the result if you pick each component individually rather than buying a prepackaged kit.

The following sections cover sound cards and speakers and give some basic instructions for installing a sound card. Chapter 3, "How To Select a CD-ROM Drive," shows you some of the quality CD-ROM drives on the market; Chapters 9, 10, and 11 list popular CD-ROM titles to round out your homegrown multimedia kit.

PC Sound Boards with CD-ROM Interfaces

Because sound boards are a must for multimedia applications (most worthwhile multimedia applications are published on CD-ROM), it makes sense for users to buy a sound board that incorporates a CD-ROM interface (a built-in connector for your CD-ROM drive) so that you can eliminate the need for yet another board in your PC. In most cases, this solution makes for a cleaner installation: you set only one set of interface-card jumpers, take up only one slot, and so on.

Most cards come with SCSI-2 connectors that allow you to choose exactly which drive you want to pair up with the audio card. Because some of the CD-ROM interfaces may not be standard, you may be limited to a choice of only a few CD-ROM drives. Although such nonstandard CD-ROM interfaces may be cheaper, you have to settle for their CD-ROM drive options, not yours.

The following sections detail the sound cards with CD-ROM interfaces currently available. Keep in mind, however, that you do not need any of these combination sound/CD-ROM cards to get full multimedia performance (these sound cards may have a proprietary CD-ROM interface—buy your own CD-ROM-drive and SCSI cards and plug them into the sound card). Many sound cards that do not provide CD-ROM interfaces can be perfectly suitable for use in your PC. In this case, a separate sound card hooked to your CD-ROM drive audio port gives you full multimedia.

Sound Blaster 16

Suggested list prices:

MultiCD (Sony, Mitsumi, Creative Labs interfaces): $199
SCSI-2: $249
MultiCD with Advanced Signal Processing (ASP) upgrade: $249
SCSI-2 with ASP upgrade: $299
Value Edition (Creative Labs interface only): $149

Sound Blaster has been around a long time. Creative Labs pioneered the acceptance of audio on the PC with this affordable, easy-to-install card, and so became a de facto standard. Most software programs list ***Sound Blaster or fully compatible*** in their installation requirements when describing the equipment needed to play the audio portions of their programs.

The Sound Blaster 16 uses a Yamaha FM synthesizer chipset to provide MIDI services and uses 8-bit AD-DAC chips for the conversion of analog sound to digital and digital to analog. The board's top sample rate is 44 KHz in stereo.

The card also incorporates a set of ADPCM signal processors, so it has the equipment necessary for compression and decompression of ADPCM-encoded CD-ROM material for XA-format applications. Sony's first CD-ROM-XA discs developed for their portable CD player, however, do not work with the ASP's ADPCM processors. Perhaps CD-ROM-XA applications will work on ADPCM-based sound boards in the future.

The board has a 4-watt on-board amplifier to drive external speakers and an external volume dial to control the output level. This amplifier has more than enough power to drive the speaker systems designed for use with PCs and can be turned off to eliminate noise if you're using an external amplifier.

If you decide to upgrade to wavetable synthesis later on, you don't have to toss out your existing Sound Blaster 16. Creative Labs offers a daughterboard (the Wave Blaster) that attaches to the Sound Blaster 16 (except the Value Edition) and replaces its FM synthesis with wavetable synthesis. It comes with Cakewalk Apprentice MIDI sequencing software. Current retail price on the Wave Blaster is $249.

Sound Blaster AWE 32

Suggested list price: $399

The AWE 32 is the new state of the art in sound cards. The built-in wavetable synthesis and DSP chip are impressive, but they're only the beginning. Add QSound 180-degree soundscape (for "3-D sound effects") and advanced WavEffects (for effects like chorus and reverb) and you've got a professional-quality sound generator—you should hear what it does for your games. You can even control many games and programs with voice-processing capabilities—the high-performance condenser microphone is included. The package also includes TextAssist text-to-speech synthesis. AWE 32 supports stereo sampling and playback at up to 44.1 KHz.

The AWE32 doesn't limit your sound selection to its built-in samples, either. If you download your own samples to it, it uses them just like other built-in instrument sounds. Don't worry about running out of storage space on the card either—you can add up to 28 MB of additional RAM.

If it offered SCSI or SCSI-2, AWE 32 would be perfect. Currently, it supports Creative Labs, Sony, and Mitsumi CD-ROM drives, which is still a respectable selection. If you want the best in home PC sound, this is it.

Media Vision's Premium 3-D

Suggested list prices:
MultiCD (Sony, Mitsumi, and Panasonic interfaces): $199
Pro (SCSI-2): $399

Listening to Media Vision's new 3-D sound cards through headphones makes games seem almost too real—even with standard speakers, the sounds appear to come from different sources. The cards use a technology called SRS (Sound Retrieval System), which is also used in high-end television systems, to provide the aural illusion of movement. Your programs don't have to be written specifically to work with SRS—it even works with music CDs.

The base system (the MultiCD) uses FM synthesis to create its MIDI sounds, but the Pro version adds wavetable synthesis and a SCSI-2 interface to justify its $200 jump in price. With this sound quality, wavetable is worth the extra money, especially if you work with MIDI. The only problem with the Pro system is that it makes you want to build a whole stereo system around your computer—if you hook your old $20 shielded speakers to it, you'll toss them out in no time.

Sampling versus FM Synthesis

There are two basic ways to produce musical sounds on demand. The least expensive way is through *FM synthesis*. This method involves using various signal generators and filters to approximate the natural sound of a musical instrument by imitating its acoustical characteristics. FM synthesis usually falls short of ideal sound because of the complexity of most natural sounds.

Sampling (usually called *wavetable synthesis*), the second approach, actually records examples of the instruments playing various notes and then plays the notes back to create the music. Although this idea is simpler than a synthesizer in some ways, the technology involved is more complex. What makes this method practical is that MIDI is used to instruct the sound board as to what it should play; although MIDI does provide for arbitrary sounds, it also has standard musical-instrument sounds. This feature means that when a program needs a piano sound, it can ask for the sound, and the board can provide the appropriate piano sample.

Cardinal Technologies: Digital SoundPro 16 Plus

Suggested list price: $150

A heavy hitter in modems and video cards, Cardinal makes one of the most budget-friendly sound cards around. The SCSI-2 version includes 16-bit stereo sound and a software upgradeable DSP chip for $150, but if you've got a Sony drive, you only need to shell out $100. To make the deal even sweeter, you can upgrade either card to wavetable synthesis for $59. The card is Sound Blaster and MIDI compatible and includes a host of sound utilities. We haven't tested this one for sound quality, but it'd be hard to go wrong with those features at that low price.

Logitech SoundMan 16

Suggested list price: $199

The SoundMan 16 by Logitech uses 16-bit ADC (Analog-to-Digital Converter) and DAC (Digital-to-Analog Converter) chips for true 44-KHz sound in and out and standard FM synthesis for sound production. A wavetable version with a SCSI-2 interface sells for $299.

The SoundMan 16 is fully configurable through software—virtually all other cards require the user to change jumpers on the board for the IRQ, DMA, and memory I/O settings.

A standard 8-bit SCSI connector for the SoundMan 16 is available as an option. Check with the manufacturer for drive compatibility and availability of CD-ROM drivers for the SCSI connector.

Gravis UltraSound

Suggested list price: $199

The Gravis UltraSound card provides 16-bit, 32-voice sound capabilities in a very affordable package. The card is based on wavetable synthesis rather than FM synthesis, making the quality far superior to some other cards on the market.

In addition, you can upgrade the wave tables to a full 6.5 megabytes of 16-bit sampled sound. The Gravis UltraSound card uses disk-based samples, rather than on-board ROM, to store the wave tables. Upgrades to the UltraSound tables are only a few floppy disks away (with ROM-based cards, you have to physically remove the ROM modules and replace them with the upgrades).

Sampling runs to full stereo 44 KHz, and the UltraSound card includes 256 KB of memory for improved throughput of sound recording or WAVE file playback. This memory is expandable on-board to a full megabyte to cache the disk-based samples.

An optional add-on daughterboard that plugs into the basic card adds a standard SCSI-2 CD-ROM interface, making your choice for CD-ROM drives more extensive than that available on other cards.

The Gravis UltraSound card offers great value; you can add modules as you need them for upgrades such as the full 6-or-more megabyte MIDI sound samples.

Speakers

The most practical way to get sound to your ears from a PC sound card is by using specially designed external speakers. These small, self-powered units come with special magnetic shielding; this shield prevents the speaker's magnets from distorting a monitor display or interfering with the viability of your hard drive. An unshielded speaker can corrupt data on a floppy disk, so the shielding is essential.

PC speakers don't have to be expensive to be effective. Unless you want chest-thumping volume as you sit at your PC, most of the speaker systems described in the following sections should be adequate for your needs. If you have to crank your multimedia to the max, you may be better off simply hooking the sound card to a full-blown stereo.

If you invest in a 16-bit sound card, you won't notice a drastic difference between it and your old 8-bit card until you plug the 16-bit card into a great stereo or buy a good pair of speakers.

The speaker systems in the following sections are just a sampling; many other brands and styles, including those that use subwoofer systems, are hitting the market. You can spend up to $600 on PC speakers alone—if you're so inclined. Look at your desktop real estate and your sound requirements. Few people require the monster speaker systems that are available, but if you intend to produce your own multimedia presentations, the investment may be worthwhile.

Labtec 88-700

Suggested list price: $99

Probably the most popular speakers on the market for PCs, the Labtec 88-700 are small, moderately priced speakers that deliver clean sound at a good price. Labtec's speakers are powered by batteries or through a DC power adapter you can plug into the wall. A nice feature is the bass, treble, and mid-range equalizers on each speaker that enable you to fine-tune the response. Each speaker has a separate volume control as well.

Sony

Suggested list price: $129 to $199, depending on model

You can find Sony speaker pairs everywhere, and the prices are right. They provide basic stereo in battery-powered enclosures that fit easily on any desk. Don't look for real high-end sound in the Sony line, however; just solid performance at reasonable prices.

Hi Tex CP-18

Suggested list price: $69

The Hi Tex CP-18 are the speakers of choice for manufacturers bundling speakers with their systems. They're a bit taller than the Sony or Labtec systems but their sound quality is about the same. The Hi Tex speakers have volume controls for each speaker. These speakers don't give you concert-hall sound, but they're an excellent value.

Roland Monitor

Suggested list price: $170 to $320, depending on model

Roland, the MIDI pioneer, makes a number of speaker systems. The Monitor series includes speaker pairs with separate bass, treble, and volume controls for each speaker. These speakers are larger than most PC speakers. They're also rugged, high fidelity, and provide higher output than the average PC speaker.

Altec Lansing ACS300

Suggested list price: $400

The Altec Lansing ACS300 speakers are favorites in the industry. Their fidelity is great, their construction is sturdy, and they require the minimum in desktop real estate. These speakers deliver real 25-watt stereo in a surprisingly small package. The price is right, too, considering the amazing quality.

Altec Lansing ACS300 speakers contain a subwoofer that delivers the cleanest bass riffs imaginable; the left and right speaker shells contain controls for bass, treble, presence, balance, and other spatial and special effects.

Altec Lansing ACS300 speakers are, for the price, the best speakers you can buy for your PC. They are highly recommended.

Altec Lansing ACS100 models are a great bargain at only $180, if you can forgo the woofer and some of the special controls and mixing capabilities. A woofer can be added later for an additional $150.

Chapter 9

CD-ROM in Business

Information is money. CDs are the most cost-effective way to disseminate information. If your business is not using CD-ROM technology—especially if you are in a professional field such as marketing, law, or medicine—you're behind the game because you can be assured that your competition is using it. CD-ROMs save you the paper chases and high costs of searching for information through expensive on-line databases. In fact, much of the database and research information discussed in this chapter was only available through on-line electronic databases until the enormous storage capacity of CD-ROM technology made wider distribution possible. CD-ROM research is convenient and cost effective; rather than contracting specialized research firms or devoting key employees to full-time research, you can train an unlimited number of employees to take advantage of CD-ROM resources on-site. By using network versions of business CDs, any number of people can access the information they need to develop sales leads, track the competition, and make informed, strategic decisions.

About This Chapter

This chapter explains CD-ROM business software, providing an overview of the capabilities of this kind of software. The chapter also covers possible application to everyday business needs and explains the flexibility and capability of the user interface and search-and-retrieval engine.

Note that many business applications are expensive. The time and resources required for publishers to gather, verify, and master information for these applications is not insignificant. In many cases, the cost of securing rights for the data is an enormous financial risk the publishers must take. For these reasons, many discs are not even sold outright; you rent or purchase a subscription to the data, much as you purchase a subscription to a newsletter or journal. For this reason, we've stated whether applications are available through a subscription, an outright purchase, or both.

And because CD-ROM information for the business sector is particularly time sensitive, we've indicated whether updates to the discs are available—where applicable—and the frequency of the updates.

The variety and magnitude of information available for businesses is staggering. This chapter provides an in-depth tour of some of the more common, less specialized, applications available. But don't let your curiosity end here; there are literally thousands of specialized databases and applications on CD-ROM; they cover virtually every conceivable business research requirement. Expand your search for CD-ROM information beyond this chapter. The best place to start to look for CD-ROMs is on CD-ROM, as described in the following section.

How To Use This Chapter

The description of each product in this chapter begins with a chart; these charts provide consistent at-a-glance information.

All the CD-ROMs highlighted here are high-quality products we can confidently recommend. We have tested every title mentioned in this chapter and written up complete reports on those CD-ROMs we felt deserved special attention. Some discs we tested were useful but not outstanding—they are listed at the end of each section. Some we haven't listed at all, believing that if you can't say something nice...well, you know. A few superlative products have been given an Award of Excellence (we explain why these titles are cream of the crop in the margin-note text accompanying the award icon).

Discs of Discs

The first category of CD-ROMs described in this chapter contains a single entry: a disc about discs. That is, the CD-ROM described in the following section contains all the information you can possibly want about CD-ROMs currently available for purchase or rental.

The CD-ROM Directory on Disc

TFPL Publishing/Pemberton Press

Operating System:	DOS 3.3 or above
Class:	CD-ROM database
Search and Retrieval:	DataWare
Updates:	Every six months
Subscription:	Quarterly
Purchase:	Yes
Licensing:	Quarterly

The CD-ROM Directory on Disc from Pemberton Press and TFPL Publishing is the most exhaustive compendium of CD-ROMs in print. This CD-ROM lists over 3,500 current CD-ROM applications in every imaginable category. And it does more than merely list titles: the listings include brief descriptions of many titles and full information regarding the developer—not just name, address, and phone, but what related products and services they provide as well as the number of employees and years in business. The directory is international in scope; it represents CD-ROMs in print from all over the world.

In addition to application information, the CD-ROM Directory on Disc also includes extensive listings for hardware manufacturers and distributors, detailing the products offered. Additional material includes retrieval and authoring software supplies and books, journals, conferences, and exhibitions for the CD-ROM industry.

The directory is updated every six months and is also available in book form.

The CD-ROM Directory on Disc is, in effect, a one-stop resource guide to the CD-ROM industry. You can search the following separate databases on the CD-ROM Directory on Disc: Titles (names of CD-ROM applications and databases), Companies (company names), Hardware (hardware product name or category), Software (software name or category), Conferences (international conference schedules and details), Journals (a comprehensive listing of journals, journal articles, and similar materials related to CD-ROMs), Books (an exhaustive bibliography of CD-ROM technology and resource books currently in print, with full bibliographic information).

The distributors, Pemberton Press, sell the CD-ROM Directory on Disc mainly by subscription, and you can purchase a multiple-year subscription. Single editions of the CD-ROM are available, but if you anticipate ongoing research into CD-ROM applications, the subscription is the better value.

General Business Discs

Many applications—not just reference, bibliographies, and databases—are moving to the roomy environs of CD-ROM. You expect to purchase spreadsheet, word processor, and database applications on traditional floppy disks. But if you purchase all these packages at once, installing them from one CD-ROM is a significant advantage.

Because some traditional applications are becoming so complex and offer so many features, they may strain your installation patience by forcing you to use 10, 15, or even 20 floppy disks just to get the program running. Some applications—especially those that include significant clip art, graphics samplers, and graphics templates—are impractical to ship on floppies; in some cases, installing these applications would require nearly 100 disks! By using CD-ROMs, developers can deliver more program for far less money. Distribution on CD-ROM for these applications is a time-saver for you—and a money-saver for application developers. One CD-ROM costs significantly less in initial production, packaging, and shipping than the horde of floppies often needed.

In addition, some CD-ROM applications can be run directly from the CD-ROM, freeing your PC hard drive for more data, applications, and utilities. If you choose to run applications from your CD-ROM drive, keep in mind that they load much more slowly than from hard disk; other disk-oriented operations also slow down.

Microsoft Works

Microsoft Corporation

Operating System:	Windows 3.1 or above
Class:	Integrated office-automation software
Search and Retrieval:	N/A
Updates:	N/A
Subscription:	N/A
Purchase:	Yes
Licensing:	Single user

One of the chief challenges of running a small office or workgroup is selecting a suite of applications that are easy for every employee to use and that work well with each other. The Microsoft Works package fits this bill nicely (see fig. 9.1). The sum here is greater than the parts because all the applications share similar interfaces, the applications can easily share information with one another, and you can install the programs from one CD, making this a veritable office in a box.

Because the tutorial doesn't cover every feature of Works, the Works CD also includes full documentation for all the components. In addition, a coupon in the CD package entitles registered users to a full printed version of the documentation. When you combine the tutorial, the on-line manual, and the program's easy, intuitive interface, however, the paper manual is probably not necessary.

This disc of products is the perfect personal productivity set for users in a small business or workgroup. The following list details the various Microsoft Works modules:

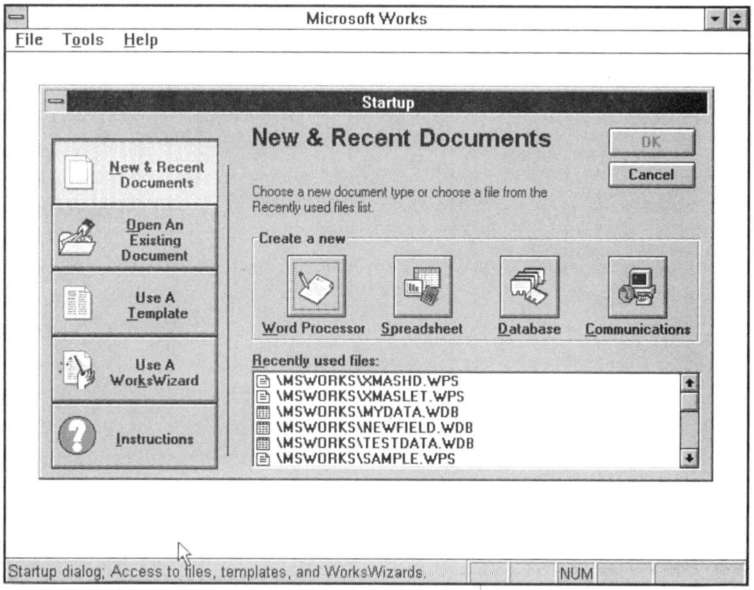

FIGURE 9.1

Microsoft Works packs a word processor, spreadsheet, database, communications program, and drawing program onto one CD-ROM.

- **Word Processor.** The Works word processor is no lightweight. It easily imports data from the spreadsheet, database, communications, and drawing components of the package. In addition, it does all the things good word processors must do: paragraph and page formatting, font selection, spelling checking, and so on.

- **Spreadsheet.** The Works spreadsheet includes basic spreadsheet functions for managing and crunching numbers. In addition, the package includes a handy graphing component with many templates for displaying your work in a variety of graphs and charts.

- **Database.** Although you won't want to keep highly complex datasets in the Works database, it's perfect for other tasks such as business addresses, contact data, and small inventories. The customizable report output is great for creating printed phone and contact lists. Predefined forms make organization and presentation easier than with most databases.

- **Communications.** The communications module is a new addition to Works. It lets you use a modem to link your computer with on-line services, computer bulletin board systems (BBSes), and other computers to exchange information. It's a mid-range, simple program—certainly not up to the level of dedicated communications programs like Crosstalk or PROCOMM PLUS for Windows.

- **Drawing.** Simple drawing tools in the Works drawing module enable you to draw freehand or with the aid of geometric tools. You can easily add the finished drawings to documents in other Works modules, this module is preferable to a high-end drawing package when you need only a quick graphic and not an elaborate presentation.

Microsoft Office Professional

Microsoft Corporation	
Operating System:	Windows 3.1 or above
Class:	Office-automation suite
Search and Retrieval:	N/A
Updates:	N/A
Subscription:	N/A
Purchase:	Yes
Licensing:	Single user

All the programs included in the Microsoft Office Professional CD-ROM are best sellers: Word for Windows, PowerPoint, Excel, Mail, and Access (see fig. 9.2). You get a workstation's worth of productivity software on a single disc (the floppy-based version must require at least 20 or 30 diskettes). When you add the fact that all the documentation, tutorials, and templates for the applications are also on the disc, you save your desktop literally pounds of printed manuals, disks, disk cases, and an assortment of slipcases. In addition, Microsoft Office Professional is priced well below what you'd spend if you bought the programs separately. Saving money and space at the same time—a great use of technology!

Saving Time

Network administrators can save a lot of time by picking up multiple packs of Microsoft Office to install on individual desktops. One disc per desktop does it; and a reduction in boxes, manuals, and assorted paper is part of the bargain.

The following sections describe each of these powerful applications in more detail.

Word Processing: Word for Windows

Word for Windows has garnered numerous awards and countless user testimonials. Microsoft's research department is famous for their prerelease testing, particularly for the last two versions of Word for Windows. Before the product hit the shelves, Microsoft's engineers went through an extensive useability study: they used actual workers in a controlled laboratory, examining people using the software and scientifically measuring how easy or difficult certain word processing chores were to accomplish. After these studies, the interface and other design elements of the word processor were further refined. The efforts show. Many confirmed users of other word processors have switched, mainly because of the ease with which complicated tasks such as reformatting, indexing, bulleting, and moving text can be accomplished in the Word for Windows environment.

This book is not the place for a full review or checklist of features, but let us say this: Word for Windows has everything you need in word processing. From simple one-page memos to book-length projects incorporating graphics, indexes, and footnotes, Word for Windows is a superior word processor. When used with the other programs in Office, Word for Windows is a key component in a smooth-running operation.

Presentations: PowerPoint

Making presentations for use on the computer screen or making full-color slides is easy with PowerPoint, a full-featured presentation package. The program includes a number of predefined presentation backgrounds and templates, making your presentations as easy as plugging your text and charts into existing slides.

PowerPoint's extensive importing capabilities—from the other components in Microsoft Office or from other Windows-based applications—allow you to produce highly sophisticated presentations with the tools you're most comfortable with. You can create presentation slides with text from a word processor, graphics from a drawing package, and charts and numbers from a spreadsheet.

PowerPoint supports a number of file formats including the SCODL file format (used by most 35-mm slide-production facilities) for turning computer presentations into slide shows. Overhead transparencies, speaker's crib-notes, and printouts of slides for handouts are other features. The automated computer-screen slide-presentation module lets you show your presentation on computer.

Spreadsheet: Excel for Windows

Excel for Windows is the Windows-based spreadsheet that has been giving Lotus 1-2-3 a run for its money. In fact, Excel for Windows lets you import Lotus files and has a cross-referenced on-line help facility and a macro program that converts Lotus command keystrokes to Excel keystrokes on the fly; Lotus users, in effect, don't even have to learn new keyboard commands.

Extensive use of templates, macros, and Windows toolbars makes former multikey and multilevel menu tasks a matter of single-clicking the mouse. Because Excel is a full-blown Windows product, it supports the drag-and-drop interface and connections to other Windows applications as well.

FIGURE 9.2

Microsoft Office Professional is all you need to run your office on one CD-ROM.

Microsoft Mail

E-mail is here to stay—and electronic mail in Windows with Microsoft Mail is an easy way to manage it. You can e-mail virtually anything you create in a Windows application with this program, and you can e-mail to virtually any computer's e-mail system: it doesn't have to be a Microsoft Mail platform.

Microsoft Office Professional doesn't include the executable files for Mail, just a single-user license. The license allows your network administrator to (legally) install a master copy of Microsoft Mail on your workstation.

One of the best features of Mail is its ability to send mail from any Windows application; no need to disturb your work or shut down an application just to use the mail. After you install it, you'll have a Mail selection on every application's File menu.

If you've wondered how to paste together the right set of programs to make your desktop work, look no further than Microsoft Office.

CorelDRAW!

Corel Corporation

Operating System:	Windows 3.1 or above
Class:	Graphics suite
Search and Retrieval:	N/A
Updates:	N/A
Subscription:	N/A
Purchase:	Yes
Licensing:	Single user

Industry giant Corel Corporation doesn't know when to quit. When other companies are offering "dozens of clip art images," CorelDRAW! includes 22,000 clip art images; when others includes "50 free TrueType fonts," CorelDRAW! includes over 800. And the main suite is nothing to sneeze at, either. It includes these professional-strength applications:

- **CorelDRAW!** The most popular drawing package in the world, CorelDRAW! is easy enough to use at home and powerful enough for professional graphics design, publishing, and advertising. It has evolved from a simple vector-graphics program (circa mid-'80s) into a graphics design monster, including bitmap and vector graphics, 3-D effects, full text layout features (including multiple pages and text wrap around irregular shapes), high-end color matching, support for virtually every graphics format (including the ability to create and edit TrueType and Adobe fonts), and an incredible number of fill options for graphics and type (including literally millions of fractal combinations).

- **CorelCHART!** A full-featured graphics chart creator with import filters for all popular spreadsheets and over 250 spreadsheet functions of its own. 90 chart types, and true 3-D charts (which include perspective, rotation, zoom, pan, and viewing angle controls).

- **CorelPHOTO-PAINT!** Corel had the corner on vector graphics early on, so what could be more natural than adding a full-featured bitmap editor to corral the rest of the market? CorelPHOTO-PAINT! includes direct TWAIN scanner support, 14 image correction filters, high-end color editing functions, resolution enhancement functions for Kodak PhotoCDs, and import functions for vector art.

- **CorelMOVE!** An animation creation/editing program that includes morphing, import and export functions from a variety of animation formats, and the ability to integrate sound with animation. True to form, Corel includes a clip media collection of over 1,000 animated figures, sounds, and props with CorelMOVE!.

- **CorelTRACE!** A bitmap-to-vector conversion program.

- **CorelSHOW!** A presentation program with over 20 transition effects, automatic bulleted lists, and a portable format for use away from your main computer.

- **CorelVENTURA!** In addition to all these other powerful "subapplications," Corel includes the number-1 long-document publishing program. While PageMaker, Quark, FrameMaker, and a few others have fought over the short-document market (restaurant menus, newsletters, advertisements, and so on), Xerox's Ventura Publisher consistently has focused on longer document management (books and longer magazines). But because long-document publishing is not something every home computer user needs, Ventura lost market share to the short-document packages. Corel took a stab at supporting longer documents in CorelDRAW! but ended up with about the same functionality as earlier versions of PageMaker. Having nailed down single-page documents (like advertisements and fliers) and having taken a few steps into the multipage document arena, Corel needed a package that could support longer documents. Rather than write their own, they snapped up the financially floundering Ventura package and revamped it to work with the rest of their tools. The packages complement each other perfectly. CorelVENTURA! now includes a much more accessible interface than the somewhat arcane early versions of Ventura Publisher, export support for Adobe Acrobat and several word processing formats, and high-end color prepress functions.

As if monopolizing the high-end graphics market wasn't enough, Corel Corporation has attacked the entry-level market as well. In a bold marketing move, they released the full Version 3 package (which originally sold for $500-$800) at the $100 price point. It includes earlier (but very capable) versions of many of the tools listed above and a wealth of clip art and fonts on CD-ROM.

Whether you're just getting started with computer graphics or you're ready for the big time, Corel has a CD-ROM solution for you.

Marketing and Sales Discs

Presentation charts, research, lead development, phone numbers, and contacts; it seems marketing and sales is *all* data. And what better place to find data than on CD-ROMs? The titles in the following sections are a few of the latest general-purpose marketing and sales tools on CD-ROM. They have many uses, are very flexible, and—of late—have become very affordable.

PhoneDisc USA: Business

Digital Directory Assistance, Inc.

Operating System:	DOS 3.3 or above
Class:	Business database, telephone listing
Search and Retrieval:	Proprietary
Updates:	N/A
Subscription:	No
Purchase:	Yes
Licensing:	Single user

Phone books are a perfect example of the utility of CD-ROM. Type a name, a partial name or number, press a key, and presto!—up pops the number and address you're looking for. One of the best products in this category of business software is PhoneDisc USA: Business (see fig. 9.3).

Individual businesspeople will want a copy of the business disc for their own desktops. If you forget the phone number for that contact and can't find his or her business card, PhoneDisc USA is there.

PhoneDisc USA has an easy-to-use interface: no searching through submenus or search-result lists to scan for the number you're after. Just type the name, and a list of numbers comes up. Most entries include full addresses and phone numbers.

You can print the results of a search, but the program does not support tagging multiple entries or tagging entries for export to disk files. Digital Directory Assistance offers database-mailing-list services if you have to compile mailing lists for marketing campaigns.

FIGURE 9.3

Look up a business across town, a potential lead across the country, or all Elvis-oriented businesses with PhoneDisc USA: Business.

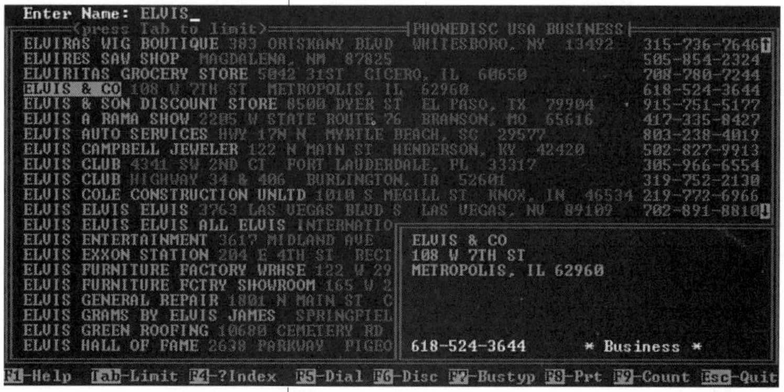

ProPhone National Business Directory

ProCD New Media Publishing	
Operating System:	DOS 3.3 or above
Class:	Business database, telephone listing
Search and Retrieval:	Proprietary
Updates:	Yearly
Subscription:	Yes
Purchase:	Yes
Licensing:	Single user and networks

The National Business Directory is one of the best phone-disc series on the market. Punch in a name, limit the search, and there's the number. Tag it. Tag a few others. You can print them, sort them, or save them to disk. The interface is easy to use, intuitive enough for any member of the office to work with after a few moment's training, and the speed of retrieval and searching is great.

As with all the phone discs on the market, you can also search the ProPhone National Business Directory by the industry-standard SIC business code. But with ProCD products, you can export the list searches to comma-delimited ASCII files so that you can quickly create databases, mailing lists, and labels.

The ProCD series is moderately priced: from the business disc to the comprehensive National Business Directory (a six-disc compilation of all residential and business listings from the U.S.). The National Business Directory also allows you to export lists to disc files and to do unlimited searching of files—without any metering at all.

ProCD also sells network packages with prices for small to very large workgroups. With a minichanger CD-ROM drive on the net and the full national directory installed and loaded, an inside sales force can have a tremendous resource at their fingertips.

GPO (Government Publication Office) on Silver Platter

Silver Platter	
Operating System:	DOS 3.3 or above
Class:	Business and government database
Search and Retrieval:	PC-SPIRS (Silver Platter)
Updates:	Bimonthly
Subscription:	Yes
Purchase:	No
Licensing:	Single user and networks

If your company or business must rely on government documents for information, strategic figures, and data, maps, or other printed resources, you *must* license the GPO (Government Publication Office) on Silver Platter (see fig. 9.4). With an astounding bibliography of over 300,000 government documents, maps, and other printed materials, this comprehensive disc lets you search for any item back to 1986.

Despite the wealth of data here, the interface and search-and-retrieval engine make record searches painless. You can perform simple searches (such as word and phrase look-ups) from the main index by entering the term and combining it with others in a Boolean or nested-Boolean operation. For example, you can enter **highway AND construction AND legislation** to see publications about legislature funding of highway construction. And you can search the entire text of the database for references to a word or group of words. You can also do searches by author, simple subject, and identifiers.

Records in the GPO are extremely detailed; they list, among other facts, the title, the year published, where and from what government office or committee they came, where to obtain a copy of the publication, the publication's OCLC number, and much, much more. All citations include the document's SUDOCS (Superintendent of Documents Classification) number. Of course, you can search for documents by this number as well.

The GPO on Silver Platter is an invaluable CD-ROM for businesses and companies that do business with the government or need to track down relevant government publications that cover finance, business, health, agriculture, and so on.

FIGURE 9.4

Short of living in the library, Silver Platter's GPO on Silver Platter is the best way to find the government document you need.

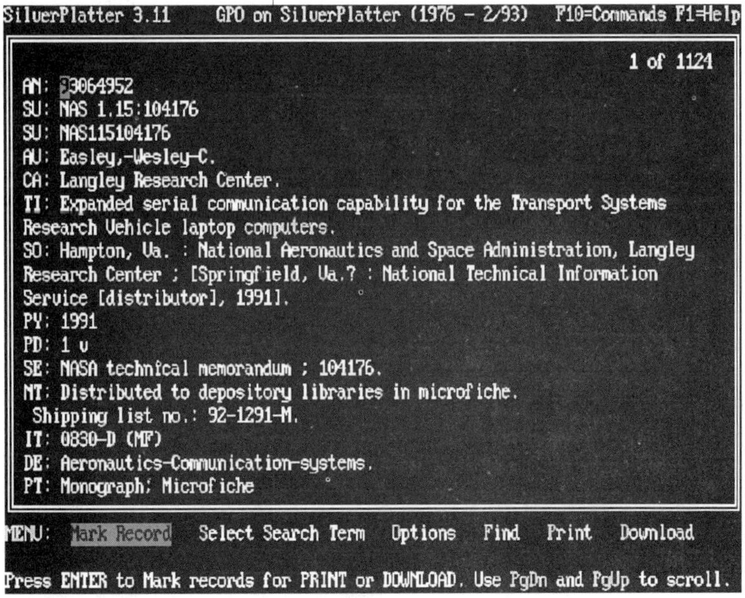

SilverPlatter 3.11 GPO on SilverPlatter (1976 - 2/93) F10=Commands F1=Help
1 of 1124
AN: 93064952
SU: NAS 1.15:104176
SU: NAS115104176
AU: Easley,-Wesley-C.
CA: Langley Research Center.
TI: Expanded serial communication capability for the Transport Systems Research Vehicle laptop computers.
SO: Hampton, Va. : National Aeronautics and Space Administration, Langley Research Center ; [Springfield, Va.? : National Technical Information Service [distributor], 1991].
PY: 1991
PD: 1 v
SE: NASA technical memorandum ; 104176.
NT: Distributed to depository libraries in microfiche. Shipping list no.: 92-1291-M.
IT: 0830-D (MF)
DE: Aeronautics-Communication-systems.
PT: Monograph; Microfiche
MENU: Mark Record Select Search Term Options Find Print Download
Press ENTER to Mark records for PRINT or DOWNLOAD. Use PgDn and PgUp to scroll.

Silver Platter

Silver Platter is the premiere CD-ROM publisher of bibliographic and abstract information. A representative sample of their products is scattered throughout this chapter. Take note of some other titles available from them:

- **COIN CD International.** Provides full text, world-wide company information: everything from earnings and credit ratings to strategy and business plans. Over 400,000 companies are listed with an additional 100,000 added each year.
- **ICC Key Notes.** Includes full text of over 220 market research reports covering 130 markets. Market size, trends, future developments, and much more are covered.
- **AGRISEARCH.** Contains five databases from African, European, Australian, U.S., and Canadian government offices for a complete bibliographic database on agriculture, food, and nutrition.
- **AGRICOLA.** Contains full bibliographic citations for U.S. agriculture and life science; citations are from 1970 to the present.
- **Food Science and Technology.** Bibliographic citations on food products, food processing, and technology are compiled and updated quarterly. Over 1,800 journals are covered.
- **VETCD.** This comprehensive bibliography of veterinary science contains over 300,000 records from the last 20 years and is updated annually.
- **AV Online.** A complete database of educational audiovisual materials that includes video tapes, films, audio cassettes, filmstrips, and more. Over 380,000 items are indexed and it's updated annually.
- **OSH-ROM.** Databases of bibliographic citations concerning occupational health and safety are compiled from the U.S., the UK, and the United Nations. The databases are updated quarterly and contain over 350,000 citations.
- **Drugs and Pharmacology.** Contains over 1,382,000 abstracts and citations covering drugs and pharmacology from 1980 to the present. The disc is updated quarterly, and 145,000 records are added each year.

MarketPlace Business

MarketPlace

Operating System:	Windows 3.1
Class:	Marketing database
Search and Retrieval:	Proprietary
Updates:	Annual
Subscription:	No
Purchase:	Yes
Licensing:	Single user

Imagine being able to key in all the characteristics for potential business clients and receive a customized list in a flash—complete with company biographies. That's exactly what MarketPlace Business delivers (see fig. 9.5). For example, your product—hand-held electronic order notebooks—may do well with businesses that have a large outside sales staff, selling over $20 million in product each year. With MarketPlace Business, all you have to do is input employee count and revenue thresholds, and up pop the numbers. You can isolate factors and generate lists according to SIC code (type of business), annual sales, number of employees, region of the country, public or private sector, and many other fields and combinations.

One thing that makes using MarketPlace Business so exciting is its ability to combine any of the fields for a truly customized result and then save the list to disk. These lists can be imported into databases for further refinement, printing of directories and reports, or output directly to printing labels for direct mailings.

Once a list is generated, you can work with a partial list so that you can experiment with a smaller set rather than the entire run.

MarketPlace Business is a direct marketer's and sales force's dream come true: lead generation. Because a product like this is only as good as its data, it's nice to know that the majority of MarketPlace's list is taken from Dunn and Bradstreet.

FIGURE 9.5

Create a direct-marketing database of leads in a hurry with MarketPlace Business.

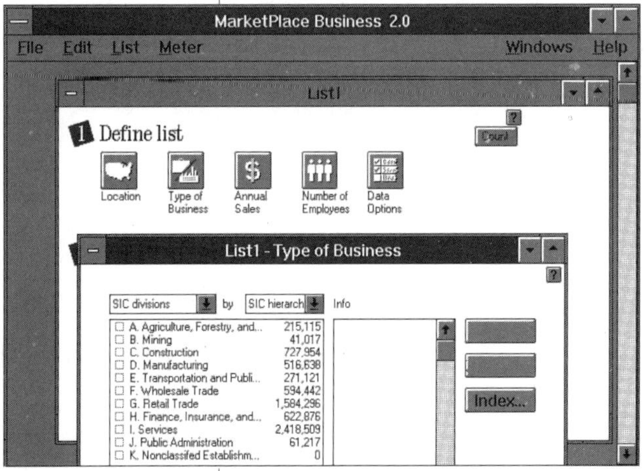

Predicasts F&S Index Plus Text

Silver Platter	
Operating System:	DOS 3.3 or above
Class:	General information database
Search and Retrieval:	SPIRS
Updates:	Monthly
Subscription:	Yes
Purchase:	No
Licensing:	Single user and networks

The wealth of information in Predicasts F&S Index Plus Text is staggering (see fig. 9.6). In one search session alone, we found references, abstracts, and full text from publications as diverse as the *Wall Street Journal*, *PC Week*, *Billboard Magazine*, and *Rubber and Plastics News*.

The search software is incredibly easy to use: the initial prompt is FIND; you type a word and refine the search with Boolean operands. The default display of the records is ALL, which gives you one article and citation after another. When you change the display to SOURCE, you can look through the search list by publication, marking and unmarking items for display, printing, or downloading to disk.

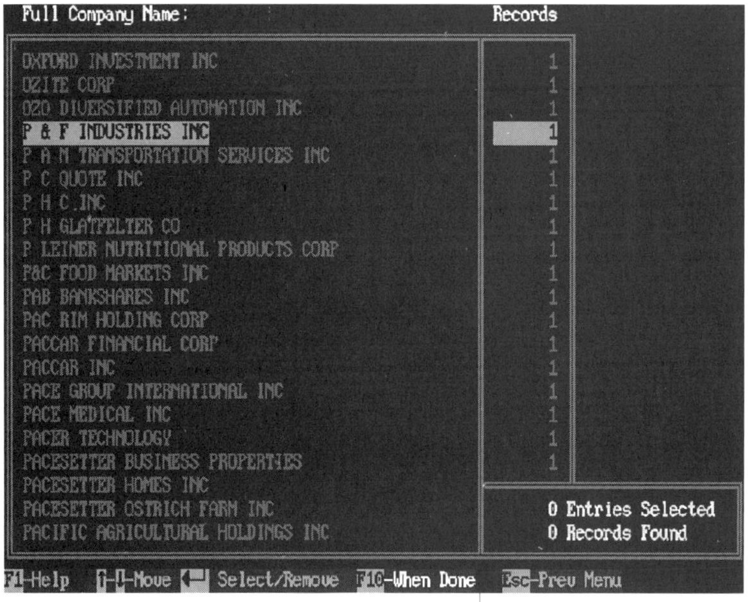

FIGURE 9.6

Full text and abstracts covering over 1,000 trade and business journals make Predicasts F&S Index Plus Text an invaluable business-research tool.

Virtually any topic—business, science, industry, finance—can be found on this disc. It's like having an entire business trade-publication library in the palm of your hand.

No amount of writing on our part can prove how powerful this information can be. With monthly updates, businesses can be instantly up to date on any number of vital issues, market trends, company strategies, and consumer research. When you buy a subscription to Predicasts F&S Index Plus Text, you buy valuable corporate information and a continuing business asset.

CD-ROM BOOK
QUE
AWARD OF EXCELLENCE

MapExpert

MapExpert is the culmination of DeLorme's Xmap-technology development effort. Its extensive database allows quick retrieval of an enormous amount of information in a way far superior to its paper equivalent. When you add its reasonable price, you can see why MapExpert clearly deserves special mention.

MapExpert

DeLorme Mapping

Operating System:	Windows 3.1
Class:	Map and geographical information database
Search and Retrieval:	DeLorme Xmap
Updates:	N/A
Subscription:	N/A
Purchase:	Yes
Licensing:	Two-level scheme

If your business involves maps of U.S. localities, chances are you can find a use for MapExpert. This application is a Windows-based computerized atlas. Its database contains just about every street in every city in the U.S.—even tiny little obscure ones like Cando, North Dakota. The program's interface lets you search by locations, by place name, by ZIP code, by area code or exchange, by street name, or by longitude/latitude.

Once you find the desired location, you can annotate the map with a broad selection of cartographic tools that allow the addition of all standard map features. You then can print the map or export it for use in another program.

MapExpert's licensing works on two levels. A limited-use license comes with the product and allows users to create an unlimited number of maps for internal use by the organization to which the software is licensed. With the second-tier license, users incur no additional cost: they just fill out a card included with the product. Once the card is completed and returned, users can create maps for limited publication and distribution. Additional rights are negotiable with DeLorme.

MapExpert has many business uses, especially for organizations that deal in real estate or find themselves frequently drawing maps for customers or internal use. Instead of photocopying existing paper maps—probably in violation of copyright law—use MapExpert to provide a highly accurate, professional map. Further advantages are custom levels of detail and annotations that make the map even more useful.

MapExpert is one of our favorite products. If you use maps, take a look at it.

FIGURE 9.7

DeLorme's MapExpert is a stunning rendition of an atlas on disc; you can probably find your own street in its highly detailed database.

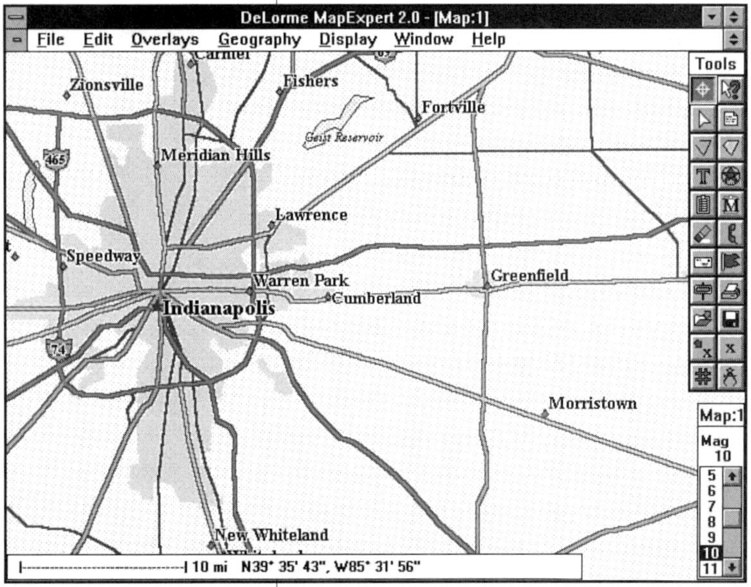

Other Marketing and Sales Discs

We also reviewed two other marketing discs worth mentioning: Multimedia Clipart, from Mediasource; and the American Business Phone Book, from American Business Information.

Although Mediasource's discs are loosely classified as "clip art," they can be more accurately called "clip media." Their discs include not only art (illustrations and photos) but sound.

The American Business Phone Book, produced yearly, is a worthwhile addition to your desktop, but it includes one slightly troubling limitation—you can look up only 5,000 numbers before the software ceases to function. Granted, most people are unlikely to look up that many numbers in a year (5,000 works out to about 20 numbers each business day), but that limitation pretty much guarantees you'll have to buy each year's update if you want to keep looking up your numbers on CD-ROM. If you want a fairly inexpensive and complete business telephone directory and are willing to put up with purchasing the annual updates, however, this one is worth a look.

Graphics Design Discs

CD-ROM has been a boon for graphic designers who used to have to buy single fonts on diskettes and clip art in printed books. Now you can buy more than 1,000 fonts on a single CD-ROM and thousands of clip art images in every conceivable image format.

The market for this type of material is such a natural fit for CD-ROM that you will find a few dozen font or clip art disc advertisements in a single pass through a computer magazine. We can't possibly cover all the material out there, so this section covers some representative collections of fonts, clip art, and *clip media* (a new category that includes sound effects and other multimedia elements).

T/Maker ClickART

T/Maker Company

Operating System:	PC and Macintosh
Class:	Clip art collection
Search and Retrieval:	N/A
Updates:	N/A
Subscription:	N/A
Purchase:	Yes
Licensing:	Single user and networks

T/Maker Company makes clip art collections for Macintoshes and PCs in most popular picture formats. The pictures are grouped by subject, and because some discs have literally thousands of individual images, you should be able to find something for any occasion. As you can see in figure 9.8, the graphics in some collections are pretty basic (that figure is from the Incredible Image Pak 2000), but that's not necessarily a problem—most clip art is designed to be easily recognized, not win trophies at art shows.

FIGURE 9.8

The Incredible Image Pak from T/Maker offers over 2,000 color graphics to fit almost any occasion.

Corel Gallery

Corel Corporation

Operating System:	PC
Class:	Clip art collection
Search and Retrieval:	N/A
Updates:	N/A
Subscription:	N/A
Purchase:	Yes
Licensing:	Single user and networks

Corel Corporation knows clip art. The most recent version of CorelDRAW!, their industry-leading graphics program, includes over 22,000 clip art images from more than a half-dozen art companies. Even if you don't use Corel programs, you can take advantage of some of that wealth of clip art on Corel Gallery, a 10,000-image disc.

The disc breaks down the graphics into 50 categories, including portraits (famous people), signs, several classifications of creatures (animals, crustaceans, birds, insects, reptiles), and borders. The artists who created the individual pieces have wildly varying styles, from radical caricature and cartoons to near photo-realistic, so you should be able to find not only the element you're looking for but match the mood you want to create.

Wayzata Clip Media

Wayzata Technology

Operating System:	PC and Macintosh
Class:	Clip media collection
Search and Retrieval:	N/A
Updates:	N/A
Subscription:	N/A
Purchase:	Yes
Licensing:	Single user and networks

Wayzata Technology (of Grand Rapids, Minnesota, not Wayzata, Minnesota) makes clip media discs for Macintoshes and PCs—mostly Macs.

Sound Library 2000 is a disc of 2,000 digital sounds for Macs. It includes enhancements for your desktop (several varieties of beeps) and for presentations (special effects, nature sounds, short phrases, and so on).

World of Motion is a disc of 100 royalty-free QuickTime film clips of people, animals, aircraft, autos, and more. Wayzata released World of Motion on a dual-format disc, which you can use for Mac or Windows (the disc also includes a QuickTime viewer for Windows in case you don't already have one). These clips are mostly fast-paced, so they're a great way to keep your audience's attention in a presentation—if you can figure out a way to work helicopters or race cars into the more boring sections.

InPrint Art Library Clipart

Allegro New Media	
Operating System:	Windows 3.1 and Macintosh
Class:	Clip art collection
Search and Retrieval:	N/A
Updates:	N/A
Subscription:	N/A
Purchase:	Yes
Licensing:	Single user and networks

InPrint's clip art collections give you high-quality photographic elements, 101 at a time. Titles include Scenic Photos (famous places and scenery), Graphic Textures (backgrounds), and Graphic Photos (see figure 9.9). Each collection works with Mac or Windows. Although 101 images may not seem like much compared to Corel Gallery's cache of 10,000, remember that these are photographs, which take up much more storage space than other kinds of graphics. InPrint also includes two versions of each picture—24-bit color and 8-bit grayscale—which also makes space something of a premium, even on a CD.

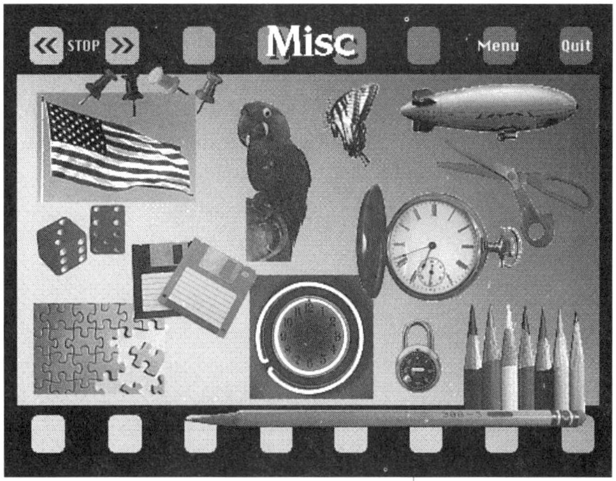

FIGURE 9.9

InPrint's Multimedia Studio shows off some of its photographic clip art.

Quantum Axcess Font Axcess

Quantum Axcess

Operating System:	Windows 3.1
Class:	Font collection
Search and Retrieval:	N/A
Updates:	N/A
Subscription:	N/A
Purchase:	Yes
Licensing:	Single user

TrueType fonts (a group of fonts that look the same on the screen as they do on the printer—theoretically) are all the rage. Since CorelDRAW! gave every graphic artist (or would-be graphic artist) the capability to easily create TrueType fonts, on-line services, BBSes, and shareware companies have been flooded with homegrown typefaces. Discs like Quantum Axcess's Font Axcess put hundreds of these fonts in one place—saving you the hours you might otherwise spend scouring CompuServe or America Online for them. In most cases (including Quantum Axcess's), the companies that make the compilation discs don't have anything to do with licensing the individual fonts, so if you find a font with a shareware registration fee and use it frequently, you still owe that fee to the font's author. Fortunately, most fonts are freeware or public domain, so registration is not an issue.

Font Axcess does more than just present a collection of fonts, however. It also includes a previewer (see fig. 9.10) that lets you see how the fonts look before you choose individual ones to install. This handy feature keeps you from clogging up your Windows installation with fonts you don't want.

FIGURE 9.10

Quantum Axcess's Font Axcess puts more than 1,000 shareware, freeware, and public domain TrueType fonts on a single disc with a handy previewer.

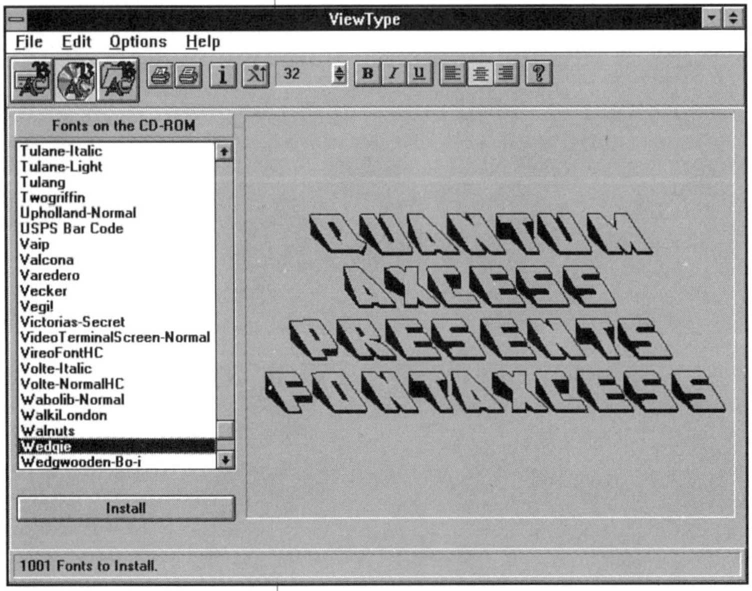

Do It On Your Desktop

Moon Valley Software

Operating System:	Windows 3.1
Class:	Desktop enhancement
Search and Retrieval:	N/A
Updates:	N/A
Subscription:	N/A
Purchase:	Yes
Licensing:	Single user

Moon Valley's Do It On Your Desktop is an enhancement for your Windows desktop, and (to justify its inclusion in this "Graphics Arts Discs" section) it should please just about any graphic artist. It runs with Program Manager, providing a graphical monitoring panel across the bottom of the screen. The panel shows you how much free memory, disk space, and system resources you have, as well as a graph of CPU usage, a count of keystrokes, and a few other handy monitors.

The monitoring is not the part that will draw in the graphically minded, however; Do It On Your Desktop pulls some wild visual tricks on your Program Manager. You can set it up to give your windows special frames (like wooden frames or the Etch-a-Sketch frame shown in fig. 9.11), change the minimize and maximize buttons to any of several elements (including fingers pointing up and down and several artistic arrows), and make the title bar look like a mountain range, a starry night, or any of several other settings.

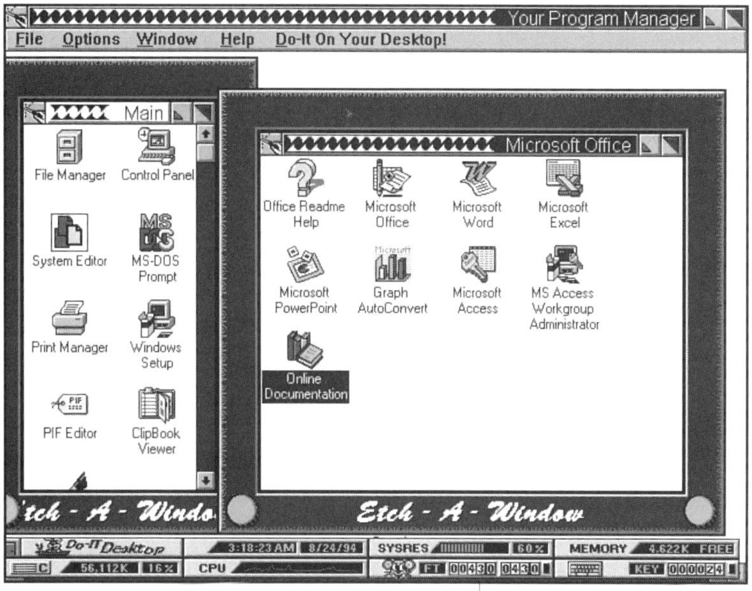

FIGURE 9.11

Do It On Your Desktop lets you change the way your desktop presents itself. Oh, and it also does sophisticated system monitoring.

Law, Accounting, and Finance Disc

Law, accounting, and finance may seem a disparate group of professions to gather under a banner for our purposes, but the following application has a great deal of crossover—especially for firms that deal with business taxes, business law involving taxes, and financial institutions heavily into investments and business partnerships. Let us emphatically state right here that the product described in the following section is merely the tip of the CD-ROM iceberg when it comes to these areas of disc information. Check out the CD-ROM Directory on Disc, described earlier in this chapter, for other sources of professional applications.

Federal Practice and Procedure, Wright and Miller

West Publishing, Inc.

Operating System:	DOS 3.3 or above
Class:	Law database
Search and Retrieval:	Proprietary (Premise)
Updates:	Yes
Subscription:	Yes
Purchase:	No
Licensing:	Single user

Law firms, law schools, and federal courthouses must all have the Federal Practice and Procedure disc by now (see fig. 9.12).It's inconceivable that such institutions would have this complex and highly detailed information in any form other than on CD-ROM. Segments can be marked, printed to disk—even in WordPerfect format—for use in word processors.

FIGURE 9.12

West Publishing's Federal Practice and Procedure is a complete guide to all aspects of federal, civil, and criminal law on one CD-ROM.

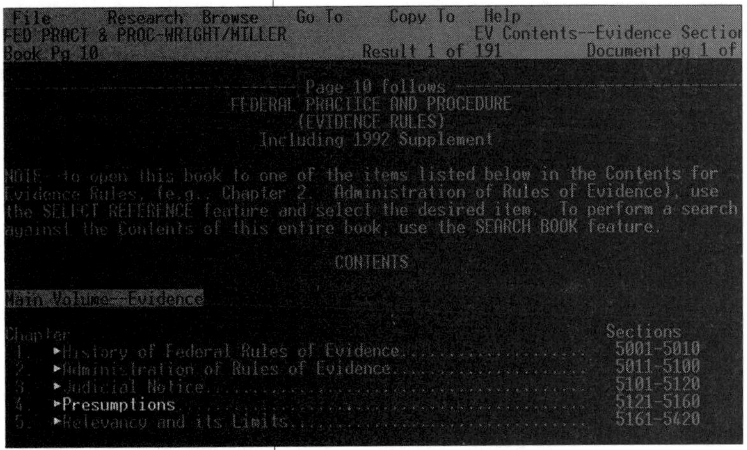

The software interface Premise uses for their legal CD-ROM discs is a logical and organized way to add numerous CD-ROM discs to the search interface of the application. You use the Premise software to add every CD to the Premise menu so that you can use one interface for all the CD-ROM applications: Bankruptcy, Federal Procedure, Tax Law, and so on. Then you select the database or book you want to work from. For example, the Bankruptcy and Federal Tax Law CD set alone comprises 16 discs, and you can search across all of them for specific data.

You can set a search for a topic or to retrieve a specific federal rule or related discussion once you know the specific title. You can search all federal procedures by areas such as main heading, title, text, footnotes, and index. The text and footnote searches alone prove the viability of researching these materials on CD-ROM. To scan footnotes and full text of all federal civil and criminal procedures by hand, with printed material, would be impossible or extremely time-consuming in most cases. With the Premise interface, all you do is enter a term under the text heading, such as **jury dismissal**, and you see a list of the appropriate procedures where the term is used.

This one set of CD-ROMs replaces an entire law library of text—and with unequaled search capabilities.

Education and Library-Science Discs

The use of CD-ROM publications, research, and bibliographies in education can fill a book in itself. Everything from agriculture education to zoological bibliographies are available through specialized publishers, distributors, and colleges and universities. Regardless of your professional educational pursuit—the preschool front to post-doctoral work—CD-ROM information on education and specialized resources for academic research are being published by the hundreds every month.

CD-ROMs won't make libraries obsolete, but they are the best hedge toward making them manageable as the information age fills shelf after shelf with new texts, periodicals, and research journals. Any library that wants to keep abreast of the books available, the books in print, and which periodicals contain what materials, will use CDs. Only CD-ROM references can provide such easy-to-retrieve information and timely updates.

Reference materials, both general and professional, that once took up yards of shelf space have been reduced to inches of easily housed CD-ROMs. The ease with which you can search the electronic references is a good argument for their existence: how can you possibly search an entire dictionary's quotations for references to one word embedded in a print version? It's no surprise that CD-ROM technology has a firm foothold in the nation's libraries already. As keepers of information, libraries can readily see the awesome advantages and utility of using this technology to disseminate and store knowledge.

ERIC

Silver Platter MLA Bibliography

Operating System:	DOS 3.3 or above
Class:	Education professionals database
Search and Retrieval:	SPIRS
Updates:	Annual
Subscription:	Yes
Purchase:	No
Licensing:	Single user and networks

This complete bibliographic database from the government-sponsored ERIC (Educational Resources Information Center) project covers over 775 periodicals on topics in education and education research. Journal, periodical, and book references are covered in detail.

You can search by topic, title, author, publication year, and institution, among others. The detailed citations also indicate the audience for the cited material (preschool teachers, for example) and what type of material it is (with major and minor descriptors).

The single ERIC CD-ROM is a gateway, so to speak, to all the available educational resources available for teachers and educators. Armed with an ERIC CD-ROM, even teachers in remote areas can do research to find articles that they then can order.

School systems and all colleges and universities (especially those offering degrees and programs in education) must have this disc subscription; it's the best means for staying abreast of the current thought on education.

MLA Bibliography

Silver Platter

Operating System:	DOS 3.3 or above
Class:	Education professionals database
Search and Retrieval:	SPIRS
Updates:	Annual
Subscription:	Yes
Purchase:	No
Licensing:	Single user and networks

Researching the literature on the topic of literature has always been productive with the Modern Language Association (MLA) Bibliography. But it's never been as easy as it is with CD-ROM.

With over 500,000 citations from journals, books, articles, and reviews covering virtually every aspect of literature and poetry, the MLA Bibliography disc represents the entire body of thought in contemporary criticism from 1982 to the present. Most libraries cannot afford the space to keep volumes from that far back on the shelves—but this CD accomplishes the task nicely.

You can search the CD for free text and look for any occurrence of a word or words in the citation or its abstract. You can also search for article titles, periodical titles, and publication dates, among others. A search for author Toni Morrison, for example, turned up 249 separate book, journal, and article citations in just under 3 seconds.

You can print the results of a search to the printer or to disk. All ISBN and ISSN reference numbers are listed; securing the actual articles is a matter of finding a library that houses the materials.

The MLA Bibliography is the master-work bibliography of literary critical texts; the CD-ROM from Silver Platter makes it more accessible, available, and alive.

The Oxford English Dictionary, Second Edition

Oxford University Press

Operating System:	Windows 3.1, Macintosh
Class:	Language database
Search and Retrieval:	Proprietary
Updates:	No
Subscription:	No
Purchase:	Yes
Licensing:	Single user and networks

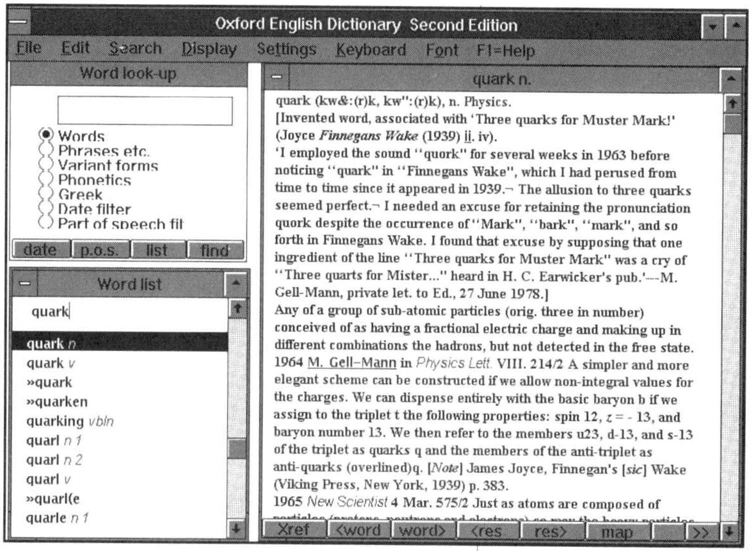

FIGURE 9.13

The Oxford English Dictionary is more malleable and usable than its printed cousin—not to mention over 10 pounds lighter.

This one application has done quite a lot to popularize CD-ROM technology. Even the most computer-illiterate, when told that the entire text of the venerable *Oxford English Dictionary* can be squeezed onto one disc, can see that CD-ROM technology is truly amazing. The people at Oxford painstakingly transferred the entire text, including its foreign and phonetic characters, to the Windows-based disc (see fig. 9.13). They then surrounded the dictionary with an extremely flexible and powerful search engine and topped it off with excellent export and printing capabilities.

You can search for words, phrases, quotations, or authors of quotations. Etymological searches can be performed as well. You can save the results of searches to disk for later use or export them to disk files. Printing from the program is also supported, and you even have the option of changing the font in which characters are printed.

The searches don't stop with the interface, however. You can build extremely complex Boolean nested searches, save them into editable scripts, and even submit the scripts to the search engine. These scripts can be saved; if you ever have to perform similar searches, it's an easy matter to edit the old script and submit the new one.

For all its power, grace, and utility, the Oxford English Dictionary is not for everyone, however. The price is steep, so only serious professionals need apply. Although the cost of developing the disc must have been high, Oxford University Press would do well to cut the price—to perhaps half its current list—to sell many more of them and recoup the initial investment many times over.

Beacon: The Multimedia Guidance Resource

Macmillan New Media

Operating System:	DOS 3.3 or above
Class:	Career database
Search and Retrieval:	Proprietary
Updates:	Annual
Subscription:	No
Purchase:	Yes
Licensing:	Single user

The Multimedia Guidance Resource is more than a resource for selecting colleges. The guide is a computer-assisted tutor for helping students select an appropriate college or university (see fig. 9.14). The Beacon set comes with a video of instruction on how to use the CD-ROM application, a pair of headphones, and the CD-ROM itself. After watching the video, students can easily boot up the software and be on their way to choosing a college.

After they peruse an initial set of menus, the software can ask a variety of questions concerning students' preferences in attending college: do they want to attend a two-year or four-year institution? Public or private? What size school will they feel most comfortable in?

From these and scores of other questions, Beacon gradually narrows the search through its database and arrives at a suitable list for the student to consider. Once the list is made, the student can print it or browse through detailed descriptions of each of the candidates.

In addition to a thorough description of each institution's resources, emphases, locale, and atmosphere, the database contains valuable admission information, guidelines, and deadlines.

Beacon is the perfect high-school guidance counselor's friend; it almost eliminates the need for the countless catalogs, brochures, and bulletins that crowd counseling offices. Students find the impartial and impersonal computer program less threatening or pressuring, perhaps, than their counselor or parents.

FIGURE 9.14

Macmillan's Beacon is a full course in choosing a college, all in one box.

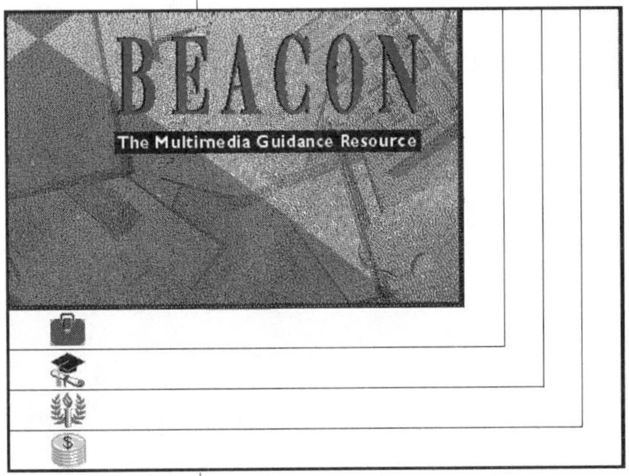

Barron's Profiles of American Colleges

LRI

Operating System:	Windows 3.1
Class:	Academic institution database
Search and Retrieval:	Viewer
Updates:	Annual
Subscription:	No
Purchase:	Yes
Licensing:	Single user

Barron's Profiles of American Colleges disc is excellent. Although not as much of a guided tour as the Beacon disc, LRI excels in search and browsing features. The Windows-based Viewer interface makes quick work of copying and pasting relevant information into a word processor or to a printer (see fig. 9.15).

Barron's outline format lends itself to free-form searches. A student or counselor can easily navigate the sections of the disc.

Barron's Profiles of American Colleges includes tips on selecting a school, factors that most schools consider during the application process, and detailed information on each of the more than 1,500 colleges and universities included on the disc. When you click the map icon, you pop up a map with the location of the college. A few of the major colleges have photos on disc, too. Some university-approved admissions forms are also included.

Because this application doesn't tie itself too tightly to a particular format, students, teachers, and even parents find Barron's Profiles of American Colleges an extremely helpful and informative disc. Its reasonable price (less than $100) makes it very attractive to the home and school environments.

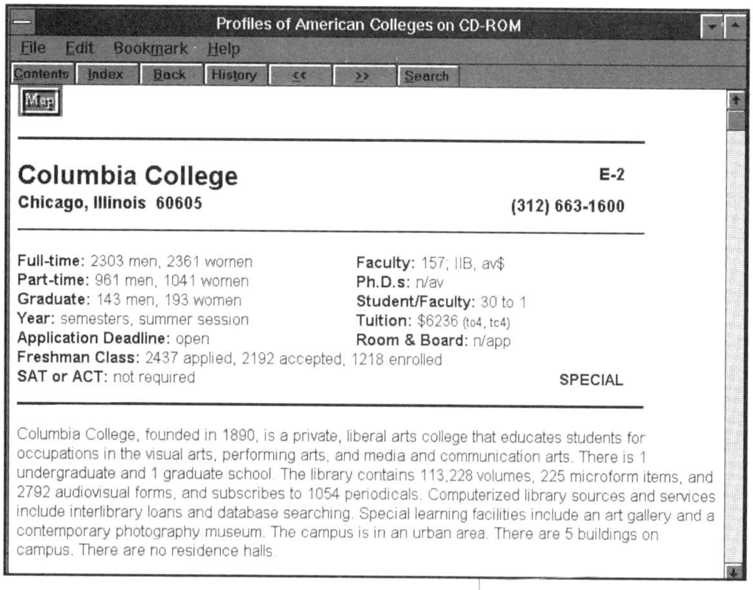

Profiles of American Colleges on CD-ROM
File Edit Bookmark Help
Contents Index Back History << >> Search
Map
Columbia College
E-2
Chicago, Illinois 60605
(312) 663-1600
Full-time: 2303 men, 2361 women
Faculty: 157; IIB, av$
Part-time: 961 men, 1041 women
Ph.D.s: n/av
Graduate: 143 men, 193 women
Student/Faculty: 30 to 1
Year: semesters, summer session
Tuition: $6236 (to4, tc4)
Application Deadline: open
Room & Board: n/app
Freshman Class: 2437 applied, 2192 accepted, 1218 enrolled
SAT or ACT: not required
SPECIAL
Columbia College, founded in 1890, is a private, liberal arts college that educates students for occupations in the visual arts, performing arts, and media and communication arts. There is 1 undergraduate and 1 graduate school. The library contains 113,228 volumes, 225 microform items, and 2792 audiovisual forms, and subscribes to 1054 periodicals. Computerized library sources and services include interlibrary loans and database searching. Special learning facilities include an art gallery and a contemporary photography museum. The campus is in an urban area. There are 5 buildings on campus. There are no residence halls.

FIGURE 9.15

Barron's Profiles of American Colleges is a perfect home or school program: it's thorough and very affordable.

Other Education and Library Science Discs

Bowker/Reed publishes some very useful, specialized discs for libraries, bookstores, and video stores. In fact, if you're in one of those industries, these discs are practically a requirement. All four of the CD-ROMs described here are from Bowker/Reed.

It's a good bet that every bookstore and library in the country has access to *Books in Print*, the ultimate list of books available through just about any source. Bowker/Reed also produces a CD-ROM version of this reference work. This disc includes capsule reviews of almost every book, ISBN numbers, suggested retail prices, publication dates, and sources. The software is easy to use and includes many thoughtful features—like the ability to use your modem to order books from any publisher that offers on-line ordering. The disc is updated monthly.

The Ulrich's Plus disc is a guide to periodicals from 200 countries. Its numbers are impressive:

- 127,000 periodicals
- 700 subjects
- 60,000 serials
- 50,000 annotations

Ulrich's Plus also offers advertising rates and contact information for most of the periodicals.

For libraries, schools, and stores that work with children, the Children's Reference Plus disc title is a veritable candy store. It lists over 84,000 books in print (and 47,000 out of print), 37,000 textbooks, 3,000 periodicals (culled from the Ulrich's list), 18,000 videos, and 5,700 audio tapes, all for children. It also includes a database of "Fiction, Folklore, Fantasy, and Poetry" for children, from 1876 to 1985.

Bowker/Reed also publishes the Video Directory disc, a list of over 90,000 videotapes cross-referenced by almost any information an inquisitive searcher is likely to know—titles, performers, directors, credits, awards (including Academy Award categories), manufacturer and distributor, subject, and dates of production and release. To help retailers, the Video Directory title also lists the order numbers and current prices through each video's distributors. And for true video buffs, Bowker/Reed provides over 1,500 movie reviews from *Variety* magazine.

Healthcare Disc

The single entry in this category is a comprehensive resource for physicians. Whether they own and operate their own small practices or are part of a large medical center, physicians will find that this timely database makes quick references and research an easy task.

Physician's MEDLINE

Macmillan New Media

Operating System:	DOS 3.3 or above
Class:	Medical database
Search and Retrieval:	BRS
Updates:	Quarterly
Subscription:	Yes
Purchase:	No
Licensing:	Single user

Physician's MEDLINE is an informative bibliographic disc that allows physicians to keep up on all current medical techniques, discoveries, and research from dozens of journals (see fig. 9.16).

The Physician's MEDLINE disc is updated quarterly. You can search the disc by author, publication date, keywords, or any text. You can browse through compiled lists of search results, print them to disk, or send them to the printer.

An affordable way for doctors to search for the information they need—without subscribing to all that they don't need—Physician's MEDLINE is a great resource for small or large practices.

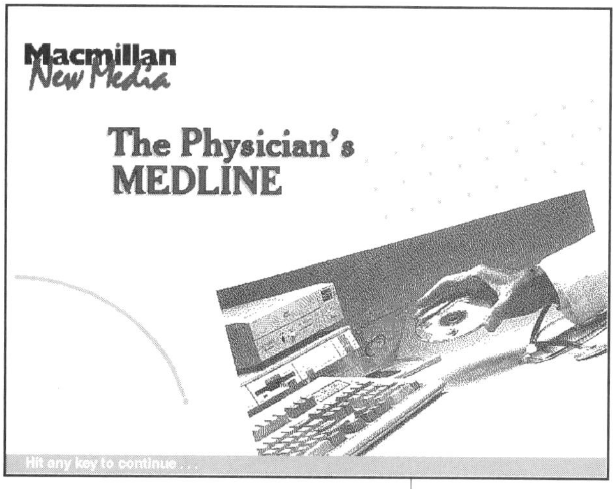

FIGURE 9.16

Physician's MEDLINE keeps any practice up to date with the click of a keyboard.

Chapter 10

CD-ROM for Home Reference and Education

Without a doubt, the revolution of CD-ROM technology will have its greatest impact where you live—at home. With a CD-ROM drive and a modest investment in software titles, you can equip your family with resource, reference, and educational tools unheard of a few years ago. Your library of discs, in a physical span of no more than six or eight inches, can hold materials that rival—or surpass—the holdings at your local library. Regardless of your interests or educational requirements, CD-ROM titles are now available to enrich your home-based work and your children's education.

This chapter explores some of the latest applications and gives you an idea of the merits and capabilities we found in installing, testing, and using the following CD applications for your home.

About This Chapter

This chapter provides an overview of the capabilities of home and educational software. The variety of products available for home and educational use is great—as you can see from the sheer length of this chapter, which presents only a sample of the titles out there. This chapter takes you on a tour of some of the better applications available.

How To Use This Chapter

The description of each product in this chapter begins with a chart; these charts provide consistent at-a-glance information.

continues

continued

A set of four icons that define the audience level of the product appears for each product. The four icons indicate that the product is appropriate for preschool children, children in the primary grades, individuals at the secondary-school level, or those at the university level and beyond. Those icons that are not valid for the product are dimmed (for example, if the software title is intended for use by primary and secondary schoolers, only those two icons are clearly visible; the preschool and university icons are in gray).

All the CD-ROMs highlighted here are high-quality products we can confidently recommend. We have tested every title reviewed in this chapter and written up complete reports on those CD-ROMs we felt deserved special attention. Some discs we tested didn't make the cut at all and weren't included in this chapter. A few superlative products have been given an Award of Excellence (we explain why these titles are cream of the crop in the margin-note text accompanying the award icon).

EXPLANATION

MPC

MPC is an acronym for Multimedia PC and refers to a specification for multimedia-capable personal computers that was written by a consortium led by Microsoft. This specification describes the minimum performance levels and equipment a PC must have to run an MPC application correctly. The original spec called for an 80286 processor, which was widely regarded as a mistake by those not involved in drafting the standard. The latest revision (MPC Level 2) requires a minimum of an 80486SX processor. MPC machines and applications can be distinguished by the MPC logo—the letters *MPC* with the image of a CD in the center of the *M*—or the MPC2 logo, which adds an arabic number 2 to the end.

Encyclopedia Discs

The encyclopedia is a natural for CD-ROM, and to be expected, more than a few encyclopedia discs are already on the market. Look at the advantages of an electronic encyclopedia:

- Occupies a mere 1/4 inch of bookshelf space, as opposed to 2 to 4 feet for the bound and printed version.
- Contains hypertext links to any document or related term.
- Lets you print documents, pictures, and maps—and carry them anywhere.
- Provides sound and video in addition to photographs.
- Lets you do searches that take seconds rather than minutes.
- There are no multiple volumes to deal with.
- Has virtually limitless search capabilities. You should closely scrutinize the capabilities and operating system requirements of these valuable reference materials to determine which best suits your needs. Make sure that you buy an encyclopedia for the environment you and your family work in the most. For example, if you do all your word processing and most of your computing in Windows, an **MPC** encyclopedia makes the most sense. If you use your machine mostly for DOS applications, look more closely at DOS multimedia encyclopedias.

Battle of the Multimedia Encyclopedias

As you try to decide which encyclopedia disc to buy, you may find the array of choices very confusing. The fact is, this product category has something for everyone. When choosing an encyclopedia, your primary concern should be how you will apply it. Microsoft Encarta, for example, is an excellent choice for a family reference: children find it easy to use, it includes educational games, and it's nice to look at. On the other hand, its contents lack the depth of some of the other choices. Think carefully about what you intend to do with your encyclopedia before you buy—you might prevent a costly mistake.

Like printed encyclopedias, CD-ROM encyclopedias have a wide range of content and depth of coverage. Some are best suited for families with younger children (there are fewer articles than are contained in a full-blown set of encyclopedias but they cover the basics very well). Others rank up there with their printed counterparts and contain tens of thousands of full-length articles, complete with maps, charts, and illustrations.

Compton's Interactive Encyclopedia

Compton's New Media

Operating System:	Windows 3.1
Interface:	Compton's Smartrieve, Windows-based mouse, and text
Multimedia:	Video, animation, sound, color graphics
Audience:	12 years and up
System Requirements:	MPC-compatible machine

Compton's Interactive Encyclopedia is virtually all an encyclopedia on CD-ROM should be. Its interface is easy for children to use, yet powerful enough for adult-strength searches and retrievals (see fig. 10.1). Button bars along the right side of the screen enable you to open indexes to graphics, sounds, atlases, slide shows, animation, videos, and more; a search box lets you specify any phrase or word for easy access to articles. Search results are presented in an indexed list; you merely highlight the appropriate article, click it, and off you go.

Articles are displayed in great-looking, easy-to-read, Windows-based fonts, with margin icons that represent pictures, charts, maps, and videos. Clicking an icon displays the multimedia element. Also in the margins are useful related-article icons for easy cross-references. Words with **hypertext** links or extensive cross-references to other segments of the encyclopedia are highlighted. Click the word and away you go to the cross-referenced material.

One of the handiest features in Compton's Interactive Encyclopedia is its virtual workspace. A miniature representation of open windows in a grid appears in the lower-right corner of the application. You can add multiple searches, videos, and articles to these miniature windows and skip back and forth among them by clicking on the grid. This feature is especially useful when you are researching a number of different—or related—topics and want to go back and forth quickly without resorting to menus or searches. The number of virtual windows you can keep open is limited to the amount of memory you have on the machine. If you exit Compton's Interactive Encyclopedia with any virtual windows open, it asks whether you want to save the workspaces—an excellent way to resume work right where you left off.

The workspaces are also ideal for multiple users. You, your spouse, and the kids can all keep your own searches and articles in

FIGURE 10.1

Compton's Encyclopedia has all the multimedia bells and whistles, including full-motion video and sound—as well as over 32,000 in-depth entries.

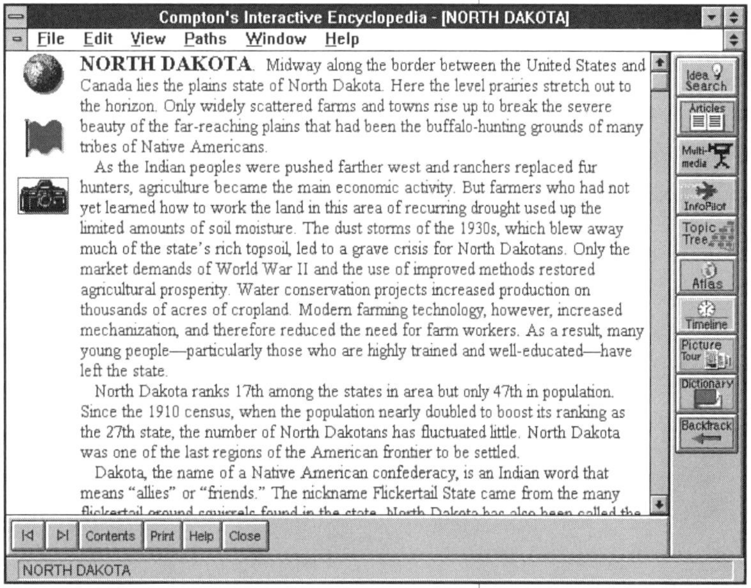

EXPLANATION

Hypertext

A *hypertext document* is an electronic document that attempts to overcome the inherently linear nature of the written word. The traditional problem with printed documents is that a cross-reference—say, to another chapter—requires you to interrupt your reading and search it out. With a hypertext link, you need only click a highlighted word to instantly display the cross-reference. In the book you are now reading, this very margin note is an attempt to provide something similar in a printed format.

separate workspaces, each saved and ready to resume when the application is fired up again.

This product's article depth and quality are superb. To give you an example, the encyclopedia contains an article on manned space flight that is well over 16 pages—not including its many pictures, videos, and sound bites.

The full-motion video is handled through Video for Windows and runs without a hitch on small or large screens attached to a 486-33 machine. Slower systems produce smaller video windows, but should reproduce just fine. A handy index of videos and animations makes it easy to browse through these exciting features with the click of a mouse.

If you have a diverse group of reference hounds in your household, this multimedia encyclopedia is the best one around. It's easy for children in junior high and above to use and powerful enough to be a constant reference for adults.

Encarta

Microsoft Corporation

Operating System:	Windows 3.1
Interface:	Text, menus, mouse
Multimedia:	Video, animation, sound, color graphics
Audience:	12 years and up
System Requirements:	MPC-compatible machine

Microsoft's Encarta is an ambitious entry in the CD-ROM encyclopedia race (see fig. 10.2). Of all the encyclopedias tested, Encarta has, by far, the most extensive multimedia displays—sound, video, animation, and graphics are virtually everywhere you turn in this disc. The viewer-based front-end is easy to use and handy for searching; hypertext cross-references throughout the book make browsing for extensive knowledge easy.

The only problem with Encarta is the quality of its text contents. It appears that Encarta has fewer entries and shorter and less complete articles than do many competing encyclopedias. This will, no doubt, be remedied in later editions. Still, the use of multimedia and its superior interface make Encarta a strong contender for your home-reference purchase.

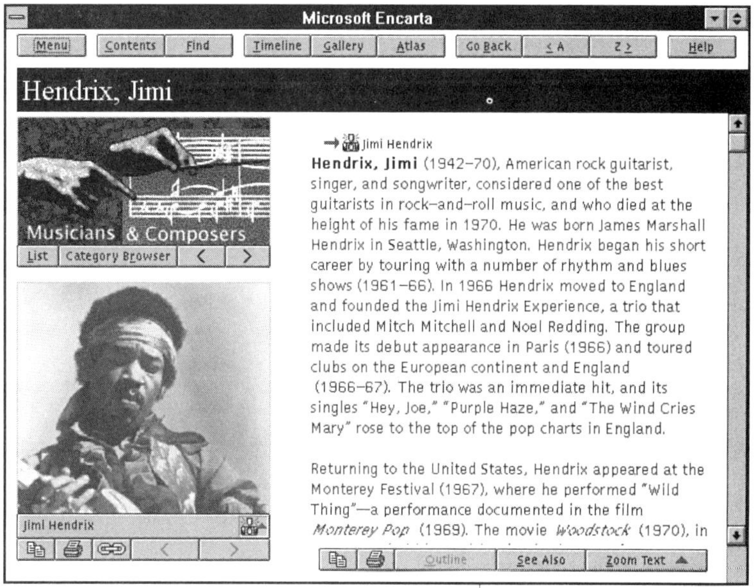

FIGURE 10.2

Microsoft's Encarta is a visually impressive multimedia exploration of the encyclopedia.

Desktop Libraries and General-Reference Discs

If you find yourself groping for dictionaries, almanacs, and other far-flung reference works while you're involved in your work, you might want to keep one of these discs permanently parked in your CD-ROM drive. By exploiting the full capacity of CD-ROM discs, publishers can pack whole collections of reference works onto one CD, making desktop libraries and general-reference applications a perfect companion to business, scholarly, and everyday writing.

Software Toolworks Reference Library

Software Toolworks

Operating System:	DOS 3.1 or above (also runs under Windows)
Interface:	Text, menus
Multimedia:	None
Audience:	14 years and up
System Requirements:	640 KB memory

The Software Toolworks Reference Library is a virtual powerhouse of useful references, all on one CD. Look what's included:

- *Webster's New World Dictionary of Quotable Definitions*
- *Webster's New World Dictionary*
- *Webster's New World Thesaurus*
- *The New York Times Public Library Desk Reference*
- *Dictionary of 20th Century History*
- *The National Directory*
- *Lasser's Legal and Corporation Forms for the Small Business*

That's a lot, and all of it is top-notch. You select which domain—or book—you want to access through a handy menu system. Once inside a book, you can use wild-card and Boolean searches to retrieve material. The interface allows you to print items to disk or to the printer and to cut and paste into your word processor; there's a configuration option that tells the application where you keep your word processor.

What makes this disc a real standout for small businesses is its legal-forms segment. Virtually all small-business contracts are included; all you need to do is fill in the particulars and go. *The National Directory* is also a great minireference to have: within seconds, you can search the database for addresses and phone numbers of all major businesses, institutions, and government offices.

The disc's interface also keeps a running, saved tally of your session searches, making it easy to skip back and forth with ease. You can mark entire texts, segments of texts, or lists for printing or cutting and pasting.

This reference is indispensable for the small businessperson and is also handy around the house. The almanac and dictionary are some of the best, and these alone may be worth the price. The Software Toolworks Reference Library was very well-behaved in a DOS window under Windows 3.1, and its DOS-alone performance was outstanding. This product is particularly great if you mainly use DOS applications, and it coexists wonderfully in a Windows environment, too.

Multimedia Bookshelf '94

Microsoft Corporation

Operating System:	Windows 3.1
Interface:	Windows Viewer 2.0, text, and menus
Multimedia:	Sound, animation
Audience:	12 years and up
System Requirements:	MPC-compatible machine

Microsoft's Multimedia Bookshelf is a perfect complement to your home-based office (see fig. 10.3). If you work in Windows, you *need* this disc. Microsoft has packed this one disc with all of these pieces:

- *The American Heritage Dictionary*
- *The Concise Columbia Encyclopedia*
- *The Columbia Dictionary of Quotations*
- *The People's Chronology*
- *Roget's Thesaurus*
- *The Hammond Intermediate World Atlas*
- *World Almanac and Book of Facts 1994*

If you're writing a speech, business proposal, or presentation—or one of the children is working on a term paper—tuck the Multimedia Bookshelf into your CD-ROM drive. The volumes included on the disc are some of the best references available today—and Microsoft made them one step better than their printed counterparts by including multimedia aspects in all volumes. *The American Heritage Dictionary*, for example, includes a pronunciation icon—simply click the icon to hear the word pronounced. *The Concise Columbia Encyclopedia* has animations of biological and natural processes such as the life cycle of volcanoes and the workings of the human heart.

Using sound to its advantage is exploited in *The Columbia Dictionary of Quotations*, where some poetry and verse is spoken—in many cases by the authors themselves. Sample musical-instrument sounds grace the dictionary as well, and the almanac contains narrative in appropriate places.

FIGURE 10.3

Microsoft's Multimedia Bookshelf '94 is the perfect Windows sidekick as you plow through your work at home—or in the office.

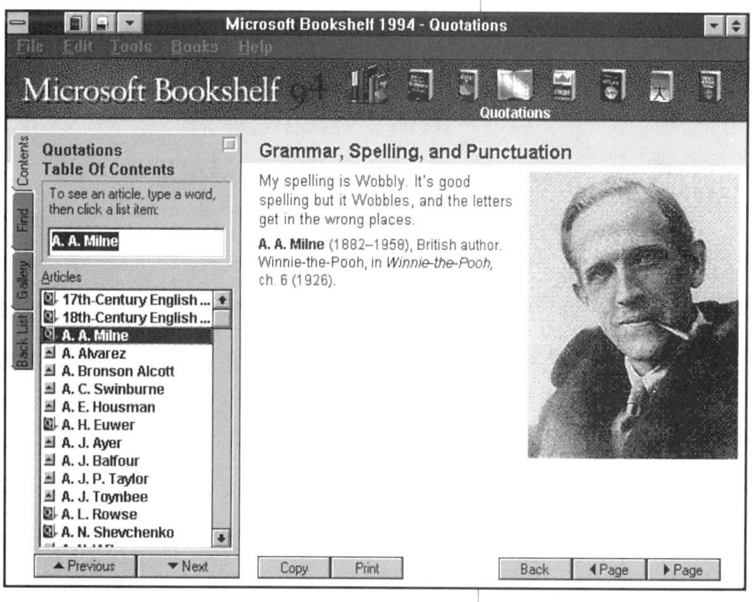

Because Microsoft's Multimedia Bookshelf is a Windows program, you can cut from the references and paste into your documents; you can also export clips of dictionary and encyclopedia graphics elements simply by pointing and clicking them into your work document.

The 1994 edition has been updated to include events in Eastern Europe and the former Soviet Union—from brand-new maps in the atlas to almanac and encyclopedia articles.

Don't expect the encyclopedia to compete with the full-blown versions (such as Grolier's and Compton's—or even Microsoft's own Encarta) described earlier in this chapter, but it's a serviceable and useful companion piece in this suite of reference materials; it'll answer most everyday questions you might need when covering general topics.

This is a must-buy for Windows users.

Miscellaneous Reference Discs

This section introduces a grab-bag of discs that can be useful—provided that you have an interest in the discs' topics. Film, magazine articles, consumer information, and a multimedia children's dictionary fill out the miscellaneous discs covered in the following sections.

Cinemania

Microsoft Corporation	
Operating System:	Windows 3.1
Interface:	Viewer
Multimedia:	Sound, color photos, movie clips
Audience:	Secondary school and up
System Requirements:	MPC-compatible machine for sound

Whether you're stumped about which videos to rent this weekend or caught up in an argument about who directed *The Elephant Man*, Microsoft's Cinemania has the answer. Die-hard movie buffs may be disappointed with the scope of the coverage—although Cinemania is great for popular titles, it is hardly encyclopedic. This Windows application gets high marks for a great interface and the inclusion of some nice multimedia touches.

Cinemania has a tremendous bibliography of films available. You can search by title, genre, actors, directors, or in some cases, screenwriters. By using a "list function," you can browse a category and tag films to add to a list; multiple lists are supported. This function makes it easy, for example, to compile a quick hit list of science-fiction movies and then print it out.

FIGURE 10.4

Microsoft's Cinemania is a film buff's dream, with an easy-to-navigate interface and tons of film information and photos.

Other sections of the application are biographies of important actors, actresses, directors, and other movie notables. *The Film Encyclopedia* contains articles on studios, specific Hollywood trends and trend-setters, and essays on particular films. The Glossary option explains movie terminology—if you've always wondered what *film noir* means, the glossary can help you out.

The Gallery section is a multimedia compendium of still photos and music from key films and sound bites of dialogue. Stills are represented by a camera icon, music with a musical staff, and sound by a microphone icon. You'll also find 20 movie camera icons in Cinemania's gallery, each of which lets you play a movie clip from one of the 20 best movies in history. When accessing any of these items, you can make a hypertext link to related articles by clicking highlighted text areas. And navigation is easy for even the most computer-phobic—the controls (appropriately enough) are laid out a lot like a VCR's remote control (see fig. 10.4).

When we last reviewed Cinemania, we said it could benefit from the type of in-depth reviews found in its hottest CD-ROM competitor—Roger Ebert's Video Companion. Microsoft must've been listening because the new edition *includes* the Video Companion as well as *Leonard Maltin's Movie and Video Guide 1994* (which alone makes up the bulk of the reviews, at over 19,000). Former *New Yorker* movie critic Pauline Kael's *5001 Nights at the Movies* adds some of the more colorful reviews (more than 2,500); these include the only thumbs-down rating for *Star Wars*, which Kael calls "exhausting" and "an epic without a dream."

Plenty of flash and a healthy dose of perspective make Cinemania a must-have for video buffs.

Sports Illustrated CD-ROM Sports Almanac

Warner New Media	
Operating System:	Windows 3.1
Interface:	Menus
Multimedia:	Full-color photos, sound
Audience:	Secondary school and up
System Requirements:	MPC-compatible machine for sound

This disc is better than a full year's subscription to *Sports Illustrated* in many ways. How could you possibly look up all the photos and articles of Shaquille O'Neill in a matter of seconds with all those printed back issues? Although not all the articles or pictures from the previous year are on the CD (the swimsuit edition isn't included, for example), many are—particularly those concerning key sporting events—and the full-color photos look great on a VGA monitor (see fig. 10.5).

FIGURE 10.5

Relive a year's worth of sports with the Sports Illustrated CD-ROM Sports Almanac.

The main table of contents gives you plenty of options: NCAA basketball and football; pro baseball, basketball, hockey, and football; horse and motor racing—the list goes on. Each option branches off to the year's review of the selected sport. Within that sport subsection, you can perform keyword searches to look up favorite teams, players, coaches, and so on.

Another main-menu choice brings you to the statistics section, from which you can search or browse through the complete statistics for any given sport. The Profiles menu option accesses full biographies on over 500 important sports figures. The Awards section is a comprehensive database of major sports awards dating back to 1931. Who won the third Superbowl? It's just a mouse click away.

Other main-menu items include a picture gallery of the year's best *Sports Illustrated* photos, obituaries for the year, and a section covering miscellaneous sports, such as bicycling and marathons.

Sound adds a dimension that the paper-bound version obviously lacks, and the CD requires no installation whatsoever—simply click the start-up batch file and go.

If you have a sports fanatic in the house, this is a perfect gift CD—all the quality, information, and excitement of *Sports Illustrated* without the paper.

Macmillan Dictionary for Children

Macmillan New Media	
Operating System:	Windows 3.1
Interface:	Toolbook
Multimedia:	Animation, color graphics, sound
Audience:	Kindergarten through grammar school
System Requirements:	MPC-compatible machine

Only a CD-ROM product can pull off this wonderful version of the old reference essential, the dictionary. The Macmillan Dictionary for Children, written and produced especially for children with help from Public Broadcasting Service (PBS) and Macmillan, demonstrates the pure utility—and fun—that CD-ROM can deliver to the learning experience (see fig. 10.6).

The dictionary's interface is clean and unconfusing—a must for the younger computer users in the house—and the variety of ways you can search for words can't be found in its printed counterpart.The multimedia aspects of this product really make it shine. Not only is the word in question pronounced when you click it, but nearly every word in that word's definition can be pronounced as well, helping your child build his or her vocabulary even further. In addition, words with alternative pronunciations are spoken one after the other, in order of preferred pronunciation.

If all that weren't enough to get your child more interested in language, the Macmillan Dictionary for Children contains three dictionary games: a spelling bee, hangman, and word search. Zak, the dictionary's ever-available tour guide and game partner, adds a playful touch whenever possible. Zak directs children to further explore aspects of the book they might overlook; Zak is like having a fun-loving teacher at your child's call.

This product is a sure winner. What better way to heighten your children's interest in language?

FIGURE 10.6

Children use an animated icon—Zak—to navigate the Macmillan Dictionary for Children.

Health Discs

Ever since Dr. Spock's baby-care book entered the households of America (and probably well before that), home health books have been perennial bestsellers. No doubt that CD-ROM health books will also do well: they're crammed with information, explanation, and in most cases, are heavily illustrated and animated.

Mayo Clinic Family Health Book, Interactive Edition

Interactive Ventures

Operating System:	Windows 3.1
Interface:	Hypertext
Multimedia:	Sound, pictures
Audience:	12 years and up
System Requirements:	MPC-compatible machine

This CD-ROM is just what its title says: a book. It's the hypertext version of the *Mayo Clinic Family Health Book*; the text of the book has been made into a hypertext document (see fig. 10.7). In hypertext, references to other material in a document are made with hot links—that is, you click specially highlighted text to "pop up" definitions, illustrations, or other information.

The Mayo book, in paper form, is an excellent reference. The hypertext, multimedia version adds the versatility of a computer database to the high quality of the basic information. Unlike paper books with their limited indexes, computerized books have unlimited search capabilities. Finding references to any particular word is as simple as typing it in a dialog box.

The book covers basic health issues from infancy to late adulthood. It also covers diseases, first aid, and how to stay healthy. The heaviest use of multimedia is a narrated guide of the human anatomy.

The Mayo Clinic Family Health Book is an excellent example of the power of computerized books—and it is still just a first-generation attempt.

FIGURE 10.7

The Mayo Clinic Family Health Book by Interactive Ventures.

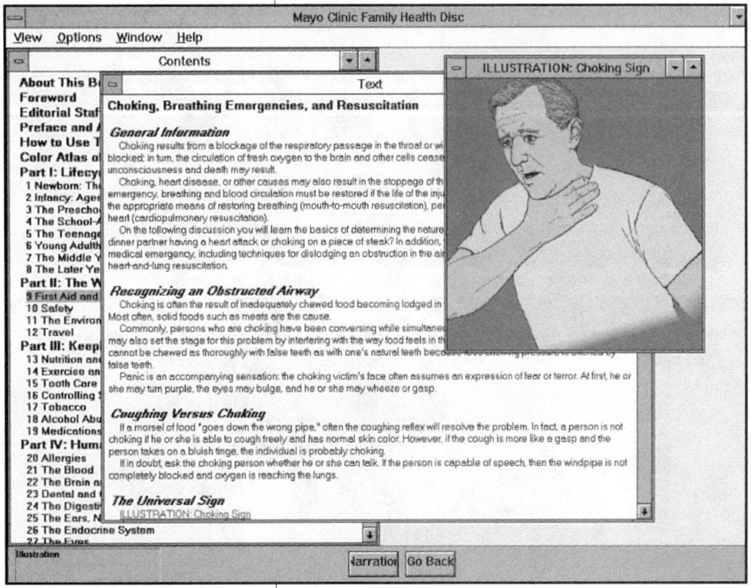

The Family Doctor

Creative Multimedia Corporation

Operating System:	Windows 3.1, DOS 3.3 or above, and Macintosh (on same disc)
Interface:	Toolbook
Multimedia:	Color graphics, sound
Audience:	Secondary school and up
System Requirements:	VGA or better display

The Family Doctor is a good general reference for the average family (see fig. 10.8). When you want just the quick facts and don't want to get bogged down in excessive detail, the Family Doctor is a perfect health reference to have around. It's an updated and expanded version of Dr. Allen Bruckheim's popular printed book; most topics are handled in a question-and-answer format.

From the main menu, you can search for topics by using a three-level Boolean search capability—three levels of IF, THEN, NOR, AND, and OR conditions. Your search results are presented in list format—simply click the ones you want to view. All full-text articles and illustrations are done in an easy-to-read font, and none of the articles is overly long or tedious. The writing is clear, informative, and easy to digest.

Also from the main menu, you can access the gallery of illustrations that accompanies the articles. All illustrations are high-resolution color bitmaps that reproduce well on-screen and on the printer. Over 300 such illustrations appear throughout the book—a useful visual aid for explaining complicated procedures and diseases.

The main menu also gives you access to a prescription drugs database. With data on over 1,600 prescription drugs, this section is valuable to all patients.

Medical terms—often tongue twisters—are pronounced for you with the MPC version (DOS and Mac versions do not provide pronunciations). To round out its features, the CD has an extensive human-anatomy guide, updated health booklets, and listings for national health resources such as support groups and information agencies and institutions.

FIGURE 10.8

The Family Doctor takes a question-and-answer approach to health information.

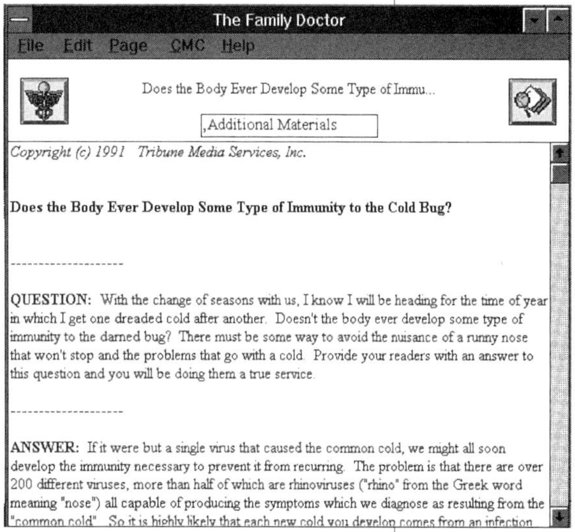

History and Current-Events Discs

For researching history and current events, powerful indexing and cross-referencing tools are a must; CD-ROM technology frees you from the restraint of paper and offers full-text searches impossible with traditional books and reference sources. The representative CD-ROMs described in the following sections range from a history of the world to maps and photos of the battle of Gettysburg.

History of the World

CD-ROM BOOK AWARD OF EXCELLENCE

History of the World

Bureau Development's product is a spectacular example of what CD-ROM can do for historical research. Containing thousands of original documents, History of the World places no restraints on how information can be searched. Bureau Development provided more than just a collection of documents and a search engine: they licensed documents not in the public domain and provided analysis to make understanding the results of your search easier.

Bureau Development, Inc.

Operating System:	DOS 3.3 or above, Macintosh
Interface:	Menus
Multimedia:	Pictures, CD audio
Audience:	12 years and up
System Requirements:	VGA or better display

The History of the World disc is an excellent example of Bureau Development's forte: the compilation of hundreds of public-domain documents into a usable database on a single disc (see fig. 10.9). The History of the World organizes more than 1,000 diverse documents, pictures, maps, and sounds into six different databases:

- **Titles.** This database allows you to access documents by title and includes two copyrighted textbooks from Harper Collins Publishers: *Civilization: Past and Present* and *Civilization: A World Phenomenon*.

- **Themes.** This arrangement of titles provides thematic access and is divided into ten categories:

  Economics
  Exploration, Discovery, and Travel
  Overviews and Narratives
  People and Letters
  Philosophy
  Politics
  Religion
  Science, Technology, and Inventions
  Society, Culture, and the Arts
  War, Conquests, and Battles

- **Regions.** This database arranges titles according to parts of the world, including the following:

  Global
  Africa
  The Americas
  Asia
  Europe
  The Pacific Region

- **Time Periods.** The editors of this database chose six time periods that they felt arose naturally from history:

  Origins of Civilization: 0 to 500 BC
  The Classical Period: 500 BC to 500AD
  The Post-Classical Period: 500 AD to 1450
  The World Shrinks: 1450 to 1750
  The Industrial Period: 1750 to 1900
  The Twentieth Century: 1900 to today

- **Pictures, Maps, and Illustrations.** History of the World offers more than 600 illustrations, including photos and maps. You can view all of them on any VGA adapter. Political cartoons supplement articles concerning political history, and photos document historical events.

- **Speeches and Eyewitness Accounts.** Thanks to the CD-ROM's capability to store audio, Bureau Development has included speeches and eyewitness accounts gleaned from the national archives in Washington, D.C. These historical sound clips range from portions of a speech by Adolph Hitler to audio from the first landing on the moon. You can hear the audio by connecting speakers or headphones to the audio output of any CD-ROM drive.

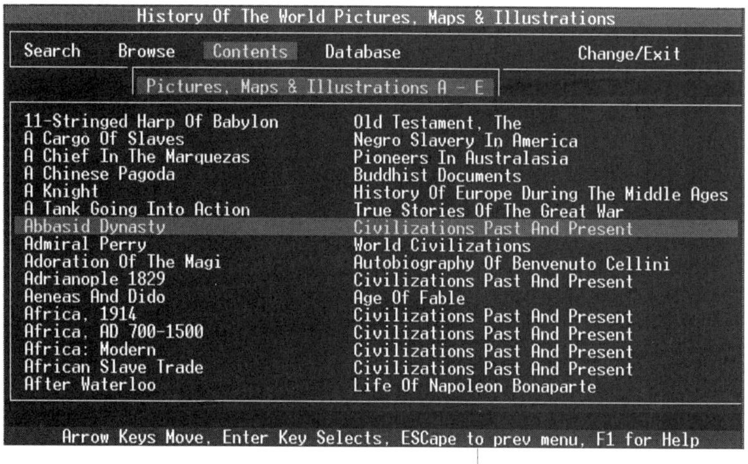

FIGURE 10.9

History of the World is a masterful example of how to best use CD-ROMs in reference applications.

Although the majority of the material on this CD-ROM is in the public domain, the editors of this disc did not just lump a bunch of material together and give it a title. It is well organized and includes useful introductory material that enhances the value of the raw data.

History of the World uses Disc Passage as its retrieval software, and although it is not the most sophisticated retrieval software in terms of search capability, it has enough capacity to do some decent searches on the huge collection of documents stored on the disc.

This disc is a must-have item for libraries, serious home schoolers, and anyone who needs to do historical research.

Twelve Roads to Gettysburg

Ebook, Inc.	
Operating System:	Windows 3.1
Interface:	MacroMind Windows Player
Multimedia:	Color graphics, photography, sound
Audience:	Secondary school and up
System Requirements:	MPC-compatible machine

Ebook, Inc. has a whole series of great multimedia titles, and Twelve Roads to Gettysburg is among the best (see fig. 10.10). Students can get a look at this momentous turning point in our nation's history with this in-depth study of Gettysburg—before, during, and well after the battle. The information on this disc is worthy of any full textbook on the topic.

FIGURE 10.10

Ebook's excellent Civil War disc, the Twelve Roads to Gettysburg, uses multimedia to its best advantage.

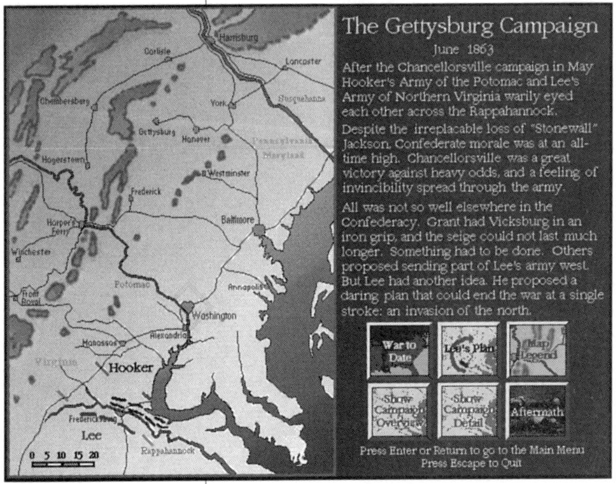

The main menu of this multimedia excursion allows you to examine these options: Campaigns and Strategies, the Battle, Gettysburg Today, and the Armies and Individuals of both the Confederate and the Union.

The Campaign segment gives you an overview of the Civil War up to the time of the Battle of Gettysburg, where the forces stood before the battle, and what each general had planned for the ensuing battle. Detailed maps of the area pinpoint troops and geographical features of the surrounding terrain.

The Battle option, the most impressive in the entire series, walks you through the battle day by day with animated troop movements depicted on the topographical maps. Each battle segment is expertly narrated.

The Gettysburg Today section is a tour of the present memorial battlefield site. The Armies and Individuals segment gives you a detailed account of troop strength, armaments, and profiles of key officers.

The entire disc is lavishly embellished with daguerreotypes, photos, and portraits set against background music from the period. Histories of the compositions are included, too.

This CD-ROM is an expertly orchestrated application. Even if you have little initial interest in the Civil War or Gettysburg, the compelling presentation made with this CD will have you riveted in no time at all. It's an excellent introduction—or review—to an important segment of this nation's past.

Science Discs

You'd think that science CDs would be flying out of developer's doors at this time. What better medium could possibly exist for reference and instruction in topics such as astronomy, physics, chemistry, and the like? As of this writing, however, few general-reference and educational CDs are available in this topic area. The ones that are available, however, are mighty impressive, particularly those developed by Knowledge Adventure, Inc., who have spent great development effort putting together some of the most engaging CD-ROM applications seen in *any* category.

Space Adventure

FIGURE 10.11

Your kids can blast off into the cosmos with Knowledge Adventure's Space Adventure multimedia learning disc.

Knowledge Adventure, Inc.	
Operating System:	DOS 3.1 or above
Interface:	Menus
Multimedia:	Video, color graphics, sound
Audience:	Primary through secondary school
System Requirements:	VGA or better display, sound card

Knowledge Adventure stakes out some important education turf with its Space Adventure title (see fig. 10.11). The videos, the interface, and the sheer fun of learning are captured in all their titles, but their talents are put to particularly good use in Space Adventure.

The main screen allows kids to choose from a variety of topics or to search for their own keywords or phrases. Among some of the main-menu icons they can choose from are a reference library, an overview of our solar system, the galaxy, our planets and moons, and space exploration.

A rotating globe lets kids zoom in on geographical areas, such as Germany, and click various sites related to space, such as the development of the V-2 rocket. Animations concerning everything from the big bang to space stations are viewed in a VCR-like controlled window, with text links to other subjects. A timeline at the bottom of the screen lets kids explore space in history as well, giving them a bird's-eye view of the creation of the solar system, for example.

The narration is great, the animation is top-notch, and the videos and games captivate even the most computer-wary kid. If you have kids, buy this disc.

CD-ROM BOOK
que
AWARD OF EXCELLENCE

Space Adventure

Knowledge Adventure's use of animation, video, sound—and most importantly, solid historical facts and figures—makes this application a spellbinding adventure for any child interested in U.S. manned space flight.

AWARD OF EXCELLENCE

Murmurs of Earth

Warner New Media combines print, audio, and data to produce a unique offering in the form of Murmurs of Earth. This title presents the information that appeared on the side of the Voyager space probe. When Voyager was launched, an optical disc—similar to a CD—went with it to educate anyone who might encounter the probe about the people and practices of Earth. Carl Sagan and others wrote the book accompanying the Murmurs of Earth disc to explain and describe Voyager's interstellar record. This is a great collector's item for any space fan.

Murmurs of Earth

Warner New Media	
Operating System:	DOS 3.3 or above, Macintosh
Interface:	Canned presentation
Multimedia:	Audio, images
Audience:	12 years and up
System Requirements:	VGA or better display

Murmurs of Earth is a record of the information sent into interstellar space with the Voyager space vehicle. It was sent in the form of a laser-disc plaque, along with what were hoped to be universally decodeable instructions for decoding the disc. The instructions started with a hydrogen atom and ended with a diagram of the timing characteristics of the disc's signals (assuming that some very intelligent extraterrestrials would find this probe).

Encoded on the plaque was an array of images, sounds, and messages from the people of Earth. These items fell into ten categories:

Pictures (118)
Some Beethoven
Greetings from then president, Jimmy Carter
A list of members of the United States Congress
Greetings from the secretary general of the United Nations
Greetings in 54 languages
Greetings from the United Nations
Greetings from whales
Sounds of Earth
Music of the world

The CD-ROM portion of Murmurs of Earth is just a small portion of this product. This product is really a multimedia book/CD set. Murmurs comes in a box designed to keep. It holds a 270-page book, *Murmurs of Earth*, published by Random House; a small book of images sent back by the Voyager space probe; and a 2-CD jewel box. This presentation provides a unique combination of traditional printed text, CD audio, and CD-ROM. It is a must-have item for space and technology aficionados and is worth having even if you can't take advantage of the CD-ROM data portion of the product. This may be the first "coffee-table" CD-ROM.

Adult-Literature Discs

Despite all the high-tech computer paraphernalia, jargon, and chipsets in your life, you probably still enjoy some old-fashioned pleasures, like reading a good book. You may not want to hear this, but CD-ROMs have invaded that formerly hallowed turf, too; now you can read a good "text file" of Sherlock Holmes, Dickens, Aristotle, or Shakespeare, all in the comfort of your favorite Super-VGA monitor. The truly conservative can print out the text files and continue reading in the traditional manner. But like it or not, these CD-ROM versions of some of the world's classics have a number of distinct advantages, for both casual readers and serious scholars:

- Less than 1/2,000 of the shelf space is required for the disc as for housing the same amount of text in bound paper form.
- Pages aren't subject to tearing or disfigurement.
- You can choose the typeface, spacing, and type size you want—excellent for visually impaired readers.
- You can search, index, and compare text for a variety of investigative pursuits into author style, language anomalies, syntactical patterns, and usage.

And if all that isn't enough, the CD-ROM versions of collected works are often a fraction of what printed editions can cost. Like them or hate them, CD-ROM collections of literature are growing quickly, for a number of economical and marketing reasons.

First, the publication of collected classics on CD-ROM is a low-cost proposition from a copyright standpoint. Dickens and members of his estate are long gone, and his work has passed into the public domain—as is the case with virtually every author collected on popular classics sets of CDs. That's not to say that the CD is cost-free; there is still the enormous burden of scanning in and carefully proofreading the electronic version of the text to ensure that it matches the author's original published version. But only a compendium of public-domain literature is feasible to publish on one CD-ROM. Imagine the cost, for example, of securing the rights to and publishing the entire works of major American writers from the 1950s and 1960s. If costs could be brought down somehow, both scholars and avid readers would be ecstatic at the prospect of receiving contemporary works on CD. Some efforts are already in the works to do just that. Byron Priess, a new multimedia publishing firm in Brooklyn, has begun to "adapt" some popular works to the CD medium, with stunning results.

Second, other marketing strategies recognize that many works that can be collected and published on CD-ROM have a wide and lasting appeal, both for the sheer joy of reading them and their invaluable use in research and education. Shakespeare's plays, for example, have lasted not simply because the works are deemed literature, but because their themes, characters, and drama still enlighten our human condition today. An illuminating examination of the human spirit and our common dilemmas is the true measure of a work's lasting value.

You can only wonder what William Shakespeare would have thought of having his voluminous handwritten scripts—his entire life's work—reduced to a string of 0s and 1s across a disc no bigger than the palm of his hand. But forget the technology; his work does still exist—whether it's in printer's ink or bits and bytes—and that, after all, is what matters.

Literature Discs You Should Look At

If you have access to the Internet, you have access to many fine collections of famous works in electronic text. If you want to compile your own collection of literature discs, however, consider these titles:

- Library of the Future, 3rd Edition (World Library)
- Great Literature: Personal Library Series (Bureau Development, Inc)
- Holmes on Disc! (Creative Multimedia Corporation)
- Monarch Notes (Bureau Development, Inc)

Discs about Animals and Such

What better topic for multimedia CD-ROMs than animals? They're colorful, we love to watch them move, and the range of sounds they produce is amazing. Throw into the mix that most kids simply love the little critters (and the large ones), and you have the basis for a perfect home CD-ROM application.

This section only scratches the surface of this topic. There are dozens of animal and wildlife applications to choose from, with more coming out every day. Some take a traditional reference approach; others use multimedia in a creative and original manner, organizing and presenting materials in a way that only multimedia can.

Dictionary of the Living World

Compton's New Media	
Operating System:	Windows 3.1
Interface:	Menus
Multimedia:	Video, color graphics, sound
Audience:	Late grammar school and up
System Requirements:	MPC-compatible machine

Although its initial menus are a bit disorienting, the Dictionary of the Living World is a superior CD-ROM application (see fig. 10.12). It isn't just a broad zoological overview of animals; it's an entire biological and entomological examination of life on the planet in multimedia format.

The initial index lists the disc's contents in alphabetical order. The list is long—over 5,000 species are covered. You can browse through the list or pull up a search interface that supports four levels of Boolean searches as well as searches for animations, photos, sounds, and videos. The search engine is fast and efficient; even children in mid-grammar school can learn to perform simple searches with little difficulty. Search results are kept in a list you can conveniently return to again and again, or you can erase the search and start over.

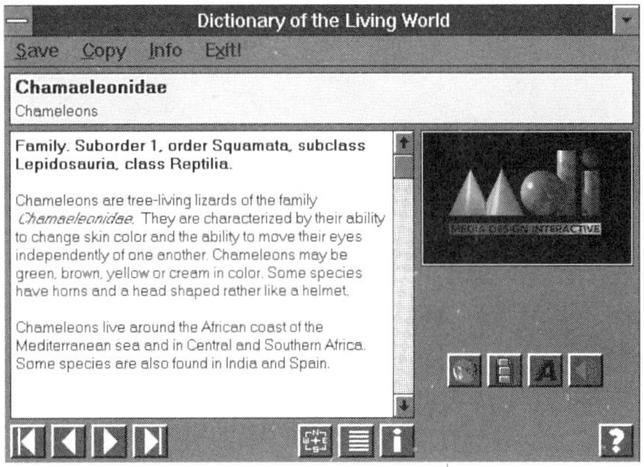

This disc's use of multimedia elements is magnificent. Sounds of various fish, fowl, animals, and insects accompany their photos; clicking the speaker icon gives you a sample. Videos are displayed in a similar way. Videos display well on a VGA monitor, with synchronized sound in some cases. The animations, however, are the most productive. The developers of this application know when to use the proper elements: the animations are instructive and easy to understand, everything that a visual aid is supposed to accomplish. The explanation of chameleon skin-color changes is a fascinating experience.

This disc takes you way beyond a simple visit with our furry friends. The Dictionary of the Living World is a serious—and valuable—learning tool.

FIGURE 10.12

The Dictionary of the Living World is a thoughtful and successful use of multimedia to illustrate science in nature.

The San Diego Zoo Presents...The Animals!

Software Toolworks

Operating System:	Windows 3.1
Interface:	Menus
Multimedia:	Video, color graphics, sound
Audience:	Late preschool through primary school
System Requirements:	MPC-compatible machine

The San Diego Zoo Presents...The Animals! provides a great trip to the San Diego Zoo without the expense of plane fares or wearing out your shoes. The organization of this disc owes its originality to the developers' keen use of multimedia. The main menu is a visual representation of the zoo; you see Rain Forest, Mountains, Temperate Forest, and other habitats (see fig. 10.13). By clicking a "zone," you are transported to that part of the zoo to examine the animals and their habitats for that region. Videos and still photography are plentiful—with the best quality on our VGA monitor being 320-by-240 pixel resolution. Full-screen videos and photos, although available on a 486 PC, are too grainy, but the smaller sizes look gorgeous.

FIGURE 10.13

Although seeing the zoo in person is the best, this disc gives you a great way to visit the San Diego Zoo without leaving your home.

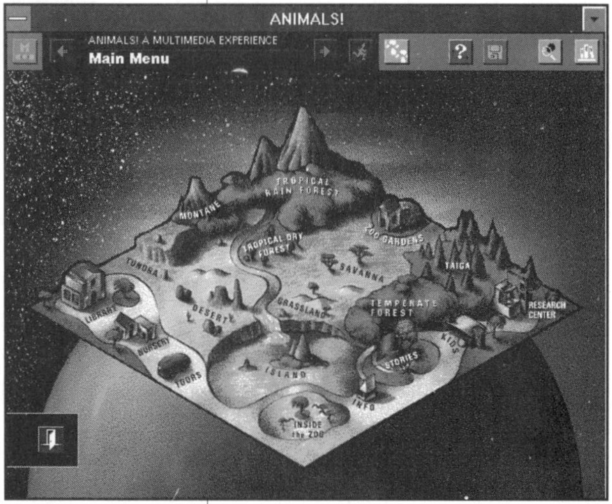

Of course, with animals come sounds, and this disc is full of them, including ambient sounds. When you enter the rain forest section, for example, you hear it drip and echo as a rain forest should. In addition to the tours of the various habitats, children can watch and listen to two dozen informative essays concerning the zoo, including visits with zoo veterinarians and a photo essay on the founding of the zoo in 1922.

Packed onto this disc are 2-1/2 hours of audio, in addition to the text, graphics, 1,300 color photographs, and 82 video clips. This CD must be stuffed to the very edges. In fact, more facts, figures, and text are available here than you can find on an unguided tour of the actual zoo itself; over 2,500 articles, descriptions, and scientific data are a mouse click away. The zoo has over 200 animals to visit, so it's a good thing they're captured on CD: you can return as many times as you like, and the gate is always open.

Children's Literature Discs

The most important things you can do for your children's education is to get them to read and to improve their reading skills. Whether they get their information from a hardbound text, a paperback book, or a CD-ROM database, they'll still be reading. And in this age of information explosion, words are where the information is.

Whatever the medium, look for stories and books that sufficiently challenge your children's skills. Watch their reading progress and suggest books appropriately. Let them explore a number of different types of books—fairy tales, science, contemporary children's stories, and so on. Above all, don't let reading become a chore for them.

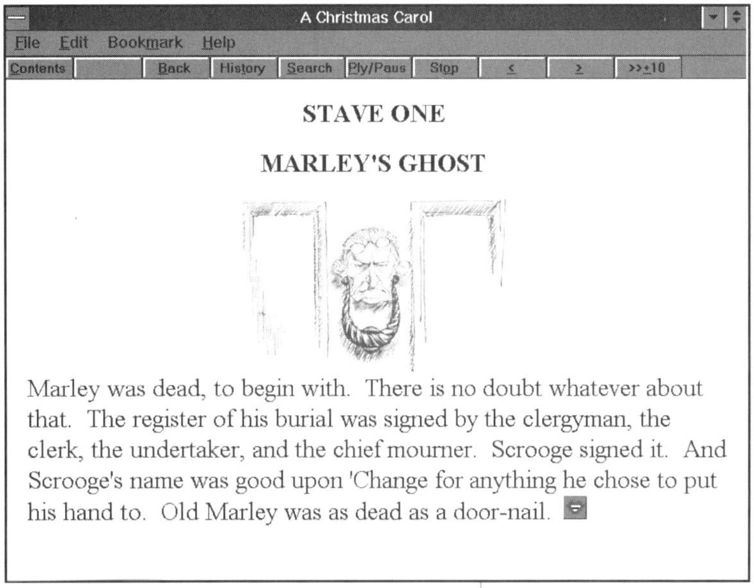

FIGURE 10.14

Charles Dickens' holiday favorite, *A Christmas Carol*, is lovingly presented in this multimedia book adaptation from Ebook.

Just Grandma and Me

Brøderbund

Operating System:	Windows 3.1
Interface:	Menus
Multimedia:	Animated color graphics, sound
Audience:	Late preschool through grammar school
System Requirements:	MPC-compatible machine

Brøderbund calls their list of children's titles the *Living Book* series—an accurate description. Children interact with the characters, the story, and objects in the animated graphics for a full and fun multimedia learning story. Although Brøderbund advises that Just Grandma and Me is for ages 6 through 10, bright late preschoolers get an enormous benefit from interacting with the pictures, characters, and unique vocabulary-building interface, too.

You can set up the story with no narration, allowing advanced readers to read at their own pace, or you can set up the program to narrate the story one page at a time. The story's words are highlighted as the narrator reads, enforcing vocabulary. At any time, the child can click any word to hear it pronounced—a real boon to teaching reading.

The fun rests not only in the clever and fun writing in this Mercer Mayer story, but also in all the surprises hidden in each frame of the story. Clicking a bucket at the beach, for example, causes a fish to leap out and splash back into the water; clicking a tree makes an animated bluebird dive-bomb the roadway and then return to its perch.

This disc also contains an interesting option: you can play it in English, Japanese, or Spanish.

The illustrations, animations, music, and story all combine for a tremendous multimedia storybook. This disc is great fun and a tremendous learning-to-read tool. Buy it for your early readers and let them loose on this brilliant reading adventure.

A Christmas Carol

AWARD OF EXCELLENCE

A Christmas Carol

Ebook's innovative use of the Microsoft Viewer for the presentation of this Dickens' classic will cause you to take a fresh look at this holiday tale. Beautiful illustrations and a databank of old-English Christmas carols round out this high-tech rendition.

Ebook, Inc.	
Operating System:	Windows 3.1
Interface:	Modified Viewer
Multimedia:	Color graphics, sound
Audience:	Late grammar school and up
System Requirements:	MPC-compatible machine

One of the primary reasons books endure despite the onslaught of film and video is that readers still respect and admire a well-turned phrase and the idiosyncratic voices of individual writers. To see a film rendition of Charles Dickens' *A Christmas Carol* is one thing—and a good thing—but to read this classic as Dickens wrote it is to experience the story in a totally new way (see fig. 10.14).

Ebook's presentation is superb. You can elect to read the text, read with narration, or read with both narration and period music. You'll also find a picture and music gallery, so that you and your family can replay the holiday carols or view the illustrations.

The best way to use this multimedia application, however, is simply to read the story. Dickens is considered a great author—and for good reason. His wit, irony, and deft storytelling skills are as apparent and enjoyable today as they were in his own time.

As with all Ebook titles, you can perform searches of the text, skip to particular pages and chapters, click archaic or difficult words to get a pop-up definition, and page through the text at your own pace.

Buy this disc as holiday entertainment for the whole family. By reading along with the text or simply listening to the narration, you and your family will undoubtedly find Ebook's adaptation of *A Christmas Carol* thoroughly entertaining and a learning experience.

The Tale of Peter Rabbit

Discis Knowledge Research

Operating System:	Windows 3.1, DOS 3.3 or above, and Macintosh (on one disc)
Interface:	Menus
Multimedia:	Color graphics, sound
Audience:	Preschool
System Requirements:	MPC-compatible machine

It's easy to see why the Tale of Peter Rabbit has won so many awards and recommendations in the short time since its release. Not only is the original story faithfully reproduced in storybook fashion, but this highly customizable storybook telling of Peter Rabbit is an educational dream come true.

First of all, parents can set up the program for a variety of options, depending on the child's experience and reading level. You can set the pace of the narration, for example, allowing very early readers to follow each word at a more suitable pace. Words can be pronounced by syllable, too, making early pronunciation of more difficult words easier to master. Other levels allow you to include designations for the parts of speech, determine whether sound effects should be included, and set the story so that it is read in Spanish.

The original illustrations are reproduced with great effect in 256-color VGA, and the narration is perfect. When readers click words and objects in the illustrations, the words are pronounced.

Because this storybook is a classic, the multimedia elements make it an even stronger learning tool. The Discis series is great. Please consider all their titles for your home learning and reading library.

Language-Instruction Discs

Here's a perfect case for CD-ROM multimedia. How better to learn a language than to hear it being spoken? How better to navigate foreign vocabulary than at your own pace? The two multimedia foreign-language systems discussed in this section are good examples of what's possible with this technology, especially for the foreign-language student in your home. If your children need additional work on their foreign-language skills, these products can help them more quickly assimilate a second tongue.

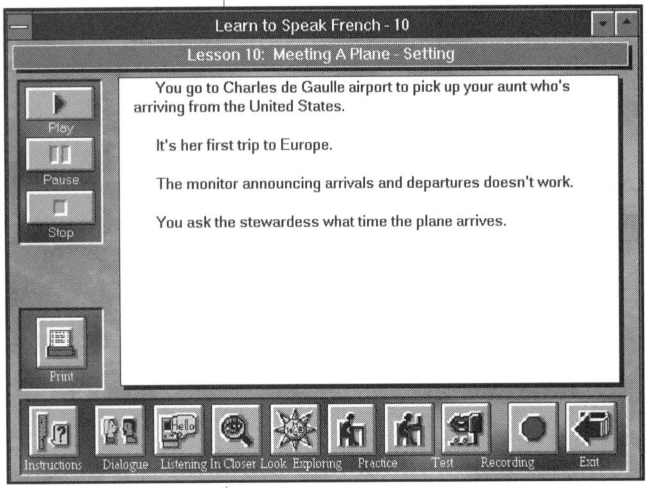

FIGURE 10.15

The Learn To Speak series from Hyperglot is a great home-study disc for virtually any intermediate learner.

Learn To Speak...

Hyperglot

Operating System:	Windows 3.1
Interface:	Menus
Multimedia:	Color graphics, sound
Audience:	Late grammar school and up
System Requirements:	MPC-compatible machine

Hyperglot publishes a series of these CD-ROM-based language tutors that are as comprehensive as any intermediate-level language text (see fig. 10.15). You can view or use the CD by starting with its table of contents, which features a parts-of-speech tutorial and a conversational tutorial. You can skip back and forth between the tutorials if you want. For example, you can read up on the common verb forms in French and then take a hypertext jump to a narrated conversation that employs many of these constructions.

The depth of coverage is great. The tutorials and conversations are well done, and the use of the CD technology—hypertext, search capabilities, and audio narration—is super.

This series is a recommended supplement to any language student's arsenal to become fluent—or conversant—in any of the major languages. The Hyperglot series features language courses in French, German, Spanish, and Italian.

Playing with Language

Syracuse Language Systems

Operating System:	Windows 3.1
Interface:	Menus
Multimedia:	Color graphics, sound
Audience:	Early primary through beginning secondary school
System Requirements:	MPC-compatible machine

Syracuse Language Systems takes a novel approach to using multimedia to its fullest in this series of language discs. Not meant as a comprehensive "from the ground up" way to learn a language, this series focuses on improving literacy and cognition in the language your student is mastering (see fig. 10.16).

The games are completely narrated in the foreign language, with instructions and questions spoken in a normal manner; in other words, the narrator doesn't slow down his or her speech for the sake of comprehension. The games themselves are a series of graphic scenarios. For example, a park near a lake shows a number of children in different activities. Speaking in the foreign language, the narrator asks the student which child is sleeping. When the student clicks on the correct child in the picture, he or she is congratulated; if the student misses, the activity of the incorrect choice is narrated, and the original question is asked again.

This disc provides an entirely natural way to learn a language, and when you think about it, it's the way we all learned our native tongue. This series of discs is not intended to replace basic language-learning courses; it reinforces and broadens the student's cognitive skills in using a foreign language. Its aim is to remove the word *foreign* from foreign-language learning, and it does a superlative job.

The discs come in a variety of languages, including Spanish, French, and German. In addition, there are various levels of difficulty within each language. You can start out with the disc Introductory Games in Spanish, for example, and then move up to the intermediate and advanced discs, each sold separately.

FIGURE 10.16

The Playing with Language series takes an interactive approach to learning, using graphics-based games for positive reinforcement.

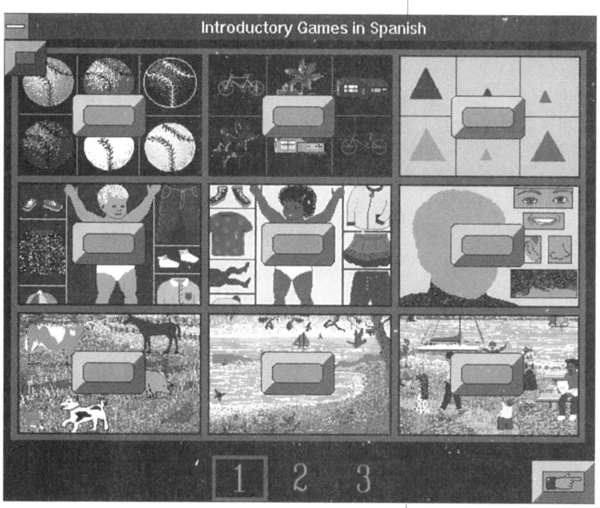

CD-ROM BOOK
QUE
AWARD OF EXCELLENCE

Musical Instruments

Microsoft's Musical Instruments CD may be the most beautiful presentation of any of the software titles we looked at. This encyclopedia includes the pictures and sounds of an enormous collection of musical instruments—from the common penny whistle to the obscure nose flute. The interface, illustrations, and high-fidelity musical samples are superb. You *need* this CD.

Music Discs

What a natural! Music instruction, history, and education on CD—the predominate media for music distribution. Of course, the multimedia CD-ROM delivers graphics, stereo sound, and tons of text to round out the music it can deliver. The following CD titles are some of the best music education and reference CDs you can find. This segment of the multimedia CD-ROM marketplace might be the fastest growing and most creative of all.

Musical Instruments

Microsoft Corporation

Operating System:	Windows 3.1 with MPC extensions
Interface:	Full Windows interface
Multimedia:	Picture, sound
Audience:	Preschool to adult
System Requirements:	MPC-compatible machine

FIGURE 10.17

Microsoft's Musical Instruments CD-ROM provides one of the most engaging MPC presentations available.

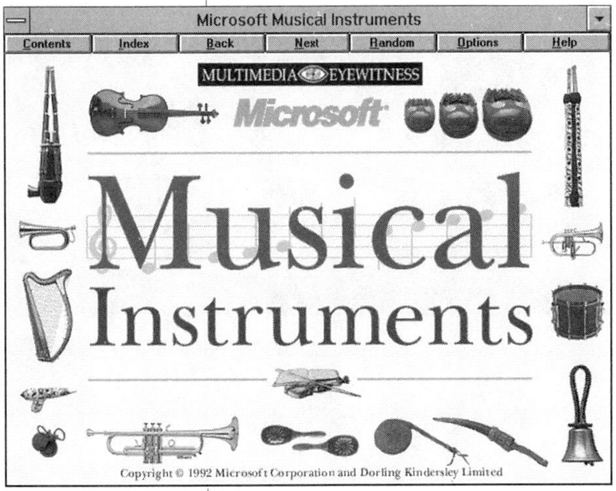

The beautiful pictures in this CD-ROM presentation come from a very well-done picture book originally published in England—and they translate well to the computer screen (see fig. 10.17). Examples of music and musical timbres cover instruments from the everyday instruments familiar to everyone, to instruments whose names and sounds you might never hear anywhere other than on this CD-ROM.

The information is organized into four formats:

- **Families of Instruments.** This section of the disc includes these categories: Brass, Strings, Woodwinds, Keyboards, and Percussion. Each category includes instruments not normally encountered but classed with the rest in their group.

- **Musical Ensembles.** Orchestras, rock bands, wind bands, chamber groups, jazz bands, steel bands, and gamelans are covered, with descriptions of the groups, their instruments, and musical examples.

- **Instruments of the World.** Laid out on a world map, this section groups instruments by region. You click a region and then an instrument to get detailed information about your choice.

- **A—Z of Instruments.** Just what it says—an alphabetical listing of all the instruments on the disc.

If you have children, or any interest in musical instruments yourself, put this disc on your required list. You'll not be disappointed.

Composer Quest

Doctor T's Music Software	
Operating System:	Windows 3.0 or above
Interface:	Menus
Multimedia:	Color graphics, sound
Audience:	Late grammar school and up
System Requirements:	MPC-compatible machine

The premise behind Composer Quest is good fun: you're given a fragment of music to listen to and then you're supposed to jump back in time to identify its composer.

The time-machine interface allows you to jump to particular musical periods—Romantic, Classical, Jazz, and so on. Once in the selected period, you can "interrogate" composers, who give you clues about the whereabouts in time of the composer of the mystery piece. These clues are biographical, musical, and historical facts about the era, the composer, and musical history. So although the clues are useful in helping you win the game, you learn a lot about music in the process as well.

The game never takes itself too seriously, and children of all ages will be entertained and challenged at the same time. In addition to the game, you can play the music tracks alone or skip along the timelines for interesting biographies and musical history. Music students of all ages will find this disc amusing and informative.

Jazz: A Multimedia History

Compton's New Media

Operating System:	Windows 3.1
Interface:	Modified Viewer
Multimedia:	Video, color graphics, sound
Audience:	Secondary school and up
System Requirements:	MPC-compatible machine

From the beginnings of jazz in the late 19th century through fusion and avant garde in the 1970s and 1980s, Jazz: A Multimedia History, from Compton's New Media, takes you on a visual, historical, and music-filled tour of the greatest influences in America's native musical form (see fig. 10.18).

The text, brilliantly written by Lewis Parker and Michael Ullman, traces the great movements in jazz throughout this century. Text is highlighted with musical scores and hundreds of still photos and video clips. Among the clips are a rare television appearance of Billie Holiday on CBS television in the '50s, and Miles Davis and John Coltrane. Many of the photos from the '20s, '30s, and '40s are from the Rutgers Institute for Jazz Studies and reproduce well on a VGA screen.

Music lovers will appreciate the numerous live music cuts on this disc, many of which have long been out of circulation. The presentation finishes up with an extensive bibliography, discography, and an interview with the authors.

Music lovers, especially jazz aficionados, will want this disc as a complement to their collection; the bibliography alone may be worth the price of this disc.

FIGURE 10.18

Video, live jazz recordings, and hundreds of photos and illustrations make Compton's Jazz: A Multimedia History a demonstration of multimedia at its best.

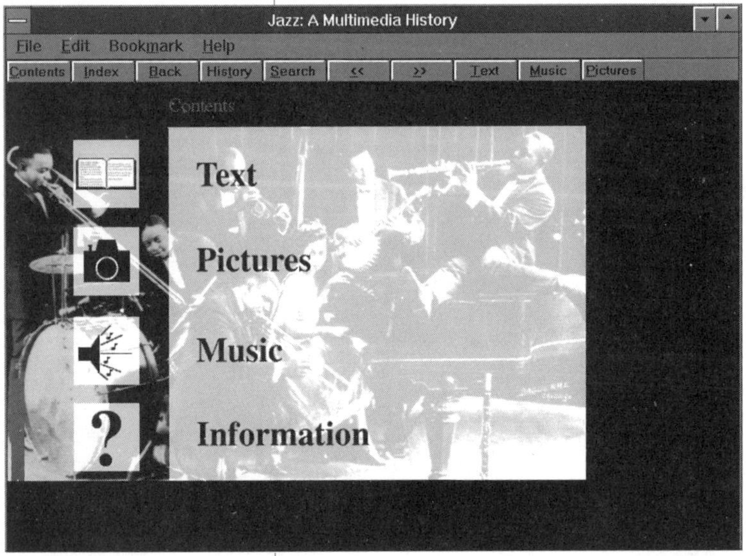

Geography, Atlases, and Travel Discs

What better place to store full-color graphics images of maps than on CD-ROM? This genre of CD-ROM publishing is growing more popular every day, with atlases, mapping programs, world tours, and travelogs finding a natural home on the ample storage medium of CD-ROM and today's full-color, high-resolution PC monitors. And that's key: the better your graphics card and display, the more utility you'll get out of these geography, mapping, and travel programs.

Street Atlas USA

DeLorme Mapping

Operating System:	Windows 3.1
Interface:	Full Windows interface
Multimedia:	Color pictures
Audience:	7 years and up
System Requirements:	VGA or better display

The low end of DeLorme's atlas products, Street Atlas USA is a marvel, particularly considering its low price. Street Atlas is a searchable street atlas, much like a paper, with two important differences. First, the searches are computerized and can be made by place name, street name, ZIP code, and area code/exchange. The second difference is the startling fact that just about every street in the U.S. is in this atlas (see fig. 10.19).

You'll have a tough time trying to stump Street Atlas USA, even when you search for obscure streets gleaned from your friends' hometowns—and this isn't just a marketing claim. What makes these searches possible is the combination of CD-ROM technology and DeLorme's Xmap technology, which allows the compact storage and quick retrieval of all those streets and other map features.

Street Atlas USA is essentially a stripped-down version of another DeLorme product, Map Expert, described in Chapter 9, "CD-ROM in Business." Compared to Map Expert, Street Atlas USA is "crippled." It is missing some features that professional map users may prefer to have, such as high-resolution export of maps and longitude/latitude data. This product's reduced capabilities, however, are offset by its reduced price, putting this disc in the reach of the home user.

Street Atlas is great for research, travel planning, and just plain fun. Put this disc on your want list.

FIGURE 10.19

Street Atlas USA contains virtually every street in the nation, all on one disc.

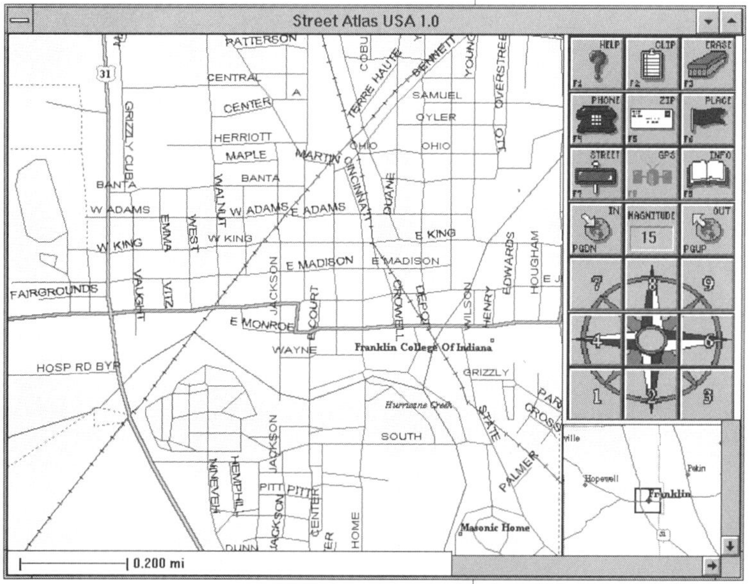

Cooking Discs

Like every other type of book that takes up a lot of shelf space (or a kitchen drawer, in this case), cookbooks are a natural for CD-ROM. Multimedia cookbooks (including animated or videotaped cooking tips and databases of ingredients and substitutions) are popping up everywhere. One drawback, of course, is that most people don't have a PC in the kitchen, and don't want to move it from the den to the countertop when dinner time rolls around.

FIGURE 10.20

Better Homes and Gardens Healthy Cooking shows the nutritional content for each dish.

Better Homes and Gardens Healthy Cooking

Multicom Publishing

Operating System:	Mac and Windows 3.1
Interface:	Full menu/icon/ button interface
Multimedia:	Color pictures, video clips, and sound
Audience:	Adults
System Requirements:	Graphics display

The cookbook to beat is Better Homes and Gardens Healthy Cooking. Not only does it offer 80 full-motion videos of cooking techniques and 400 health-conscious recipes, but its database can find recipes that match the ingredients you've got on hand, print out shopping lists for a weekly menu plan, and show you the calorie and nutritional information for every recipe (see fig. 10.20). And you don't have to worry about getting spaghetti sauce on your keyboard—every recipe is printable. For a little multimedia spice, all the international recipes play ethnic music while you read them.

Lifestyles of the Rich and Famous Cookbook

Compton's New Media

Operating System:	Windows 3.1
Interface:	Full menu/icon/ button interface
Multimedia:	Color photo- graphs, audio, video
Audience:	Adult
System Requirements:	Graphics display

Cockney mogul Robin Leach serves up a collection of the stars' favorite morsels on this impressively produced platter. Not only do you get illustrated recipes for dozens of extravagant dishes, you also can view videos of some of the stars over the stove. No, you won't see a video of Ivana Trump's blintzing tips, but you will see a segment on her life and career as produced for the Lifestyles of the Rich and Famous television show. The disc also includes interviews with Jerry Lewis, Eva Gabor, Joan Collins, and Martha Stewart (the video describes Martha as "the super-guru of home entertaining"), among others.

The real stars of this disc, the recipes, are fit for just about every taste and lifestyle (see fig. 10.21). From Katie Couric's chilled cream of carrot soup to the sinful chocolate tulips from Liz Taylor's most recent wedding, you get meals to suit everyone from the health-conscious to the...well...*less* health-conscious.

The disc also includes cooking tips—or at least one cooking tip. We may have been doing something wrong during our review, but no matter what we tried, the Tips button on the menu bar always gave us the same tip: "Herbs," which contains extensive advice on using herbs instead of salt.

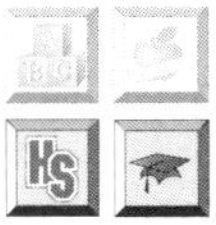

FIGURE 10.21

A sample from Robin Leach's extravagant Lifestyles of the Rich and Famous Cookbook.

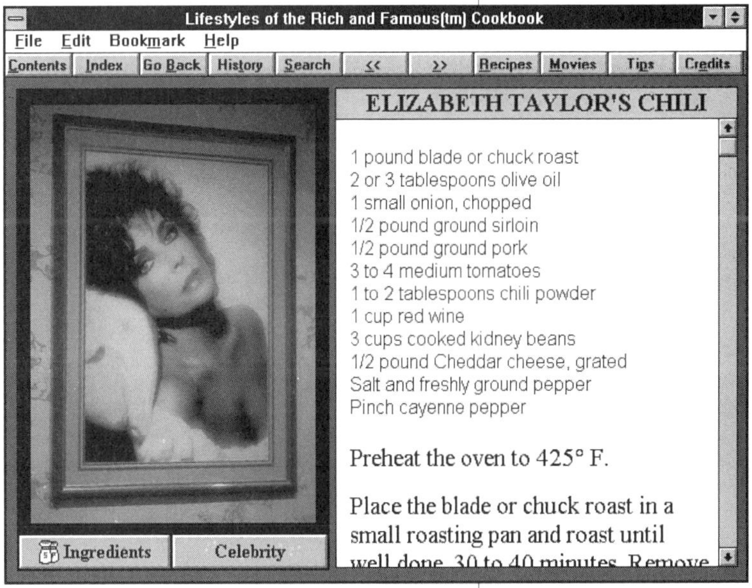

Chapter 11

CD-ROM for After Hours

You've spent a long hard day at your home computer researching tax code or assembling a bibliography of articles concerning your company's competition. And your children just want to do something on a rainy day besides watching even more TV. A CD-ROM game can be just the answer; after all, we all have to have some fun. And CD-ROM games are the best entertainment values going right now.

In this chapter, we've done our best to round up the latest and greatest CD-ROM gaming titles. In each review, we'll give you a thumbnail sketch of the game's objectives and play as well as a handy specification checklist to make it easier to determine which titles are compatible with your system. We've organized the titles into categories: Action/Adventure, Arcade and Board, Mystery, Children's, and Music discs. We've also estimated the audience level for each, with tips on content where appropriate.

Today's Game Technology

If you've been following PC game technology for the last several years, you've noticed a significant change. Games are more sophisticated, employing 3D graphics and animation lavishly rendered in full color; sound has evolved from simple *blips* and *beeps* to full-stereo MIDI orchestration accompanied by speech; and game complexity has grown accordingly, with engaging story lines, plots, and characters. PC games have traditionally been installed on the hard drive of your computer; but all these advances and improvements in sound, graphics, and story eat tons of disk space. For example, Origin's Wing Commander II—the most advanced space shoot-'em-up ever produced—needs over 25 megabytes of hard drive real estate when fully installed—without the speech modules!

It's easy to see why game producers have embraced CD-ROM technology as the development medium of choice. No longer hamstrung by the limited and valuable space of customer's hard drives, they now have over 600 megabytes of development elbow-room in which to let their creations run wild. The only restriction imposed on the game producers when moving to CD-ROM is the drive's relatively slow speed. Remember, the best CD-ROM drives have access times (that is, the time it takes to find data) in the 200-to-280 millisecond range; most hard drives can access data under 20 milliseconds. Transfer rates (that is, the time it takes to move data), of course, are also much slower for CD-ROM and contribute to the challenge of delivering the game in a format that is not distracting or annoyingly slow. The most ingenious developers have cleverly minimized the effects of slow CD-ROM drive speed by **caching** significant portions of their games in computer memory just before playback.

EXPLANATION

Caching

The useful concept of caching is used in most computer technology. Caching leverages a smaller amount of faster, more expensive storage for dynamic use; the slower, cheaper media provides mass storage. Caching works like this: data that is needed now—or that a program guesses will be needed soon—is moved from slower storage (CD-ROM, disk, and so on) to faster "storage" (RAM, fast disk, and so on). This process allows the required data to be retrieved in a timely fashion. Caching is especially useful to games where the goal is smooth animation or sound, and a still or silent pause is not problematic.

Pauses for drawing data from the CD into cache are timed to occur between scenes or game levels, where they are less noticeable and don't affect the playability of the game. Other developers use a disk cache or copy bit-intensive files to the hard disk, which is a less desirable but understandable alternative for some action-packed games that need many megabytes of data on faster media.

There's good news on both fronts—CD-ROM technology and game development. First, CD-ROM access times and transfer rates are improving steadily. And game developers are getting more adept at porting existing games or developing new games to accommodate the new technology. As a consumer, you'll do well to keep one thing in mind: because games and other multimedia applications require the most horsepower you can provide, you'll see the best possible results—and enjoy your play all the more—if you purchase the fastest CD-ROM drive you can afford. See Chapter 3, "How To Select CD-ROM Drives," for a full rundown on current CD-ROM drives and their specifications. If you already own a CD-ROM drive and want to increase its performance, you can include more caching buffers on the drive or consider a commercial CD-ROM-caching program.

The Current State of the Gaming Art—and What's Next

The sound, animation, and graphics capabilities of your system determine whether you get the optimum use of the multimedia technology that has been exploited to its fullest by today's game producers. We've already mentioned the need for a fast CD-ROM drive—MPC Level 1 compliance (single-speed CD-ROM) is already too slow for many of today's games. But even your graphics adapter, sound card, and speaker systems must be up-to-date to get the full effect of some of the latest gaming thrills. For example, speech recorded to CD in 16 bits becomes gravelly and scratchy when played on an 8-bit card; through inferior speakers, the mellow tones of Don Pardo doing voice-overs in Space Quest IV, for example, become a tinny representation of his voice. Similarly, music takes a heavy hit in quality when played over 8-bit systems. Animations run faster and more smoothly if your system is at least a 486SX 25 MHz (MPC Level 2 minimum spec) and has a solid accelerated graphics card. That's not to say that slower systems can't run the latest CD-ROM software—developers must be careful not to go too far, too fast, and leave behind an installed system base that can still benefit from their latest software. But the industry—and games in particular—are moving toward this type of configuration for the best results in gaming and multimedia performance:

- A 486SX 25 MHz or better processor
- 4 megabytes or more of RAM
- Accelerated Super-VGA adapter
- 16-bit sound card with DAC (Digital-to-Analog Converter)
- Amplified speakers with bass boost or subwoofers
- 300 millisecond CD-ROM drive with 64 KB buffer and double-speed transfer rate or better

Speech and Sound

Most games on CD-ROM now incorporate some speech. Sierra Online (one of the most innovative game producers and one of the first to incorporate speech into their games) has gone so far as to develop lip-syncing technology into their speech-enhanced games. Characters actually look as though they are mouthing the words rather than moving their lips in some poorly dubbed Godzilla-like movie. In earlier disk-based versions of games, speech was used sparingly—or not at all—because of space limitations. (Remember that one minute of speech takes several megabytes of disk space.) As a result, disk-based versions of games relegated all story narration and instruction to text boxes floating amid the graphics panels. With speech-enhanced CD-ROM games, the panels are gone, giving the player an unobstructed view of the action or story.

Most high-end games incorporate MIDI (Musical Instrument Digital Interface) or Red Book audio (audio stored on the CD) music as background for their games now. Only a true 16-bit sound card can reproduce these effects accurately. Cards that incorporate sampled sounds do an even better job and may become increasingly affordable and prevalent in the months to come.

Graphics and Animation

Most games—even those on CD-ROM—have been limited to EGA and VGA resolutions. The technology exists to use higher resolution and provide more detailed graphics, but developers must create their games for a home market where the predominant display adapter has been a standard VGA—or even an EGA. That's changing. A handful of titles now support Super-VGA displays up to 800 by 600 pixels and over 35,000 colors, nearly doubling the resolution of graphics and adding a 16-fold increase to the number of colors artists can paint with. For an eye-popping look at what's possible in Super-VGA graphics and animation, look at a release by Virgin Games: The 7th Guest features lush, realistic detailing and smooth animation as you move from room to spooky room in a haunted house; this type of realism can be rendered only with a high-resolution video card. Increasingly, game developers will move to the higher-resolution platforms; most no longer support EGA displays or adapters.

Some developers are beginning to experiment with full-motion video as well. Interplay, Virgin, CMC, and Sierra Online have all released or are about to release game titles that incorporate some elements of video through custom overlay, Video for Windows, or through Micromind's Projector technologies.

Computer gaming is an art form where some developers are concerned. Those in the forefront, as mentioned, are already utilizing the best in sound, graphics, and animation. They prefer to offer products with the best animation, graphics, video, and sound that technology allows. And more and more users are upgrading their systems—which is good news. Once a significant number of systems have higher-end displays and sound capabilities, software developers can begin to fully exploit the capacity of CD-ROM and the latest generation of 16-bit audio cards.

About This Chapter

This chapter describes some of the most innovative game titles available on CD-ROM. Although this chapter describes several dozen titles, hundreds more are available. For information about additional game titles, look at Que's *1995 CD-ROM Buyer's Guide*, which lists hundreds of CD-ROMs.

How To Use This Chapter

The description of each product in this chapter begins with a chart; which provides consistent at-a-glance information.

A few superlative products have been given an Award of Excellence (we explain why these titles are the cream of the crop in the margin-note text accompanying the award icon).

Action/Adventure Discs

Get set for some thrilling contests when you pop one of these action/adventure discs into your CD-ROM drive. Some of the best games on the software shelves fall into this category. Be prepared for lots of nifty graphics, walls of sound, and stunning animation. If you've ever played Dungeons and Dragons—or ever wanted to—you'll find something to love in the titles presented here.

Getting Help

If you get so frustrated you can't stand it anymore, hints and tips are available for many popular games—CD-ROM-based or otherwise—on CompuServe's Games forum. You'll probably need a Universal Hint viewer for the hint files (also available on the forum). Type **GO GAMERS** at the CIS prompt.

Space Quest IV

Sierra Online	
Operating System:	DOS 3.3 or above, Windows 3.1 with MPC extensions
Interface:	Point and click
Pointing Devices:	Mouse, keyboard, joystick
Sound:	All major cards
Graphics:	256-color VGA
Audience:	Ages 15 and up

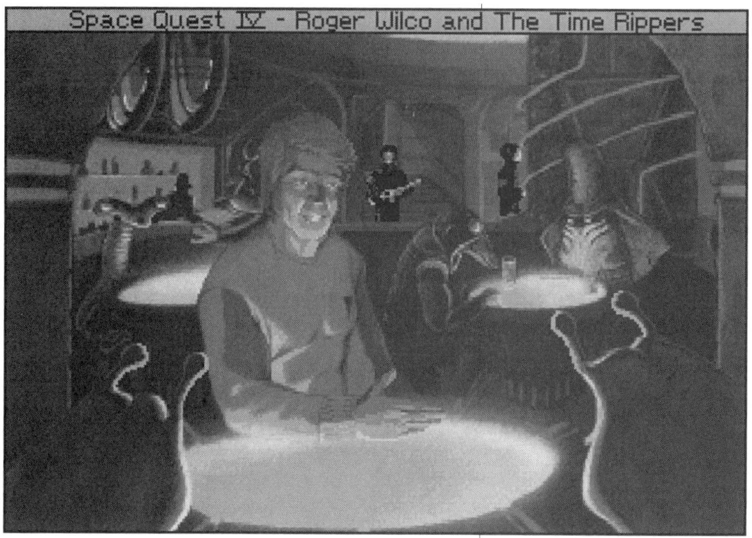

FIGURE 11.1

Space Quest IV on CD-ROM is campier than ever with narration and voice-overs adding new dimension to an old favorite.

Sierra Online's Space Quest series is another long-lasting success story. The main character in all the titles is Roger Wilco; he began the series as a janitor aboard an intergalactic garbage scow, only to have fate step in and launch him through a series of adventures throughout the known—and unknown—universe. The series is decidedly tongue-in-cheek, and the hero is as reluctant as he is unlucky. You guide Roger through his exploits, and hopefully, to victory (see fig. 11.1).

In this fourth installment—Alien Time Rippers—Roger finds himself chased out of a back-galaxy dive by a cadre of storm troopers. While making his escape, he's rescued by a stranger who has, as Roger puts it, "an overgrown hair dryer" that rips open an escape hatch. Roger leaps through, only to find himself back on his home planet—Xenon—many decades into the future.

The puzzles, conundrums, and scavenger hunts in the game are difficult. There are even a number of interesting arcade-style hurdles to leap as you progress through the many levels, and Roger (in harmony with the rest of the cast) is as sarcastic and hapless as ever. For example, when Roger finds himself suddenly transported back to an episode from Space Quest I, the scenery looks odd: it's in 16-color EGA graphics. One of the characters quips, "That's all we had back then." To enhance the off-beat mood, you also get narration with the pizzazz and aplomb that only Don Pardo can provide.

This is definitely a teens-and-up kind of game, if for nothing else than the quips, situations, and level of difficulty. The humor, we're sure, may not be for everyone, but then neither are role-playing games. This kind of CD-ROM game, however, really shows what the technology—and creative developers—can do.

Wing Commander/Ultima VI: The False Prophet

Origin	
Operating System:	DOS 3.3 or above
Interface:	Menu
Pointing Devices:	Joystick, mouse
Sound:	All major cards
Graphics:	256-color Super-VGA
Audience:	Ages 12 and up

In Wing Commander/Ultima VI: The False Prophet, Origin has combined two of its most popular titles on one CD-ROM (two games for the price of one on this two-CD set that takes up only a fraction of the shelf space of the disk-based version). Nothing has been enhanced from the diskette-distributed version, but if you don't own either and want a good Origin sampler, this is a good CD to start with.

FIGURE 11.2

Wing Commander II, complete with 80 missions, great stereo sound, and full speech, is the best space game on the shelves.

Wing Commander

One of the programs on this combo-CD is the ground-breaking Wing Commander. Its use of detailed graphics and animation upped the ante in the PC game industry and competitors have been trying to catch up since.

In this role-playing action game, you're a pilot aboard a space station behind the battle lines. The Kilrathi, a lion-like race of aliens, is bent on destroying the human race and occupying its worlds. A routine escort mission to the front gets you wrapped up in the heat of battle—despite the objections of one of your former superior officers. Subsequent missions get more furious and heated, with as many as 12 high-speed enemy fighters involved in the fray.

Because you fly a variety of ships and missions, Wing Commander is tricky to master—but a built-in flight simulator or trainer and advice from the more seasoned pilots in the lounge are enough to help you rack up kills on subsequent missions. Before each mission, you're briefed and sent out. You control the ship's path and all armaments. Often you fly in formation with one or more pilots—with communication between ships a must in coordinating a successful mission. Surviving a mission is tough, and when you die—and you will—you have the option of replaying the mission until you come out unscratched. And if living through a Kilrathi cat-fight isn't enough, you can vaporize yourself docking your craft improperly, so handle your landings with finesse as well.

The missions, the graphics, and even the sounds are great. It's easy to see why the hard-drive version of this game was so popular—even when it ate up 15 megabytes of precious disk space. Packing this and Ultima VI on one disc is worth the price.

Wing Commander II Deluxe Edition

If the missions in Wing Commander I weren't enough, get the deluxe edition of Wing Commander (a separate purchase, but worth it). Slip this CD into the drive and hang onto your joystick (see fig. 11.2). This CD contains over 80 missions, all of Wing Commander II, the optional Special Operations I and II packages, and the Speech Accessory Pack—all of which can overwhelm the average home-based PC hard drive. There are, in fact, more missions here than on *all* the diskette-based versions.

After a near-disaster at the end of Wing Commander I, you are court-martialed and relieved of your combat status. Renewed fighting and a quirk of fate push you back into the battle—against a superior officer's wish. You're fighting many of your own crew members as well as the Kilrathi in this episode.

The formula here is the same as the original—more briefings and more space battles. The addition of speech and a more complex story line, however, make this a superior game to the original Wing Commander. The action is just as tough to master, with the addition of a few unexpected enemy wrinkles to keep even the best fliers from getting too cocky. If you want to see high-speed action at its best, test out this CD.

Ultima VI: The False Prophet

The Ultima series may never die—through time, interplanetary travel, and underground, its various permutations and story line just keep going. Each new chapter, it should be mentioned, gains a more sophisticated interface, richer graphics, and better stories.

Ultima VI: The False Prophet is the sixth in the series and is included with Wing Commander on one CD. This time, you are taken once again to Britannia—a medieval world of knights, villains, supernatural powers, and magic. The hero—Avatar—must take on the hordes of Gargoyles who have escaped from the underworld to threaten all of Britannia. The Gargoyles lay siege to important Britannia strongholds and places of knowledge, so it's imperative that you, Avatar, come to the rescue. Hints are given that the Gargoyles have risen in search of something that can make them even more powerful, so your fight is one against time as well.

The Ultima interface is easy to use: you move your band of collected characters around the countryside and through village and city by clicking the mouse. You can rearm or use items any member is carrying by selecting their character. Like most role-playing games, you amass a small band of multitalented assistants and find a way to defeat the enemy by collecting armor, money, and jewels; most importantly, you must build your strengths and spell-casting abilities.

Myst

Brøderbund	
Operating System:	Windows 3.1 or Macintosh
Interface:	Point and click
Pointing Devices:	Mouse
Sound:	All major cards
Graphics:	VGA
Audience:	Ages 12 and up

CD-ROM BOOK
QUE
AWARD OF EXCELLENCE

Myst

All right, we'll admit it's pretty trendy for books and magazines to give awards to Myst right now, but we're not just hopping on the bandwagon. This is one of the most artistic games—visually and conceptually—we've ever seen. This is the one to get the new video card and big screen monitor for.

Adventure games used to be strictly text-based: you typed commands to move around and perform actions and saw text explaining what happened. Then the games sprouted still pictures and sounds to go with the basic text interface, so that you saw or heard what happened after you typed your commands. Newer adventure games have animated characters, music, and speech, and you can choose icons instead of typing commands, but the games are still not far from their roots. Myst, however, is a giant leap forward in the evolution of adventure games—there are no commands at all, just you in a virtual world. When you enter Myst's world, there is no menu, no status screen, just a new reality you have to interact with. You point at objects and click them to perform actions, and you click the surroundings to move around.

Myst is very subtle, which makes it an eerie and exciting experience. You may find helpful objects, but they don't go out of their way to be found—a pleasant change from games that visually highlight important objects with different colors or lighting.

It's also beautifully illustrated, with over 2,500 near-photorealistic images including rich textures like marble and cherry wood (see fig. 11.3). Most of the exterior scenes have a misty quality and subtle animations (moving water, flying birds in the distance), which adds to the realism and eeriness of the journey.

In short, put down this book and go buy this game. And get a glare filter while you're out—you'll be glued to your screen for a while.

FIGURE 11.3

Stepping out of a building into the virtual world of Myst.

Critical Path

Media Vision

Operating System:	Windows 3.1
Interface:	Point and click
Pointing Devices:	Mouse
Sound:	All major cards
Graphics:	256-color Super-VGA
Audience:	Ages 12 and up

Actress Eileen Weisinger stars in this intensely realistic game as Kat, a helicopter pilot you must help escape from a dangerous fortress. The twisted Generalissimo Minh is the mastermind behind this highly booby-trapped facility, but he is also your only source of clues—he's kindly left a notebook of mysterious ramblings laying around in the control center, which you've now taken over.

You communicate with Kat through a communications module—you click on the direction you want her to go or on the Alert button, and she responds by voice. You also have some control over the Generalissimo's booby-traps through a slightly-damaged control panel.

Critical Path is dramatic and exciting, but it's more movie than game—you watch more than you play. Kat spends a few minutes walking from dangerous scene to dangerous scene; in most cases, you only have to push one or two of the right buttons to get her out of it. Still, deciphering the villain's notes and knowing which buttons to press is something of a challenge. The action and special effects are straight out of Hollywood, as is the dialogue (which includes some network-TV-level swearing).

Loom

LucasArts	
Operating System:	DOS 3.3 or above
Interface:	Point and click
Pointing Devices:	Mouse, keyboard
Sound:	All major cards
Graphics:	256-color VGA
Audience:	Ages 10 and up

Loom is an adventure game with a musical twist. As the hero of this game, you must collect magical spells and powers by weaving musical passages—the more you collect, the more power you receive. Spells include Invisibility, Terror, Healing, and Night Vision. As a novice spell weaver, you must collect as many spells as possible because your journey to restore the master loom is fraught with obstacles and puzzles (see fig. 11.4).

FIGURE 11.4

Gather spells, power, and musical ability with LucasArts' Loom.

The graphics here are a great lure to children of virtually any age. The gathering of spells from musical notes is a tricky—and fun—way for children to learn notation: they must assemble the spells by writing the notes on staffs within the Book of Patterns, a booklet included with the game.

The sound effects and music are great, and the narration is suitably other-worldish. If your child likes music and puzzle-solving, this is a good game, although not as challenging as some other titles in the LucasArts list.

Sam and Max Hit the Road

LucasArts

Operating System:	DOS 3.3 or above
Interface:	Point and click
Pointing Devices:	Mouse, keyboard
Sound:	All major cards
Graphics:	256-color VGA
Audience:	Ages 12 and up

Sam and Max Hit the Road is a great example of what video game makers have been trying to accomplish for years—professional-quality animation that is totally user controllable. The characters move smoothly—walking, gesturing, and bouncing around—like real cartoon characters instead of the dressed-up stick figures gamers have been stuck with for years. When the characters speak, their lips are synced (more or less) with their words. One of the best things we can say about this game (and Maniac Mansion's Day of the Tentacle, another LucasArts title) is this: it's so good, you don't notice the technology.

Don't be fooled by the fact that the title characters are a bunny and a dog—this ain't kids' stuff. Sam and Max are accurately described on the box as "twisted," "bizarre," "quirky," and "deranged" (especially Max).

FIGURE 11.5

A typically twisted scene from the beginning of Sam and Max Hit the Road.

The game follows them on a hilarious trek through America's sleaziest tourist traps, and it's so close to the truth as to embarrass travelers of all ages.

Check out Sam and Max for one of the most purely entertaining games around.

Maniac Mansion's Day of the Tentacle

LucasArts

Operating System:	DOS 3.3 or above
Interface:	Point and click, text
Pointing Devices:	Mouse, keyboard
Sound:	All major cards
Graphics:	256-color VGA
Audience:	Ages 12 and up

Sharing the animation quality and (slightly less twisted) wit of Sam and Max Hit the Road, Day of the Tentacle is another of LucasArts' titles that can entertain any age group. Most of the characters are human, except for the villain, who is a power-mad disembodied purple tentacle with superpowers gained from drinking toxic waste. At the start of the story, the tentacle is safely tied up out of harm's way, but a well-intentioned nerd (you) frees it before remembering that's not such a good idea.

From the outset, Day of the Tentacle presents itself as a farce—and shows that LucasArts can poke fun at itself. In one of the early scenes, for example, your character sees a calendar with a picture of Darth Vader, and exclaims, "It's a calendar from my favorite movie!"

Later in the game, you control any of three different characters, depending on which of three time periods you're in. You'll need items from each time period to stop the Tentacle, which means you'll spend a fair amount of time passing items from one time period to another through the time machine (formerly a portable toilet).

Flawless animation and hilarious complications make this game well worth picking up.

FIGURE 11.6

A disembodied tentacle is the villain in this funny, graphically superior title.

Arcade and Board Game Discs

No longer do you have to fiddle around with folding game boards, tiny markers, and dozens of playing cards. Board games have hit the big time. CD-ROM provides the perfect medium for interactive play. Everyone has at least seen the ubiquitous Solitaire game being played on a computer; with a few of these game CDs tucked into your game-table drawer, you won't ever have to worry about finding a gaming partner again. Your PC is ready and waiting to take you on—and you can even tell it how smart to be.

And if you've never been the type to sit around playing parlor games but prefer the screaming fun of the local video arcade, you may never again have to leave the comfort of your family room to find a satisfyingly hair-raising game. Open the disc case, put the disc in the drive, double-click the icon, and you're off!

Jones in the Fast Lane

Sierra Online	
Operating System:	DOS 3.3 or above, Windows 3.1 with MPC extensions
Interface:	Point and click, text
Pointing Devices:	Mouse, keyboard
Sound:	All major cards
Graphics:	256-color VGA
Audience:	Ages 12 and up

If you don't get enough of trying to make it in the big city, Jones in the Fast lane is for you. This computerized board game challenges you to take your choice of character (two female, two male) from destitute poverty—no job, no place to live, not even decent clothes—to the top of the corporate ladder.

The game begins when you choose goals in each of four iconically represented areas: money (dollar bill), happiness (smiley face), education (diploma), and success (briefcase). Each move takes one "Jones" week. During each week—elapsed time is displayed on a clock at the bottom of the board—you must move your character from place to place and make choices about how to spend your money and time.

At each stop along the way, you hear and see characters, from the rent-office manager—who somehow seems to dislike you even as she thanks you for the rent—to the professor at "Hi Tech University," who is reminiscent of a Three Stooges character.

Jones in the Fast Lane is a relatively easy game to play and is definitely more fun with multiple players—the game supports up to four. The software plays the game's namesake, Jones, if you are without human companionship.

Jones in the Fast Lane runs under DOS or in an MPC window—and does the MPC job quite well. It expects a 640-by-480-by-256 color display driver for Windows, but runs under higher resolution with no problem.

Jones in the Fast Lane is definitely not designed for young children (who would not understand its basic premises). There is nothing objectionable in the game, however.

MegaRace

Software Toolworks

Operating System:	DOS 3.3 or above
Interface:	Point and click
Pointing Devices:	Mouse (recommended), keyboard
Sound:	All major cards
Graphics:	256-color SUPER-VGA
Audience:	Ages 12 and up

MegaRace uses cutting-edge video technology (morphing, computer animation, and live-action video) to enhance an animated arcade game. You're "Enforcer," a game show contestant in a broadcast by VWBT—Virtual World Broadcast Television. Several cities are being overrun by evil car gangs, and your challenge is to stop the speed punks with one of several specially equipped cars. You do battle with the car gangs on the high-speed freeways of their virtual worlds.

Your host is the delightfully annoying Lance Boyle, a live actor (Christian Erikson) who makes irritating game show host chatter between rounds. Lance points out several times throughout the game that it's only a game and nobody's really getting hurt, which would probably get a little old for most gamers if he weren't so obnoxiously sincere about it.

The actual arcade sections of the game are fast-paced, fun, and interesting. The speedways include hairpin turns, loop-the-loops, and corkscrews, all of which keep you off balance and alert. The music is upbeat and changes for each challenge level to keep from getting monotonous.

Another point in MegaRace's favor is that its special effects don't distract from the game play. All the high-tech full-motion video effects go on between rounds on the track, so even if you've got a slower PC or CD-ROM drive, you won't see any jumpiness or delays while you're playing.

Battle Chess

Interplay

Operating System:	DOS 3.3 or above
Interface:	Point and click
Pointing Devices:	Mouse
Sound:	All major cards
Graphics:	256-color VGA
Audience:	Ages 12 and up

Battle Chess plays like a standard chess game, but it adds a new dimension to the pieces—they really take part in animated duels (see fig. 11.7). If you move your Queen into a space occupied by your opponent's Bishop, for example, they really face off on the chess board—until the Queen summons up some magic and disintegrates him. Each piece interacts with others differently, so you may not see the same type of confrontation twice in a whole game. Some of the skirmishes last quite a while, with all the action of a Hollywood fight scene, but you always know who's going to win—they haven't changed the game *that* much.

FIGURE 11.7

The Blue Queen checks the Red King in a scene from Battle Chess.

Although Battle Chess is obviously great for chess buffs, it is also entertaining enough to keep newcomers interested while they learn the classic game.

Bicycle CD-ROM Collection

Swfte

Operating System:	DOS 3.3 or above
Interface:	Menu
Pointing Devices:	Mouse (recommended), keyboard
Sound:	None
Graphics:	CGA, EGA, MCGA, and VGA
Audience:	Ages 12 and up

If you like cards, get the Bicycle CD-ROM Collection. Poker, cribbage, bridge, and solitaire are all here on one moderately priced disc (see fig. 11.8).

The cards are sharp and clear in VGA resolution, and using the cribbage board is far easier with a mouse than not. Play against the computer—if you dare—and be prepared for a real challenge.

The Solitaire module includes seven different varieties of solo cards, including Canfield, Klondike, and Little Spider. The Poker segment allows for stud and draw, both of which can have wild-card play as well.

The documentation is top-notch, and the back of the book even has a quirky collection of card trivia, card-making lore, and various anecdotes about Bicycle's long history. The price is very reasonable, and all the cards you'd care to play are all on one disc.

FIGURE 11.8

The Bicycle poker game is one of four in this collection's deck.

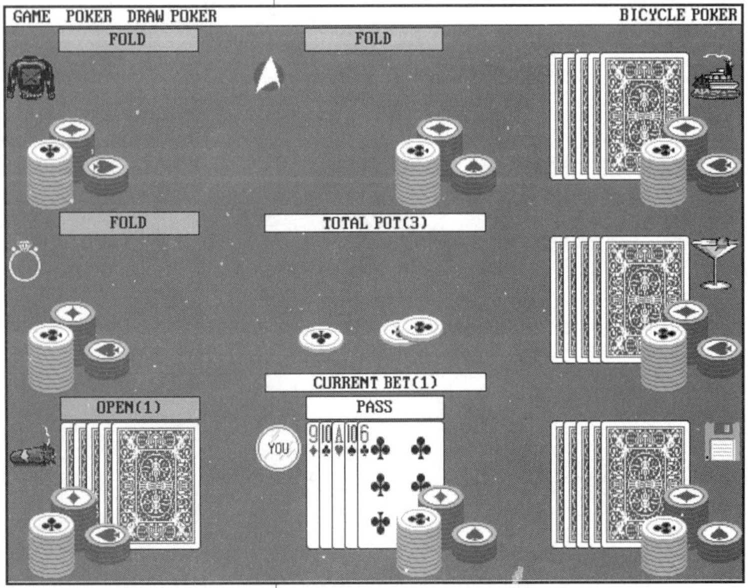

Mystery Game Discs

Elliot Roosevelt, move over. There's a whole new genre of mystery writers lurking in the shadows. Mystery games are the perfect alibi for maintaining the illusion that you use your CD-ROM drive only for educational purposes. Challenge yourself to a round with one of the titles reviewed here and see whether or not your powers of deduction don't improve! If you're ready to play Watson—or the Great Sleuth himself—the world of mystery on CD-ROM awaits you.

Who Killed Sam Rupert?

Creative Multimedia Corporation

Operating System:	Windows 3.1 with MPC extensions
Interface:	Menu, point and click
Pointing Devices:	Mouse
Sound:	All major cards
Graphics:	256-color VGA
Audience:	Adult

If just watching *Perry Mason* or *Murder She Wrote* isn't enough, Who Killed Sam Rupert? may appease the budding gumshoe in you (see fig. 11.9). As the story opens, you arrive on the scene of the murder of Sam Rupert in the wine cellar of his popular and elegant restaurant, Sam's. Your assistant gives you a run-down on the initial crime scene and then you're left to investigate. By picking various menu options, you can search the entire restaurant, perform careful forensic examinations of the actual murder scene and body, interview various suspects, and read Sam's appointment books and phone messages. Suspect interviews are QuickTime for Windows videos that pop onto the screen; all other options are VGA photos you can examine in some detail. Printed records of alibis, Sam's guest reservations, and recordings of his phone messages are also available to sift for clues.

Once you determine which suspects you want to interview in depth, you must pass a press conference. There, reporters ask you questions about the crime scene, possible suspects, and events leading up to Sam's death. If you don't answer at least seven of the ten questions correctly, you're sent back to do more investigation.

The sound and video make this game an interesting, interactive whodunnit.

FIGURE 11.9

Test your sleuthing skills in the multimedia game Who Killed Sam Rupert?

CD-ROM BOOK

AWARD OF EXCELLENCE

Sherlock Holmes

If the use of video and sound weren't innovative enough, ICOM's genuinely challenging Sherlock Holmes adventures will keep you sleuthing for hours.

Sherlock Holmes, Volumes I, II, and III

Viacom

Operating System:	DOS 3.3 or above
Interface:	Menu
Pointing Devices:	Mouse
Sound:	All major cards
Graphics:	256-color VGA
Audience:	Ages 12 and up

It's almost unfair to lump all three of these Sherlock Holmes volumes together, but they all follow the exact same format and interface (see fig. 11.10). At the start, you choose from three separate cases and then are given a brief video introduction to the current case. From there, you—as Holmes—must find the murderer. From a convenient interface, you select addresses to visit (such as Scotland Yard, the Coroner, and other official—and unofficial—establishments). At each venue, you see a short video clip of your interview. Make sure that you take careful notes—each scene contains valuable clues to the solution of the mystery.

FIGURE 11.10

Sherlock Holmes Volume III: High-quality video and genuinely tough murder cases send you through Arthur Conan Doyle's London.

Other resources for sleuthing include Holmes' personal files of notable personages in London and copies of the *London Times*—in both print and electronic format—which you can browse for the off-beat clue or connection.

Once you believe you've gathered enough clues to make an arrest, you appear before a judge. Be careful—he'll want to know many things before putting your suspect on trial, and he's impatient with detectives who waste his time with half-baked theories.

Although all the fun is in the solving, you can rate your effectiveness by Watson's summary of your work at the end of each case—the higher the score, the worse you've done. Watson lets you know what the perfect number of moves would have been. We're not sure even the "real" Holmes is that effective.

This is a thoroughly enjoyable game, much more sophisticated than any other whodunnit on the market—either diskette-based or disc-based titles. If you love mysteries and a great challenge, get Volume I. We're sure you'll be become a VIACOM-Holmes addict and pick up the other volumes as well.

7th Guest

Virgin	
Operating System:	DOS 3.3 or above
Interface:	Point and click
Pointing Devices:	Mouse (recommended), keyboard
Sound:	All major cards
Graphics:	256-color SUPER-VGA
Audience:	Ages 12 and up

Wow! That's the first and only word out of your mouth after starting 7th Guest. This game is so far ahead of the pack in graphics, sound, and animation, it leaves you nearly speechless.

Before we even attempt to describe the game itself, we must point out that this game is, in all earnestness, in a class by itself. Using high-resolution 3-D modeling software to develop the realistic interiors of the haunted Stouf Mansion, Virgin has produced the only game on the market that approaches the full meaning of the phrase *interactive adventure*. Because of its astounding graphics clarity, you feel as though you're in the corridors of a real house. A trip down a spider-clogged drainpipe, playing chess, and looking through telescopes and microscopes take on unparalleled realism. The house sets, the sound effects, and music are all a boost to the game as well. Live video of ghosts—and an extensive introduction to the house's past and that of its builder, Stouf—add yet another layer of complexity. When you consider the wealth of graphics, sound, and video, it should come as no surprise that the program is shipped on two CDs.

The setting is a small New England town; you visit the reputedly haunted Stouf mansion in search of clues to the murder of a journalist and the secrets the house is supposed to guard. You have a booklet of clippings collected on the house and its builder (the toymaker Stouf) and related articles about the town, including a mysterious virus that killed a dozen children before the disease just as mysteriously disappeared.

As you wander the mansion, you're beckoned or warned off available directions of travel by an animated skeletal hand—the cursor changes according to function. A rolling, disembodied eye indicates one of Stouf's many puzzles left behind in the house; a skull with a pulsating brain indicates the location of the puzzles; and a mask shows where a ghostly vignette may be played out.

All the rooms in the Stouf mansion are not immediately available. Solving Stouf puzzles opens rooms, each of which contains valuable clues about the many mysteries of Stouf and his mansion. You'll enjoy the puzzles as much as the animation.

The game's cover says that this is the future of interactive games. For once, marketing hype comes up square with the truth. If you have the equipment needed to play this game, buy it. You won't regret it—even if you're a confirmed game snob.

CD-ROM BOOK
QUE
AWARD OF EXCELLENCE

7th Guest

Get this one. The graphics, sound, animation, and full-motion video all push the envelope of current technology. If that weren't enough, the game is engaging and full of challenging logic puzzles. A must have!

Children's Game Discs

While you're busy stocking up your CD-ROM library with new game titles, don't forget the younger members of the family. For the same reasons you want to play games on the computer, the Little League crowd wants their time on-line, too. Kids learn basic computer skills as they navigate the graphical mazes and respond to audio cues; they improve reasoning skills and bone up on the principle of cause and effect. And if you're still looking for a plausible excuse for forking over the credit card for a *children's game*, try this one: *you* might enjoy it, too!

Beyond the Wall of Stars

Creative Multimedia Corporation	
Operating System:	Windows 3.1 with MPC extensions, Macintosh
Interface:	Menu
Pointing Devices:	Mouse
Sound:	All major cards
Graphics:	VGA
Audience:	Ages 12 and up

CMC bills Beyond the Wall of Stars as an interactive multimedia adventure story; although that's quite a mouthful, it's an apt description. A science-fiction story set on a dying planet named Caledon, from which a delegation of galactic travelers sets out to find Taran—a world fabled to be habitable and capable of helping the dying race. As a participant in the story line, you choose the captain of the mission from eligible crew members. You also make key decisions, such as whether to answer a distress signal coming from a nearby planet or continue with your rescue mission. Each decision, of course, alters the ultimate outcome of the story. And each twist adds new subplots and characters to the story's roster (see fig. 11.11).

The interface is easy to work with and, unlike some games and stories, the sound track for this adventure is perfect for its purposes. (Some scores become as irritating as off-key humming after prolonged play.) Although the animation isn't very sophisticated, that's not why you bought this ticket. Here, it's all story—and it's a full story, too: you won't be able to finish it in one sitting. The interface includes a bookmark feature for just that reason. You can place multiple bookmarks within the story so that you can explore different branches of the story line or so that more than one person can read the story.

Goferwinkel's Adventures

Creative Multimedia Corporation

Operating System:	Windows 3.1 with MPC extensions
Interface:	Menu
Pointing Devices:	Mouse
Sound:	All major cards
Graphics:	256-color VGA
Audience:	Ages 5 to 11

With the most eye-popping color in any CD-ROM we've seen, Goferwinkel's Adventures is a multimedia comic book that is especially good fun for the younger set. It's a comic book they can control, playing or replaying scenes in Goferwinkel's struggle to get safely to the Lavender Land.

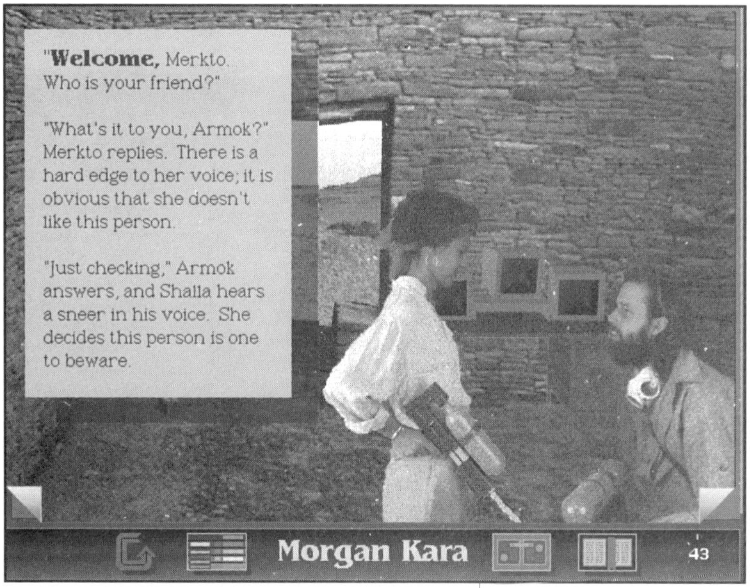

"Welcome, Merkto. Who is your friend?"
"What's it to you, Armok?" Merkto replies. There is a hard edge to her voice; it is obvious that she doesn't like this person.
"Just checking," Armok answers, and Shalla hears a sneer in his voice. She decides this person is one to beware.
Morgan Kara
43

FIGURE 11.11

Beyond the Wall of Stars is an interactive novel—you choose among the many plot alternatives.

The sound and voices are a great addition to a snappily drawn cartoon. Preschoolers will especially love this game, which also helps them learn to use a mouse and get used to using computers.

EcoQuest: The Search for Cetus

Sierra Online

Operating System:	DOS 3.3 or above, Windows 3.1 with MPC extensions
Interface:	Point and click, text
Pointing Devices:	Mouse, keyboard, joystick
Sound:	All major sound cards
Graphics:	256-color VGA
Audience:	Ages 12 and up

With the EcoQuest: The Search for Cetus role-playing game, Sierra Online takes you on an adventure under the sea (see fig. 11.12). The hero is Adam, son of a marine biologist who helps his father nurse a dolphin back to health after it's trapped and nearly killed in a drift net. As he plays with the recuperating dolphin, Adam discovers it has surprising powers. He learns that the dolphin was on a mission when it was nearly killed and he determines to let it go.

FIGURE 11.12

Kids help Adam and Dolphinius, the dolphin, save an underwater world in EcoQuest.

Adam joins his new-found sea friend, Dolphinius, on an ocean trek through ancient ruins, an underwater sea-life city, and an abandoned ocean-floor, oil-drilling rig. Adam—and you—get points for helping sea creatures, picking up trash, and bettering the ocean environment. And, of course, you get points for solving the many puzzles and hunts along the ocean floor.

As you can tell, EcoQuest has a decidedly proenvironment bent. There's much here about the way toxins, garbage, and other wastes affect plant and animal life in the oceans. According to Sierra Online, the facts have been checked with oceanographers; the game does a good job of imparting facts about marine biology and ocean ecosystems.

The game is definitely geared to an older child (some of the puzzles are too difficult for younger players to solve on their own). The theme, story, and characters are well-suited for children under 12 and adults to play together, however.

The Adventures of Willy Beamish

Dynamix

Operating System:	DOS 3.3 or above
Interface:	Menu
Pointing Devices:	Mouse (recommended), keyboard
Sound:	All major cards
Graphics:	256-color VGA
Audience:	Ages 12 and up

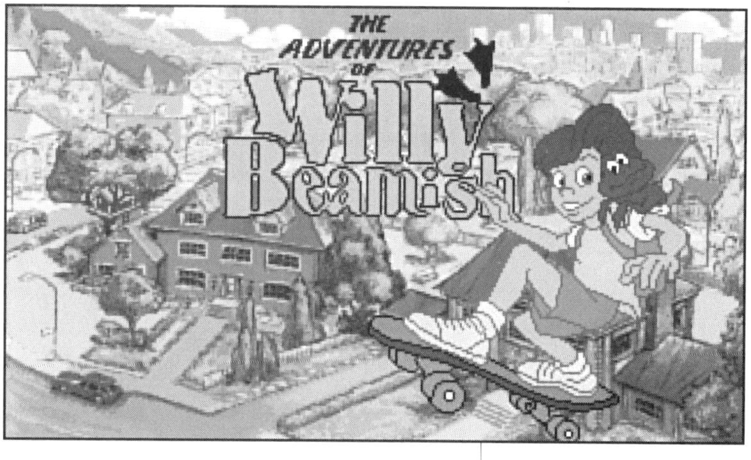

FIGURE 11.13

Willy Beamish is for kids—especially for those over 18 years old.

The Adventures of Willy Beamish is a pure joy to play with older kids. It's an adventure game with a twist: everything is cartoons and you play the part of Willy Beamish, a preteen boy with energy, mischief, and problems to spare (see fig. 11.13).

Willy's biggest dream is to enter the Nintari Video Game Championship—but the competition requires money, which Willy doesn't have. With his friends and his pet frog, Willy devises a way to earn his way to the games: enter the frog-jumping contest and win first prize.

As Willy struggles to get his frog ready for competition, other story lines develop—the town is plagued by a mysterious sludge, workers are laid off, and Willy's father, we discover, is in for trouble. Only Willy can save the town and his dad.

Throughout this gorgeously painted cartoon, you control Willy's actions, help him solve the puzzles he needs to get ahead in the game, and ultimately triumph over evil. Many of the game's puzzles are arcade-action based; others require pure gray-matter skills, striking a good balance for both of this game's potential audiences.

The sound, music, and voices are superb and enhance the wacky, Saturday-morning cartoon atmosphere of Willy's world. We hope Dynamix doesn't stop with one Willy under its belt. Willy is a fresh concept that older kids will enjoy playing with their parents—a welcome way to bridge a computer generation gap. Let the kids handle the arcade action, and you help out with the brain teasers.

Where in the World Is Carmen San Diego Deluxe

Brøderbund

Operating System:	DOS 3.3 and above, or Macintosh
Interface:	Menu
Pointing Devices:	Mouse, keyboard
Sound:	All major cards
Graphics:	VGA
Audience:	Ages 12 and up

The *Deluxe* in Where in the World Is Carmen San Diego Deluxe stands for more sound, more voices, more of everything than the original program (which was released more than three years ago). The interface is vastly improved as well, making navigation around the world and through the clue lists much easier (see fig. 11.14).

The premise of Where in the World Is Carmen San Diego is that you play a rookie gumshoe for the Acme Detective Agency—dedicated to foiling the evil band of Carmen San Diego's world-wide network of art and jewel thieves. Once you're assigned a case by headquarters over your communicator, you must select a spot on the globe to jet to for clue searching. When you land somewhere that plays a part in the criminals' crime or flight, you receive valuable additional information on their whereabouts. Clues are, of course, tied to geography, language, religion, and cuisine of various countries throughout the world.

The voices—of the chief, your travel agent Shirley, and various witnesses—make this game a lot more fun than the original. Actual still-life photos of representative landmarks and clips of native music—from the banjoes of the U.S. to the Irish harp—are used when you arrive in each country.

The cases are a challenge for most kids, and the clues may send them immediately to your multimedia CD-ROM encyclopedia for answers.

FIGURE 11.14

Your global pursuit of master criminals in Where in the World Is Carmen San Diego is controlled with your Acme Communicator.

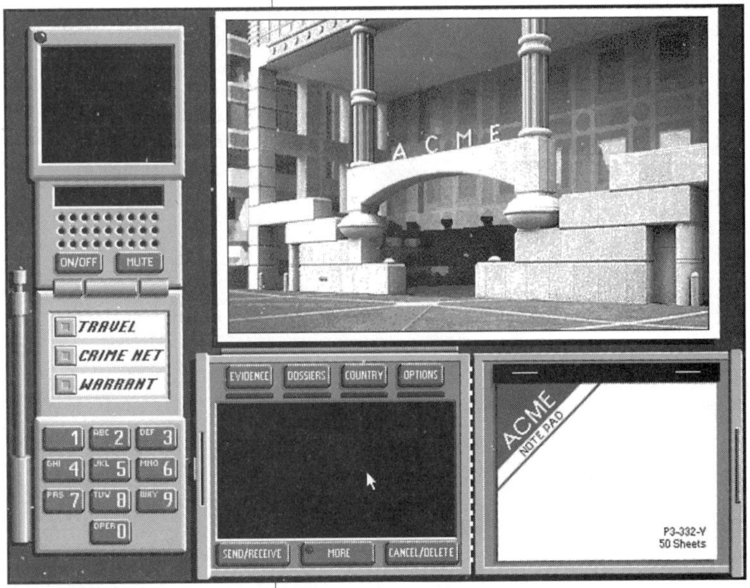

Music Video Discs

There's a new development in the CD-ROM world that should surprise nobody—disc-based music videos. Huge stars like Peter Gabriel, the Beatles, and the artist formerly known as Prince have released CD-ROM versions of their music and videos, some including features like the ability to remix songs, remake the videos, and tour strange virtual worlds.

In addition to the ones we review here, look for David Bowie's interactive disc, Jump, and more projects from TRI (who has recently changed his name from Todd Rundgren—the new moniker is said to stand for "Todd Rundgren Interactive").

The Beatles: A Hard Day's Night

Vicarious Entertainment

Operating System:	MPC, Macintosh
Interface:	Menus, icons, buttons
Pointing Devices:	Mouse
Sound:	All major cards
Graphics:	VGA
Audience:	Adult

The Beatles: A Hard Day's Night is an enhanced computer-playable version of the madcap 1964 movie. You can watch the entire 90 minutes, with the special prologue added in 1982, all on your Mac or Windows screen. The disc also includes some of the early short films by director Richard Lester, the entire text of the script, the trailer released for theaters in 1964, an essay about the Beatles by critic Bruce Eder, and trivia about the movie and the players.

From an historical perspective, A Hard Day's Night is interesting because it's the inspiration for many of the directing/photography styles used in today's music videos. Weird camera angles, rapid-fire montage editing, and actors spending whole scenes out of character mugging for the camera are commonplace today, but when Lester released this movie 30 years ago, he was called everything from *avant-garde* genius to talentless idiot.

If you're more interested in entertainment than historical perspective, A Hard Day's Night wins there too. This is the Beatles at their young, energetic, irreverent best, before scandals and supergroup tensions made serious, sometimes angry, men out of them.

FIGURE 11.15

Watch your favorite Beatles movie on your computer screen and access lots more info about the Fab Four.

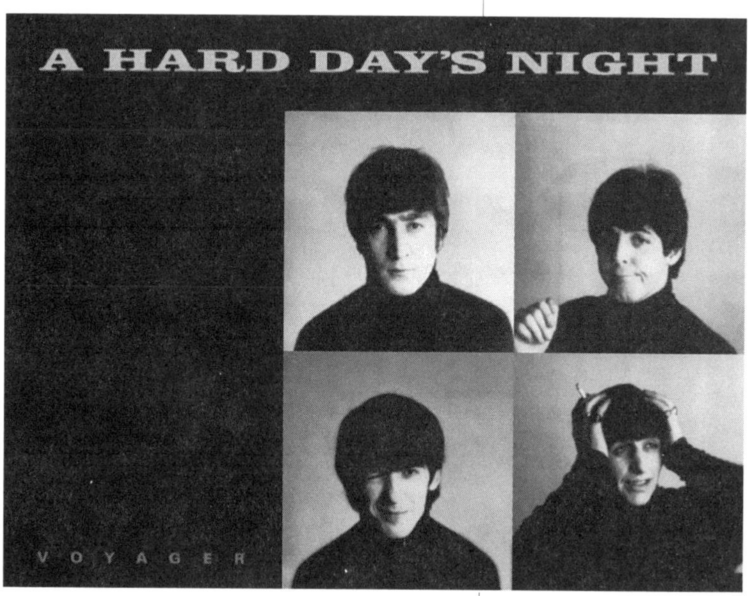

Interactive

GraphixZone	
Operating System:	Macintosh, Windows
Interface:	Point and click
Pointing Devices:	Mouse
Sound:	All major cards
Graphics:	256-color super VGA
Audience:	Adult

Many professional music offerings on CD-ROM have been geared to virtual reality. The artist formerly known as Prince (who now signs his name as a symbol nobody knows how to pronounce), has released Interactive, a disc available for Mac and PC. It is as much a video game as a musical experience, with special challenges and puzzles in a world you travel through by clicking your mouse on your destinations (definitely reminiscent of some new games like Myst). You can remix some of the music, play the six included songs and four full-length videos in the studio, and tour several beautifully rendered rooms.

A word of caution: this one's not for kids. If you know anything about the Purple One, you know he's not going to be playing on the Family Channel any time soon.

XPLORA 1—Peter Gabriel's Secret World

InterPlay	
Operating System:	Macintosh
Interface:	Point and click
Pointing Devices:	Mouse
Sound:	Macintosh
Graphics:	256-color
Audience:	Adult

Another intriguing virtual reality experience is XPLORA 1—Peter Gabriel's Secret World. Currently available only for Macintosh, this disc uses full-motion video to give you a feel for being backstage at the Grammys, at a concert with Gabriel, and all through a music studio during the making of the recent album, US. You can remix some of the music, play instruments with your mouse, and even re-create a video for "Digging in the Dirt" (one of the four full-length videos included on the disc). You also take part in something like a treasure hunt, using your own personal attaché case to store the goodies you pick up on your tour. Your options change as you pick up different items (backstage passes, for example). Peter Gabriel himself even pops up on-screen periodically to help out.

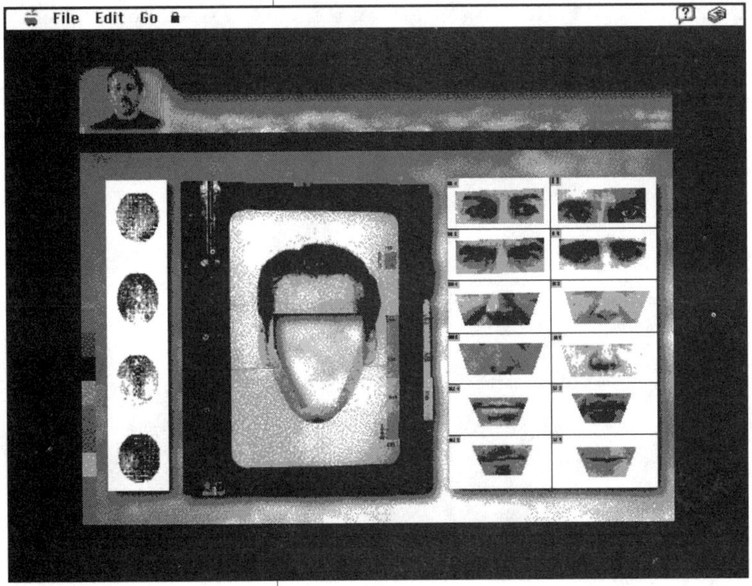

FIGURE 11.16

Join Peter Gabriel on a treasure hunt, take a backstage tour, or remix and re-create a music video.

Chapter 12

Copyright Law

As you've seen in the preceding chapters, CD-ROM publishers are distributing hundreds of megabytes of art, sound files, photography, and film clips on each of their CD-ROMs. How you use these files depends solely on the publisher's agreement with the owners of the source material. Unfortunately, the owner of the source material is often not the publisher; therein lies the complication.

Copyrights

> *The Congress shall have Power...To promote the Progress of Science and useful Arts, by securing for limited Times to Authors and Inventors the exclusive Right to their respective Writings and Discoveries....*
>
> —Article II, Section 8
> Constitution of the United States

In the simplest of terms, copyrighted material on a CD-ROM is owned by another party—an individual artist, a news organization, or an estate. The distribution of the material does not mean that it belongs to the purchaser. This concept is one you're familiar with: when you purchase the latest Stephen King novel, you don't dash to the nearest copy machine to run off copies for your friends and family. The book is a copyrighted work, with rights belonging to the author of the book. Only with the author's and publisher's permission can you run off a copy for your brother—and you'll find it very difficult to secure that permission. The livelihoods of the author, publisher, and even the bookstores that carry King's works all depend on adherence to copyright laws.

Without copyrights, the publishing business could not survive. This idea is so fundamental that its roots appear in the Constitution of the United States. Without it, cheap copies of printed works would turn up everywhere, with no royalty or profit for the author, the publisher, or their distributors. Works would be altered without regard to the original, changing the intent of a work. Finally, the quality of the work would suffer, injuring the reputation of the author and the publisher, making future products unmarketable.

CAUTION

Seek Legal Advice

Because of the intricacies and ambiguities involved in copyright law, you are advised to contact a lawyer if you are protecting a work of value.

For these reasons, **copyrighted** works are always designated as such. The copyright symbol (©) and words describing the extent and scope of the copyright appear at the beginning of the text, alerting purchasers to their obligations when buying the work.

Copyright Notices

Because the U.S. is a signatory to the Berne convention, it is no longer necessary for an explicit notice to appear on a work for that work to be protected. Instead, an implied copyright exists for all original works. This doesn't mean that you can find yourself in trouble for using a work with no copyright notice; rather, the originator can notify you and tell you to stop using the work. The ultimate protection is registration of a copyright, which costs about $20 and provides evidence that an individual or corporation is the originator.

Taken to its extremes, a world without copyrights would gradually grind to a halt—authors would refuse to produce, publishers would stop the presses, and bookstores would close shop. In essence, copyrights provide the incentive to produce new works in an environment protected from theft. Copyrights control and ensure quality and accurate representation.

CAUTION

User Beware

Just because a work does not bear a copyright notice does not mean that it is a public-domain item. If you are unsure of a work's status and you cannot contact the owner, it's probably best not to use it.

It's easy to see that the authors, publishers, and distributors benefit from copyright law, but what about the consumer? As we explained, the alternative—no copyright protection—virtually eliminates the incentive to publish, making new works scarce or nonexistent. But copyrights, paradoxically, protect the *consumer* in a variety of ways:

- Copyrights ensure that the product you purchase is in the form and content intended by the author and publisher; what you get is what they wanted you to get—the decision to purchase is left to you.
- Copyrights make it less likely that undeserving works are brought out as products. With the work itself protected, the publisher then invests in paper, printing presses, warehouses, delivery trucks, and marketing campaigns to get the product in front of the consumer. No business can long survive delivering products no one will purchase. Publishers, therefore, secure the rights to works that are marketable. A certain level of quality is virtually ensured.
- Copyrights make publishing a competitive business. Rights to the most marketable materials go to the publishers that pay the best price. These publishers, in turn, spend time and money marketing the works to recoup their investment. In this environment, works are more visible and subjected to greater scrutiny, and the public is more informed on the quality of individual products.

Public Domain

Once a published (or unpublished) work no longer has rights assigned to it, it falls into what is known as the **public domain**. A work may be in the public domain if any of these conditions arise:

- The work's copyright has run out and is no longer in effect.
- The **holder** of the copyright has released the work into the public domain and relinquishes all rights.
- No rights were ever assigned or claimed for the work and its use has been widespread.

Copyrights do run out. The length of the copyright depends on the type of work produced, how the creator of the work copyrighted the material to begin with, and what types of rights might survive the creator and be passed to heirs.

Work created before copyright law was enforced or work created long ago and no longer copyrighted falls into the public domain. Shakespeare's plays and Nathaniel Hawthorn's novels, for example, fall into this category. The plays and the novels may be reproduced at will, with no royalties or fees paid to anyone.

Anyone can use public-domain materials for whatever purpose without obligation to any other party. No fees, royalties, or permissions must be paid or secured for the use of public-domain materials, nor are there restrictions on how they can be used—a scene from Macbeth, for example, can be used to sell sleeping pills.

Fair Use

Life under copyright law has become complicated, however. The introduction of VCRs, tape recorders, computer media, and duplicating machines has made enforcement of copyrights difficult and has deadened the public's sensitivity to copyright law.

When it is so easy to reproduce copyrighted material, the consumer may feel that no law is being broken. This is not the case. Technically, any reproduction of a copyrighted work—in any form—is an infringement on the holder's rights. If you use a copyrighted photograph in a sales brochure without securing the copyright holder's permission, you've violated the law. If you copy a film clip and use it in a marketing presentation without permission, you're liable under the law.

These cases of infringement are easy for most of us to determine. Other areas are less definitive. What if you use that same photograph on an invitation to a New Year's Eve party and distribute it to a select group of friends? Or you use that film clip to illustrate script-writing techniques in your high school English class?

To address this issue of personal use, the courts have produced what is known as the Fair Use Doctrine. This doctrine covers four points—or criteria—for determining whether use of a copyrighted work can be claimed as "fair use" rather than falling under the strict terms of copyright law. These criteria are as follows:

1. The purpose and character of the use, including whether such use is of a commercial nature or is for nonprofit educational purposes.
2. The nature of the copyrighted work.

CAUTION

Don't Lose Control

If you want to make one of your own works available, it is best to do so by first copyrighting the work and then by offering it for use with no fee. If you place the work into the public domain, you have no control over it whatsoever and you may regret your decision later.

3. The amount and substantiality of the portion used in relationship to the copyrighted work as a whole.

4. The effect of the use on the potential market value for the copyrighted work.

In a nutshell, the doctrine protects your personal use of a copyrighted product if:

1. You will not profit from the reproduction.

2. The work's individual copyright protection is taken into consideration—for example, laws covering printed text differ from those protecting music.

3. You use only a portion of a work.

4. Your use does not adversely affect the profit to be made by the holder of the copyright.

The first example—using a commercial, copyrighted photograph on invitations to a New Year's Eve party—hits some of the fair-use criteria and violates others. For example, you are using the work in its entirety, making your use a clear violation of point number 3. Copyright laws governing photography insist on a per-use basis as well: you must pay a sliding-scale fee for a work depending on the number of appearances the photo will make. Yet you clearly are not affecting the market value of the photo or using it for profit. Your potential for breaking the law here seems evenly split.

The second example is more easy to determine. First, your intent is nonprofit and educational in nature; showing a high school English class a film clip does not make anyone any money—unless you charge admission. Second, the nature of film copyrights allows the use of brief segments for criticism. Third, your clip constitutes only a brief segment of the entire work. And finally, your presentation of the clip in no way lessens the market value of the entire film. In fact, such a "tease" of a clip may cause the entire class to rent the film on videotape after viewing the segment in class.

The bottom line with fair use is not simple to determine, but you should keep a few things in mind. If the use is noncommercial in nature—that is, it promotes a nonprofit enterprise—it may fall under fair-use protection. If your use does not constitute a loss in profit for the copyright holder, and especially if you use only a small portion of the work, you should be protected by the fair-use provision. The courts have a long way to go on this issue, however.

In a suit brought before the U.S. Supreme Court (*Sony vs. Universal Studios*), the court ruled that taping a TV show for personal use at a later date did not constitute a copyright infringement. The reasoning was that the consumer would tape the show for viewing later and had no intention of distributing the product for profit. But look at the number of fair-use clauses the ruling violates!

Furthermore, software companies instruct individual users (for good reason) to make backup copies of distribution diskettes in the event that an original diskette is damaged.

All these ambiguities make copyright law and fair use an affair potentially fraught with confusion and liability for consumers and small businesses.

CD-ROM and Copyright Law

Materials contained on a CD-ROM are subject to the same copyright laws as other media. What may confuse the issue, however, is that CD-ROMs may contain more than one form of original work. Text files, of course, are subject to the laws pertaining to written works. Music files fall under the laws protecting recorded materials, and film clips and photos have laws protecting them as well. In effect, CD-ROMs can carry virtually every known type of copyrightable material.

Publishers may also find themselves in need of securing rights from a number of different sources, adding to production costs. Royalties are another complication. For example, the use of a copyright-protected photograph on a CD may be subject to royalty payments only if the consumer uses the particular photo in a commercial enterprise, such as a printed advertisement; all the text on the disc may be subject to author royalties based on the number of discs sold to customers.

For this reason, copyright clearinghouses have emerged as an important catalyst in the CD-ROM publishing business, helping CD-ROM publishers and copyright holders more efficiently secure and sell rights to works in a timely fashion. By using such clearinghouses, the publishers spend less time internally negotiating rights and more time producing and distributing products. Copyright holders are ensured that their rights are protected in a uniform manner, and they don't lose royalties or spend significant time in negotiation. Authors can even submit materials and their standard copyright terms to such clearinghouses for publishers to choose from.

Your Copyright Responsibilities

As discussed, the capability of CD-ROM to contain a variety of different media makes it susceptible to all types of copyright law. The potential for confusion and abuse—by both copyright holders and consumers—is as vast as the storage capacity of the disc itself.

Let's take a seemingly innocuous example. You purchase a CD containing a huge database of sound effects and music files. One of the files is a recording of the opening of the popular TV show *Star Trek*: "Space. The final frontier..." intones William Shatner, with the familiar theme from Star Trek playing under his voice over.

If you use this music/voice clip in a multimedia presentation to promote the more spacious interior of a new minivan at a trade show, are you violating copyright law? Probably. The music is, without a doubt, copyrighted. The excerpted words of the opening may also constitute an infringement. And furthermore, using Star Trek to promote a new car model clearly violates the fair-use doctrine of infringement (using the Star Trek identification to profitably market a vehicle). But it came on a disc with so many other effects, who would know what is in the public domain and what is not?

CAUTION

Beware the Lack of Notice

Some publishers are not nearly as forthright as they should be. You'll be surprised to find, for example, that purchasing a certain commercial series of photographs on CD does not give you the right to reproduce the photos in any form without permission. You find that out, however, only after you open the disc package—making a refund of your money nearly impossible. The outside of the disc case has no clear mention of this provision. Another vendor, however, makes it abundantly clear that you must pay fees for the use of any images contained on the enclosed disc. And you're alerted to this before you open the disc case.

Most CD-ROM publishers are extremely responsible when they market their discs and **clearly state**—on the outside packaging—that the contents are either public domain or copyright-protected materials. There should be further warnings in the software program itself that tell you precisely what you can—or cannot—do with the materials.

Protect Yourself

When using clip media from any CD-ROM—either for fair use or commercial purposes—read all the fine print included with the disc and in the software itself. Take your cues from this information.

For example, the copyright use for Digital Directory Assistance's PhoneDisc USA is clear, concise, and unambiguous:

> This product a) may be used only by the purchasing end-user and may not be made available for any other use by loan, rental, service bureau, or other arrangement; b) may only be used for reference purposes; use for commercial direct mail or telemarketing of more than 100 listings per month is strictly prohibited; c) may only be used with a single microcomputer permitting access by one individual at one time; d) may not be made available to multiple users at one time through networking or any other means without obtaining a separate networking license from DDA.

This is the first paragraph on the back of the PhoneDisc USA case; it gives the business user very clear guidelines for the use of the product. According to Digital Directory Assistance, in a nutshell, you can't do these things with the disc:

- Use the disc for mailing lists
- Allow more than one person to use the disc at one time or loan it to any other person
- Use the disc for extensive telemarketing

Most importantly, you make your purchasing decisions about this CD accordingly. If you need a disc for telemarketing, you know this is not the product for you.

Other publishers are not as clear in their copyright notices. If you have questions regarding fair use or copyrights of a particular piece of media, call the publisher before you use the media in a commercial enterprise. Get the use restrictions or copyright guidelines in writing—for example, have them fax this information and explanation.

When determining whether your use of clip media falls under the fair-use doctrine, make certain that you are covered in at least two of the four areas of the guidelines—making absolutely certain that your use does not infringe on profits to the copyright holder.

Make no assumptions about public domain. Never use entire works or substantial portions of works unless they are clearly and irrevocably presented as public-domain property. Use of an entire chapter from Herman Melville's *Typee* from the Library of the Future disc may seem perfectly acceptable—Melville's work is in the public domain, after all. But the notice on World Library's disc—stamped on the disc itself, the outside package, and in the title screen of the software—clearly states:

> Unauthorized reproduction, lending, or distribution of text or programs contained on this disc is strictly prohibited.

Fair use would be applicable, however. Because of the collision of copyright law and the licensing of software databases like the Library of the Future, the application of a concept like "fair use" is not clear cut.

An Editorial on the Future of Copyright Law

For CD-ROM publishing to truly flourish, new rules must be set. Copyright laws must become more uniform, universal, and, above all, understandable. Most infringements today are probably caused by confusion and the wide distribution of copyrighted materials. Laws must reflect this wider distribution and make compliance an easier feat for the average business and consumer.

The current copyright laws are out of date. The current laws never anticipated the explosion in the information industry, nor could they anticipate the technologies that make information so readily available (and easily duplicated). Congress needs to revamp laws to reflect the use of media clips, text, and information in an age where dissemination of copyrighted materials should be opened up—and not hamstrung—by copyright law. Make certain that copyright holders are fairly compensated, but make compliance less bothersome and confusing.

Some proponents of reform suggest that an industry-wide tariff be placed on each CD-ROM sale, provided that the use of the information on the disc is for limited commercial application; the proceeds would go to a common copyright-royalty fund from which copyright holders would be paid according to some as-yet-to-be-determined schedule. In this scenario, you in essence comply the moment you make your CD-ROM purchase. Opponents of this measure believe that the tariff penalizes those users who never intend to use the products for any commercial reproduction.

Until copyright laws are streamlined or reformed, we need to be vigilant. Individuals, finally, must be educated and responsible for the use of CD-ROM-based materials; intentional abuse of the laws will only restrict the number and nature of materials available for distribution on CD-ROM. Companies publishing CD-ROM materials need to follow the lead of vendors who supply clear, concise, and easy-to-follow instructions regarding the nature of the copyrighted material contained on the discs.

Chapter 13

When One CD-ROM Isn't Enough

So your business has a CD-ROM drive or two installed, and some employees are finding information faster than ever before. Productivity is increasing, cost of research is dropping, but the hassles of adding a CD-ROM drive to every employee's desk who could benefit from the technology is getting a bit much. The demand for CD-ROM information is increasing. Thankfully, there are ways to ensure that your use of CD-ROM is cost-effective and efficient.

When Enough Discs Aren't Enough Any More

If you want to network large numbers of CD-ROM discs, consider CD-ROM drive arrays or a CD-ROM changer. These technologies have distinct benefits in networked environments, and you need to evaluate them separately. Each has its own advantages and disadvantages for distributing data across a network, whether it's a large, multiserver Novell NetWare network or a smaller peer-to-peer environment such as Windows for Workgroups.

This chapter introduces you to the following kinds of advanced CD-ROM hardware:

- **CD-ROM changers.** A **changer** is a CD-ROM drive that accepts multiple discs in a cartridge, much like the audio CD changers you see in homes and autos. Each disc on a CD-ROM changer is usually assigned a separate drive letter (for example, the game CD can be drive G, the encyclopedia CD can be drive H, and so on), although you can "combine" all the discs in the changer and refer to them by a single drive letter.

TIP

Changers and Arrays

For single users who need massive CD collections at their disposal or for a disc collection that is infrequently used, a changer is an ideal, cost-effective solution. If you expect even moderate traffic to the disc collection, however, consider a CD-ROM array.

- **CD-ROM jukeboxes.** A jukebox is similar to a changer except that it can have multiple CD-ROM drives and uses a robotic-arm mechanism to change discs.
- **CD-ROM arrays.** An array is a string of disc drives chained together. Arrays are usually fixed; that is, if there are four disc drives chained together in an array, you cannot add a fifth drive to the chain. You can, however, chain arrays together.
- **CD-ROM towers.** Tower systems offer all the benefits of arrays and go one further: they are expandable. Manufactures offer tower systems that can accommodate up to 18 disc drives—sometimes more. You can start with a few drives and add more drives whenever you need more power.

CD-ROM Changers

You're already very familiar with the technology used to stack a number of CDs on a network even if you've never seen a CD-ROM changer. The most popular CD changers are the Pioneer series of CD minichangers that use the same **cartridge** found in the Pioneer audio CD players. The similarities don't end there, either. Changers assign drive letters to every CD held in the cartridge. When a user on the network or on a standalone PC requests data from one of these "drives," the changer loads the appropriate disc into the CD-ROM reader. There is only one physical drive, but the drive designations are assigned to the individual discs for identification purposes: users, or their applications, know that drive K, for example, holds the corporate customer database and drive L holds the company's product literature.

EXPLANATION

Magazines and Cartridges

A magazine (also known as a cartridge) is a special case that holds up to six CD-ROM discs for use in a changer. It allows the changer to mechanically "change" discs as they are needed.

Changers also can be programmed to treat all the discs as one massive database, allowing the search and retrieval of data to span all the CD-ROMs in the magazine. A company with enormous databases on discs can then "publish" them on the network as one dataset; the users and their applications need not know that the actual data resides on many different platters or discs.

The CD-ROM changer is especially useful when organizations have to keep massive amounts of infrequently used data available at all times. Because there is only one physical drive, a user requesting a single bit of data can access the changer at any given time. Requests from other users looking for data on another disc loaded in the changer's magazine must wait, or retry their request later when the changer is available.

Changers are also useful to individual users who must keep massive databases or research resources at their fingertips. Without a changer, the user must sift through a stack of CDs, unload the current CD from the drive, and then load the CD with the appropriate data. With a changer, this activity is unnecessary. Applications can be configured to expect to find data on a given CD with an assigned drive letter. Multiple magazines of CDs can also be configured. For example, a librarian can load one magazine of CDs containing all literature and language databases, another magazine full of CDs with biology and chemistry abstracts, and yet another magazine with general-reference CD-ROM applications. Each magazine is a self-contained and defined library of information.

A law firm can pack one changer with bankruptcy CD databases, another with tax law CDs, another with state statutes, and yet another with an archive of the firm's past legal briefs.

The advantages of a CD changer are simple. The cost for changers is significantly less than buying the equivalent number of drives. For example, the Pioneer DRM-602X, a six-disc changer, sells for about $900 through some distributors. The price of six stand-alone drives is considerably more—nearly four times as much, in fact.

The disadvantages of changers relate mainly to networked CD environments. The minichanger is, in fact, one drive. If you expect access to the changer by a large number of people across the network, a changer cannot get the job done. Speed is another consideration. Although the disc-swapping speed is greatly improved in the newer changer models, users can expect a 6-to-15-second delay between their request for data and the actual loading and access of the CD.

Pioneer

Pioneer was the first to manufacture CD-ROM changers. Their minichanger series is the most affordable solution around. The drive accepts, as we've said, standard Pioneer CD cartridges, available where Pioneer audio CD drives are sold.

Pioneer DRM-602X

Interface:	SCSI, SCSI-2
Access time:	300 ms
Data transfer rate:	307 KB/s
Data buffer:	256 KB
CD-ROM formats supported:	ISO 9660, High Sierra, CD-DA
Suggested list price:	$1,095

The DRM-600-A was Pioneer's first changer and has now been replaced by the DRM-602X. Both the DRM-602X and DRM-604X hold standard six-disc magazines. The back of each unit has standard RCA audio output jacks, dual SCSI ports for easy daisy-chaining of SCSI devices either before or after the changer, a grounded power input, and a SCSI ID switch.

The front of each unit has a disc-eject button; headphone jack with volume control; power, drive busy, and audio indicator lights; and an AC power switch.

Pioneer DRM-604X

Interface:	SCSI, SCSI-2
Access time:	300 ms
Data transfer rate:	614 KB/s
Data buffer:	128 KB
CD-ROM formats supported:	ISO 9660, High Sierra, CD-DA, CD-ROM-XA (Mode 2, Forms 1 and 2), Rock Ridge, CD-R mastered discs
Suggested list price:	$1,495

EXPLANATION

QuadSpin

A number of vendors, including NEC, Texel, Toshiba, and Chinon, supply high-speed versions of their drives. The Pioneer minichanger offers what the company calls *QuadSpin*—speeds up to four times the base delivery rate for data.

EXPLANATION

Jukeboxes

CD-ROM jukeboxes are the functional equivalent of the jukeboxes you know from Pop's Soda Shoppe. They use a robotic arm to change compact discs in a standard CD-ROM drive, much the way the 45 rpm records were placed on a normal turntable.

The DRM-604X **QuadSpin** minichanger has all the front-panel and back-panel features of the DRM-602X. An additional LED on the front panel of the DRM-604X indicates when the drive is in QuadSpin mode.

The DRM-604X is, without a doubt, a killer CD-ROM configuration. The 614 KB/s transfer rate is unexcelled at the time of this printing, making the QuadSpin the best drive around for accessing massive data chunks—from archived, scanned photos to full-motion video. The number of formats supported also make this a good all-around CD-ROM reader, regardless of your data types.

This changer also boasts a quick five-second disc-swapping mechanism, making delays to disc far less bothersome than earlier versions. Using CorelSCSI!, it's a simple matter to hook the QuadSpin onto an Adaptec, Future Domain, or other supported controller.

Although the price may seem high, look what you get with the DRM-604X in terms of functionality: virtually all CD formats are supported; the drive has the highest transfer rate available; its SCSI-2 interface makes it a snap to configure; and you have the equivalent of six CD-ROM drives in one case.

This drive is highly recommended for power CD-users, small businesses with extensive reference requirements, and smaller networks and workgroups where archived data is needed at a moment's notice. The DRM-604X is a great CD-ROM product that has no competition in its class.

CD-ROM Jukeboxes

Changers generally use a mechanism that holds all the discs in a turntable, cassette, or magazine. Another technology—the **jukebox**—uses an array of discs in a "library." The jukebox is so named because of its similarity to the familiar machines that play 45 rpm records in restaurants and bars.

Pioneer

Not surprisingly, Pioneer offers CD-ROM jukeboxes in addition to their popular CD changers. Although most other companies make jukeboxes that hold 50 to 200 discs, Pioneer markets jukeboxes on each side of those numbers—a "personal jukebox" that holds 18 discs and a huge 500-disc jukebox.

Pioneer DRM-1804X

Interface:	SCSI-2
Access time:	300 ms
Data transfer rate:	614 KB/sec
Data buffer:	128 KB
CD-ROM formats supported:	CD-DA, High Sierra, Rock Ridge, CD-ROM-XA, Multisession PhotoCD, CD-R
Suggested list price:	$2,495

The DRM-1804X personal jukebox has a single drive mechanism, but holds three 6-disc magazines. One unique aspect of the DRM-1804X is that the optical mechanism is at the top of the machine, so you put your CD-ROMs in upside down. This feature is said to protect the head from dust and other contaminants that normally settle on face-up optics.

Pioneer DRM-5004X

Interface:	SCSI-2
Access time:	300 ms
Data transfer rate:	614 KB/s
Data buffer:	256 KB
CD-ROM formats supported:	CD-DA, High Sierra, Rock Ridge, CD-ROM-XA, Multisession PhotoCD, CD-R
Suggested list price:	From $18,995 (2 QuadSpin drives) to $21,995 (4 QuadSpin drives)

The newly released Pioneer DRM-5004X holds five 100-disc magazines and runs up to four quad-speed CD-ROM drives. Disc switching takes just under 30 seconds. Clearly suited to large offices or universities, it features a premium price—from $18,995 to $21,995, depending on the number of QuadSpin CD-ROM readers included. Pioneer is expected to offer a configuration that includes up to four CD-ROM *recorders* in place of the readers. A setup with one quad-speed recorder and three readers is expected to cost $24,995.

TAC Systems

Although Pioneer has led the way in six-disc magazine technology, it does have some competition in the higher-end jukebox solutions that may be more applicable to large law firms or sites that require access to more than six CDs at one time. One such company is TAC Systems.

TAC JukeDrive

Interface:	SCSI-2
Access time:	300 ms
Data transfer rate:	153 KB/s
Data buffer:	64 KB
CD-ROM formats supported:	CD-DA, High Sierra
Suggested list price:	From $10,595 to $18,595

The TAC JukeDrive comes in 50-disc, 100-disc, and 200-disc configurations. The 50-disc configuration lets two drives operate off the same unit so that two users can simultaneously access the 50-disc library (provided that both users do not request the same disc). The 200-disc JukeDrive can accommodate four drives, increasing the number of simultaneous accesses.

In all the TAC JukeDrive systems, the software loads each CD at its disposal and catalogs the disc labels, adding them to a menu that can be accessed by networked users. TAC Systems claims that JukeDrives can be daisy-chained for a maximum of over 11,000 on-line CDs. All the TAC systems use Hitachi drives and support most CD-ROM formats, with the exception of CD-ROM-XA.

Users of TAC JukeDrive systems tend to be government agencies, communications companies, large law firms, procurement companies, and research institutions that generate a lot of in-house data.

Other Vendors

Companies and government institutions and agencies are finding it economical to archive data with CD-R technology and then make the recorded data available to certain users over a network with jukeboxes. Other vendors of jukebox solutions are also delivering products now, most based on third-party drive and robotic mechanisms.

CD-ROM Arrays

CD-ROM arrays are a cost-effective way to "publish" CD-ROM data across a network so that a large number of users can simultaneously access discs. In essence, arrays or towers (towers are described later in this chapter) are a series of connected, individual drives. Each drive can hold a unique data disc; the array allows multiple users to access the CD library at the same time. In fact, text-based discs can accommodate three or four users on one disc with little degradation in performance across the network.

Arrays are ideal for high-traffic data. If many users need to access your company's disc library, an array is the most economical solution.

Arrays come in a variety of configurations, depending on the manufacturer. Four-disc arrays are common. Some OEM vendors supply *towers*—expandable array systems to which the user can add drives as budget and expansion of data CDs demand.

For example, you can buy a 12-bay tower system with only three or four drives installed. As your system grows, you can plug in additional drives and make minor configuration modifications to the software.

Fixed arrays allow only the number of drives for which the cabinet was originally configured. But fixed arrays can be daisy-chained, providing a way to add drives in four-drive or six-drive increments.

If you anticipate that four drives, for example, is the maximum needed for a given segment of your network, a fixed array is sufficient. If you know that expansion of your datasets is only a matter of time, an expandable tower configuration is not only more economical, but also entails far fewer installation and configuration hassles.

Toshiba TXM-3401A4

Interface:	SCSI-2
Access time:	200 ms
Data buffer:	64 KB
Data transfer rate:	300 KB/s
CD-ROM formats supported:	CD-DA, CD-ROM-XA
Drives in array:	4
Suggested list price:	$3,575

The Toshiba TXM-3401A4 is a four-drive fixed-array system that packs four Toshiba double-speed CD-ROM drives in one compact enclosure. The unit has a good cooling-fan system and standard SCSI ports on the back, allowing you to daisy-chain units or add the TXM-3401A4 to an existing SCSI chain of devices.

Because the drives are based on the standard Toshiba drive mechanisms, there is support for CD-DA, ISO 9660, CD-ROM-XA, and PhotoCD formats.

The industry-high 200 ms average access time makes this array system fast at getting to data; it certainly out-performs most other arrays in a networked environment.

Other Arrays

JVC, Todd Systems, and other manufacturers and OEMs make fixed-array systems. See Appendix G, "Miscellaneous Hardware and Software Vendors," for company information.

CD-ROM Towers

Tower systems are expandable versions of arrays that allow you to start out small—with two or three drives—and add as demand grows. Many third-party OEMs have begun putting together comprehensive network tower systems, using off-the-shelf CD-ROM drives in custom-designed cabinets. The clear differentiating factors among tower systems are these:

- Ease of expansion
- Software
- Drives used

TAC Systems

TAC Systems offers a full line of tower systems. You can purchase towers with any number of Hitachi drives installed and add more drives as your needs expand. The maximum tower configuration available for TAC Systems is 18 separate drives in one enclosure. In addition to manufacturing a wide variety of tower systems, TAC can build custom towers to fill your specific needs.

Todd Systems

Todd Systems offers a veritable buffet of array, fixed-array, and tower systems limited only by your imagination and budget. Todd was one of the first companies to offer tower solutions in networked environments and has the experience to custom-build systems for almost any CD-ROM requirement.

Chapter 14

Creating CD-ROMs

14

For compiling and publishing your own in-house databases or other CD-ROM materials, consider **mastering**, or recording, your own CDs. The technology for in-house production of CDs has advanced enormously, making production a mere question of budget rather than expertise. Corporate databases, inventories, and archives can be recorded, distributed, or put in vaults for safekeeping. CD-R drives make distribution of massive amounts of data throughout a company cost effective.

If you'd like to get into professional CD-ROM publishing, you can have your **CD-R** discs professionally duplicated hundreds or thousands of times—a process that is usually much cheaper than duplicating your own CDs on a CD recorder.

This chapter shows you how to make your own CD-ROMs for internal or commercial use. It lists some of the current crop of CD recorders, tells you how to contact professional CD pressing companies, and lists some of the software tools you can use to create multimedia presentations for CD-ROM.

How To Master Your Own CD-ROM Data Discs

Many companies are finding that archiving data or publishing company databases on CD-ROM discs is an affordable and productive way to get information quickly to customers, employees, and the public. The major drawback to recording your own CDs in the past has been cost: initial CD-R drives typically cost $15,000 or more. Prices have plummeted in the past two years, however.

The dye-based recordable media used in CD-R drives has also come down substantially in price, with single blank discs selling for under $20.

CD-R makes a lot of sense for organizations that have large sets of data that must be periodically distributed to a wide audience. Catalogs, transaction records, and the like can require large amounts of storage, making them difficult and costly to distribute by

EXPLANATION

Record Your Own

Some special CD-ROM drives can create CDs. These CD-R (or CD-Recordable) drives use special, blank media for the recording of data in standard CD formats such as CD and CD-ROM-XA.

EXPLANATION

CD-R

The use of the term *CD-R* in this chapter refers to the recording of accessible data on a CD-ROM recordable disc.

EXPLANATION

Premastering and Mastering Software

Premastering is the process of formatting the data on the PC in the way it will be placed on the disc; *mastering* is the process of copying the data onto an actual CD. Premastering can occur in the computer's RAM (if there is enough) but is usually done on the hard drive or on a tape drive.

conventional means. Compact disc, however, offers a simple, low-cost alternative.

Understanding the Premastering Process

The best CD-R drives in the world are useless without **premastering and mastering software**. Without these important tools, the recorded CD-R discs are not compatible—or readable—by standard CD-ROM drives. Although you can write data to CD-R drives with many software packages, only full-featured premastering systems allow you to record in industry-standard formats and offer a variety of other features.

Premastering, or logical formatting, is the process of converting your data—a company database, archival data, or scanned images—into a format that is accepted by the standard CD-ROM drive. Chapter 2, "CD-ROM Specifications Explained," describes many of these formats, such as ISO 9660, PhotoCD, and CD-ROM-XA.

When you use software to premaster data, it accepts your DOS-based data as input and produces as output a disc image of the data in the logical format that will be transferred to the blank CD. For this reason, premastering software needs massive amounts of hard drive storage space to record the disc image—up to 640 megabytes, or the equivalent of the final CD.

Because hard drives are expensive, the best premastering software supports large-capacity tape drives—4-mm and 8-mm drives are the most popular and have capacities in the 2-to-6-gigabyte range. The premastering software can then take your finished data or data application and store it in logical format on inexpensive tape. An added benefit of using tape as an intermediary storage point for premastering is that you can make multiple, different masters, store them on a tape or tapes, and then run a series of CD-R discs from one tape session.

But Aren't Tape Drives Expensive?

There are pros and cons to the use of tape in the mastering process, however. The tape drives themselves are $2,000 to $7,000, even though the tape itself is cheap. If you don't anticipate mastering a large number of different discs at one time, a large hard drive, devoted strictly to storing the premastered disc image, may be more economical. Hard drives in the 600-megabyte range are currently going for about $800. If your network or workstation needs tape backup, on the other hand, consider a 4-mm tape drive that can serve as both a backup for the system and as a premastering facility for disc production.

All premastering software is not created equal. Beyond the CD-ROM formats supported, a number of other factors must be accounted for. For example, because of the unique, spiraling track of the CD-ROM's recorded surface, data recorded on the inner tracks of the disc is more quickly accessed than data on the outer rim. Premastering software should allow you to determine where datasets, or files, are placed on the disc—reserving the most frequently accessed files for the inner tracks and relegating the least-used data to the farther reaches of the disc. Organizing your data in such a way increases the disc's performance.

In addition to optimizing the placement of data, the software should conserve space—that is, it should recognize blank areas within an image and eliminate them. When dumping a disc image to tape, for example, the software may read blank sectors of the hard drive and transfer them intact to the disc image, resulting in wasted CD-ROM disc space.

Simulation of the finished product from the hard disk is also a key ingredient in good premastering software. It's best to run data from its *disc image* to see whether everything runs smoothly and the data is properly accessible before you make the expensive commitment to record the data on a blank disc. Recording to a CD-ROM is an expense in not only media, but valuable time: CDs take anywhere from a half hour to an hour to write, and (except on a few specific drives) you can't interrupt the process in the middle and start over—it ruins the disc. Some premastering software even simulates CD-ROM access times in test mode, allowing you to better determine how optimized your data is for the end user or the end user's application.

In general, you'll want to record your own CDs in the ISO 9660 format, which makes them compatible with the widest possible range of CD-ROM drives. Specialty applications (such as multimedia and PhotoCD) may mean you have to use different formats, however. For storing text-based or simple image-based databases, the ISO 9660 format is more than adequate.

Once the disc image of your data is saved and tested, the simple task of mastering begins. The mastering software reads the disc image from the hard drive or tape and transfers it to the CD-R drive, imprinting your data on a standard CD-ROM-format recordable disc. The recorded disc can be accessed, copied, or sent to a mastering facility where multiple copies can be mass-produced after making a production master from the CD-R disc.

Looking at Premastering and Mastering Software

One of the factors fueling the expansion of CD-R use is the availability of a number of top-notch premastering and mastering software packages. Early-issue mastering software was difficult to use and required a great deal of formatting knowledge to use effectively; most mastering software is now turnkey in nature and is compatible with virtually all the standard CD-R drives on the market.

There are two ways to premaster a disc. In the first, you build an actual image on a physical disk or tape. In the second, you create "virtual disc images" on the fly. In other words, the software builds the image directly from the disk files and transfers the image to the recordable disc as it goes along, eliminating the need for large hard drives or auxiliary tape systems. However, virtual-image software also prevents you from testing your data's viability and usability before committing it to CD-R disc. You can test your data, however, with the first method, and using a staged area for disc images makes multiple copies of one image relatively painless.

Note that most CD-R drives now come bundled with at least some premastering software. Although this software may be less sophisticated than more full-featured—and full-priced—premastering packages, for most data-storage purposes, the bundled software may be just fine. The following sections describe just a few stand-alone premastering programs.

Tempra CD Maker

The Windows-based Tempra CD Maker mastering software from Mathematica has a number of features to recommend it:

- Allows individual tagging of files, directories, and partitions to be recorded
- Has a selection of ISO 9660 or High Sierra formats
- Provides simulation of CD for data testing

The Tempra CD Maker supports the Philips CD recorder and retails for about $1,495.

Mathematica also plans to sell a hardware/software package that includes a Philips CD-R drive and a full range of Mathematica authoring and animation tools.

SimpliCD

A longtime leader in the use of CD-ROM in the UNIX marketplace, Young Minds now sells a Windows-based ISO 9660 formatter. Featuring a completely menu-and-button-driven interface, SimpliCD is an easy way to set up single-speed, double-speed, and (soon) quad-speed discs. SimpliCD retails for around $1,100.

CD-Prepare and CD-Record

DataWare Technology has two premastering and mastering software components: CD-Prepare and CD-Record. These software titles are pretty self explanatory: The Prepare product produces a disc image—not virtual—that it stores on disk or tape. The disc image can be tested before you use CD-Record to send it to the disc in the recorder.

CD-GEN

The CD-GEN software from CD-ROM Strategies, Inc., supports most CD-ROM file structures and formats and has many additional features. It allows simple ordering of data for dataset optimization on the CD-ROM disc and provides support for all major CD-R recorders (including the Sony CDW-900E and the Philips CDD 521).

CD-GEN allows you to perform premastering in multiple sessions to tape—a godsend for those who are tight on hard drive space or for those who want to create discs over a period of time.

The simulation portion of the program allows you to test data access from a disc image. You can even tweak the simulated CD-ROM drive's specifications to see, for example, how the data reacts on a 600-ms versus a 200-ms CD-ROM drive.

As a bonus, the CD-GEN software can also perform on-the-fly CD-R images, bypassing the creation of the disc or tape image.

Although many software developers have taken premastering and mastering software and broken them into separate, complimentary packages, CD-ROM Strategies has delivered a full-function, all-in-one solution to recording CD-R data.

Looking at CD-R Drives

Large manufacturers have begun releasing CD-R drives, making prices very competitive. Bare drives—just the CD-R mechanism itself—run in the $3,000 to $7,000 range. Premastering and mastering software add from $1,200 to $3,000 to the final cost. Many companies are beginning to offer CD-R hardware/software bundles that slash costs even further. As competition heats up, look for continued price drops.

JVC, Philips, Sony, Ricoh, Pinnacle Micro, and Meridian Data all have competitively priced systems shipping now. Other systems have been announced but are not yet shipping. Keep in mind that CD-R may be the fastest growing segment in the CD-ROM industry; prices should fall and capabilities should increase dramatically over the next 12 months.

The hardware/software packages described in the following sections provide entire solutions to moving data onto CD-R discs.

Pinnacle Micro RCD-202

The RCD-202 from Pinnacle Micro supports the recording of virtually all CD-ROM formats. CD-DA, PhotoCD, and mixed audio/data formats are supported. The drive has a standard SCSI interface and RCA jacks (see fig. 14.1). The Pinnacle Micro internal, half-height unit is an exceptional value at $3,995.

External	
Compatibility: PC, Macintosh, or MPC-compliant	
Interface: SCSI, SCSI-2, or Proprietary	
Formats supported: CD-DA, ISO 9660, High Sierra, CD-ROM- XA, PhotoCD	
Average access time:	3000 ms
Transfer rate:	153 KB/s
Data buffer:	64 KB
Software included: Premastering, mastering	
Suggested list price:	$3,995

FIGURE 14.1

The Pinnacle Micro RCD-202.

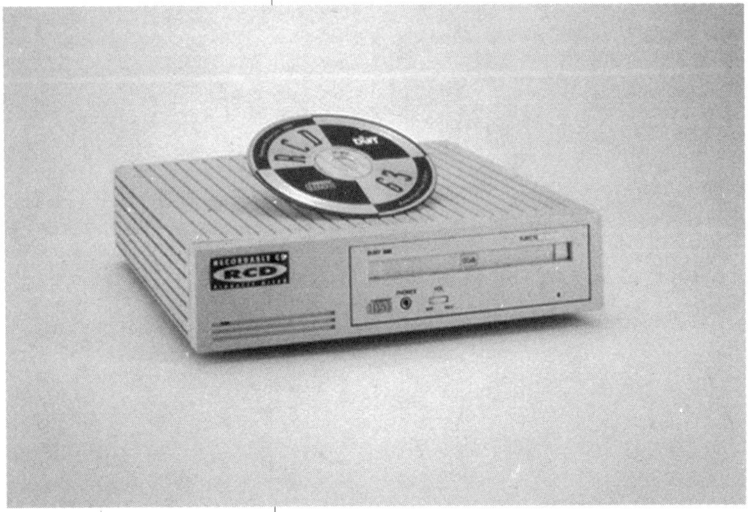

Meridian Data Personal SCRIBE 500

External	
Compatibility: PC, Macintosh, or MPC-compliant	
Interface: SCSI-2	
Formats supported: CD-DA, ISO 9660, High Sierra, CD-ROM-XA, PhotoCD	
Average Access time:	350 ms
Transfer rate:	153 KB/s
Data buffer:	64 KB
Software included: Premastering, mastering	
Suggested list price:	$7,995

FIGURE 14.2

The Meridian Data Personal SCRIBE 500.

Meridian ships a whole system—drive, software for mastering, and SCSI adapter and cables. The Meridian Data Personal SCRIBE 500 supports ISO 9660, CD-DA, and PhotoCD formats (see fig. 14.2).

The Meridian package includes the following:

- Personal SCRIBE software for CD mastering
- CD-ROM recorder, cable, and interface card
- One blank CD

Personal SCRIBE 500 is an affordable, highly versatile system that should be at the top of any list for consideration. Meridian Data has a strong presence in the optical field (the company claims that nearly 75 percent of all published CD-ROM titles originated on a Meridian hardware/software system). For in-house data duplication, archiving, or distribution, the Personal SCRIBE 500 is a perfect solution.

Other Meridian Data Innovations

Meridian also sells a networked CD-R drive and has announced a joint venture with Kodak to provide multi-session PhotoCD capabilities across a network. The NETSCRIBE 1000, like the Personal SCRIBE 500, packs all hardware and software into one bundle. The basic NETSCRIBE 1000 package also has NetWare support for up to five users. A networked CD-R enables multiple users to archive valuable data and images to the CD-R for off-site storage or use in an array for publishing the finished data to the company network. The five-user NETSCRIBE 1000, including all hardware and software, is $13,995.

Meridian Data is best known for its CD-ROM networking software: CD-Net. CD-Net is used to network multiple CD-ROM drives under the Novell NetWare operating system. When considering array systems or jukeboxes for use across the network, Meridian CD-Net may be the best software solution available.

Philips 521WR

External

Compatibility: PC, Macintosh, or MPC-compliant	
Interface: SCSI-2	
Formats supported: CD-DA, ISO 9660, High Sierra, CD-ROM-XA, PhotoCD	
Average Access time:	350 ms
Transfer rate:	153 KB/s
Data buffer:	64 KB
Software included: Premastering, mastering	
Suggested list price:	$5,995

Philips offers full CD-R publishing packages running under Microsoft Windows and for the Macintosh System 7. Not only do the publishing systems include all the necessary hardware for mastering CDs, the Windows-based mastering software handles ISO 9660, High Sierra, CD-DA, and PhotoCD formats. Software upgrades allow the 521WR to record CD-ROM-XA and CD-I format discs as well.

JVC
Personal ROMMaker

External

Compatibility: PC, Macintosh, or MPC-compliant	
Interface: SCSI-2	
Formats supported: CD-DA, ISO 9660, High Sierra, CD-ROM-XA	
Average Access time:	300 ms
Transfer rate:	153 KB/s
Data buffer:	128 KB
Software included: Premastering, mastering	
Suggested list price:	$9,995

JVC offers premastering software and hardware solutions for both Macintosh and DOS machines (see fig. 14.3). The system's software creates a disc image on a hard drive that is a part of the JVC system. Once the disc image is created, you can test the data in its disc-image format. From the hard drive, the JVC software can then move the data to a CD-R.

FIGURE 14.3

The JVC Personal ROMMaker is a new, low-cost, CD-ROM archiving system that supports Macintosh and DOS machines.

The JVC system includes everything you need to create CD-R discs, including a large hard drive for data-disc images and CD-ROM image testing.

Sony CDW-900E

External

Compatibility: PC, UNIX, Macintosh, or MPC-compliant	
Interface: SCSI-2	
Formats supported: CD-DA, ISO 9660, High Sierra, CD-ROM-XA, MMCD	
Average Access time:	350 ms
Transfer rate:	154 KB/s
Data buffer:	64 KB
Software included: Premastering, mastering	
Suggested list price:	$7,995

Sony's CDW-900E is a double-speed transfer-rate drive that supports major CD-ROM formats (ISO 9660 and High Sierra) as well as Sony's format for its MMCD player. Unlike other CD-R drives on the market, the Sony cannot read standard CD-ROM discs.

Executive CDs

Sony's MMCD (multimedia CD) player uses standard CDs written in a proprietary format to provide a platform for multimedia applications in a portable package. The software offerings for this player are mostly targeted at the traveling business executive; titles include foreign-language instruction and business-database applications.

When used with the recently announced Sony Multimedia Authoring software, the CDW-900E makes an ideal system for producing prototype CD-ROM-XA application titles. It is *not* good for standard CD-ROM distribution of data, however. The drive and software are sold primarily to application developers.

How To Develop CD-ROM Applications

When it comes to CD-ROM applications, data isn't everything. To produce a usable, standalone, CD-ROM application, there's a lot more to do than dump the contents of your company's customer list onto a disc and turn it loose on the sales force. For example, although 99 percent of Prophone's excellent business phone-number CD-ROM is just that—names and phone numbers—it would be a useless lump of data without its fine search-and-retrieval software.

That's the bottom line in producing high-quality CD-ROM applications: the interface. Big databases require elegant front ends. Multimedia applications with mounds of sound, video, and text need a system for pulling it into a useful tool.

Although you won't be able to build your own multimedia CD-ROM by the time you finish this chapter, we guarantee you'll have a good understanding of the hard work that goes into producing all the fine CD titles we've described in this book.

The first (and perhaps the only obvious) decision a CD-ROM developer must make is what form the application will take. That is, will the application be primarily text or primarily other media, such as graphics, video, or sound. Multimedia and text-based applications share some similarities in the development process, but tools for creating the two basic types of CD-ROM applications are vastly different. Each application type poses a different set of challenges for the developer.

Multimedia development adds another layer of complexity to the development process. Not only must text and graphic elements be indexed for later retrieval, but sound, video, and animation may also play a large part in the finished product. Fortunately, a number of multimedia development products are now on the market, easing the construction of complex software titles.

Text-based applications are usually databases of information from which users need to extract and compile data. The applications may include graphic images, but their primary purpose is to communicate text information.

Because the meat of the application is the database's text, two factors are critical in molding the lump of textual data into a solid application: the indexing of the text and the software that performs the searches.

First of all, the text must be in a format that the indexing software can read. For example, Microsoft's Viewer can read only Microsoft Word files. Other indexing software accepts only ASCII text or RTF (Rich Text Format) files. Fortunately, the better packages can import a variety of standard word processing formats for the indexing process.

Indexing Applications

Text-based CD-ROM authoring software includes utilities for indexing the database of text. A thorough indexing of a volume of history, for example, would compile all references to every word—and its location in the volume. The compiled index serves as the gateway for the user front end.

To continue with the example of a history volume, assume that the indexing software found all occurrences of the name *Richard Nixon* in your 2,000-page history volume. The compiled index has *Richard Nixon* pointers and cross-listings to specific sections of the volume that contain references to the former President. When a user queries the application for "Richard Nixon," the software goes to the index and provides the user with a list of chapters or articles that contain the queried text. This list comes from the stored, compiled index.

Indexing, then, plays a critical role in an application's performance—whether it is text based or multimedia based. For example, you would never want a complete index of all the text in a database: indexing words such as *the* and *and* serves no purpose. These words are called *noise words*; good indexing software provides a way to exclude such words from the index-building process. You can usually submit such a list to the software before indexing. Here's a partial list of typical noise words:

a
an
and
that
the
there
which
would

You get the picture. Unless you're doing textual analysis concerning an author's writing style, indexing noise words is a waste of CD-ROM space.

Other irrelevant words may not be as readily apparent as noise words. For example, it would be similarly useless to index all the occurrences of the word *CD-ROM* in this book—you'd be presented with a list of nearly every page in this book. In the development of text-based applications, proper and economical indexing is the key to building a good end product.

Aside from the exclusion of noise words, indexing must also mirror the uses the data will be put to in the application. For example, Bowker/Reed's Books in Print on CD-ROM allows you to search the contents of the database for given predefined fields. No other indexing is necessary in this application. To simplify the search interface in Books in Print, you can search by any of the following fields:

Author
Title
Publisher
ISBN
Audience

(Other fields are available in the application; these are just some examples.) When searching for a book in this database, why would any user need a text that is 100-percent indexed? The developer, in constructing the application, indexes only those elements that the application (and therefore the user) would want to search for. The result is a faster application, a less confusing interface for the user, and a vast conservation of the CD-ROM disc space used to hold the compiled indexes. Not to mention a time-saver in the initial indexing and preparation process.

Unless the developer is submitting an entire text for thorough indexing to the software, the indexing process can be a tedious one—a trained operator or the developer must make decisions about what gets indexed, what can be left out, and what categories various words or fields fall into. This is a necessary and time-consuming evil of building text-based CD-ROM applications. But the effort pays off in the finished product.

We'll say it again: in application development, the index is the key to a successful CD-ROM.

Using Search-and-Retrieval Software

If you've ever looked at text-based CD-ROM applications, you've noted that they all basically allow you to search for items or citations by submitting a request to the application. Most are menu based, offering a variety of options for requesting data; others merely present you with a stark and uninviting question mark.

Welcome to the user interface and search-and-retrieval engines. Search-and-retrieval front ends are available to developers as a tool kit—the indexing software puts tags in the text; the search-and-retrieval software uses the compiled index to find citations, present choices to the user, and go to and retrieve the chosen text or field.

Obviously, not all search-and-retrieval engines are created equal. And not all are suitable to every type of application task. Before we go into the features of search-and-retrieval software, let's look at the individual components of this application front end.

Text-based search software usually incorporates a text menu from which the user chooses various options and actions. The menus may be as simple as "Search" and "Print" options or as complex as a multilayered, pull-down menu of Boolean operands, clipboards for marked text, and printer configurations. In some search-and-retrieval software development kits, the search interfaces are not customizable and offer the developers little freedom to add their own items or menu choices. Other development kits allow a complete customization of the interface. But despite interfaces with limited customization, you'll begin to recognize similar interfaces if you use a variety of CD titles from different developers. You'll also begin to favor—and **detest**, perhaps—the capabilities or shortcomings of the various engines.

There's good reason for the use of standard interfaces. Unless the application is so unique in the presentation of its material that it needs a custom search-and-retrieval engine, a ready-made interface allows the CD publisher to more quickly produce the application and bring it to market. Why reinvent the wheel when there are a number of great packages available?

The interface is intimately tied to the capabilities of the search-and-retrieval software that lies beneath the surface. Menu items and options, then, are often based in large part on the underlying capabilities of the software.

Note that the primary areas of search are clearly defined for the user at the outset—no other options are allowed at this stage. If the *Movies by Titles* and *Essays* options are menu items, you must branch to these areas before continuing. This arrangement may be a

NOTE

Good Data, Bad Interface

Based on our experience, the contents of a CD-ROM application may not be enough to persuade us to use it if it has a search-and-retrieval engine we've grown to dislike. All the data in the world is not worth the aggravation of certain limitations.

plus—users are guided to areas in which the developer expects they may have an interest. The downside of this menu system is a limited view of the entire database; options for wider searches open up only after a category has been selected. This particular interface allows the developer to program the initial menu choices—but that is all. From a development standpoint, this particular engine is extremely easy to implement and produces highly effective full-text applications. The look and feel of the interface during the searches (as is true for most search-and-retrieval engines) is identical for all applications that use this software for development.

Flexibility and logic are key in the choice of an interface front end. For a video guide, the Folio front end with its main-menu choices is a better interface than a cryptic search option. The individual who will browse a video database expects a simpler approach to finding information.

Looking at Search-and-Retrieval Engines

As you might expect, the search-and-retrieval engines that lie underneath the interfaces have different capabilities as well. Some search engines provide you with a list of choices you then can view one at a time; you return to the list after each viewing. Other engines require you to perform the search each time you view a listing. Still others allow you to compile a list of citations and print the entire set—to the screen, to a disk, or to a printer. Again, the purpose of the application determines the best type of retrieval. For most applications, however, the more options available to the user for retrieval, the better. And unless the developer anticipates fundamental confusion in using search techniques, the broadest possible search capabilities should be provided.

Aside from how the citations are retrieved—to the screen, the printer, or to disk files—another consideration in retrieval software is the way text is displayed. In World Library's Library of the Future (Windows edition), for example, you can display text in individual windows with automatic scrolling (see fig. 14.4). The Folio engine for DOS also layers the screen with window on top of window of retrieved text when you retrieve more than one item, allowing you to skip back and forth between retrieved citations at will. But note: a retrieval engine that piles up cross-references on the screen for an electronic software manual would be completely inappropriate for reading Dickens' *Bleak House* on a monitor. The *Bleak House* application—and its ultimate use: reading—require a totally different interface design to make it useful.

FIGURE 14.4

World Library's interface for Library of the Future allows speed-selectable automatic scrolling of text (AutoScroll) for reading literature without paging with the mouse or keyboard.

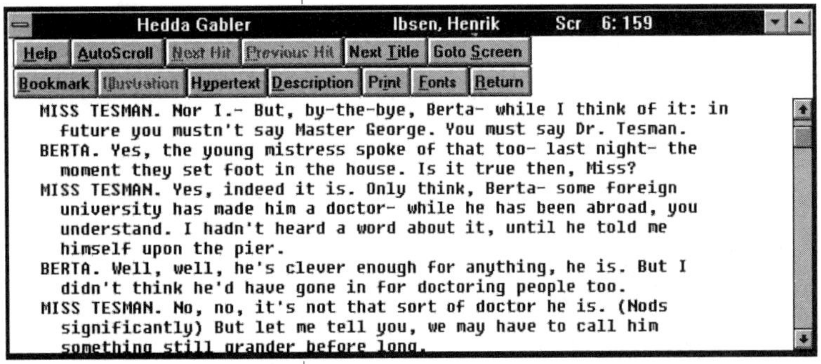

Hedda Gabler
Ibsen, Henrik
Scr 6: 159
Help
AutoScroll
Next Hit
Previous Hit
Next Title
Goto Screen
Bookmark
Illustration
Hypertext
Description
Print
Fonts
Return
MISS TESMAN. Nor I.- But, by-the-bye, Berta- while I think of it: in future you mustn't say Master George. You must say Dr. Tesman.
BERTA. Yes, the young mistress spoke of that too- last night- the moment they set foot in the house. Is it true then, Miss?
MISS TESMAN. Yes, indeed it is. Only think, Berta- some foreign university has made him a doctor- while he has been abroad, you understand. I hadn't heard a word about it, until he told me himself upon the pier.
BERTA. Well, well, he's clever enough for anything, he is. But I didn't think he'd have gone in for doctoring people too.
MISS TESMAN. No, no, it's not that sort of doctor he is. (Nods significantly) But let me tell you, we may have to call him something still grander before long.

Understanding Search Terms and Operations

Depending on the search-and-retrieval engine in the developer's application, you may or may

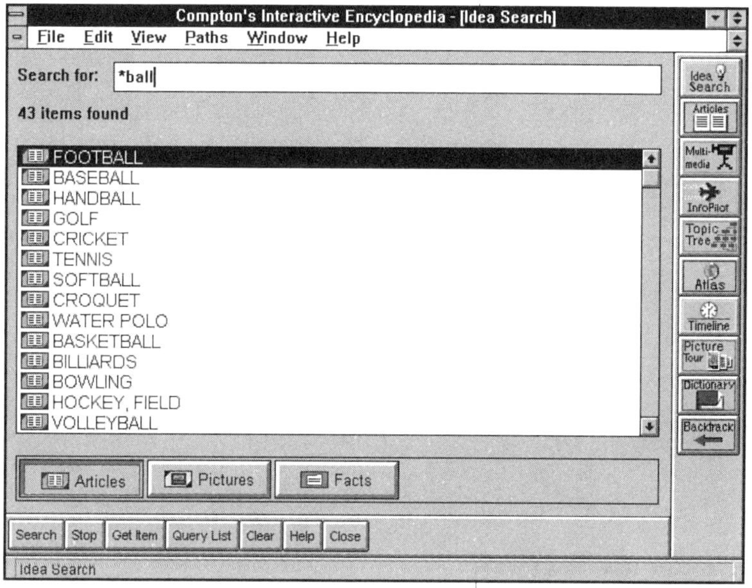

FIGURE 14.5

The use of the wildcard asterisk (*) before the word *ball* in the search calls up all articles in the encyclopedia that end in *ball* as well as any article that contains *ball* as part of the text (or any part of any word in the text).

not be able to do a large number of types of searches. Here are some of the types of searches that may be allowed, based on the search-and-retrieval software:

- **Wildcard.** Just as you use wildcard operations in DOS, some search engines allow you to use wildcards when searching databases. For example, if you use ***ball** in a search of Compton's Interactive Encyclopedia, you get the results shown in figure 14.5.

- **Boolean.** Boolean searches—or Boolean logic—are a series of search techniques in which inclusion or exclusion of a combination of elements produces a set of results. For example, a search of our history text with the Boolean expression **Nixon AND Vietnam** results in a list of all articles that contain mentions of *both* Nixon *and* Vietnam. Here are other examples of Boolean operation:

  OR: automobile OR car

  NOT: automobile NOT Ford

  Good search software allows *nested* Boolean operations. For example, **automobile AND car NOT Ford** produces references to any article that contains the words *automobile* and *car* but not if the word *Ford* is also mentioned.

  In addition to nesting, some search software allows Boolean *proximity* searches. If a word falls within the same sentence, paragraph, or page, it is a candidate for the <u>**proximity**</u> search. The search **automobile AND Ford SENTENCE** produces all citations in which *automobile* and *Ford* fall in the same sentence.

- **Phrase.** Search software that allows phrase look-ups is especially useful in full-text documents. You input the exact phrase you are looking for, and the search engine finds the text string within the database of text. Entering **Four score and seven years ago** for our history CD-ROM, for example, takes you to Lincoln's Gettysburg Address.

  Phrase searches are also useful for finding all occurrences of phrases in a collection of texts in one database. Entering **Oedipus complex**, for example, calls up all the references to this Freudian term in Quanta's Monarch Notes. Any application that uses full text should allow phrase searches.

NOTE

Proximity: How Close Is "Close"?

Proximity searches in some software allow proximity values, expressed in numbers, for determining hits or misses. Using **automobiles AND Ford > 5**, for example, ensures that all text that includes the words *automobile* and *Ford* within five words or less of each other is a hit; any other condition is a miss.

- **Field.** Applications based primarily on fixed-field databases (that is, databases in which data exists exclusively in one strictly defined field or another) provide searches within any given field; they may also allow the addition of wildcard searching within any given field. A search for **Morris*** in the Last Name field in a phone-directory database should result in a list of all last names beginning with the letters *morris*: Morris, Morrison, Morrisey, and so on.

Indexing Graphics

Most development packages (although not all) allow the indexing and retrieval of standard graphic elements such as PCX files. And some development packages support only a limited number of graphics formats. If a developer wants to use scanned artwork or product photos in a CD-ROM application, and the scanning software only supports certain graphics formats, the developer must convert the art and photo scans to one of the retrieval software's supported formats. Developers must also take into consideration what resolutions the application-development software supports; it makes no sense to scan or create high-resolution elements if the intended platform does not support the higher resolutions or the retrieval software cannot display it properly.

SGML

To help provide a basis for standard transmission of text from one operating system and application to another without massive reformatting, the SGML (Standard General Markup Language) has been adopted by a number of software application and publishing groups. This language, originally intended for publishing text electronically in a number of desktop publishing and document archiving applications, is already in use in a number of CD-ROM application-development packages. Although it is not an indexing convention, SGML allows any SGML-aware application to format and display text in a uniform manner, despite the text's origin or the platform on which it is used (DOS, Mac, UNIX, and so on). CD-ROM authoring programs that accept SGML-formatted text can easily import documents for use in applications across platforms, regardless of the source of the document. Features of the SGML format also allow for some indexing, making the data preparation and indexing procedure even less complicated.

SGML tags, on the highest level, identify types of documents, which is useful in a many-faceted database. Descriptive tags are used for incorporated elements, such as charts, graphs, or graphics files. Finer-level tags are used for definitions of headings, subheadings, and other subdivisions and special-case text-handling and formatting conventions.

Use of SGML in the data-preparation stage of development smoothes the integration of text retrieval and display in the final stages of development. And as we said, many data-preparation programs accept text with SGML tags—and many add-on packages for popular word processors can add SGML tags to existing word processor documents.

Indexing and Search-and-Retrieval Software

There are dozens of indexing and search-and-retrieval packages available now. All provide developers with tools to index data and provide an interface to the search-and-retrieval engine. These packages permit the developer—for a fee (usually by royalty on a bulk basis)—to include the software on the disc as a part of the application. Other packages charge only for the development software; some allow the developer to include **run-time modules** free of charge.

EXPLANATION

Run-Time Versions

Run-time versions of software (in this case, of search-and-retrieval packages) are free-standing engines that run independently of the development software on the disc and are usually provided free of charge or for a small royalty fee (charged to the developer).

In addition, some development packages allow a full range of search capabilities—from limited field searches to nested Boolean operations and a full complement of graphics indexing and display capabilities—and may also be useful in developing products across different platforms. The trend in development packages, in fact, is toward cross-platform development in which database and multimedia objects are usable in nearly identical formats in any operating system.

This multiplatform strategy lets publishers drastically reduce production costs, and, hopefully, pass on these savings to consumers.

ROMware

Nimbus' ROMware development search-and-retrieval package allows DOS, Windows, and multimedia options. The package is strong on full-text indexing and use of graphics in a DOS environment. The company also makes ROMview, a Windows-based equivalent of the DOS-based ROMware.

The interface is customizable, and searches can be compiled. Searching by phrase and nested Boolean operations is possible; text blocking is also supported. Toolkits for further customization (such as BookFace) allow creation of various display characteristics for specific applications.

Here's an added bonus for developers: Nimbus is also a full-service CD-ROM production facility that provides everything from project consultation to warehousing of finished products.

KAware

The KAware DOS-based development package allows for extensive interface customization. For an excellent example of the flexibility KAware has—particularly with fixed-field databases—see the TFPL CD-ROM Directory, which lists thousands of CD-ROM titles, software distributors, hardware manufacturers and much, much more. The TFPL disc has an extensive array of searchable fields—made possible by the KAware indexing and search-and-retrieval engine. Searches can be further refined within fields or subfields, making it easy for searches to zero-in on specific results.

Another of KAware's retrieval features is its ability to combine previous searches into a printable or disk file. You can also omit certain searches from the compiled list, making misses and mistakes easy to prune from your finished work.

Folio Views and Folio Views for Windows

Although Folio got its biggest boost in the development of on-line technical manuals and software troubleshooting guides, users with little experience also can index and build a standard interface for a text database. One of the best examples of the use of Folio outside the software-manual arena is in Infobases' American History CD. The Folio interface allows for extremely flexible searches on full-text databases. Text is compressed after conversion to the Folio database; a wide variety of word processing formats are supported.

Add-in modules allow developers to scan and perform optical character recognition on text, and then import the text directly into Folio Views. Applications created with Folio Views let users create annotations, bookmarks, and shadow files that can be saved for later reference.

The DOS version of Folio Views has support for graphics files that are stored and viewed separately.

The Folio system is, perhaps, the easiest for the uninitiated to use. The straightforward way in which Folio imports and indexes full-text databases is a painless process. The newer OCR and graphics features make it a perfect development tool for businesses that want to distribute data in stand-alone format in a hurry, and that want to spend as little time as possible making subsequent updates.

The Windows-based version of Folio Views adds font and screen configurations to Folio's excellent basic search-and-retrieval engine. All the ease-of-use in the DOS product is preserved, and there are the additional WYSIWYG features of Windows fonts and formatting. Another great feature for the Windows version is support for OLE: graphics, sound, and even video objects can be imbedded anywhere in Folio Views once they're named and stored.

Font, hierarchy, and highlighting styles can be set as well. Folio text databases developed under DOS can be used with the Windows version, and vice-versa. Print versions of any Folio Views documents retain all formatting.

CD Author/CD Answer

Dataware has been in the CD-ROM development business since there was a CD-ROM development business. Their popular authoring and retrieval development systems are available for every platform from DOS to Windows to the Macintosh. CD Author has utilities that convert and index data; the package also allows users to customize menus from a library of predefined interfaces. The retrieval package, CD Answer, supports a variety of searches, all selectively available during application development: the developer decides how much—or how little—the application will be able to search.

Dataware recently announced multiplatform support for their authoring system, allowing one application to be ported to UNIX, DOS, Apple, Windows, MMCD, and other formats. This flexibility allows developers to quickly deliver products to a number of operating systems and CD formats in a short development cycle. The CD Author/CD Answer system also supports multiple formats recorded to one disc, allowing data on a single disc to be shared by UNIX, DOS, and all other platforms. According to Dataware, over 400 CD-ROM titles have been developed to date using their software.

Dataware's Windows-based package has all the features of the DOS package as well as Windows-based customizable menus, dialog boxes, and buttons. The Windows version supports many of the Windows MCI extensions, allowing the inclusion of graphics and sound objects.

Windows-Based Multimedia Application Development Software

Because Windows multimedia development may involve text, graphics, video, and sound, the multimedia development tools described in the following sections are often more akin to storyboards for the production of films rather than systems for retrieving data. Some of these development tools (most notably Asymetrix's Toolbook) have data-query functions; others only allow selection of prewritten scripts or menu choices and have little opportunity for branching or searching. It's important to note that most of these systems are primarily used for other multimedia presentations rather than CD-ROM-based applications; disk-based and kiosk-based presentations are the most prevalent. There's one exception in this group: a number of commercial applications have been developed using Toolbook.

Smartrieve

Compton's Smartrieve would easily fall into the multimedia authoring category were it not for its extensive search-and-retrieve capabilities. Actually a set of tools, the Compton package allows developers to index a variety of text, graphics, and sound files and formats for use with Compton's search-and-retrieval engine. SMARTBUILD, naturally, is the database indexing and building software; SMARTDR is the retrieval engine that allows the simultaneous search of multiple databases (sound, graphics, or text). A library of user-customizable subroutines for interfaces is included in the SMARTAPI utilities. Another feature of the Smartrieve system is that it allows Compton to build in their Virtual Workspace windows to all applications, giving users a thumbnail view of previous searches, available merely by clicking the representation. Within workspaces, text and graphics can be cut and pasted.

Compton is using these development tools to provide software titles on a variety of platforms including Apple, Tandy, and MMCD.

Toolbook

Asymetrix's Toolbook was one of the first multimedia authoring tools available and is still one of the most favored. Unlike some other development tools, Toolbook is easy to use and extremely versatile in creating text-links and hypertext cross-references.

What makes Toolbook so easy to use is the extensive set of templates included in the basic software package. Users can plug text and graphics into predefined panels and easily customize a wide range of dialog boxes, radio buttons, and menus.

Video and animations in any Windows-supported format can be included as well; OLE support lets you add sound and other objects from a number of Windows-based applications (from spreadsheets to paint programs to word processors).

A number of multimedia publishers have developed titles using Toolbook, and for good reason. Development is straightforward and developers can use off-the-shelf Windows applications to develop all the necessary multimedia elements. Perhaps the biggest reason for its popularity is that Toolbook includes a royalty-free run-time module with its already reasonably priced development kit. Developers both large and small can put together an application and distribute it freely. Examples of Toolbook-developed CD-ROMs include Warner New Media's Desert Storm and EduQuest's National Parks.

The only drawback to Toolbook is its reliance on a page philosophy; in other words, screens full of data are presented one at a time and must be linked by scripts to produce more than one contiguous page of information.

To be fair, however, the scripting capabilities in Toolbook are powerful; if developers take the relatively short time to learn the Toolbook language, they can construct incredibly detailed, linked, hypertext creations. Toolbook's level of hypertext creation and maintenance is more difficult to achieve with other packages, even with the object-oriented application-development tools.

IconAuthor

IconAuthor, the multifaceted authoring toolkit from AIMtech, is one of the most feature rich of any Windows-based multimedia development software available.

The latest version of IconAuthor supports OLE and DDL, making it possible to include any and all Windows-based graphics, sound, text, and video elements from standard Windows applications.

IconAuthor uses a flow-chart approach to application development. A toolbar running along the side of the development space allows the developer to select, in icon format, any type of supported element. The developer then assigns the appropriate text, animation, or other object to the icon and moves down the flow chart, building the application one element at a time.

The program uses extensive branching, and can attach many conditions to events. For example, if you click the mouse during the play of an animation, the application can ask whether you want to see the animation full screen, to continue playing it, or quit. In addition, the branching supports extensive database management of multimedia elements and allows extensive conditional use of objects in many layers.

With its easy-to-understand objects, flow-chart construction, and extensive support of video and branching capabilities, IconAuthor is a full toolbelt for creating the most complex—and exciting—multimedia presentations.

HSC Interactive

HSC Interactive is a trimmed-back version of its big-brother application, IconAuthor. Interactive supports fewer branching elements and has fewer predefined object elements that you can use in the flow-chart builds for finished applications than does IconAuthor.

Other capabilities missing from HSC Interactive, when compared to IconAuthor, are the database management of elements and some graphics-format support. The presentations you develop with Interactive may not be as complex as those possible with IconAuthor, but Interactive is also more than five times less expensive than AIMtech's high-end product.

Authorware

Macromedia's multimedia development package is the top in its class—and the most expensive. Run-time version royalties, similarly, are also top of the heap in terms of price.

But with the price comes a variety of features and performance that many of the other development packages lack. The Authorware system is similar to IconAuthor in its icon-based, flow-chart approach to building applications.

Branching and conditions for branching to other events are even more extensive than those available in other packages, and the latest version of Authorware allows multiple events to occur simultaneously—providing for multitasking multimedia, as it were. For example, while viewing a Video for Windows clip about the first moon landing, you can hit the *A* text button to pop up a related text article or a biography and still photo of Neal Armstrong.

The video formats supported by Authorware include DVI, Video for Windows, and QuickTime for Windows, making it the most video-intensive multimedia development kit available today. OLE and DDL support allow the use of any Windows-based element.

Completely customizable button bars, menus, and dialog boxes round out this one-stop multimedia authoring solution.

StudioXA

Mammoth Micro recently released this cross-platform development tool for producing MMCD (CD-ROM-XA), OS/2, and MPC multimedia titles. The StudioXA authoring system does everything from capturing and storing audio, video, and graphics elements to formatting the data for true XA interleaving of audio and video. Toolkits for sizing video and touching up graphics elements are also included. Video can be captured at rates up to 15 frames per second.

Most importantly, the developer can preview the multimedia production at any time during its creation and any portion of the production can be viewed and edited. Developers can create screen layouts as well as button bars, radio buttons, hot spots, and scroll bars—all without any programming knowledge. Buttons can be scripted to any element or action within the presentation.

Most importantly, StudioXA formats the finished piece in the XA disc format, ready to be recorded onto any CD-R that supports the XA specification. XA-formatted files, of course, can also be premastered onto tape. Developers can preview the finished CD in simulation of a CD-ROM-XA. Most important to developers, Mammoth's companion software, PlayerXA, allows applications created with StudioXA to be played on MPC, OS/2, or MMCD formats with no modification to the original application.

User-Tested, Author-Recommended

Before we leave the discussion of application development tools, we'd like to express our preferences. After reviewing and using well over 150 CD-ROM titles for this book—and in our professions—we've come up with a few favorite user interfaces:

Text-based: Folio Views

Windows-based: Microsoft Viewer

Multimedia-based: Authorware

How To Master, Produce, and Print CD-ROM Applications

Once developers have completed and debugged the CD-ROM application, the premastering and mastering process begins. If developers use premastering software that simulates CD-ROM usage, they can even test the application's performance and make adjustments accordingly.

After debugging and premastering, developers can record the final CD-ROM application on a CD-R disc to produce a formatted CD-ROM disc that can be used to produce a *one-off*.

What's a One-Off?

A *one-off* is a single production copy of a CD-ROM made for testing purposes. The developer sends the CD-R disc or tape master to a one-off facility or full-production house to have a production disc made. This disc is used for extensive testing of the application before a full production run is made. Major developers use multiple one-offs for field testing before making the costly commitment to a full production run.

A number of one-off companies have started up over the last two years; many of them are not even attached to full-production facilities. Their sole reason for existence is to offer one-off test discs and limited-run production CDs. In many cases, these small shops are better suited to providing discs for limited-use CD developers; as a rule, larger full-service facilities don't consider taking projects with very small production runs.

CD-ROM Production Facilities

A number of independent and large commercial facilities are available to the CD-ROM developer for mass production of the final application. Most facilities in this competitive environment offer complete one-stop CD-ROM production.

One successful independent, Nimbus Corporation, offers a full gamut of CD-ROM-production services from data conversion all the way to warehousing. Nimbus, and other full-service facilities, can provide these services:

- Prepare and convert data
- Premaster and master data
- Create master discs and one-off productions
- Take care of full production runs, including quality control
- Provide disc and jewel-case imprinting and packaging
- Arrange shipping and warehousing

Other services available through some facilities include drop shipment of orders to distributors and order fulfillment. In some cases, the last developers may see of their code before it arrives shrink-wrapped in the final package is the CD-R or tape they send to the facility.

The Optical Publishers Association

Independent publishers, in particular, are advised to join the Optical Publishers Association. This Ohio-based professional organization is a clearinghouse of information for CD-ROM application developers. The association provides members with industry updates on a quarterly basis concerning the latest in hardware, software, and production technologies and techniques; a monthly publication, "Digital Publishing Business," focuses on the business aspects of CD-ROM development and production. The association's founder, Richard Bowers, compiles an extensive bibliography of background and technical books and papers on the CD-ROM industry.

Association members also receive information regarding related technical associations, trade shows, and technical seminars and workshops.

Aside from member benefits, the Optical Publisher's Association has taken a proactive role in such issues as multimedia standards development and standards in the interpretability of search-and-retrieval software.

The Optical Publisher's Association may be reached at the following address:

PO Box 212668
Columbus, Ohio 43221

Or you can contact the OPA on CompuServe; just type **GO CDROM VENDORS**.

Chapter 15

CD-ROM on the Road: Going Portable

For those of you whose work keeps you on the go, the notebook computer and its liberating portability have been the answer to a prayer. Yet if you adopt CD-ROM technology, are you going to be tied to a desk again?

The answer, thankfully, is a resounding *no*. Although still in its infancy, portable CD-ROM technology is mature enough for consideration. The small but competent selection of portable, battery-powered drives, integrated notebook machines, portable computers with CD-ROM capability, and specialized CD-player hardware offers enough choice to get you going in this emerging field.

Choosing Your Poison

The decision about what sort of portable CD-ROM hardware to buy is made easier by the somewhat limited selection available. However, you still must decide just what you hope to accomplish with your portable CD-ROM before you can make a choice. Let's take a look at the three classes of hardware—portable drives, integrated notebook systems, and integrated lunchbox systems—and what they offer.

Portable Drives

Portable CD-ROM drives are built using the same technology as Sony Corporation's ubiquitous Discman portable CD player. Portable CD-ROM drives are relatively lightweight and battery-powered. Unfortunately, most are also noticeably slower than their desktop counterparts (a notable exception is Media Vision's Reno, with its 180 ms access time). The slow speed is because the sled that moves the laser pickup is not designed to move quickly—a relatively unimportant thing when you use the drive for music, but very noticeable when you use the drive to access data.

Although the slow-moving sled affects *seek time* (the time it takes the drive to find the next item), it does not hurt the data transfer rate, another important speed specification.

You may want to buy a portable CD-ROM drive for two basic reasons. If you already own a notebook or portable computer and don't look forward to investing in another, a portable drive can add CD-ROM capability to your existing computer. Most portable drives connect to the parallel port of your machine, using either a parallel-to-SCSI adapter or some proprietary adapter. A CD-ROM drive that uses the SCSI scheme is clearly the preference.

The other reason you may choose a portable drive is cost. No, portable drives are not inherently cheaper than packages with integrated CD-ROM drives; but if you intend to use CD-ROM at your desk as well as on the road, the portable drive can pull double duty and save you hundreds of dollars.

The following sections describe some of the portable drives currently available. Each drive is rated with up to five disc icons (five being the best rating) based on any features that make the drive exceptional. If a drive has no disc icons, it's not bad (we tried to stay away from bad drives all together), it's just average. The list is not intended to be exhaustive. Because of the nature of portables—they require a state-of-the-art design just to make them work—there are really no bad portables on the market. Base your choice on specifications and price.

CD Technology Porta-Drive Model T4100

External (Portable)

- ✔ PC compatible
- ✔ Macintosh compatible
- ✔ MPC Level 2 compliant

- ✔ PhotoCD, single session
- ✔ PhotoCD, multisession

Interface:

- ✔ SCSI
- ✔ SCSI-2
- Proprietary

Average access time	320 ms
Transfer rate	300 KB/s
Buffer	64 KB

Audio:

- ✔ Standard RCA jacks
- ✔ Headphones
- ✔ 4-pin CD audio out

Suggested list price: $450

Comments: Average specs, and an average price for a portable.

CD Technology Porta-Drive Model T3401

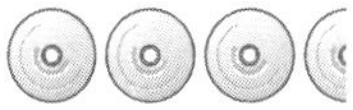

External (Portable)

- ✔ PC compatible
- ✔ Macintosh compatible
- ✔ MPC Level 2 compliant

- ✔ PhotoCD, single session
- ✔ PhotoCD, multisession

Interface:
- ✔ SCSI
- ✔ SCSI-2
- Proprietary

Average access time	200 ms
Transfer rate	330 KB/s
Buffer	256 KB

Audio:
- ✔ Standard RCA jacks
- ✔ Headphones
- ✔ 4-pin CD audio out

Suggested list price: $700

Comments: Very good specs but priced beyond comparable (and even better) drives.

The T4100 is CD Technology's new star. Weighing in at 1 pound, it's obviously great for travel, but they didn't skimp on the features to make it so. It includes a headphone jack and volume control, a SCSI/SCSI-2 interface, and your choice of a Mac or MPC version of America Alive GUIDisc—a multimedia tour of the U.S. You can add a battery pack for 2 hours of continuous operation. The specs aren't stellar, but certainly aren't bad for a portable.

The price of the CD Porta-Drive Model T3401 includes drive, caddie, power supply, enclosure, and instructions. SCSI cards are sold separately by the company, but Adaptec, Future Domain, and Procom SCSI adapters should be fine if you use the appropriate Toshiba drivers.

CD Technology also sells a parallel-to-SCSI adapter—a SCSI-on-the-printer-port solution for the external drives. This adapter makes it possible to easily attach either drive to a notebook computer that has no slot available for a SCSI card. The adapter also is an ideal solution for those who are squeamish about opening up PCs and messing with SCSI interface cards.

CD-ROM BOOK

QUE

AWARD OF EXCELLENCE

NEC MultiSpin-3XP

NEC's triple-speed portable drive has it all. It's priced below many double-speed portables, has a SCSI-2 interface, and blows away the competition on performance. The NEC name doesn't hurt, either.

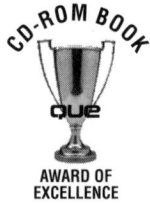

NEC MultiSpin-3XP

External (Portable)

- ✔ PC compatible
- ✔ Macintosh compatible
- ✔ MPC Level 2 compliant

- ✔ PhotoCD, single session
- ✔ PhotoCD, multisession

Interface:

- ✔ SCSI
- ✔ SCSI-2
- Proprietary

Average access time	195 ms
Transfer rate	450 KB/s
Buffer	256 KB

Audio:

- ✔ Standard RCA jacks
- ✔ Headphones
- 4-pin CD audio out

Suggested list price: $415

Comments: Portable doesn't get any better than this. Low price, stellar specs, and NEC quality.

Notice that the NEC MultiSpin-3XP portable offers the same performance as its desktop counterparts, the 3XI and 3XE (described in Chapter 3, "How To Select CD-ROM Drives"). This portable MultiSpin drive is more than adequate for multimedia tasks, including full-motion video in QuickTime for the Mac or Video for Windows. As a bonus, the sticker price on this triple-speed drive compares favorably with some double-speed drives.

Liberty 115 Series

External (Portable)

✔ PC compatible
✔ Macintosh compatible
✔ MPC Level 2 compliant

✔ PhotoCD, single session
✔ PhotoCD, multisession

Interface:
✔ SCSI
✔ SCSI-2
Proprietary

Average access time	200 ms
Transfer rate	300 KB/s
Buffer	256 KB

Audio:
✔ Standard RCA jacks
✔ Headphones
4-pin CD audio out

Suggested list price: $649

Comments: It's fast but the price is a drawback. Because Liberty sells mostly direct, this is one case where MSRP is real.

The Liberty model 115CD-P has a parallel-port SCSI adapter. All systems—Macintosh, PC with host adapter, or PC with parallel port—ship with cable, power cord, and software for drive installation. An optional padded carrying case is $29.

Liberty Systems

Liberty Systems is best known for bundling a variety of mass-storage devices with SCSI and parallel-to-SCSI interfaces. The company specializes in removable-media drives (such as Syquest systems) and high-end optical products. The 115CD-P portable CD-ROM reader is a Toshiba drive in a Liberty enclosure with parallel-to-SCSI, Macintosh, and standard PC SCSI connection options. The 115CD-P prices out lower than the CD Technology Porta-Drive T3401, which is based on the same Toshiba XM-301 drive mechanism.

Media Vision Reno

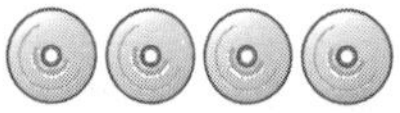

External (Portable)

- ✔ PC compatible
- ✔ Macintosh compatible
- ✔ MPC Level 2 compliant

- ✔ PhotoCD, single session
- ✔ PhotoCD, multisession

Interface:
- ✔ SCSI
- ✔ SCSI-2
- Proprietary

Average access time	180 ms
Transfer rate	306 KB/s
Buffer	64 KB

Audio:
- ✔ Standard RCA jacks
- ✔ Headphones
- ✔ 4-pin CD audio out

Suggested list price: $349

Comments: Fast and cheap—but hard to find as of this writing. Look for more price cuts and availability problems, especially with Media Vision's well-publicized financial problems. Some distributors won't carry Media Vision because they are waiting to see how the company weathers the storm.

Media Vision's Reno is a portable powerhouse, boasting a super-fast, 180-ms access time and a very low retail price. You can separate the drive from its computer interface, turning it into a portable audio CD player.

Toshiba TXM-4101A

External (Portable)

- ✔ PC compatible
- ✔ Macintosh compatible
- ✔ MPC Level 2 compliant

- ✔ PhotoCD, single session
- ✔ PhotoCD, multisession

Interface:
- ✔ SCSI
- ✔ SCSI-2
- Proprietary

Average access time	320 ms
Transfer rate	300 KB/s
Buffer	64 KB

Audio:
- ✔ Standard RCA jacks
- ✔ Headphones
- 4-pin CD audio out

Suggested list price: $415

Comments: Average specs but the street price might make up for it if you're on a budget.

The TXM-4101A is Toshiba's portable version of its double-speed drive, identical in specs to its internal (XM-4101B) and external (XM-4101L) models, described in Chapter 3, "How To Select CD-ROM Drives."

The Notebook Solution

If you don't already own a notebook computer, or if ease of transportation is a key requirement, an integrated notebook solution may be the answer for you. These machines are standard notebook computers with CD-ROM drives directly adapted to the case of the machine. In the past year, several major manufacturers have introduced multimedia notebooks with integrated CD-ROM drives, sound capabilities, and speakers.

IBM ThinkPad

All IBM's popular ThinkPad notebooks are powerful enough for multimedia. When you add the 3545 docking station ($685), you can take your CD-ROM titles on the road with you. The 3545 fits the ThinkPad 360, 750, or 755 so perfectly, it doesn't look tacked on. However, the docking station does make the notebook look a little different—much thicker, and the built-in stereo speakers put semicircular wings on each side of the keyboard. The 3545 doesn't include a CD-ROM drive, but it has a SCSI interface on board and a bay for a slim-height drive. IBM's slim-height double-speed CD-ROM drive is $449. The docking station also comes with one 16-bit ISA slot and two PCMCIA slots.

Texas Instruments TravelMate 4000M

The Texas Instruments TravelMate 4000M is a true multimedia notebook. It includes integrated 16-bit stereo sound, MIDI, audio in and out ports, and a microphone port. Local bus video with 1 MB of video RAM is standard, as is a SCSI-2 interface, making the 4000M perfect for desktop use as well as travel. The caddieless CD-ROM drive is integrated into the optional portable docking station—not the computer—but the docking station attaches securely to the computer and looks built in. As a bonus, the docking station includes stereo speakers. Street prices for the 4000M are around $4,000 for the 486SX/25 model with a 200-MB hard drive and an active-matrix 8.4-inch color screen. The 486DX4/75 model with a 340-MB hard drive and the 8.4-inch active-matrix color screen costs under $6,000. The budget-conscious may consider the 486SX/25 model with a 9.4-inch monochrome screen and a 120-MB hard drive (just under $3,000), but you may want to carry around a color Super-VGA monitor for professional presentations.

Toshiba T6600C/CD

Toshiba's T6600C/CD Mobile Multimedia Computer is not quite a notebook, weighing in at over 17 pounds, but is a very capable (and highly expandable) machine for traveling presentations. Its case includes room for two full-length 16-bit ISA cards as well as one PCMCIA Type II card. The 101-key keyboard is detachable and is complemented by a Logitech Trackman pointing device (which can be held in your hand for slideshows). The base configuration is a 486DX2/66 with 8 MB of RAM (expandable to 40 MB), a 510-MB hard drive, a 1.44-MB floppy drive, and an internal double-speed CD-ROM drive. Naturally, the T6600C/CD includes a full set of ports for external devices, including serial, parallel, PS/2, VGA, and SCSI. And the system is topped with a 10.4-inch TFT-LCD active-matrix color display. The T6600C/CD includes DOS, Windows, UltraFont, Asymetrix COMPEL,

Asymetrix MediaBlitz, and EZ-SCSI software, all for a suggested retail of $8,299.

Zenith Data Systems Z-Noteflex

Zenith Data Systems recently released its Z-Noteflex multimedia notebook, which (like the Texas Instruments TravelMate 4000M) includes a double-speed CD-ROM drive and amplified stereo speakers in its portable docking station. The Z-Noteflex is built around an Intel 486DX4 CPU and local bus video, so it can function very adequately as a desktop PC. One interesting innovation is the removable color LCD display with its own stand, which can sit on a desktop or conference table a few feet away from the main unit. Each Z-Noteflex is custom-configured with your choice of RAM, hard disk, and other options, so pricing varies with your choices.

Lunchbox Options

Portable machines using desktop components in a "luggable" case are often referred to as *lunchbox* machines. This name derives from the form of the box itself: it is reminiscent of an oversized lunch box. Many options are available because a lunchbox machine does not require much sophistication to integrate a CD-ROM—thanks to the fact that the lunchbox case accepts standard components. As you may expect, the standard components become a double-edged sword: quality of components and construction is extremely variable in this market.

If you don't need battery power or exceptionally small size, and you think you want an expansion slot or two for special hardware, the lunchbox machine may be just what you are looking for. If you do intend to buy a lunchbox from a local or mail-order clone dealer, please do a lot of research first! You may easily find yourself with a machine that doesn't work quite right and a dealer who cannot—or will not—fix it. Get references from the company and call the users; ask about durability and solidity of the product and the quality of service from the seller. Call at least three vendors of lunchbox systems, then decide.

The Dolch Mach from Dolch Computer Systems

One company we can unequivocally recommend in the lunchbox-computer market is Dolch. These guys have been making high-end portable systems since it was possible. Although Dolch also offers a line of traditional-style systems, its latest product is truly state-of-the-art for portable equipment.

The newest technology from Dolch is called the Mach. It is a scalable, liquid-cooled, rubberized, multimedia machine—please don't slobber on the book. Let's look at that in slow motion:

- **Scalable.** Unlike other transportable machines, the Mach is built in layers called *MultiSlice modules*. Each two-inch-thick module offers four slots and a drive bay. The slices plug into a passive backplane that connects them to the CPU. This means you can add to the capacity of the Mach—with drives or slots—and even change the CPU, right up to the capacity of the power supply.

- **Liquid-cooled.** One of the things that makes traditional lunchbox machines larger than they might otherwise be is the need to circulate air through the case. Even with the provided air space, these machines can get hotter than you like. Dolch got around this problem—and greatly reduced the machine size—by employing a more efficient liquid-cooling technology. Liquid cooling enables Dolch to equip a Mach with processors as powerful—and as hot—as the 486DX2/66. This is a serious advantage.

- **Rubberized.** The enclosure for the Mach is made from a metallic alloy and then covered with a sexy black silicone rubber. This makes it one of the most rugged machines around—in addition to its other virtues.

- **Multimedia machine.** The Mach is certainly no slouch in the multimedia arena. The machine is available with a CD-ROM drive, of course, but it also sports an active-matrix color display and a hi-fi audio system good enough to make a presentation to a large room.

Clearly, the Dolch is a superior machine. But as you expect, it is not a cheap machine. The price varies along with the very flexible configuration options, but you can expect to see a retail list price of about $20,000 on a well-outfitted multimedia presentation machine (street prices are less, of course). On the other hand, if you need what the Mach can do to get your work done—or you have lots of money to burn—the price may be worth paying: there is nothing else like the Mach on the market. If seeing that price tag almost killed you, look at Dolch's more traditional lunchbox systems, which share the commitment to quality that the company applied to the Mach.

Chapter 16

CD-ROM in the Family Room

You may already have a Sega Genesis or Super Nintendo video game system in your home. These second-generation game systems are nearly as plentiful and popular as VCRs in this country. Within the next few years, these seemingly innocuous, mindless game machines will begin to mature into full-fledged computer systems. The key to the expansion of these game platforms lies in CD-ROM.

Although the main focus of this book is the enormous impact CD-ROM technology has on your PC, CDs are invading your family room as well. A number of home-entertainment and education systems are shipping now—or will ship very shortly—which will drastically alter perceptions about standard video game systems. With the storage capacity of CDs added to existing systems or as a part of wholly new home systems, video games, entertainment, and education in the family room will take a bold new direction.

The Future of Home-Entertainment Systems

Although you may already be accustomed to the *zaps*, *zings*, and animations of video-arcade action blaring from your TV set, soon you can hear and see a guided museum tour, preschool phonics lessons, or the illustrated text of one of your favorite novels. In short, your preteen video-game fanatics may have to compete with the rest of the family for access to the new and expanded systems.

Like all evolving technology, however, there's good news and bad news. The good news is obvious: game systems add education and reference sources to the mix of offerings, making them complete family systems. The bad news is that these systems require an investment in hardware and CDs above and beyond what you may already have invested in

NOTE

More Terms

For the purposes of this chapter, when we refer to *home-system CDs*, we are describing those entertainment and game systems that hook up to your TV.

your PC-based CD-ROM setup. **Home-system CDs**, with a few exceptions, are incompatible with your PC CD-ROM drive (and with each other), and there is little likelihood that this will change.

The high-tech home in the next few years might have a PC with reference, education, and entertainment CDs in the den and a different set of similar CDs for the family-room system. Many people will choose one system over the other—a PC or home-entertainment system—and for good reason. Building a library for two competing CD formats can get expensive in a hurry, and you may find yourself analyzing which system makes the most sense for your home.

Keep a few things in mind: PC-based CD-ROM reference and business applications have a tremendous head-start on the evolving home systems. A PC armed with a CD-ROM drive is a formidable business and research tool that home-based systems will never quite rival. The home systems, on the other hand, will be simpler to use, and their CD titles will be aimed at broader, more consumer-oriented topics. You won't see a comprehensive U.S. history CD on a Sega Genesis system anytime soon—quite possibly never.

So you may have no choice: your PC may have a CD-ROM for reference, research, and occasional education or game CDs, and your family-room system may have a collection of entertainment, light education, and many game CDs. There's no denying the two types of systems have their own niches for home use—but no one can predict which will dominate the home market.

Purchasing any of these systems requires some caution. Many are in direct competition with each other and offer no compatibility. A disc for the Sega CD system, for example, is useless on the Philips CD-I, and vice-versa. Who'll win? Who'll survive? Atari and Magnavox home-game systems were once all the rage in American homes; today they're all but forgotten in the wake of Nintendo and Sega (although Atari is trying for a comeback). Buying a Philips CD-I or a Sega CD player is, in many ways, an unprotected investment. Although they offer a significant library of CD titles now, there is no guarantee that software developers will continue to support any of these platforms in the future.

Just as software drove the PC marketplace, so too will software development grow or stall the acceptance of home-based entertainment systems. CD-ROM makes the expansion of these systems practical, but the creativity, usefulness, and mass appeal of home-system CD titles are the only factors that can ensure their success.

CD-ROM Upgrades to Current Game Systems

Most of the big home-game systems have shipped or announced CD-ROM drive upgrades to their current products. As expected, the CD titles for these systems will remain predominantly games. The storage capacity of CD gives software developers the chance to expand their use of graphics, music, and—in many cases—actual video in their products, making video games more sophisticated than ever.

In the past, game developers for these systems packed their software onto ROM-based memory contained in plug-in game cartridges. There's a limited amount of space for these ROMs in the cartridge cases, however, and the ROM chips themselves, despite price decreases, are many times more expensive than the pressing and production costs of a single CD-ROM disc.

Consider the real estate as well: the most ambitious game cartridge has, at the high end, 40 megabytes of ROM storage. As you know, the CD-ROM disc can accommodate over 600 megabytes of data. Even luxuriously scored and painstakingly animated video games have elbow room to spare when developed for a CD-ROM attached to the game system.

It's no wonder that these home systems, in competition with one another and other emerging technologies, have stepped up the pace by introducing CD-ROM drive add-ons for their basic systems.

TurboGraphx

A division of NEC, TurboGraphx was the first video-game system with a CD-ROM add-on. The basic system is 16 bit—meaning its internal processor uses a 16-bit-wide data path, allowing faster refreshes and more complex video manipulation and sound reproduction than earlier 8-bit game systems.

The TurboGraphx CD add-on includes a set of sample CD game titles, cables for attaching the CD unit to the basic TurboGraphx system, and outputs for amplified stereo sound hookup to your home stereo.

The TurboGraphx system—even though it is one of the first CD systems—has had disappointing sales despite its relatively reasonable $599 price tag. In many areas, it is difficult to find, and software titles for this machine—in either cartridge or CD format—are on the wane as a result. Although the system is technically on a par with Sega or Super Nintendo in its use of graphics and sound, it hasn't had the market success of its rivals.

It's unclear whether the parent company, NEC, will continue to push the system aggressively enough in the face of stiff competition with Sega and Nintendo. The dwindling number of titles for the system by third-party developers is also an indication that this platform may be in deep trouble.

Sega CD

Sega rolled out their CD system for the 1992 Christmas buying season and was in for a shock: the initial production run of the Sega Genesis CD add-on sold out in a matter of days. The demand for the CD-ROM unit surpassed all the company's early predictions. Since then, a number of big-name software developers have come on board to roll out software CDs for the Sega CD—Electronic Arts, Sony, and Konami, to name a few—and others are scrambling onto the bandwagon.

The Sega CD unit plugs into the top of the existing Sega Genesis system and is literally held fast by the plug and a bracket, making the unit connect solidly to the Genesis base. Plugs in the back allow you to connect the unit directly to a stereo unit or to your TV's stereo jacks for CD-quality sound effects and music.

Sega got ambitious with the CD unit. Although the base Genesis system already uses a 16-bit microprocessor, an additional processor was

EXPLANATION

CD+G Equals Karaoke

CD+G stands for CD audio plus graphics. This format provides the capability to play CD audio along with titles, still pictures, and song lyrics synchronized to the music. This CD format may be best suited for karaoke-style discs—music playing along with on-screen lyrics.

added to the CD unit for faster graphics. The CD also carries an on-board memory chip for storing game scores or game place markers.

The CD unit ships with a number of CD software titles, including ICOM Simulations' popular Sherlock Holmes, an interactive, live-video mystery game (also available for the PC) in which the player helps Holmes solve one of three mysteries. The point-and-click interface of the Holmes title is controlled with the standard Genesis game pad. The live-video segments reproduce well on the home screen but not as crisply as on a PC-based Super-VGA screen. Other titles that ship with the unit include titles previously released on cartridge: Battle Axe, Sol-Feace, and Shinobi. The entire package—CD-ROM drive plus bundled titles—has a suggested list price of $229.

With all that storage space to play with, a few early game titles prove the merit of using CD-ROM technology for gaming. Sony's CD-publishing division has produced Sewer Sharks, a full-motion video-arcade game set in the future. You play the part of a Sewer Jockey, piloting a super-fast subterranean craft that must sweep the sewers of assorted mutated vermin—everything from 100-pound sewer rats to the ultimate in sewer mutants: the dreaded ratagator.

The action on this game is fast and furious, with excellent music and voice overs. Only a storage technology like CD-ROM can give you this much video in an arcade-style game. If this game alone is any indication of what creative software developers can produce for the Sega CD system, the platform should be a continued success.

In addition to game CDs, a few **CD+G** discs are available for the Sega CD system. One CD+G title allows you to create your own music video, selecting a variety of still images to run in sequence with any of the music tracks on the disc.

Not one to stand still in the swift waters of the $2 billion gaming industry, Sega has recently released Sega CDX—a portable machine that plays Sega CD games and audio CDs, as well as Genesis cartridges. Street price is under $400.

3DO

This company is something of a dark horse in the game-system market right now. 3DO is a wholly new company with resources and cooperation formed from Electronic Arts, Time-Warner, and Matsushita. In fact, it's rumored that the three principal companies kicked in a total of $200 million to start up this home-entertainment newcomer.

At the 1993 Consumer Electronics Show in Las Vegas, the 3DO company released initial specifications for the 3DO platform to a number of third-party developers. These specs no doubt sent a shock wave through corporate headquarters at Sega, Nintendo, and others.

The 3DO system includes the following:

- A 32-bit RISC processor
- A double-speed 300 KB/s CD-ROM drive
- CD-quality sound and 3D sound synthesis

The 32-bit RISC processor provides an enormous boost in power over existing home systems. Formerly the domain of only high-end graphics workstations, RISC processing was hardly expected to show up in a home gaming system. The fast CD-ROM drive invites the use of extremely detailed 3D graphics and animations. The high-powered DSP (Digital Signal Processor) for sound allows the 3DO Multiplayer to produce 3D sound effects—the placement of sound around the listener at specific points in the room. At an early demonstration at the Intermedia Multimedia trade show in San Jose in March 1993, demonstrations of the 3DO graphics and animation capabilities were, in a word, stunning.

Major investor Matsushita is the biggest manufacturer of 3DO-compatible systems (marketed in the U.S. as the Panasonic REAL system), but other companies are quickly hopping on the bandwagon. Creative Labs has announced the 3DO Blaster, an add-in card that will allow you to play 3DO titles on your PC.

So how does 3DO combat the competition from Atari's 64-bit Jaguar (profiled in the next section of this chapter)? With their own 64-bit PowerPC upgrade for existing 3DO systems and new graphics and sound chips, of course. The upgrades should be available for Christmas '95. (Incidentally, the 3DO representative we spoke with says Atari's claim to 64-bit leadership is bogus—she said they use a 64-bit data path with a 16-bit processor, as opposed to 3DO's native 32-bit RISC processor.)

Only a few technical drawbacks stand in 3DO's way to make a significant impact in home entertainment. The CD-ROM drive that ships with the unit as an integral part of the system (not as an add-on) is not compatible with other CD-ROM disc formats (although it does read Kodak PhotoCDs).

Pricing for the 3DO Multiplayer system is around $700—more expensive than its Sega and Atari rivals on the low end but in the same ballpark as the Philips CD-I players on the high end.

When you add education and reference materials to its video-game base, the 3DO system may be a big winner.

Atari Jaguar

Atari, the former video-game dreadnought, is trying to climb back into the ring—and it's bringing a secret weapon that has shocked the industry (especially 3DO). Atari's Jaguar is a *64-bit* RISC system, priced well under $500 even with its $200 CD-ROM module. Released in a few major metro areas before Christmas 1993, the Jaguar flew off the shelves. Since then, however, Atari has yet to stage the kind of marketing offensive that made them legendary in the game market in the early '80s. The graphics, sound, and full-motion video of the (relatively few) Jaguar game titles is truly amazing, and the machine is more than powerful enough to run nongame applications. If the word gets out on the Jaguar (and Atari starts getting them into stores), Atari could have another winner on their hands.

Philips CD-I

Philips took the lead with family-based education and entertainment systems with the introduction of the CD-I, or CD Interactive, in 1991 (see fig. 16.1). The CD-I is not positioned

FIGURE 16.1

The Philips CD-I system, with over 150 software titles, has superior video and animation capabilities.

to compete with the game systems, although a number of game titles have appeared. The chief thrust of its software development has been in education and home reference—an area in which Philips has garnered a lot of third-party development support.

The CD-I system hooks up to the inputs of your TV or stereo. Connecting it to your stereo is the best bet because the CD-I unit can also play audio CDs—after all, Philips was one of the inventors of the audio CD. Another plus for the Philips system is that it can read Kodak PhotoCD discs. The system comes with an infrared remote. An optional children's trackball (an oversized, brightly colored trackball and button pad that even small children can operate) is also available.

The Philips system is widely available at electronics and department stores and is heavily promoted in vertical markets as well. For example, a number of large businesses have developed CD-I discs for in-house training and point-of-sale kiosks for trade shows. With a dual-marketing strategy—business and home use—Philips is keeping the CD-I system on its feet during a long, slow take-off period.

The software titles for the Philips CD-I fill a 35-page catalog, and several more titles have been announced for shipment in the near future. The current title count is over 150; here's a quick look at a few titles:

- **A Visit to Sesame Street: Numbers and A Visit to Sesame Street: Letters.** Two separate titles use the famous Sesame Street gang to interactively teach your preschooler numbers and letters through games and toys. Children explore a number of Sesame Street haunts including Big Bird's nest, the Count's castle, and Bert and Ernie's house.

- **Stickybear's Reading.** This program was a monster hit on the PC, and the CD-I version is more colorful, animated, and full of music. Stickybear helps children build sentences, learn words, and improve their use of language. The program can switch between English and Spanish, making this a useful early learning tool for Spanish.

- **Richard Scarry's Busiest Neighborhood and Richard Scarry's Best Neighborhood.** Sold separately, these two Scarry discs feature interactive visits to Busytown. Both discs are designed to aid preschoolers in a variety of prereading exercises.

- **Children's Musical Theater.** Various animal musicians help children put together their own music scores, with choices of instruments, musical styles, and lyrics.

- **Mother Goose: Hidden Pictures.** Objects are hidden in 26 pictures depicting Mother Goose fairy tales. Once children find all the hidden objects in a picture, an animated scene starts up.

- **Children's Bible Stories.** A series of discs with high-quality animation and music depict David and Goliath, Noah's Ark, the Story of Samson, and other Bible stories.

- **Tell Me Why, I and II.** These two discs adapt the popular *Tell Me Why* books to the CD-I format, answering in story and animation popular children's questions about how things work. Topic areas include the body, the zoo, and our world.

- **Story Machine: Star Dreams and Story Machine: Magic Tales.** Both these titles supply children with backgrounds, characters, and objects for creating their own stories. Once the characters are chosen, children can begin to write the story with screen text. Star Dreams is a space adventure; Magic Tales has a fairy-tale theme.

Aside from a wide base of software titles both shipping and announced, another indication of CD-I's health—despite soft sales—is Philips' recent announcement for add-on modules for the CD-I system.

Philips recently released a **full-motion-video** upgrade cartridge for the CD-I system that allows CD-I titles to display up to 72 minutes of live-motion video and sound. The sample videos we saw at the Intermedia trade show in San Jose were laser-disc quality images—better than VCR in clarity—with full stereo soundtracks. One of the first interactive full-motion video titles, *Voyeur* (the focus of Philips' aggressive television advertising campaign), is a fine example of using live actors in interactive video games.

The new Philips cartridge carries an MPEG-I video-compression chipset that decompresses the CD-I disc-based video for display on your TV. The cartridge also has 1 MB of memory for buffering sound and video, essential for the 30-frames-per-second of live-motion video and stereo sound. Philips maintains that the new cartridge also allows developers of CD-I titles to produce higher quality animations.

Pop-up VCR-like controls on-screen allow the user to freeze, rewind, or fast forward the video with a remote control.

Recently, Philips also introduced a portable version of the CD-I, which is targeted at business applications, sales presentations, and the interactive tutorial market.

The Philips 220 CD-I system with remote and Compton's Interactive Encyclopedia has a suggested list price of $499. Magnavox makes two CD-I players, both with slightly less functionality than Philips's 220: the 200 (a $399 unit with Compton's and the Kether game) and the 450 (a $299 unit with Compton's and 2-Player Tennis). Other CD-I titles range in price from $15 to $60. You can also buy a $249 digital video adapter that allows you to play CD-based movies and games with full-screen digital video.

NOTE

Do the Video Squeeze

What makes full-motion video possible is the use of *video-compression algorithms*—special software that "squeezes" the digitized video images into a size that is practical to store.

Kodak PhotoCD

Some industry insiders joke that Kodak wanted out of the photo-developing business and that the Kodak PhotoCD was their ticket out. The PhotoCD format has already had clear and overwhelming support from the CD-ROM industry. The Kodak PhotoCD unit for the home audience is targeted at customers who want to view their photographs on TV in full color. All Kodak PhotoCD units also play audio CDs (see fig. 16.2).

The PhotoCD scenario is this: you take a roll of exposed film to a neighborhood developer who ships the roll to a Kodak PhotoCD processing center. The film is developed and scanned at high resolution and imprinted on a special recordable CD disc. The finished product is shipped back to your developer. The key to the PhotoCD's success lies in its capability to record multiple photo sessions on one CD; you continue to bring in the same PhotoCD disc until it's filled up and then you start a new disc.

FIGURE 16.2

Targeted at the photography hobbyist, the Kodak PhotoCD allows amateur and professional photogs to view their work on standard televisions.

As a subset of the CD-ROM-XA specification, Kodak PhotoCDs can display photos along with titles and narration or audio soundtracks. Kodak now has three consumer PhotoCD players on the market, all of which are multisession:

- **PCD 270.** This is the lowest priced model, offering basic picture viewing and the ability to tag photos to be deleted from the playback session. The CD unit "remembers" which photos have been deleted, making it unnecessary to reprogram it each time the disc is used. The player also has an autoplay feature that cycles through selected photos. Suggested list price for the PCD 270 is $379.

- **PCD 870.** This model has advanced viewing features not available on the PCD 270. For example, users can select a portion of a photo for enlargement. Multiple-disc memory is also included, allowing you to create custom carousels of photos from many discs that the unit remembers. The suggested list price for the PCD 870 is $449.

- **PCD 5870.** This unit is identical in function to the PCD 870 but has a five-disc turntable that lets you play a series of photo or audio CDs. This player also has an on-screen display for programming photo series and numbering images. The suggested list price for the PCD 5870 is $549.

Compatibility

As you've read through the categories of home CD-ROM systems, you may have noticed that some systems are compatible, to a limited degree, with other systems. Let's run through the systems quickly to summarize these limited compatibilities. This information may sway your decision one way or another in selecting either a PC or home CD-ROM system. Please note: for the most part, game, education, and database applications developed for the PC are ***not*** usable in any home-game system.

- **PC CD-ROM Drives.** If your computer's CD-ROM drive is XA ready, and the manufacturer specifies that it has multisession capabilities, the drive can read PhotoCDs if you add special PhotoCD-viewing software to the PC. (Some drives are only single session—they can read only the first recorded session on the PhotoCD.) Virtually all PC CD-ROM drives are capable of playing audio CDs.

- **Sega, Atari, Turbographx, and 3DO.** The Sega and 3DO systems are incompatible. In addition, they cannot read any PC, PhotoCD, or CD-I formatted discs or applications. However, they do play audio CDs.

- **Philips CD-I.** The CD-I system is incompatible with PC and game-system CD formats. The CD-I does play PhotoCDs and audio CDs, however. Some PC-compatible and Mac-compatible CD-ROM players are now supporting the CD-I standard, though.

- **Kodak PhotoCDs.** The Kodak system is for photo and audio CDs only. The PhotoCDs are compatible with any multisession PC CD-ROM drive, however.

What does all this incompatibility mean? Either you live in a two-CD environment—one set of CDs for your PC and yet another for your home—or you choose one over the other. If all you're interested in for your home is education, games, and very little reference, the CD-I system may be a perfect fit. Upgrading an existing home PC to a multimedia PC that uses CD-ROMs can easily cost more than your initial investment in the Philips or Kodak system once you add a sound card, speakers, and the CD-ROM drive itself (provided you buy quality components). You may find a home-based multimedia PC worthwhile for business and reference work and may want to invest in the Sega, Atari, or 3DO unit for games.

And if all that doesn't cause enough confusion, there are other factors entering the fray: if the 3DO Multiplayer is even a moderate success, look for other traditional CD-ROM drive manufacturers to jump on that wagon for one important reason: 3DO, unlike its home-system rivals, actively seeks to license their technology to other companies (like Panasonic, who recently released the 3DO-based REAL system).

We wish there was better news—that one system would fit all needs. At the very least, we wish a home-based system would take some PC-based CDs. After all, when the initial-investment dust settles, it's the cost of CD-ROM applications and software that runs up the tab. Although that's good news for the software suppliers, it's bad news for the consumer.

Chapter 17

Video on Disc: CD-ROM and Full-Motion Video

We've spent the entire book lauding the storage capacity of CD-ROMs. By now, you probably have the impression that this technology is virtually inexhaustible when it comes to storing applications and sound. Not so. Emerging multimedia technologies have found a way to make even CD-ROM discs seem cramped for space. The introduction of full-motion video to commercial and limited-distribution applications has done more to fill CD-ROMs in the last year than all software applications combined.

What Is Full-Motion Video?

Photographs or still-images from motion video depend on the resolution at which they're captured and displayed; the amount of storage space required for a single image varies according to its resolution. Common television resolution, for example, contains approximately 480 horizontal lines—actually rows of dots or **pixels**—and up to 450 vertical lines. The most common PC standard for image processing and display is VGA—640-by-480 resolution. The multiple of this number—the horizontal by the vertical—yields the number of pixels in the image, which for VGA is 307,200.

That's fine for black-and-white images (you can store a black-and-white 640-by-480 resolution still image in 307,200 **bits** without compression). But most video is color; to add "true color"—a representation of more than primary colors—you must compound your pixel storage requirements by a factor of 24. Each primary color is assigned a full byte—8 bits—for storage. This leap to 24-bit color multiplies the storage requirements for a single image by 24, bringing the total for a single frame of a full-color 640-by-480 resolution image to 921,600 bytes—nearly a megabyte!

EXPLANATION

Pixel

The term *pixel* is a contraction of two words: *picture* and *element.* A pixel is the "atomic" component of an image displayed on the computer.

EXPLANATION

Data Elements

The term *bit* is a contraction of BInary digiT. A bit is the atomic—read *smallest, indivisible*—element used to represent data in computer memory. A bit is binary, that is, it can only have one of two values: 1 or 0. Bits are grouped together to represent symbols and for easier manipulation. The most common grouping is eight bits, called a *byte*. One byte can represent 256 different values. In the case of text, these are the 256 characters in the ASCII (American Standard Code for Information Interchange) character set. A *nybble* is four bits—or half a byte. Although the nybble is useful in some obscure cases, it certainly shows that some computer scientists have a sense of humor.

But one image does not a video make. The standard frame rate that must be achieved for film and video to be considered "full-motion" is 30 frames per second. Multiply, then, the storage space for a still image (921,600 bytes for a single full-color image) by 30 to get the storage requirements for a single second of video: the staggering number of 27,640,000 bytes! One second of full-motion, full-color video requires over 27 megabytes of storage space. A 30-second commercial, then, with absolutely no sound, cannot fit on a single CD-ROM.

Video Choices

Multimedia developers are presented with tough choices. They must either find a larger and more economical storage medium for the production and distribution of applications that contain full-motion video, or work with what's available. They've chosen the latter because, at this point, no other storage medium can deliver as much for the money as CD-ROM. Shortcuts, technology, and creative development have all been deployed to deliver the best possible video in such a "cramped" space.

Compression

One way to reduce storage space is to compress the images before they are stored on the disc. A number of compression standards are available now, and we'll discuss some of them later. The best compression techniques employed today can reduce most frame sizes by a factor of 20. In other words, our original 27-megabyte 1-second video image can be stored in just over a megabyte of space using advanced compression techniques.

But it's not just the space requirements that necessitate compression. When pulling a multimegabyte file off a disk or disc for use as live video, the number of bytes that must be continuously transferred to display a smooth video is beyond current commonly available processor or disk subsystem speeds. Compression enables much more video information to be delivered in a short period of time, improving the flow of the video frame delivery.

Compressed data is not directly useful, however: it must be decompressed before it's sent off to an application for display. The compression and decompression must be performed by hardware or software using the same type of compression standards, which further complicates widespread use of video in PC applications. As you may expect, competing compression techniques are currently being used. No single compression/decompression standard has emerged as the dominant standard.

Squeezing Data

You may wonder how it is possible to "compress" data. After all, a megabyte of data is a megabyte of information, isn't it? Well, not really. In the simplest terms, compression is easy to understand: it involves the removal of redundant information from the stored data.

Let's take a look a simple compression scheme called RLE (Run Length Encoding). With RLE, any time there are strings of the same value (for example 50 1s in a row), the value 1 is not stored 50 times. Instead, the value 1 is stored once with a note about the number of times it appears in a row. This technique works very well, particularly with simple images. Variations on this idea make up the more sophisticated schemes.

Compression comes in two varieties—hardware and software. Each, as you probably guessed, has advantages and disadvantages.

Hardware Compression

Hardware compression and decompression is performed by a specialized set of microprocessors called DSPs—Digital Signal Processors. These specialized chips contain software code for the compression algorithm used to compress incoming images. Most hardware compression also uses memory *buffers*—memory that stores the incoming frames before they are processed—so that the compression chipset can "keep up with" the flow of incoming data. Hardware-compression chips are found on hardware-compression boards that plug into the standard PC expansion bus.

Hardware decompression works in the opposite manner. When an application requests a compressed file from storage, the board accepts the compressed data in its buffer and, using the encoded algorithm, "replaces" the data that was removed from the compressed image. Once decompressed, the image is passed to the display through the application.

The chief advantage of hardware compression for video is computational power. The hardware performs the computer-intensive tasks of compression and decompression on the expansion card through the DSPs and related chips and buffers, saving the computer's main CPU and memory for the running of applications.

The obvious disadvantage is that computers must all have hardware compression cards conforming to the compression-board manufacturer's implementation of that particular compression algorithm. For this reason, video-compression boards have been expensive—hovering in the $1,000 range and scaring off all but the most ardent video-application developers and users.

Software Compression

Software implementation of decompression and compression is no different, in practice, than the hardware equivalent. Instead of using DSPs, coprocessors, and on-board memory to compress and decompress images as do hardware compression boards, software video compression uses the PC's main CPU and main RAM for all operations.

The important advantage of software compression is its portability: the PC need not have special hardware in place to use the video contained in the application. This arrangement allows application developers to write for a common platform of installed PCs and makes their applications instantly usable by a majority of users. The application must include a "run-time" version of the decompression software (a utility that reads and decompresses the video and passes it along to the display when necessary).

The chief disadvantage to software-based compression and decompression is the toll it takes on a PC's performance. Reading video off a CD-ROM causes some delay, and decompressing using the PC's CPU and memory causes further delays. Most systems with less than a 80386-25 MHz processor will experience loss of frames and a jerky playback of video because of the resource-hungry nature of software decompression.

Other Video Economies

Compressing images is one way of making the most of storage space for video, but other techniques can be used as well. Although 30 frames-per-second is optimal for viewing motion video, a reduction in the number of frames-per-second can obviously cut the storage requirements. Video cut down to 15 frames-per-second is not uncommon in PC multimedia applications—but the results are noticeable. Further reductions can be made by reducing the pixel count. For example, our original 640-by-480-pixel window for images can be cut by 75 percent to 320 by 240, dramatically reducing storage requirements. The image is reduced in size, not in quality, so the PC displays a smaller version of the full-screen image. Similarly, reduction in the color depth from 24 to 16 or even to 8 bits trims down the size of video images considerably.

All these size-reduction techniques come at a cost. The image quality of a 15-frames-per-second video at 320-by-240 resolution is video, to be sure, but not the video you're used to seeing on your TV. For most current PC-based applications and presentations, such video may be just fine—but it lacks the realism of full-screen, truly full-motion video.

Video Application Development for CD-ROM

For software developers to incorporate video into CD-ROM applications, they need some additional hardware and software development tools. The process of including video in an application involves three steps:

1. The capture of video from an analog source, such as a camcorder, television, or VCR.

2. The processing of the image into the appropriate digitized format.

3. The incorporation of the video into the overall software application.

Capturing video from an analog source requires a video-capture board capable of processing 15-frames-per-second or more. A number of capture boards are on the market now. Most cards have standard RCA and S-VHS inputs that enable the easy hookup of a VCR, camcorder, or TV monitor directly to the PC card. The card processes the incoming analog signals, changes them to digital bits, and stores the incoming data on a hard drive or removable media device. Most capture boards do not employ compression or decompression techniques, so the digitized video is stored in its full, bloated state and can eat up a lot of storage in a short period of time. Other capture boards have hardware compression features and can save video files to the primary storage device in a proprietary compressed format.

Once the image is captured, it may have to be converted to the appropriate format for the application to use. Some capture boards include drivers that prepare the data, before storing it, for a number of video formats. Many multimedia authoring tools on the market today have extensive support for a variety of video formats; including video is just a matter of telling the application where the video clip is stored and when the multimedia presentation should use the clip. IconAuthor, Toolbook, Macromedia Director, and many other Windows, Macintosh, and DOS-based authoring toolkits allow easy integration of video—and provide a number of more sophisticated uses, such as assigning video to hot spots, radio buttons, and menu items.

PC Video Standards

As we mentioned—and cautioned—a number of technologies are available for the compression, decompression, and digitization of video for PCs. Each has different features, strengths, and drawbacks. Some are strictly hardware based; others are software based. Many can be found implemented in both hardware and software. For the purposes of this book, we'll give you a thorough overview of the **video standards** currently available.

Indeo

Developed by Intel Corporation (the same folks that bring you the main CPU in your PC), the Indeo algorithm for compressing and decompressing video is independent of hardware or software. Intel incorporates the Indeo technology on all its DVI hardware compression/decompression boards; a slightly modified version of Indeo is incorporated in Microsoft's Video for Windows. Besides Microsoft, a number of third-party manufacturers have licensed the Indeo technology from Intel for use in their hardware and software products.

One of the chief advantages to Intel's Indeo compression/decompression algorithm (abbreviated as *codec*) is the inclusion of adaptive playback of Indeo-encoded clips. That is, the software dynamically adapts its playback for the platform it's running on. For example, a 386-based PC may play an Indeo file at perhaps one-quarter screen and a 15 frames-per-second rate; a 486 (because of its increased horsepower) may play the same video at half-screen and 25 frames-per-second. Intel has licensed the Indeo technology to Apple (for use with Apple's QuickTime video) and to IBM (for use with IBM's Ultimedia video).

Video for Windows

The addition of Video for Windows to the Microsoft Windows environment makes it possible to use Intel's Indeo codec with Windows AVI (Audio Video Interleaved) files. What some people do not realize, however, is that the Video for Windows product also has built-in support for the new Motive codec from Media Vision. To make things even more flexible for developers and users alike, the Video for Windows software can incorporate virtually any new codec that comes along—all users need to do is add the new codec module to Video for Windows.

Another strength of the Microsoft addition is its ability to take advantage of any available hardware assistance. For example, if the Video for Windows driver detects an Intel-based hardware codec, it dynamically adjusts to take full advantage of the hardware support, providing the application with full-screen, 30 frames-per-second video instead of using scaled-back windows in the applications.

Microsoft's AVI

Just as Sony developed and proposed the XA specification for CD-ROM drives to effectively interleave audio and video, Microsoft developed its own audio-video interleaving scheme (which Microsoft named with the simple acronym AVI). The AVI format does not depend on the data format of the drive but on the format of the data itself. Video is distributed on the disc in small segments by using files in the DIB (Device Independent Bitmaps) format. The DIB files contain compressed video frames. Audio is contained in separate WAVE or MIDI files. The Video for Windows player reads the appropriate DIB and WAVE files and synchronizes them appropriately during playback.

Microsoft touts the AVI format as being platform independent. This arrangement makes it possible to move AVI applications to other operating systems and to store them on any current or yet-to-be developed media.

NOTE

Video Clips and Local Bus

In the course of testing CD-ROM applications that had multimedia video clips, we noted some incompatibilities with local bus video cards and some QuickTime and Video for Windows clips. We've had reports from other users as well. One vendor noted that video cards incorporating some local bus chipsets were, indeed, incompatible with some older implementations of video under Windows. At any rate, if you experience trouble playing back or capturing video through local bus VGA adapters, first contact the adapter's manufacturer—an updated driver may solve these problems.

MPEG

The MPEG, or Motion Picture Experts Group, codec standard was developed before the Indeo standard. The MPEG specification adheres strictly to the 30 frames-per-second playback rate, ensuring that video is smooth and free of lapses. (Lapses occur in other codec schemes when lesser frame counts are used.) All MPEG implementations to date are hardware based because of the enormous processing that must occur to decompress images at such a high frame rate and at full-screen resolutions.

Although MPEG shows the greatest long-term promise in delivering the most video in the least time and space, hardware platforms that use it are only now being delivered and costs have yet to come down significantly.

QuickTime

Traditionally ahead of the Windows platform in multimedia, the Macintosh has had support for a video format—QuickTime—built into its operating system since 1991. QuickTime features fast dithering (so that high-resolution movies can be shown on lower-resolution screens) and compression/decompression. It has a completely modular structure, making it easy for developers to add new features or optimize existing features.

In the summer of 1994, Apple introduced version 2.0 of QuickTime. Major enhancements include radically increased speed (up to 30 frames per second—up to twice as fast as the previous version, 1.6), MPEG support, SMPTE (movie/sound syncing) features, and the ability to play QuickTime movies across a network. QuickTime 2.0 also supports MIDI sequencing, a technique that takes up much less storage space than the WAVE recording used by most other video formats.

Apple also has some exciting QuickTime products on the close horizon. QuickTime VR (Virtual Reality) is an interactive version of QuickTime, geared more to presentations and graphical applications than movies. It incorporates the "hot spot" technology (areas of a picture that cause other actions when you click them with a mouse) with QuickTime's full-motion video, resulting in truly interactive movies. One of the first titles to use the technology is Simon & Schuster's *Star Trek: The Next Generation Interactive Technical Manual*, which gives you free run of all areas of the Enterprise.

QuickTime for Windows

Apple has also released its QuickTime video player for use with Windows. Developers now can use any previously developed QuickTime for Macintosh videos on the Windows platform. The QuickTime Video for Windows format is already showing up in a number of multimedia PC-based applications; software developers that want to work with both Mac and Windows CD-ROM applications will probably prefer using QuickTime than any other video technology (*The Beatles: A Hard Day's Night*, for example, is all QuickTime on both Macintosh and Windows platforms).

Apple has also announced QuickTime 2.0 for Windows, which incorporates the features of QuickTime 2.0 for Macintosh (described in the preceding section).

Video Capture and Codec Boards

If development of video applications for CD-ROM is to be efficient, using a codec board or a software codec during video capture is a near requirement. Codec boards, as we mentioned, allow the developer to move the compression and decompression calculations from the main system CPU to the codec board itself, freeing the system for other application chores. Boards that support software codec—mostly those that have drivers compatible with Video for Windows—are a reasonable alternative to more expensive hardware codec systems. Following are some currently shipping video capture and codec solutions for Macs and PCs.

MediaVision Pro Movie Spectrum

MediaVision's Pro Movie Spectrum is one of the lowest-priced Video for Windows-supported capture boards. Compression of captured video is through the Motive hardware codec, located on the board. The board supports only 15 frames per second in a 160-by-120 window. Suggested list price is $349.

SuperMac Technology Video Spigot

The Video Spigot from SuperMac can capture video at 15 or 30 frames per second, but the frame rate depends on resolution—the higher the rate, the smaller the window. The highest resolution is 320 by 240. The Video Spigot uses its own proprietary hardware codec. Street price is around $375.

Creative Labs Video Spigot for Windows

With a $300 sticker price, Creative Labs' Video Spigot for Windows is a low-priced powerhouse for video. Although it doesn't support the high resolutions of its big siblings, the Video Blaster series (described in the next section), Video Spigot for Windows is perfect for entry-level video production and playback. The maximum window size is 320 by 240, but you can use full 24-bit color (16.7 million colors) in your videos. The product includes S-VHS and composite inputs (so that you can connect it to just about any video source) and supports the NTSC, PAL, and SECAM video standards.

Creative Labs Video Blaster SE and FS200

The two versions of the Video Blaster from Creative Labs use the drivers in Video for Windows for capture compression. The Video Blaster SE, which replaces the earlier Video Blaster, supports up to 800-by-600 resolution at 256 colors, up to 19 frames per second, and includes Aldus Photostyler SE, all at a suggested retail price of $329. The FS200 is the next step up, and has up to 800-by-640 resolution at 64,000 colors (up to 2 million colors at lower resolutions) at a suggested retail price of $449. Each version supports a variety of composite input sources, including VCRs, laser discs, and video cameras; the FS200 supports NTSC and PAL television standards.

Radius VideoVision Studio

High-end video pioneer Radius has created a professional-quality video capture solution for Macintosh (complete with professional-level pricing—$1,700 to about $3,500 for different versions). Its external port station lets you link up to 15 video and audio devices into it for mixing and editing. The results are full-screen, full-motion video at 60 fields per second, up to 24-bit color. It should be clear that this system is geared for the highest-level production quality. If you just want to add basic video to presentations, you can get capable equipment for much less—but if you want to make animations for MTV's *Liquid Television*, check out the VideoVision Studio.

IEV International ProMotion

ProMotion from IEV supports input up to a resolution of 1024 by 768 and comes with AVI drivers for Windows. The card is capable of 30 frames per second and permits editing and storage of individual video frames. Suggested list price is $995.

Logitech MovieMan

At a suggested retail price of $299, Logitech's MovieMan is an inexpensive way to get your feet wet in digital video production and playback. It includes a SCSI adapter, 16-bit stereo audio (at 44.1 KHz), and a solid software library including Adobe Premiere (video production in Video for Windows and QuickTime formats) and photo-editing software for still captures. It captures video and audio at 30 frames per second in a 320-by-240-pixel frame, and compresses at roughly 4:1.

Cardinal Technologies SNAPlus

The SNAPlus card from Cardinal Technologies supports 30 frames per second through Video for Windows drivers that ship with the product. Standard video, S-VHS, and RGB inputs and outputs allow the SNAPlus to not only capture video for application development but allow video output from the PC to standard VCRs and camcorders. The Windows drivers allow direct manipulation of computer-interface controllable VCRs, such as the NEC PV-S98a, so that the video tape can be controlled and edited through the SNAPlus software. Individual frames can be edited and stored in the DIB format. Live video can be displayed on-screen in true color in resolutions as high as 800 by 600. Captured video depends on Video for Windows for display resolutions 320 by 240. Suggested list price is $995.

Intel ActionMedia II

The ActionMedia II card from Intel features an on-board coprocessor and a hardware implementation of the Intel Indeo codec. The system is capable of 30 frames per second and full-screen or can scale back to 15 frames per second in a 320-by-240 window. The ActionMedia card includes audio capture as well, and has support for Microsoft Windows as well as DOS. Suggested list price is $1,295.

Intel Smart Video Recorder

Intel's entry-level video processor is packed with features and includes some pretty impressive video production software. The maximum on-screen video window is 320 by 240 (a quarter of a screen on a VGA monitor) at 15 frames per second, but you can get up to 30 frames per second in a smaller (160-by-120) window. It accepts input from composite and S-VHS sources, in NTSC or PAL formats. The software bundled with the Smart Video Recorder makes it as close to a turnkey system as you're likely to find at this level. It includes Microsoft Video for Windows, Asymetrix Compel presentation software, and Asymetrix MediaBlitz audio/video production software. As a bonus, Intel includes Firstlight's Gatekeeper CD-ROM, a disc of clip media with 150 movie clips, music, and other useful presentation elements.

Chapter 18

The Future of CD-ROM

You have to expect the obvious: a technology as hot and versatile as CD-ROM will continue to evolve and improve. In the next few years, we'll see enormous changes in CD-ROM drives and applications. Even though we're impressed—and rightfully so—with the technology as it stands today, increases in speed, capacity, standards, and application development will make many of these initial CD-ROM products seem quaint by comparison.

The good news is that we are not dealing with a "flash-in-the-pan" technology. Wide acceptance by consumers, developers, and major manufacturers ensure that CD-ROM technology will be a continued success. If you purchase CD-ROM technology now for your business or home, you're not buying into the next Edsel. Applications and standards will evolve in an orderly fashion, ensuring that what you buy today should be useful many years from now.

Engineers are working hard to make a good thing even better. In this chapter, we examine some of the impending advances in CD-ROM technology and application development. You can be assured that most of what we talk about here is **not pure conjecture**—manufacturers and developers have gone on the record in announcing many of the future advancements we discuss here. In other cases, a clear view of the current state of the market can give you an indication of what is to come. But that same marketplace can be cruel—a new, unexpected advance in one corner of the technology marketplace can change things overnight.

Increases in Performance

One constant you can count on in the computer world is this: if a new technology is

NOTE

We're Not Making This Up

We stand by our discussions in this chapter as informed and reasonable opinions of the future state of the CD-ROM market, but offer no guarantees on our prognostications. In the computer marketplace, there's no such thing as sure bets or bug-free software—just change, constant change.

developed, its main focus is on improving performance. Speed is nearly everything in computers. Faster video displays, hard drives, I/O busses, processors—you name it. CD-ROM drives are certainly not immune to these pressures. It's not enough to have video from CD-ROM, it's better to deliver it at 30 frames per second on a full screen. Accessing a database of graphic images shouldn't require a pause from the drive, right? One of the clearest focuses of the CD-ROM manufacturers in the coming years will be speed and performance increases. Both initial access times and data transfer rates will improve in the next generation of CD-ROM drives.

Access Times

As this book went to press, the fastest average access time for any CD-ROM drive was NEC's quad-speed drive—clocking in at 180 milliseconds. Remember that *access time* is the average time it takes the drive to position the read-beam on the disc and begin transferring data. When you compare CD-ROM access times with hard drives, you get an idea of how much room there is for improvement: the typical hard drive nowadays has an average access time of 10 to 20 milliseconds (ms).

The physical make-up of the CD-ROM drive itself contributes to its slow access time. The motor and tracking device that position the reading mechanism must seek across a spiral of data, positioning itself as closely as possible to a disc segment in front of the address of the requested data; the mechanism then reads through the initial data until it arrives at the location it needs. All this takes time, valuable time. Improvements in the speed of the positioning—or the stepper motors—as well as more precise initial reads will contribute to improved average access times. There's some question about how fast—*reliably* fast, that is—the drives can be pushed. The physical distance and format of the data suggest that access times will never approach that of hard drives. But as soon as you say something can't be done, someone'll go out and prove you wrong.

By the end of 1994, most major manufacturers will have drives in the sub-200 ms access class. This will put pricing pressures on the lower-end drives, and you'll see drives with perfectly acceptable 200-ms, 250-ms, and 300-ms access times going for much less than they are now.

Transfer Rates

By increasing the spin rate and buffering of a drive, you can also increase its transfer rate. Remember: one of the keys to providing full-motion video is to increase the rate at which the computer—and its display—can receive the huge data files associated with video. Many manufacturers are shipping double-speed drives that adapt to the data task at hand. When Red Book audio is played, the double-speed disk slows to the speed required of CD-based audio, but when other data tasks are requested of the drive, it spins and reads at twice the speed of a normal CD player. Refer to Chapter 2, "CD-ROM Specifications Explained," for more information about colored-book specifications.

Several new drives have *quad-speed capabilities*—four times the normal CD player transfer rate. If you want to use compressed, full-motion video in a full-screen display, the quad-speed transfer rate is ideal. Although compression and the computer's own memory and CPU resources can and will pick up much of the "slack" in such applications, the delivery of the data at a higher rate increases the overall performance of applications.

Until applications that require and can utilize the speed of quad-speed drives become more widespread, transfer rate will not be a high priority. When Pentium-powered PCs and more sophisticated multimedia applications become more plentiful, quad-speed—and possibly higher—drives will gain popularity. And as with most other technologies, the ever-dropping prices will help the popularity of the drives.

Increases in Capacity

Just when you thought 640 megabytes was enough storage to ship any imaginable software application, some hot-shot developer comes along and ruins the whole thing. Live video, stereo sound, and complex Super-VGA animations and graphics are already stretching the bounds of the once-unfathomable depths of CD-ROM storage. Developers are working now on increasing capacities, but a number of obstacles stand in the way.

The first obstacle is purely physical—there's only so much real estate on a CD-ROM disc. The only way to get more bits and bytes into that space is by cramming more information into the allotted space.

Compression

By compressing all forms of data used on the CD-ROM—sound, graphics, and text—developers can squeeze much more data into the same amount of space. The problem of *how* to squeeze the data is an issue, however. For every type of data, there are literally dozens of compression techniques available. Some are obviously more efficient and dominant than others, but so far, no one compression technology is a standard for any given data type. With a multiplicity of compression options available, software and application developers are at risk of choosing the "wrong" compression technology—that is, they may commit to a compression scheme that may not be supported in the long term by a large number of hardware manufacturers. For more details about video-compression "standards" and technology, see Chapter 17, "Video on Disc: CD-ROM and Full-Motion Video."

Compression—either through specialized microprocessor chips or through software that uses the PC's CPU and memory—offers a solution for getting more bits on the disc. Complications arise when applications need hardware compatibility or when using the PC's resources slows down the performance of the majority of today's installed computers.

As an example of the utility of compression techniques, an XA-encoded CD-ROM application can hold up to seven hours of audio—seven times the current, uncompressed capacity.

Audio Compression and Nonconformity Issues

The use of compression for audio is a perfect example of the utility of compression techniques. Sony proposed the CD-ROM-XA specification for the purpose of incorporating compressed audio in synchronized interleaving with graphics or video. This audio compression calls for the use of a specialized hardware chip to both encode the audio data during development and, most importantly, to decode and use the data on the application or playback end. This specialized code within the chipset is called ADPCM. For a drive to utilize XA-encoded audio, it must incorporate an ADPCM chip on the drive itself or, possibly, on the sound card to which the drive is patched.

To further complicate the implementation of the XA specification in ADPCM hardware, there are compatibility issues with actually implementing the hardware—in other words, not all ADPCM chips are created alike. As a result, the XA format has not gained momentum in the marketplace. Microsoft has developed its own interleaving and compression techniques for use with Windows, for example, with its DIB (Device Independent Bitmap) and AVI (Audio Visual Interleaved) file formats.

As a rule, software implementations of compression techniques are more portable and adaptable than hardware-based solutions. Software compression and decompression of data takes a heavy toll on the host system's resources, though; increasingly computational-intensive applications in combination with decompression tasks may force many systems to a noticeable crawl.

The important thing to remember is that compression and compression techniques are in a state of competition right now. Time, the marketplace, and continued advances in technology are the only factors that can push the competition into standardization. In the meantime, the designation *XA-ready,* for example, not only indicates that the drive is capable of being easily upgraded for audio compression in the XA specification, but that it also is multisession PhotoCD compatible. Of course, such a drive is backwards-compatible with all previous CD formats.

More Dots Per Inch: Blue-Light Lasers

Data compression is not the only answer to packing more bits on a disc. Why not pack the pits and lands—the basic CD-ROM data—closer together? Lasers used today in every CD-ROM are red-light lasers. They have distinct physical properties based on the wavelength of the light they project. This wavelength determines how precise and how small the pits of a CD-ROM's data can be. Blue-light lasers, under heavy research and development now, have a shorter wavelength than the current red-light lasers. With a shorter wavelength, data can be packed more tightly because the actual pits and lands can be much smaller, and tracks can be packed more closely together.

There are a number of technological and marketing concerns for manufacturers to address. First, because of the greater density of the data, blue-light lasers will be more susceptible to disruption and corruption of data. Also, the technology needed to mass-produce such mechanisms reliably does not exist today. This last hurdle has proved historically to be nearly insignificant: if there is sufficient demand, manufacturing develops accordingly.

Lastly—and perhaps most importantly—blue-light laser CD-ROM drives would, in all likelihood, be unable to read current CD-ROM discs. The data from the current generation of discs would be too widely dispersed, in effect, for the narrower beam to accurately read.

Dual-light lasers could be produced, but at an enormous cost.

Although the blue-light laser CD-ROM is currently only in research and development, its capabilities may hasten both its demand and initial production. It's estimated that the capacity of a blue-light CD-ROM disc could be four to six times that of the current CD-ROM. A disc with more than 2 gigabytes of room makes a multitude of video and sound applications practical and affordable. More tightly-packed data also means higher transfer rates (assuming the discs will spin at the current rates or higher).

Standards: A One-Size-Fits-All Future?

As popular and truly useful as CD-ROM technology is, its market base is severely fragmented. Even in its computer-based form, there are separate data and disc formats for DOS, Macintosh, and UNIX platforms. CD-ROM applications that are to have any sense of portability across different computer environments must currently be shipped with different operating-system interfaces and, in some cases, multiple-format discs (one-half of the disc may be in DOS and the remainder in Macintosh format, for example).

And if formatting for different operating systems is not enough, for CD-ROM applications to truly become a mass-market consumer item, the reconciliation of the remainder of the CD-ROM formats must happen. Remember that CD-ROM is incorporated into such home-use units as the Philips CD-I and even the Sega Genesis game system. Asking families to invest in CDs for their home-entertainment system and then reinvest in similar titles for the PC that sits in the den as a work tool is asking too much. The strategy is not geared to increasing acceptance and wide availability.

Rumors on the Standards Front

It's no surprise that some major manufacturers are eyeing the possibilities of increasing portability—especially across home-entertainment and PC-based systems. Companies are beginning to realize that a CD-ROM application that can be popped into a unit attached to the TV *and* in the PC in the den can increase the sales of both hardware platforms—as well as have a tremendous effect on software-application development. If the PC-based system and the home-entertainment system use compatible CDs, software developers can reach a larger market and focus on providing better titles rather than waste development efforts porting similar applications to many different hardware platforms.

Rumors are strong that Sony is developing a CD-ROM-XA drive for use in both Nintendo's and Sega Genesis's newer systems. If the drives are truly XA-compliant—that is, if they are to the Sony spec—information applications developed for one platform (say the PC) would be usable on the home-based Nintendo or Sega system, too. Besides giving the game developers a more expanded platform for zapping aliens and running mazes, it would effectively allow many reference, educational, and business-oriented CD-ROM applications to migrate easily into consumer's family rooms.

Finally, the Sony CD-ROM-XA specification and Philips CD-I format are so close in actual details as to be virtually the same. Key elements are different, however, and those are enough to discourage computer-based developers from crossing the line into CD-I territory. If the Philips system could be modified in some way to use XA-compatible discs, Philips would instantly double the number of applications for the system and increase acceptance among users who have already invested—or are about to invest—in primarily PC-based CD-ROM applications.

And Yet Another Size

Sony recently announced the availability of yet another CD-ROM format—or rather *form factor*. The latest is a 3.5-inch version of the current CD-ROM format. This scaled-back CD-ROM, according to the company, is perfect for laptop computers and can replace one of the floppy drives in larger PCs, much as the 3.5-inch floppy is gradually pushing out the 5.25-inch disks.

This small form-factor CD has a formatted capacity of nearly 200 megabytes, and Sony promises that will increase in the coming months. This new disc format—and the drives that use them—may have made developers a lot more nervous if the new drives had incorporated another file format as well. Fortunately, the new 3.5-inch discs and drives will use the standard CD-ROM High Sierra and XA formats.

Because the standard formats will be used on the smaller discs, CD-ROM software developers can ship products on both sizes of disc or make scaled-back versions of their products for the smaller drives. Truth be told, most CD-ROM applications that are primarily text-based consume barely a third of current CD-ROM discs—the rest is blank, unused space. Shipping sophisticated multimedia applications on dual media may be more troublesome because data may overrun the capacity of the smaller discs.

What's the Verdict?

What will come to pass? The introduction of other home-based systems, such as the 3DO system, and the proliferation of PC-based drives may further fragment the market. On the other hand, these same pressures may force unlikely alliances, as in the Sony-Nintendo arrangement. The only outcome that benefits you as a consumer is increased compatibility and portability of CD-ROM formats and applications. Better titles—at more reasonable costs—will be the direct result of even a partial reconciliation between even a few of the competing formats.

Will we ever arrive at a one-drive-fits-all future? We doubt it. Some formats will simply disappear as that technology loses the fight to become a widely distributed product. Other formats will evolve into even more complex—and incompatible—technologies that address more sophisticated data applications.

In the meantime, buying, installing, and using a CD-ROM drive for your PC—whether at work or on your home PC—is a sound investment with a great future.

Appendix A

Drive Manufacturers in This Book

The following is a list of CD-ROM drive manufacturers whose products are described in this book. Note that this is not a comprehensive, all-inclusive list of CD-ROM drive manufacturers; a number of companies produce products that we thought were inappropriate for this book, and there were some companies who wished not to be included.

Apple Computer
1 Infinite Loop
Cupertino, CA 95014
Phone: (800) 538-9696

CD Technology, Inc.
766 San Aleso Ave.
Sunnyvale, CA 94086
Phone: (408) 752-8500
Fax: (408) 752-8501

Chinon America, Inc.
660 Maple Ave.
Torrance, CA 90503
Phone: (310) 533-0274 or (800) 441-0222
Fax: (310) 533-1727

Hitachi Multimedia Systems Division
3890 Steve Reynolds Blvd.
Norcross, GA 30093
Phone: (404) 279-5600
Fax: (404) 279-5699

Laser Magnetic Storage International Company
4425 ArrowsWest Drive
Colorado Springs, CO 80907-3489
Phone: (719) 593-7900
Fax: (719) 599-8713

Liberty Systems
160 Saratoga Ave.
Santa Clara, CA 95051
Phone: (408) 983-1127
Fax: (408) 243-2885

Media Vision
47300 Bayside Parkway
Fremont, CA 94538
Phone: (510) 770-8600
Fax: (510) 770-8648

MicroSolutions Computer Products
132 W. Lincoln Highway
DeKalb, IL 60115
Phone: (815) 756-3411
Fax: (815) 756-2928

Mirror Technologies
5198 West 76th Street
Edina, MN 55439
Phone: (612) 830-1549
Fax: (612) 832-5709

NEC Technologies, Inc.
1255 Michael Drive
Wood Dale, IL 60191-1094
Phone: (708) 860-9500

Philips Consumer Electronics Company
One Philips Drive
P.O. Box 14810
Knoxville, TN 37914-1810
Phone: (800) 845-7301

Pioneer New Media
2265 E. 220th Street
Long Beach, CA 90810
Phone: (800) 444-OPTI
Fax: (310) 952-2990

Procom Technology
2181 Dupont Drive
Irvine, CA 92715
Phone: (800) 800-8600 or (714) 852-1000
Fax: (714) 852-1221

Sony Corporation of America
1 Sony Drive
Park Ridge, NJ 07656
Phone: (201) 930-6432

Plextor
1605 Wyatt Drive
Santa Clara, CA 95054
Phone: (408) 980-1838
Fax: (408) 980-1840

Toshiba America Information Systems, Inc.
Disk Products Division
9740 Irvine Boulevard
Irvine, CA 92718
Phone: (714) 583-3111
Fax: (714) 583-3133

Appendix B

CD-ROM Software Developers and Publishers

This appendix lists the names, addresses, and phone numbers of the main software manufacturers discussed in this book. Software developers include everyone from developers of search-and-retrieval software to database-compilation companies.

AimTech Corporation
20 Trafalgar Square
Nashua, NH 03063-1973
Phone: (603) 883-0220

ALDE Publishing
6520 Edenvale Blvd.
Eden Prairie, MN 55344
Phone: (612) 835-3401

Allegro New Media
387 Passaic Ave.
Fairfield, NJ 07004
Phone: (201) 808-1992

American Business Information
5711 South 86th Circle
Omaha, NE 68127-0347
Phone: (402) 593-4565

Applied Optical Media Corp.
1450 Boot Road
Building 400
West Chester, PA 19380
Phone: (215) 429-3701

Bowker Electronic Publishing
121 Chanlon Road
New Providence, NJ 07974
Phone: (908) 464-6800

Brøderbund
500 Redwood Blvd.
Novato, CA 94948
Phone: (415) 382-4400 or (800) 521-6263

Buckmaster Publishing
Route 4
Mineral, VA 23117
Phone: (703) 894-5777

Bureau of Electronic Publishing
141 New Road
Parsippany, NJ 07054
Phone: (201) 808-2700

Compact Publishing
P.O. Box 40310
Washington, D.C. 20016
Phone: (202) 244-4770

Compton's New Media
2320 Camino Vida Roble
Carlsbad, CA 92009-1504
Phone: (619) 929-2500

Corel Systems Corporation
The Corel Building
1600 Carling Ave.
Ottawa, Ontario, Canada K1Z 8R7
Phone: (613) 728-8200 or (613) 728-3733

Creative Multimedia Corp.
514 N.W. 11th Ave.
Portland, OR 97209
Phone: (503) 241-4351

Dataware Technologies
222 Third Ave.
Cambridge, MA 02142
Phone: (617) 621-0820

DeLorme Mapping
P.O. Box 298
Freeport, ME 04032
Phone: (207) 865-4171

Digital Directory Assistance
5161 River Road
Bethesda, MD 20816
Phone: (301) 657-8548

Discis Knowledge Research
45 Sheppard Ave. East
Suite 410
Toronto, Ontario, Canada M2N 5W9
Phone: (800) 567-4321 or (416) 250-6537

Disclosure Incorporated
5161 River Road
Bethesda, MD 20816
Phone: (800) 843-7747

Dr. T's Music Software
124 Crescent Road
Needham, MA 01294
Phone: (617) 455-1454 ext. 226

Dun's Direct Access
Three Sylvan Way
Parsippany, NJ 07054
Phone: (800) 526-0651

Dynamix
1600 Mill Race Drive
Eugene, OR 97403
Phone: (503) 343-0772

Ebook, Inc.
32970 Alvarado-Niles Road
Suite 704
Union City, CA 94587
Phone: (510) 429-1331

Eduquest
6269 B Variel Ave.
Woodland Hills, CA 91367
Phone: (818) 992-8484

Electronic Press
124 Mt. Auburn St.
Cambridge, MA 02138
Phone: (617) 225-9023

Grolier Electronic Publishing
Sherman Turnpike
Danbury, CT 06816
Phone: (800) 356-5590 or (800) 285-4534

Healthcare Information Systems
2335 American River Drive
Suite 307
Sacramento, CA 95825
Phone: (916) 648-8075 or (800) 468-1128

HW Wilson
950 University Ave.
Bronx, NY 10452
Phone: (800) 367-6770 or (718) 588-8400

Hyperglot Software Company
5108-D Kingston Pike
Knoxville, TN 37939
Phone: (615) 558-8270

Infobases International, Inc.
1875 S. State St.
Suite 7200
Orem, UT 84058-8078
Phone: (801) 224-2223

Information Access Company
367 Lakeside Drive
Foster City, CA 94404
Phone: (800) 227-8431 or (415) 591-2333

Interactive Ventures
2900 Lone Oak Parkway
Suite 122
Eagan, MN 55121
Phone: (612) 686-0779

InterOptica
300 Montgomery St.
San Francisco, CA 94104
Phone: (415) 788-8788

Interplay Productions
17922 Fitch Ave.
Irvine, CA 92714
Phone: (714) 553-6655
Fax: (714) 252-2820

Knowledge Adventure
4502 Dyer St.
LaCrescenta, CA 91214
Phone: (800) 542-4240 or (818) 542-4200

Laser Resources, Inc.
20620 S. Leapwood Ave.
Carson, CA 90746
Phone: (310) 324-4444

LucasArts Entertainment
P.O. Box 10307
San Rafael, CA 94912
Phone: (415) 721-3300

MarketPlace Information Corp.
Three University Office Park
Waltham, MA 02154
Phone: (617) 894-8371

Matthew Bender and Company
11 Penn Plaza
New York, NY 10001
Phone: (212) 216-8094 or (800) 223-1940

Media Vision
47300 Bayside Parkway
Fremont, CA 94538
Phone: (510) 770-8600

MicroProse Software
180 Lakefront Drive
Hunt Valley, MD 21030
Phone: (410) 771-0440

Microsoft
One Microsoft Way
Redmond, WA 98052-6399
Phone: (206) 882-8080 or (800) 426-9100

National Geographic Society
1145 17th St., N.W.
Washington, D.C. 20036
Phone: (202) 775-6583

Oxford University Press
200 Madison Ave., 9th Floor
New York, NY 10016
Phone: (212) 679-7300 ext. 7370

Pemberton Press
462 Danbury Road
Wilton, CT 06897-2126
Phone: (203) 761-1466

Penton Overseas, Inc.
2740 Impala Drive
Carlsbad, CA 92008-7226
Phone: (619) 431-0060 or (800) 748-5804

ProCD New Media Publishing
8 Doaks Lane
Marblehead, MA 01945
Phone: (617) 631-9200

Quanta Press
1313 Fifth St. S.E.
Suite 223A
Minneapolis, MN 55414
Phone: (612) 379-3956

Random House Reference & Electronic Publishing
201 E. 50th St., 3rd Floor
New York, NY 10022
Phone: (212) 751-2600

Sierra OnLine
P.O. Box 485
Coarsegold, CA 93614
Phone: (209) 683-4468

Silver Platter Information
100 River Road Drive
Norwood, MA 02062-5026
Phone: (800) 343-0064 or (617) 769-2599

Software Toolworks
60 Leveroni Court
Novato, CA 94949
Phone: (415) 883-3000 ext. 566

Syracuse Language Systems
719 E. Genesee St.
Syracuse, NY 13210
Phone: (315) 478-6729

Texas Caviar
3933 Steck Ave.
Suite B115
Austin, TX 78759
Phone: (512) 346-7887

Tiger Media
5801 E. Slauson Ave.
Suite 200
Los Angeles, CA 90040
Phone: (213) 721-8282

Trilobyte
110 S. 3rd St.
Jacksonville, OR 97530
Phone: (503) 899-1113

UMI
30 N. Zeeb Road
Ann Arbor, MI 48106
Phone: (313) 761-4700 or (800) 521-0600

Virgin Enterprises
18061 Fitch Ave.
Irvine, CA 92714
Phone: (714) 833-8710

The Voyager Company
1351 Pacific Coast Highway
Santa Monica, CA 90401
Phone: (914) 591-5500 or (800) 446-2001

Warner New Media
3500 W. Olive Ave.
Suite 1050
Burbank, CA 91505
Phone: (818) 955-9999

Wayzata Technology
2515 East Highway 2
Grand Rapids, MN 55744
Phone: (218) 326-0598

West Publishing
610 Opperman Drive
Eagan, MN 55123
Phone: (800) 328-0109

World Library
12914 Haster St.
Garden Grove, CA 92640
Phone: (800) 443-0238 or (714) 748-7198

Ziff Communications Company
One Park Ave.
New York, NY 10016
Phone: (212) 503-4400

Appendix C

Useful CD-ROM Utilities

CD-ROMs are great, but there's always room for improvement. Even the new high-speed drives can get faster with caching software, and several companies now offer software to help you manage music CDs and graphics CDs (including PhotoCDs).

This appendix shows you some of the current software tools that can make your experience with CD-ROMs easier and faster.

Caching Software

Caching software makes your drive seem faster by doing a little high-tech predicting. Caching software doesn't actually speed the drive up, it just anticipates what data on the drive you're most likely to want and puts that data into RAM (or on your hard drive) where it can be accessed much more quickly than from the CD-ROM drive.

Your computer works with most data very quickly, but you've probably noticed it appears to slow down when you work with programs or data on your CD-ROM drive (or a floppy drive), especially when compared to the speed of working with files on your hard drive. The speed difference is because the CD-ROM drive delivers data much more slowly than the hard drive. The computer sends a request to the drive and the drive has to find the data and transfer it back to the computer (see Chapter 1, "What Is CD-ROM?" for more information about how CD-ROM drives find data on discs and why it takes so long). Once the data is in the computer's memory or on the hard drive, however, it can be accessed almost immediately.

Caching software steps in between the computer and the CD-ROM drive, processing requests from the computer and data delivery from the drive. The caching software uses time when the CD-ROM drive would normally be idle to load some of the disc's data into RAM or onto the hard drive, into what is called a *cache*. When your computer requests some information from the CD-ROM drive, the caching software checks to see whether that data is in the cache. If so, the data is delivered immediately, otherwise the data request is passed on to the CD-ROM drive.

The caching software's "guesses" as to what data you'll ask for next are based on some simple principles:

- Because one of the most requested pieces of data from a CD-ROM drive is the directory, the directory is almost always loaded into the cache
- Odds are that when your software asks for a piece of data, it will ask for the same information in the near future
- It's also a good bet that when your software asks for a piece of data, the next request the software makes is for the information immediately following it

Most CD-ROM drives have hardware-based caches built in (some caches are as large as 1 MB), but software caches give you much more flexibility and, usually, more cache space.

Several companies make CD-ROM caching software for DOS-based systems. One of the easiest to find is MS DOS 6.22's SMARTDRV. Although SMARTDRV is primarily hard-disk caching software, the new version does a fine job on CD-ROMs. Norton's Speedrive boasts a 30x speed improvement (depending on the application) for CD-ROM drives, running neck-and-neck with Lucid Corporation's capable but not-quite-as-sophisticated Lighting CD software. Other companies have adapted hard-disk caches to work with CD-ROM drives as well, including PC-Kwik and Online Computer Systems.

One Macintosh cache is FWB's CD-ROM Toolkit. It improves the drive's apparent performance up to 18 times and includes other utilities for working with CDs (including an audio CD manager).

Caching CD-ROMs with SMARTDrive

How much easier can it get? SMARTDrive version 5.01 (included with DOS 6.22) caches CD-ROM drives automatically so that you don't have to do *anything* to get it to work—assuming that you've already installed SMARTDrive. If you haven't installed it yet, add a line like this to your AUTOEXEC.BAT file:

```
C:\DOS\SMARTDRV.EXE
```

This line must appear *after* the line that loads your CD-ROM extensions (usually MSCDEX), or SMARTDrive won't know you've got a CD-ROM drive. SMARTDrive automatically sets up read and write caching for hard disks and read caching for CD-ROMs and other drives (floppies, INTERLNK drives, and so on—but not network drives).

In the unlikely event that SMARTDrive's caching causes any problems with one of your discs, you can disable SMARTDrive's CD-ROM functions without affecting its caching of other drives. At the DOS prompt (not in a Windows

DOS box), type **SMARTDRV** with the drive letter of your CD-ROM and a minus sign, like this:

```
SMARTDRV D-
```

This example assumes that your CD-ROM drive is drive D. This change affects only the current session—when you restart your computer, SMARTDrive returns to the settings from the AUTOEXEC.BAT file. To reenable CD-ROM caching without restarting the computer, type the same command but use a plus instead of a minus after the drive letter, like this:

```
SMARTDRV D+
```

If you want to permanently disable CD-ROM caching in SMARTDrive, use the /U switch when you load it in the AUTOEXEC.BAT file, like this:

```
C:\DOS\SMARTDRV /U
```

This command tells SMARTDRV not to load its CD-ROM functions at all. If you use this switch, you can no longer use the + and – switches from DOS to affect SMARTDrive's CD-ROM caching.

Other Utilities

Speed is not the only element with room for improvement in CD-ROMs. The interfaces for the discs vary widely in quality and functionality, and some discs are purely collections of files (graphics files, sound files, or text) with no interface at all. All CD-ROM drives play audio CDs, but in most cases, you need software for that as well.

Corel Corporation makes the CD Power Pak, a collection of Windows utilities that solve almost every CD-ROM problem. Not only does the CD Power Pak include caching software to speed up your disc, it also has utilities to manage audio CDs, sound files, and (no surprise, coming from Corel) graphics. Corel CD-Audio manages audio CDs, including impressive features like sampling to your hard disk. Photo CD Lab converts photo CD images to several other formats and lets you create catalogs and slide shows of your photos. CorelDRAW! users will recognize CorelMOSAIC, the graphics manager included in the CD Power Pak. CorelMOSAIC includes search, preview, and printing functions, and will let you create catalogs of your graphics. And true to form, Corel includes plenty of samples with its CD Power Pak—150 sound clips and 100 royalty-free photos.

Another popular utility from Corel is CorelSCSI! for PC or Macintosh. It includes SCSI diagnostics tools, an audio CD player, and extensive PhotoCD manipulation tools. CorelSCSI! also includes an optimized CD-ROM extensions driver, CORELCDX. It functions much like Microsoft's MSCDEX and even uses most of MSCDEX's command-line parameters.

Aris Entertainment makes MPC Wizard, a diagnostics and setup package for Windows. Version 2.0 includes an accessible overview of the MPC specifications, as well as MPC1 and MPC2 tests for your video, audio, and CD-ROM drive. One of MPC Wizard's most impressive features is its driver library. If you need to replace a lost video driver, CD-ROM driver, or sound-card driver, you'll probably find it right on this disc. Even if you have the original driver diskettes, you may want to use the MPC Wizard's easy driver installation program instead of the (typically horrible) installation program from the hardware manufacturer.

And who better to help you manage your PhotoCDs than Kodak? Their Shoebox software lets you save, edit, and catalog PhotoCDs; you can even save clips from different PhotoCDs to your hard drive.

Appendix D

Where To Buy: Hardware and Software Vendors

Look around at the nearest shopping mall: most computer hardware and software shops now stock CD-ROM hardware and software. Their prices are reasonable, in most cases, with up to 25 percent off the suggested list prices. Egghead Software, Electronique Boutique, Circuit City, CompUSA, Best Buy, and others are finally offering the software end of the business for games, home-based reference, and business applications. Drive availability and selection is, at best, abysmal in most other chains and mall stores, with only low-priced—and mostly low-quality—multimedia upgrade kits available.

For the majority of the industrial-strength business applications, particularly those that entail a subscription-based fee, you have to deal directly with the manufacturer or through specialized distributors. Discounts, if any, are slight.

Mail-Order Sources for Hardware and Software

By no means is the following list of **mail-order firms** for hardware and software exhaustive—we've narrowed the list to those with which we've had direct experience, or those we know have excellent reputations for good prices, support, and service.

TIP

Mall or Mail Order?

You don't have to settle for the drives offered by the chains—their selection can't compare to mail order. The reputable mail-order firms we list here carry a wide array of drives, SCSI cards, cables, and accessories—and their prices are as much as 30 percent off list. Most carry CD-ROM software as well, and even have bundling prices: when you order a drive, they offer special pricing on a wide selection of CDs.

ComputAbility

P.O. Box 17882
Milwaukee, WI 53217
Phone: (800) 558-0003
Fax: (414) 357-7814
Visa and MasterCard accepted

ComputAbility was founded in 1982 and is on the cutting edge of multimedia with a wide product line spanning everything from CD-ROM game software to high-end video-editing and laser-disc players. Most of the products discussed in this book are available at ComputAbility—from SCSI cables to video compression boards—and their prices are extremely competitive. Some of the CD-ROM drives they carry include the following:

- NEC
- Toshiba
- Hitachi
- Plextor

Sound cards from Turtle Beach, MediaVision, and Creative Labs are available separately or in the bundled multimedia upgrade kits we spoke of in Chapter 3, "How To Select CD-ROM Drives." ComputAbility is also a good source for speakers and SCSI host adapters. We've ordered Adaptec cards from ComputAbility on numerous occasions—they're always priced right and arrive within days. ComputAbility carries the full Altec Lansing series of ACS speaker systems, too.

Computer Discount Warehouse (CDW)

2840 Maria Drive
Northbrook, IL 60062
Phone: (800) 326-4239
Fax: (708) 291-1737
VISA, Discover, and MasterCard accepted

CDW has been in the mail-order business for over a decade. They have a few Midwest showrooms and discount stores, but their primary business is mail order. The company stocks a good selection of CD-ROM drives, including the following:

- NEC
- Toshiba
- Hitachi
- Plextor

Prices are excellent—usually 25 percent or more below list—and delivery and support are good. CDW also carries sound cards, an extensive assortment of SCSI adapters, and some multimedia upgrade kits. Ask about CD-ROM software bundling when you order a drive—they regularly run specials for drive purchasers, offering an assortment of CD-ROM starter titles for a low price.

The motto at CDW is *ask for it*. With over 15,000 items in stock, they usually have—or can get quickly—whatever item you're looking for.

Dustin

20969 Ventura Blvd.
Suite 13
Woodland Hills, CA 91364
Phone: (800) 274-6611
Fax: (818) 884-6611
VISA, Discover, and MasterCard accepted

Dustin claims to be the largest seller of CD-ROM software and hardware on the planet. They may be right. They offer an extensive line of software titles and multimedia upgrade kits from Creative Labs and MediaVision. Although their drive selection is limited, their software title list is impressive. And they offer extensive discounts on titles when you purchase a drive or multimedia upgrade kit. For example, the regular price of ProPhone software is $219; when you order it as part of a bundle, the price is $79.

Elek-Tek

7350 North Linder Ave.
Skokie, IL 60077
Phone: (800) 395-1000
Fax: (708) 677-1081
Visa and MasterCard accepted

Elek-Tek started out in the calculator business—the high-end HP calculators, back before the PC market was even a reality. So they've been in the business since the beginning of the PC boom. They carry an extensive line of software titles, multimedia kits, and drives. Technical support and service is very good.

TigerSoftware

9100 South Dadeland Blvd.
Suite 1200
Miami, FL 33156
Phone: (800) 888-4437
Fax: (305) 447-0738
Visa, MasterCard, Discover, and American Express accepted

TigerSoftware is more than just software. The company has a great reputation in the mail-order business and offers an extensive line of software and hardware products, including multimedia upgrade kits, CD-ROM drives, and speakers. The main CD-ROM drive product they sell is NEC, with some other brands as well. TigerSoftware makes extensive use of bundling—check for prices on a number of options or ask for their latest catalog.

Mail-Order Sources for CD-ROM Software Titles

Following are mail-order sources for CD-ROM titles. These firms specialize in CD-ROM software and offer a wide range of the latest titles at a substantial discount. They'll probably beat the prices of many chain and mall stores.

Mr. CD-ROM

123 South Woodland St.
Winter Garden, FL 34787
Phone: (800) 444-6723
Fax: (407) 877-3834
Visa, MasterCard, and American Express accepted

Plenty of titles, fast delivery, and great discounts are a few of Mr. CD-ROM's highlights.

Walnut Creek CD-ROM

4041 Pike Lane
Suite D
Concord, CA 94520
Phone: (800) 786-9907
Fax: (510) 674-0821
Visa, MasterCard, and American Express accepted

Walnut Creek specializes in compilations of public-domain software on CD-ROM as well as an extensive library of programming source code. In addition, the company carries a complete line of the most popular CD-ROM software titles available today.

CD-ROM Warehouse

1720 Oak St.
Lakewood, NJ 08701
Phone: (800) 237-6623
Visa and MasterCard accepted

The folks who brought you MacWarehouse, MicroWarehouse, and Data Comm Warehouse are at it again. CD-ROM Warehouse stocks all major titles for the Mac and PC, as well as drives and multimedia kits. They offer several hardware/CD-ROM and multiple-CD-ROM bundles.

Appendix E

Additional Sources for Information

The CD-ROM industry is dynamic and fast growing. Periodicals are a good source of information concerning product announcements; electronic information services are *the* best source for contacting fellow CD-ROM users; and company bulletin-board services are a must for obtaining the latest software drivers and software program revisions. The more information you have at your disposal, the better your CD-ROM expertise.

Magazines, Journals, and Newsletters

To keep up to date with the latest in technology and application development, you should check in periodically with at least some of the following publications. Stores with large magazine racks and computer stores should have a large selection of these periodicals.

CD-ROM Professional

462 Danbury Road
Wilton, CT 06897-2126
Phone: (800) 248-8466
Annual subscription price: $44.95

CD-ROM Professional, published bimonthly, is slick, well-designed, and always on top of what's new in the industry. Articles are written by professionals in the business, so the content is always accurate and appropriate. Geared as much toward the CD-ROM publisher as the end-user, the magazine has a lot of ground to cover—and to its credit, it does it well.

CD-ROM World

Meckler Corporation
11 Ferry Lane West
Westport, CT 06880
Phone: (203) 226-6967
Annual subscription price: $39 (personal), $87 (institutional)

Published monthly, *CD-ROM World* covers CD-ROM news from all over the globe. It has reviews, news, and user articles highlighting the uses of CD-ROM in a variety of educational, manufacturing, and other professional work situations.

New Media

901 Mariner's Island Blvd.
Suite 365
San Mateo, CA 94404
Phone: (415) 573-5170
Fax: (415) 573-5131
Price: $3.95 per issue

The multimedia market—from Apple Macintosh to PC to CD-ROM and beyond—is growing rapidly. *New Media* has staked out this considerable turf as its base of coverage in articles ranging from multimedia authoring software to game and reference reviews. Although the magazine is oriented toward the consumer and entry-level developer, it is written for the average user and is a pleasure to read and always up to date.

Wired

544 Second Street
San Francisco, CA 94107-1427
Phone: (415) 904-0660
Fax: (415) 904-0669
Annual subscription price: $20; $36 for two years

Wired is a monthly explosion of post-information-age news, views, and techno-editorial that is a joy to read and look at. Visually and intellectually alive, the content may not be for all readers, but you owe yourself at least one look. Not technology specific, *Wired* is more a guide to what's fringe, off the edge, or looming on the electronic horizon.

Business and Legal CD-ROMs in Print

Meckler Corporation
11 Ferry Lane West
Westport, CT 06880
Phone: (203) 226-6967
Annual volume price: $55

Business and Legal CD-ROMs in Print is an annual review and digest that targets this most vital area of CD-ROM publishing. Any legal or business research professional needs this volume to keep up to date.

Information Searcher

14 Hadden Road
Scarsdale, NY 10583
Annual subscription price: $24

Targeted at teachers, researchers, and library professionals, this quarterly newsletter covers both the on-line and CD-ROM markets in reviews, strategies, and tips. *Information Searcher* includes curriculum guides, conference coverage, and a CD-ROM directory for schools.

Electronic Sources

Following is a listing of the most popular CD and BBS reference sources for CD-ROM users. Note that CompuServe has an expanded CD-ROM vendor and user forum. Also note that nontraditional methods for accessing information about CD-ROMs can be found in places such as the Internet and other professional organizations that host electronic forums on America OnLine, CompuServe, BIX, and Prodigy.

Meckler CD-ROMs in Print

Meckler Corporation
11 Ferry Lane West
Westport, CT 06880
Phone: (203) 226-6967
CD-ROM version: $95
Printed version: $95

Meckler CD-ROMs in Print is a great disc-of-discs. Virtually all CD-ROMs in print, in the U.S. and throughout the world, are referenced on this disc. Multimedia, hardware manufacturers, and much more, are indexed and searchable. The disc is an excellent value and has a printed counterpart.

Nautilus

7001 Discovery Boulevard
Dublin, OH 43017
Phone: (800) 637-3472
Fax: (614) 761-4110
Per issue price: $9.95 (plus $1.50 shipping and handling)
Annual subscription price: $137.00 (includes shipping and handling)

A unique, multimedia CD-ROM magazine on CD-ROM disc, Metatec's Nautilus is filled with multimedia presentations, sound samples, photography, industry interviews, full-motion video clips, and shareware in a variety of categories. Worth a look if you're new to CD-ROM; you can get a sample disc of a past issue for $4.95.

The CD-ROM of CD-ROMs

1547 Palos Verdes Mall
Suite 260
Walnut Creek, CA 94596
Phone: (800) 786-9907
Fax: (510) 947-1644
Price: $39.95

The CD-ROM of CD-ROMs is an encyclopedia of CD-ROMs, software, and hardware. Over 4,000 North American discs are listed with reviews of 500 products. Screen captures of many programs are shown as well. Contact information for over 4,600 companies is provided. All this comes in a polished Windows interface with a good search engine.

CD-ROM Forum

This CompuServe forum is devoted to CD-ROM enthusiasts—both corporate and home. The CD-ROM forum is a clearinghouse for news, tips, and CD-ROM-related shareware programs. Libraries and topics include PhotoCD, CD audio, and Nautilus (the CD-ROM magazine from Metatec). To access the forum, type the following at any CIS prompt:

GO CDROM

CD-ROM Vendor's Forum

Software and hardware manufacturers sponsor the CD-ROM Vendor's forum on CompuServe. Among the vendors on-line in this forum are the following:

- Trantor
- Meridian Data
- Bowker Electronic Publishing
- Best Photo Labs
- One-Off CD Shops
- Nimbus Information Systems
- QuickScan
- Bureau of Electronic Publishing

Other vendors are expected to come on board in the coming months. The forum includes demos, driver updates, press releases, and other information in addition to access to company representatives. To access the forum, type the following at any CIS prompt:

GO CDVEN

Multimedia Forum

The Multimedia forum on CompuServe hosts vendors and users of all multimedia equipment and software: Macintosh, Amiga, PC, and many other platforms are represented. Vendor representatives are available to answer questions, and shareware and demos can be found as well. To access the forum, type the following at any CIS prompt:

GO MULTIMEDIA

BIX

Byte magazine's information service (BIX) has a CD-ROM forum for users, developers, and manufacturers. Library files include demos and shareware. Select CD.ROM from the forum menu for access to the CD-ROM forum.

Internet

The Internet—that wonderful jungle of tons of information on virtually every conceivable topic—has, as you might imagine, a CD-ROM information forum with archive files and information files. The Internet address for this forum is **cdrom.com**.

Optical Publishing Association

P.O. Box 21726
Columbus, OH 43221
Phone: (614) 442-8805
Fax: (614) 442-8815

The Optical Publishing Association is for CD-ROM software title developers and publishers. They publish a newsletter, sponsor seminars, and offer discounts on industry-related publications, as well as conduct market research and offer expert advice for all aspects of CD-ROM publishing. If you're a publisher or are seriously considering marketing your own CD-ROMs, OPA membership is a good investment.

Appendix F

Care and Feeding of CD-ROMs

CD-ROM discs are extremely durable. Properly cared for, they should last indefinitely. They are not indestructible, however. When audio CDs were introduced, for some reason a rumor began that there was nothing you could do to hurt them. It didn't take long for the truth—or lack of truth—in this statement to be shown. Take a few precautions and you won't need to worry about your discs. If they do get damaged, there may still be hope.

Handling CD-ROMs

If you read about how a CD-ROM drive works in Chapter 1, "What Is CD-ROM?," you know that the surface of a disc is essentially a transparent surface. It must allow a finely focused beam of laser light to pass through it twice—first to the metallic layer beneath the plastic (which contains the data) and then back to the receptors. Dirt, scratches, fingerprints, and other imperfections interfere with the retrieval of the stored data.

In the case of an audio CD, there is a great deal of leeway in surface imperfections. Audio is a predictable, analog signal. It is possible for a CD player to interpolate (that is, make an educated guess) about any missing data. It works like this: assuming the scratch or dirt doesn't obliterate too much data, the circuitry of the player simply looks at the values before and after the unreadable information and "guesses" that the missing value is between the two. Although the guessed value may not precisely match the missing value, because the data represents sound, it would take quite a few missed guesses to make the sound detectably different.

Computer data, on the other hand, has no such predictable pattern. It is absolutely necessary that a 1 be retrieved as a 1 and a 0 as a 0. Because small scratches are a fact of life, the

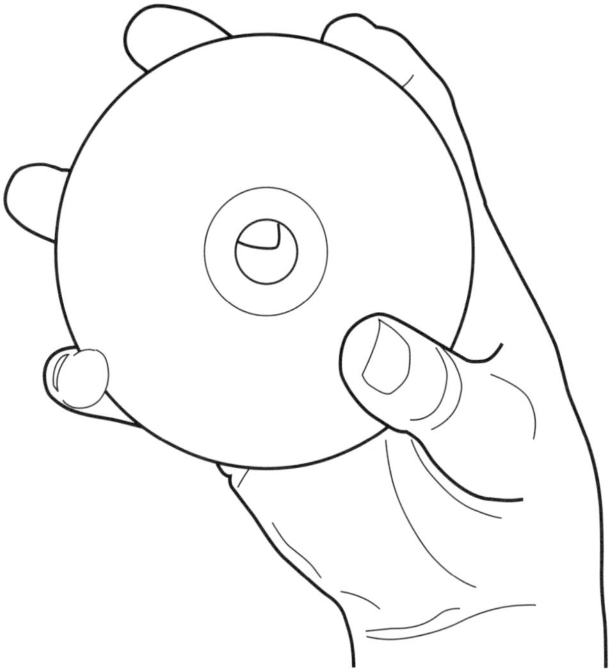

FIGURE F.1

Handle the disc by its edges to avoid putting fingerprints on its surface.

CD-ROM must incorporate a scheme that makes it somewhat forgiving of such small damage. This scheme is called ECC (Error Correction Code). With ECC, a disc can sustain some surface damage and still be usable. ECC works by recording data redundantly. That is, it uses a scheme that makes possible the reconstruction of any bit from the surrounding bits. While ECC does allow a CD-ROM to tolerate some degradation, your best bet is to handle your discs carefully enough to keep the surface in good condition.

- **Treat your discs as you do photographic negatives.** Hold discs only by the edges (see fig. F.1). Keep them free from dust. Store them in containers when not in use. The goal is the same in both cases: keep the surface free of scratches, fingerprints, and dirt.

- **If you must put a disc down, do it with the working surface up.** When you place a CD-ROM on your desk or other surface, make sure that you place it with the *unprinted surface up*. Doing so helps avoid getting dirt on the disc's surface or scratching it when trying to pick it back up.

- **If your drive uses caddies, buy enough caddies for all your commonly used discs.** Caddies are relatively inexpensive—certainly cheaper than the CD-ROMs they protect. If all your commonly used discs are in caddies, you never actually have to handle the discs themselves.

Storing CD-ROMs

The CD is basically a plastic sandwich with an aluminum filling. It really does not require too much in the way of special storage. Commonsense precautions should suffice.

- **Try to keep your CD-ROMs at room temperature.** Although CD-ROMs can tolerate a fairly wide temperature range without visible damage, extreme heat can be hazardous to their health. In addition to warping the discs by overheating, cyclic heating and cooling can damage the metallic layer inside the disc. A well-manufactured disc should last indefinitely, but, like any storage medium, radical changes in environment can damage it.

- **Keep your CD-ROMs in their packages when not in use.** If a CD-ROM is not in use (or in a caddie), store it in its package to help prevent dust or other contamination from getting on the disc. Dust itself does not damage the disc, but if enough accumulates, read errors can result. This means the disc must be cleaned, which is where the potential for damage lies. It is very easy to damage a disc while cleaning it. (The cleaning method itself may scratch the disc surface, or the dust may be abrasive enough that wiping it from the surface does damage.) Keeping the disc in its package also limits the possibility of scratching the surface while handling it.

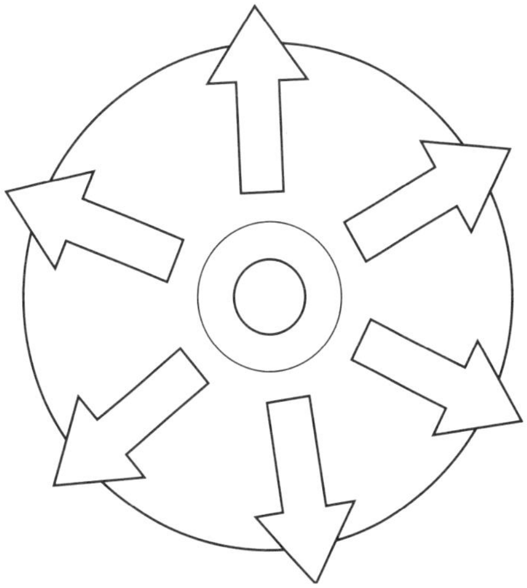

FIGURE F.2

Cleaning strokes should be made from the center to the edge of the disc to limit scratch damage.

Cleaning CD-ROMs

If you follow the precautions on handling and storage, you should rarely need to clean your discs. When you do, however, a little care will make damage to them unlikely.

- **Use a very soft, lint-free cloth.** The plastic surface of the disc is soft. Paper towels, for example, scratch it. The cloth you choose should be of the type for cleaning lenses—you can find one at a photographic supply house. In fact, any lens-cleaning accessory is potentially useful for cleaning CD-ROMs.

- **Use radial strokes from the center to the outside edge to remove the dust.** Although the natural tendency is to wipe the CD in a **circular** fashion—this being the easiest—this method is the most likely to cause damage that the ECC can not overcome. Wipe from the inside out (see fig. F.2).

- **Use a CD-approved solvent to remove contamination more tenacious than dust.** Make sure that the label specifically states the solvent can be used for cleaning discs. Spray the area on the disc and let the cleaner sit for a while to allow the solvent to remove the spot without rubbing—which must be avoided. In extreme cases, careful washing in the sink with mild dish soap and not-too-warm water is also okay. Follow the same radial-cleaning method as for dust.

Using compressed gas—available in office-supply or photo stores—is good for preventative maintenance. You will find that if dust is allowed to accumulate, the spray alone cannot remove it. The dust adheres to the surface of the disc and requires mechanical action to remove.

NOTE

Why Not To Wipe in a Circular Motion

Because the information on the CD-ROM is recorded in a spiral, any scratch you may cause by wiping the disc in a circular fashion has a chance of obliterating a whole string of pits, making a large part of the data unreadable.

Commercially available CD-cleaning systems are just fine for CD-ROMs. They are designed to provide the radial cleaning action and often come with some sort of liquid for use in conjunction with the machine.

In Case of Damage...

Even if you've done everything right in handling, storing, and cleaning your discs, mistakes do happen. Fortunately, there are a few things you can do to **restore** a damaged disc to near-new condition.

NOTE

Are You Sure It's the Disc?

Before you try any of these cures, make sure that the disc is the problem. Try the disc in more than one drive. If it works on another system, the problem is probably in the drive itself.

CD Polish

There are various brands of polish intended for removing small scratches from CD-ROM discs. You can find these products in audiophile stores or through magazines.

Metal Polish

Liquid metal polishes—like Brasso—are very similar in composition to the CD polish just mentioned. Use these polishes sparingly and with a very soft cloth to get rid of small surface defects.

TIP

Keep Polishing Radially

When you rub the disc with toothpaste (or any other polish), remember to rub from the center of the disc to its edge rather than around the disc. The abrasives in polish are intended to repair existing damage, not cause additional damage. Although it may not make any difference if you polish around the disc, it's probably best to keep your cleaning strokes consistent.

Toothpaste

Yes, toothpaste—preferably one designed to give you "shiny white teeth"—can work wonders on more severe damage. Use your finger and gently **polish** out the defect with a small amount of the toothpaste using short, reciprocating strokes. Carefully rinse the residue and then use a CD polish or metal polish to smooth the surface more if necessary. This procedure should be something of a last resort because it actually takes away microscopic portions of the disc's coating—it is possible (though unlikely) that you might damage the disc rather than cure it.

Professional Plastic Polishes

In the most extreme cases, when the disc is irreplaceable and the damage is more than toothpaste and metal polish can repair, it may be possible to use methods normally reserved for working with lucite and other plastics after machining. These methods involve using successively finer grits of abrasive paper and ending with liquid-based polishes. These techniques require some skill and some practice. You can get the materials—and advice on their use—from a local plastic-supply store. If you resort to this method, practice on some scrap plastic or a junk disc first; take your time when doing the job on the real disc.

Drive Maintenance

There isn't too much you have to do to maintain your CD-ROM drive. Its main enemy is the omnipresent dust in homes and offices. Dust can have detrimental effects on the mechanical components of the drive, but its most likely effect is to cover the laser's collimating lens. When this happens, all your discs falsely appear bad.

If you have a dirty lens, there are two courses of action available:

- Disassemble the drive and dust the lens with a soft brush or pressurized air.
- Buy a CD lens-cleaning disc from your local audio store.

The first option is probably beyond most of us. Very frequently, CD-ROM drives are sealed internally—an attempt to prevent the dust problem in the first place. This is a double-edged sword: if the drive does get dirty, you can't easily open it for cleaning.

The second option is easy and should work. Lens-cleaning discs have a small, velour-like material attached to the disc; they instruct the drive to seek across the disc, wiping the lens as it seeks. Some discs just put the velour "brush" on the data track; when the drive attempts to initialize the disc, the lens is cleaned. Most drives then spit out the disc because it cannot be read.

Appendix G

Miscellaneous Hardware and Software Manufacturers

Hardware and software vendors—from makers of speakers to multimedia boards—described or mentioned in this book are included in this appendix. Also included are vendors for which we could not devote space in the main text of this book but that are still worth mentioning.

Adaptec
619 Millpitas Blvd.
Millpitas, CA 95035
Phone: (408)945-8600

AimTech Corporation
20 Trafalgar Square
Nashua, NH 03063
Phone: (603) 883-0220
Fax: (603) 883-5582

British Telecom Directory Products Unit
1st Floor, Columbia Center Market Street
Bracknell
Berkshire RG12 1JG
United Kingdom
Phone: (+44) 344-861961
Fax: (+44) 344-860872

C-Cube Microsystems
1778 McCarthy Blvd.
Millpitas, CA 95035
Phone: (408) 944-6300
Fax: (408) 944-6314

Canadian Center for Occupational Health & Safety (CCOHS)
250 Main St.
East Hamilton, Ontario, Canada L8N 1H6
Phone: (905) 572-2981
Fax: (905) 572-4419

Canadian Telebook Agency
301 Donlands Ave.
Toronto, Ontario, Canada M4J 3R8
Phone: (416) 447-4005
Fax: (416) 467-7886

Capitol Disc Interactive
2121 Wisconsin Ave., N.W.
Washington, D.C. 20007
Phone: (202) 965-7800
Fax: (202) 965-7815

CBIS, Inc.
5875 Peachtree Industrial Blvd.
Building 100
Norcross, GA 30092
Phone: (404) 446-1332
Fax: (404) 446-9164

CD Romics
P.O. Box 221085
San Diego, CA 92122
Phone: (619) 546-8278

CD-ROM Galleries, Inc.
512 Gertrude Ave.
Aptos, CA 95003
Phone: (408) 685-2315
Fax: (408) 685-0340

CD-ROM Strategies
18 Chenile
Irvine, CA 92714
Phone: (714) 733-3378
Fax: (714) 786-1401

CEDROM Technologies, Inc.
1290 Van Horne Ave.
Suite 209 Outremont
Quebec, Canada H2V 4S2
Phone: (514) 278-3373
Fax: (514) 270-4162

Claritas/NPDC, Inc.
201 N. Union St.
Alexandria, VA 22314-2645
Phone: (703) 683-8300

CMC - Creative Multimedia Corporation
514 N.W. 11th Ave.
Suite 203
Portland, OR 97209
Phone: (503) 241-4351
Fax: (503) 241-4370

Compact Publishing, Inc.
4958 Ashby St., N.W.
Washington, D.C. 20007
Phone: (202) 244-4770
Fax: (202) 244-6363

Compton's NewMedia
345 Fourth St.
San Francisco, CA 94107
Phone: (619) 929-2500 or (619) 929-2555
Fax: (415) 546-1887

CoSA (Company of Science and Art)
14 Imperial Place
Suite 203
Providence, RI 02903
Phone: (206) 628-4526
Fax: (401) 274-7517

Crowninshield Software, Inc.
1050 Massachusetts Ave.
2nd Floor
Cambridge, MA 02138
Phone: (617) 965-3383
Fax: (617) 661-6254

Dai Nippon Printing Company, Ltd.
1-1 Ichigaya-Kagacho 1-chome Shinjuku-ku
Tokyo, Japan 162-01
Phone: (+81) 3-266-2910
Fax: (+81) 3-266-4599

Dataware Technologies, Inc.
222 Third St.
Suite 3300
Cambridge, MA 02142-1188
Phone: (617) 621-0820
Fax: (617) 621-0307

Diaquest, Inc.
1440 San Pablo Ave.
Berkeley, CA 94702
Phone: (510) 526-7167
Fax: (510) 526-7073

Digidesign, Inc.
1360 Willow Road
Suite 101
Menlo Park, CA 94025
Phone: (415) 688-0600
Fax: (415) 327-0777

Digital Audio Labs
14505 21st Ave. North
Suite 202
Plymouth, MN 55447
Phone: (612) 473-7626
Fax: (612) 473-7915

Digital Video Arts, Ltd.
Twining Center
715 Twining Road
Dresher, PA 19025
Phone: (215) 576-7920
Fax: (215) 576-7932

The DMR Group
57 River St.
Wellesley Hills, MA 02181
Phone: (617) 487-9000
Fax: (617) 237-3528

DNASTAR, Inc.
1228 S. Park St.
Madison, WI 53715
Phone: (608) 258-7420
Fax: (608) 258-7439

EarthInfo, Inc.
5541 Central Ave.
Boulder, CO 80301
Phone: (303) 938-1788
Fax: (303) 938-8183

The EDGE Interactive Media, Inc.
150 S. El Molino Ave.
Suite 201
Pasadena, CA 91101
Phone: (818) 304-4771
Fax: (818) 796-0132

Electronic Arts, Inc.
1450 Fashion Island Blvd.
San Mateo, CA 94404-2064
Phone: (415) 571-7171
Fax: (415) 571-1893

Electronic Press
101 Rogers St.
Cambridge, MA 02142
Phone: (617) 225-9023 or (800) 342-1338
Fax: (617) 868-7738

Elmsoft, Inc.
7954 Helmart Drive
Laurel, MD 20723
Phone: (301) 470-3451

Folio Corporation
2155 N. Freedom Blvd.
Suite 150
Provo, UT 84604
Phone: (801) 375-3700
Fax: (801) 374-5753

Gaylord Information Systems
P.O. Box 4901
Syracuse, NY 13221
Phone: (315) 457-5070 or (800) 962-9580
Fax: (315) 457-8387 or (800) 272-3412

GEOVISION, Inc.
5680 Peachtree Parkway
Norcross, GA 30092
Phone: (404) 448-8224
Fax: (404) 447-4525

The H.W. Wilson Company
950 University Ave.
Bronx, NY 10452
Phone: (212) 588-8400 or (800) 468-1128
Fax: (212) 538-7507

Henco Software, Inc.
100 5th Ave.
Waltham, MA 02154
Phone: (617) 890-8670 or (415) 691-5805
Fax: (617) 890-7671

Hewlett-Packard Company
100 Mayfield Ave.
Mountain View, CA 94043
Phone: (415) 691-5587
Fax: (415) 691-5484

Highland Software
1001 Elwell Court
Palo Alto, CA 94303
Phone: (415) 493-8567
Fax: (415) 493-4506

Hitachi Software Engineering Co., Ltd.
6-81 Onoe-cho Naka-ku
Yokohama, Japan 231
Phone: (+81) 45-681-2111
Fax: (+81) 45-681-4914

I.S. Grupe, Inc.
948 Springer Drive
Lombard, IL 60148
Phone: (708) 789-0710
Fax: (708) 627-4086

Image Concepts
33 Boston Post Road West
Marlboro, MA 01752
Phone: (508) 481-6882
Fax: (508) 481-4406

Imagetects
7200 Bollinger Road #802
San Jose, CA 95129
Phone: (408) 252-5487
Fax: (408) 252-7409

InfoAccess
2800 156th Ave. S.E.
Bellevue, WA 98007
Phone: (206) 747-3203
Fax: (206) 641-9367

Infolink, Inc.
750 N. 200 West
Suite 307
Provo, UT 84604
Phone: (801) 375-7507
Fax: (801) 375-7537

Information Access Company
357 Lakeside Drive
Foster City, CA 94404
Phone: (415) 378-5200 or (800) 227-8431

Information Handling Services, Inc.
15 Inverness Way East
Englewood, CO 80112
Phone: (303) 790-0600
Fax: (303) 799-4085

Information Navigation, Inc.
4201 University Drive
Suite 102
Durham, NC 27707
Phone: (919) 493-4390
Fax: (919) 489-5239

Information Technologies Group, Inc.
7315 Wisconsin Ave.
Suite 1100 W.
Bethesda, MD 20814
Phone: (301) 961-8580
Fax: (301) 961-8892

Inmagic, Inc.
2067 Massachusetts Ave.
Cambridge, MA 02140
Phone: (617) 661-8124
Fax: (617) 661-6901

Innotech, Inc.
110 Silver Star Blvd.
Unit 107
Scarborough
Toronto, Ontario, Canada M1V 5A2
Phone: (416) 321-3838
Fax: (416) 321-0095

Intechnica International, Inc.
P.O. Box 30877
Midwest City, OK 73140
Phone: (405) 732-0138
Fax: (405) 732-4574

Interplay Productions
17922 Fitch Ave.
Irvine, CA 92714
Phone: (714) 553-6665
Fax: (714) 252-2820

Iterated Systems, Inc.
5550-A Peachtree Parkway
Suite 650
Norcross, GA 30092
Phone: (404) 840-0310
Fax: (404) 840-0029

JAPAN Media
Tempelhofer Damm 4 1000
Berlin, Germany 42
Phone: (+49) 30-785-1713
Fax: (+49) 30-785-1993

Knowledge Access International
2685 Marine Way
Suite 1305
Mountain View, CA 94043
Phone: (415) 969-0606
Fax: (415) 964-2027

Knowledge Garden, Inc.
12 Technology Drive
Suite 8
Setaucket, NY 11733
Phone: (516) 246-5400
Fax: (516) 246-5452

KnowledgeSet Corporation
888 Villa St.
Suite 410
Mountain View, CA 94041
Phone: (800) 456-0469
Fax: (415) 968-9962

KWA, Inc.
7125 W. Jefferson Ave.
Suite 342
Lakewood, CO 80235
Phone: (303) 987-1729
Fax: (303) 987-2262

LaserLaw Corporation
1720 Loraine St.
Enumclaw, WA 98022
Phone: (206) 825-4093
Fax: (206) 825-9607

Library Systems & Services, Inc.
200 Orchard Ridge Drive
Gaithersburg, MD 20878
Phone: (301) 975-9800
Fax: (301) 975-9844

LinksWare Corporation
812 19th St.
Pacific Grove, CA 93950
Phone: (408) 372-4155
Fax: (408) 646-1045

Logical Data Expression
5537 33rd St., N.W.
Washington, D.C. 20015
Phone: (202) 966-3393

Macromedia, Inc.
600 Townsend
San Francisco, CA 94103
Phone: (415) 252-2000
Fax: (415) 442-0190

Magnetic Press, Inc.
588 Broadway
New York, NY 10012
Phone: (212) 219-2831
Fax: (212) 334-4729

Mammoth Micro Productions
1700 Westlake Ave. North
Suite 702
Seattle, WA 98109
Phone: (206) 281-7500
Fax: (206) 281-7734

Management Information Technologies, Inc.
5 Vanderbilt Motor Parkway
Suite 403
Commack, NY 11725
Phone: (516) 265-3518

Maxwell Data Management, Inc.
275 East Baker St.
Suite A
Costa Mesa, CA 92626
Phone: (714) 435-7700
Fax: (714) 751-1442

MECC
6160 Summit Drive North
Minneapolis, MN 55430-4003
Phone: (800) 685-6322
Fax: (612) 569-1551

Mentor Graphics Corporation
8005 S.W. Boeckman Road
Wilsonville, OR 97070-7777
Phone: (503) 685-7000
Fax: (503) 685-1202

Meridian Data, Inc.
5615 Scotts Valley Drive
Scotts Valley, CA 95066
Phone: (408) 438-3100
Fax: (408) 438-6816

Microboards
308 Broadway
P.O. Box 130
Carver, MN 55315
Phone: (612) 448-9800
Fax: (612) 448-9806

MicroRetrieval Corporation
One Broadway
Building 100
Cambridge, MA 02142
Phone: (617) 577-1574
Fax: (617) 577-9517

Midisoft Corporation
P.O. Box 1000
Bellevue, WA 98009
Phone: (206) 881-7176
Fax: (206) 883-1368

National Geophysical Data Center
Mail Code E/GC1
325 Broadway
Boulder, CO 80303
Phone: (303) 497-6826
Fax: (303) 497-6513

Nippon Courseware Co., Ltd.
4-16-6 Kuramae Taitoh-ku
Tokyo, Japan
Phone: (+81) 3-35687-9800
Fax: (+81) 3-35687-9822

OCLC Online Computer Library Center, Inc.
6565 Frantz Road
Dublin, OH 43017-3395
Phone: (614) 764-6000 or (800) 848-5878
Fax: (614) 764-6096

ON Technology, Inc.
One Cambridge Center, 6th Floor
Cambridge, MA 02142
Phone: (617) 374-1400
Fax: (617) 876-0391

Online Computer Systems, Inc.
20251 Century Blvd.
Germantown, MD 20874
Phone: (301) 428-3700
Fax: (301) 428-2903

Open Text Corporation
180 Columbia Blvd.
Suite 2110
South Waterloo, Ontario, Canada N2J 1P8
Phone: (519) 888-7111

Optical Access International, Inc.
500 West Cummings Park
Suite 3250
Woburn, MA 01801
Phone: (617) 937-3910
Fax: (617) 937-3950

OptImage Interactive Services Company
1501 50th St.
Suite 100
West Des Moines, IA 50266
Phone: (515) 225-7000
Fax: (515) 225-0252

Optimus Publishing, Inc.
Database Division
155 E. Boardwalk Drive
Suite 300
Ft. Collins, CO 80525
Phone: (303) 226-3466
Fax: (303) 226-3464

Optisys
8620 N. 22nd Ave. #109
Phoenix, AZ 85021
Phone: (602) 997-9699
Fax: (602) 944-4051

Optivision, Inc.
4009 Miranda Ave.
Palo Alto, CA 94304
Phone: (415) 855-0200
Fax: (415) 855-0222

Pacific CD Corporation
P.O. Box 31328
Honolulu, HI 96820
Phone: (808) 949-4594
Fax: (808) 949-4594

Palisade Corporation
31 Decker Road
Newfield, NY 14867
Phone: (607) 277-8000
Fax: (607) 277-8001

Pennsylvania Department of Education, State Library, Education Media Services
333 Market St.
11th Floor
Harrisburg, PA 17126-0333
Phone: (717) 787-6704
Fax: (717) 783-5420

Personal Bibliographic Software, Inc.
525 Avis Drive
Suite 10
Ann Arbor, MI 48108
Phone: (313) 996-1580
Fax: (313) 996-4672

Personal Library Software, Inc.
2400 Research Blvd.
Suite 350
Rockville, MD 20850
Phone: (301) 990-1155
Fax: (301) 963-9738

Pinnacle Courseware, Inc.
4340 Stevens Creek Blvd.
Suite 202
San Jose, CA 95129
Phone: (408) 249-8383
Fax: (408) 249-8393

Pixel Productions
67 Mowat Ave.
Suite 547
Toronto, Ontario, Canada M6K 3E3
Phone: (416) 535-3058
Fax: (416) 535-2794

PRISM Interactive Corporation
751 Roosevelt Road
Building 7, Suite 200
Glen Ellyn, IL 60137
Phone: (708) 469-1215
Fax: (708) 469-1452

Research Information Systems, Inc.
Camino Corporate Center
2355 Camino Vida Roble
Carlsbad, CA 92009
Phone: (619) 438-5526
Fax: (619) 438-5573

Skak Technology
800 Airport Blvd.
Suite 320
Burlingame, CA 94010
Phone: (415) 340-1700
Fax: (415) 347-6675

Simmons Market Research Bureau
420 Lexington Ave.
New York, NY 10170
Phone: (212) 916-8900
Fax: (212) 916-8918

SoftWright
791 South Holly St.
Denver, CO
Phone: (303) 329-6388
Fax: (303) 329-0901

Sterling Resources, Inc.
10 Forest Ave.
Paramus, NJ 07652
Phone: (201) 368-8725
Fax: (201) 368-9024

Sun Moon Star Group
1941 Ringwood Ave.
San Jose, CA 95131
Phone: (408) 452-7811
Fax: (408) 452-1411

TerraLogics, Inc.
600 Suffolk St.
Lowell, MA 01854
Phone: (508) 656-9900
Fax: (508) 656-9999

TextWare Corporation
1910 Prospector Ave.
P.O. Box 3267
Park City, UT 84060
Phone: (801) 645-9600
Fax: (801) 645-9610

Thunderstone/Expansion Programs International, Inc.
11115 Edgewater Drive
Cleveland, OH 44102
Phone: (216) 631-8544
Fax: (216) 281-0828

Tiger Media, Inc.
5801 E. Slauson Ave.
Suite 200
Los Angeles, CA 90040
Phone: (213) 721-8282
Fax: (213) 721-8336

Titus Software Corporation
20432 Corisco St.
Chatsworth, CA 91311
Phone: (818) 709-3692
Fax: (818) 709-6537

TMM, Inc. (Total Multimedia)
299 West Hillcrest Drive
Suite 200
Thousand Oaks, CA 91360
Phone: (805) 371-0500
Fax: (805) 371-0505

TMS, Inc.
110 W. 3rd St.
P.O. Box 1358
Stillwater, OK 74076
Phone: (405) 377-0880
Fax: (405) 372-9288

UniDisc
3941 Cherryvale Ave.
Suite 1
Soquel, CA 95073
Phone: (408) 684-2191
Fax: (408) 464-0187

United States Geological Survey (USGS) National Geomagnetic Information Center
Box 25046MS
968 Denver Federal Center
Denver, CO 80225-0046
Phone: (303) 273-8494

User Interface Technologies (U.I.T.) Corporation
P.O. Box 1698
Idyllwild, CA 92549
Phone: (909) 659-4580

Viacom Simulations, Inc.
648 S. Wheeling Road
Wheeling, IL 60090
Phone: (708) 520-4440
Fax: (708) 459-3418

Virgin Games, Inc.
18061 Fitch Ave.
Irvine, CA 92714
Phone: (714) 833-8710
Fax: (714) 833-8717

The Voyager Company
One Bridge St.
Irvington, NY 10533
Phone: (914) 591-5500
Fax: (914) 591-6484

VTLS, Inc.
1800 Kraft Drive
Blacksburg, VA 24060
Phone: (703) 231-3605
Fax: (703) 231-3648

Wayzata Technology, Inc.
2515 East Highway Two
Grand Rapids, MN 55744
Phone: (218) 326-0597
Fax: (218) 326-0598

Young Minds, Inc.
1910 Orange Tree Lane
Suite 300
Redlands, CA 92374
Phone: (909) 335-1350
Fax: (909) 798-0488

Index

Symbols

A

D

E

F

G

I

N

O

P

Q

R

S